GOSPEL GLEANINGS

GOSPEL GLEANINGS

Critical and Historical Notes
on the Gospels

by

THOMAS NICKLIN
Formerly Warden of Hulme Hall, Manchester

LONGMANS, GREEN AND CO
LONDON • NEW YORK • TORONTO

LONGMANS, GREEN AND CO LTD
6 & 7 CLIFFORD STREET LONDON W 1

ALSO AT MELBOURNE AND CAPE TOWN

LONGMANS, GREEN AND CO INC
55 FIFTH AVENUE NEW YORK 3

LONGMANS, GREEN AND CO
215 VICTORIA STREET TORONTO 1

ORIENT LONGMANS LTD
BOMBAY CALCUTTA MADRAS

First published 1950

Printed in Great Britain by William Clowes and Sons Ltd, Beccles

FOREWORD

I AM glad to write these few lines to commend Mr. Nicklin's work to the careful consideration of those who have the wisdom to read it. His subject needs no recommendation, and all learned, thoughtful studies of it are to be welcomed. This book covers much ground and it is ground long fought over. But there is always room for fresh and independent enquiry and for clear exposition of the conclusions to which it leads. The author is not afraid to challenge many widely accepted opinions and to make his own reconstructions and conjectures. He will not in either case expect to find easy agreement. But it will be strange if he does not persuade candid readers to "think again" and to reflect with profit upon an argument set out with admirable lucidity and force. I had the good fortune as a boy to sit at Mr. Nicklin's feet, and it has been a privilege to repeat that happy experience and to encourage others to share it.

ALWYN DUNELM.

May 1947.

PREFACE

IN laying before the reader for consideration this little volume of Gospel studies I crave his indulgence if repetitions and contradictions are yet to be found in its pages. Long periods of interruption have from time to time broken the thread of thought and argument, and memory has failed to repair the injury, and this the more so as failing eyesight and at last blindness came to me. A caustic critic has denied that it is justifiable to write again on a period of history on which so many books and by so eminent authors have been written, a period, too, for which the documentary evidence has been so thoroughly examined and is limited in compass. Such criticism ignores the fact that the masses of papyri unearthed in the last sixty years have given a new perspective to that evidence, and that where cultural, intellectual and religious developments come under review in a story, each generation, as it takes the impress of its own age and environment, inevitably assesses the events of the past in a new light and must interpret them after its own fashion. For the present work no more shall be claimed than this: it has been my aim to achieve an industrious and independent study of the documents, a humble and persistent search in them for any involuntary revelation or undesigned coincidence, an unfettered readiness to ponder fresh theories, and an adherence to the conceptions affirmed by orthodox theology. If some of my conclusions and suggestions should provoke the reader's resentment and antipathy, I would desire to shelter myself behind the shield which Dr. Coulton in his autobiography has recovered to our use, the courageous and confident dictum of St. Gregory the Great, "melius est ut scandalum oriatur quam ut veritas relinquatur," and I would ask that the evidence and argument should be weighed impartially without inclining the scales either in favour of the novel or of the customary.

Since my work was completed and given its final shape, several volumes have appeared which I could have wished to bring into relation with arguments I have advanced and the conclusions I have drawn. (1) The posthumously published work of my friend Mr. R. O. P. Taylor *The Groundwork of the Gospels* has in my judgment dissipated the airy and subjective theories of the last sixty years. They were built upon imaginary re-creations of the first Christian age whilst there were at hand masses of records revealing the actualities of the time. These Mr. Taylor has studied, and the conventionally repeated traditions of the professors and lecturers are seen to be the artificial idols of the divinity school. Some of my contentions will be found to be confirmed and argued at greater length in my friend's book. (2) Dr. Kilpatrick's *The Origins of the Gospel According to St. Matthew* supplies some needful collateral appraisal of the First Gospel which should be added to what I have written, but the taint of the just-mentioned idols to some degree vitiates the reasoning and he underestimates the intransigence of unbelieving Jews before A.D. 70. Yet arrangement for liturgical use will well explain some chronological dislocations and repetitive doublets, and while we might hold Matthew conceivably to have written his *Oracles* in Aramaic for the Mesopotamian diaspora, a Greek Gospel for Phoenicia accords with the belief that our Lord spoke Greek in Galilee. (3) If some special cause may explain the possibility in an isolated case of a derangement in an archetype, wholesale and general derangements must be judged unacceptable as a buttress to the theory that Lazarus wrote the Fourth Gospel as maintained by Mr. Hugh Redwood in *The Book of Lazarus*. (4) My suggestion that St. Luke has transmitted to us factual material [1] communicated to him by St. John and that that Apostle in what he has written has been mindful of the other's record will explain the features in the Fourth Gospel which are noted by Mr. John W. Hoyland in his *Christ and the Saving of Civilization*, and will at the same time entirely negative his interpretation of them.

---

[1] e.g. details in the story of the Transfiguration, the eucharistic institution, words from the Cross.

CONTENTS

PART III. *DOMINICAL TITLES*

PART IV. *THE LORD'S HUMANITY*

PART V. *WAYSIDE JOTTINGS*

INTRODUCTION

IT is now over fifty years since I first became interested in attempting to reconstruct the history of the events attested or reflected by our four Gospels.

About a quarter of a century ago the thought took shape in my mind that fresh consideration should be given to the question how recent discussion of the synoptic problem had affected the basis of the old harmonizations of the Gospels. From that time onwards at intervals I recurred to the question, without achieving anything definite. Meanwhile, much work was published by others—by Professors Sanday and W. M. Ramsay—to name two only. Later I turned aside to what had previously[1] engaged my attention—the examination of the dating of the chief Gospel events, following up suggestions of Dr. Kirsopp Lake and Lieut.-Col. Mackinlay. This led to my opening discussions on these topics at several clerical gatherings and giving courses of lectures on the Gospel history. Finally, in connexion with two courses of Lenten addresses I printed, but did not publish, a *Tentative Harmony of the Gospel Records*, and now at last am emboldened to do what several years ago I was pressed to do, viz. to outline the story that this harmonization suggests as representing the actual course of events.

I shall divide the subject into two parts, which can be treated separately since they do not in point of fact stand or fall together:

(i) The chronological order of the events recorded for us; and

(ii) The historical dating of the chief events.

It may be useful to state at the outset what may be called the Postulates of the Harmony I have attempted.

(1) Mark's Gospel is in broad outline chronologically consecutive and historically trustworthy, but at several points he has parenthetically interposed or trajected certain incidents

---

[1] *Journal of Philology.* Vol. 27, pp. 232 ff. *Guardian* 20 Sept. 1899.

which it suited his purpose to introduce without attending to their chronological setting—thus Mark's record is accurate except, as Papias said, in the matter of chronology.

(2) Matthew groups utterances of different periods together, but gives a more understanding reproduction of some argumentative discussions and sometimes by interpretative phrases gives the true spiritual significance of a saying of our Lord where the letter might be misunderstood.

(3) St. Luke's express claim (i. 1–4) warrants our using his Gospel to guide us towards a correct chronological order, and the apparent fidelity of the *Acts* to the words and thoughts of the speakers justifies the acceptance of his representation of the words and thoughts of those who figure in the Gospel narrative. St. Luke indeed follows and attests Mark's chronological order, but his copy has lost Mark vi. 46–viii. 27, and he corrected the order of Mark i. 15–21, where Mark placed the Call of the Four Disciples so as to explain their intimacy with our Lord in verse 29.

(4) Though John fuses into his narrative expository reflections and comments, the chronological and geographical framework of the incidents and of the teaching that he records is historical. He had knowledge of Luke's Gospel, and had as one of his objects the correction and clarification of points that were liable to mislead or to be obscure in the third Gospel, e.g. John iv. 47–53 explains Luke iv. 14–44; and this, it should be noticed, Matt. iv. 12, undesignedly confirms. John explains the significance of Luke's repeated statement in Luke ix. 51–xix. 28, that our Lord was making His way to Jerusalem, and he makes clear that in Luke xxii. 15 "desire" has the connotation of vain desire, as in Luke xvi. 21.

These summary statements are examined more fully in later chapters and submitted to the reader's judgment. They are not the first improvisation of a theory to integrate the phenomena, but the latest and so far as has hitherto appeared the only impregnable reconciliation and co-ordination of them all. Here it may be appropriately mentioned that of all the works dealing with the Gospels which I have studied few if any have not yielded some valuable contribution. The list of these works is too lengthy to give in full, but it is right to name Keim, Schaff,

Abbott, Milman, Godet, Huck, Foakes Jackson, Mimpriss, Westcott, Willoughby Allen, Plummer, Howard, Wright, Tischendorf, Balmforth, Prut, Trench, Farrar and Latham, besides others mentioned in the text and numerous articles in the *Journal of Theological Studies*, *Expository Times* and *Church Quarterly Review*.

Two observations may be intruded here by way of comment on the postulates mentioned above.

(1) A further example of the way in which the Fourth Gospel corrects or clarifies the Synoptic and in particular the Lucan record deserves special attention. Mark expressly states that on Palm Sunday after entering the Temple our Lord did no more than look about him. On Monday he places the expulsion of the traffickers from the Temple and the next day the priests' demand for the Lord to name the source of His authority. The First and Third Gospels, possibly deducing the notion from Q, give this expulsion as occurring on Palm Sunday; i.e. at the point where first in the Synoptic narrative our Lord comes to the Temple. At the same time it is observable that the First Gospel brings together what Mark relates as happening on Monday and Tuesday in regard to the barren fig-tree. Luke shows similar uncertainty as to the exact dating of the incidents, for he assigns to "one of the days" the priests' challenge for the naming of the authority. John makes it clear that the first visit to the Temple was shortly after the Baptism and that it was then that the merchants were expelled. The Synoptists' narratives gave no opportunity to insert this before Holy Week. Mark knew that it did not occur on the Sunday and Matthew connects the priests' challenge with their jealousy of our Lord's healing of disease in the Temple precincts. St. Luke's historical sense was sound, but he had not the material to disentangle the whole. St. John's knowledge enabled him to supply what makes all intelligible and consistent with the evidence of the other writers.

(2) Bishop Headlam's *Life of Christ* not only supplies an illuminating picture of the circumstances and environment amid which the Gospel narrative moves, but in general traces the course of events as we may believe them to have occurred. Notwithstanding this, the bishop seems to be led away by one

idol of the modern critic. He holds that the Second Gospel is a better authority than the Third, because the Second is a source and the Third is secondary. Dispassionate reflection is enough to show, when once the question is broached, that this valuation of authorities is too simple to be acceptable in history, however adequate in palaeography. For textual criticism, an old MS. from the hand of an ignorant scribe is of more value to us than one worked over by a critical scholar, but only because we prefer ourselves to infer the correct text and our critical methods are more scientific and trustworthy than those of ancient copyists. But even here if a copyist with several older but blundering MSS. before him, wrote out faithfully what he judged to be from point to point the best attested text, inserting no conjectures of his own, but selecting now from one MS., now from another, we should not, merely because he was secondary to the older MSS., value his text as inferior to one of those MSS., if it alone survived, while the others on which he had drawn were lost. Still more does this consideration apply to the valuation of historical documents. Were it otherwise, there would be no point in any later historian, however well equipped with impartial and scientific judgment, embarking on the re-telling of a story once recorded, in however slip-shod a fashion. Moreover, as it happens, we have the definite criticism made from a very early date that, so far as chronological order is concerned, Mark is not so good an authority as Luke. To carry this line of argument to a point, just as the textual critic will estimate a secondary MS. such as has been described, after an independent examination of its merits, so with the secondary Gospel of Luke, resting as it does not only on Mark but on other authorities now lost to us, we have to estimate the value of his chronological arrangement on its merits. The bishop gives one definite test by which he is led to the conclusion that Mark is the more trustworthy, but a reference to the actual Lucan text shows that the bishop has done an injustice to the Third Evangelist. As will be seen later, after a period of popularity when hearers from all parts were attracted to our Lord's preaching, commissioners, so to say, were sent down from Jerusalem to appraise the orthodoxy of His teaching. The bishop takes it that Luke mistakenly supposes such commis-

sioners to have appeared early in the Ministry, but it is clear
that what is in reality said by the evangelist (v. 17) is that there
was still a collection of hearers—including lawyers—from all
parts, including Jerusalem. This aggregation of listeners is in
agreement with the statements of Mark (iii. 7–8) and Matthew
(iv. 25), and with Luke's subsequent narrative of the Ministry
(vi. 17). There is no ground here for ranking him below Mark
in accuracy of chronological arrangement.

These general considerations prompt a closer examination
of the phenomena exhibited by our Gospels. This examination may naturally be divided into several sections which for
clearness may be grouped under separate headings.

PART ONE

THE GOSPELS

Chapter One

The Earliest Copies of Mark and their Pagination

St. Luke wrote his Gospel having at hand the Second Gospel as one of his authorities. Subject to minor reservations or modifications, this hypothesis is now generally adopted. Accordingly the chronological arrangement of the two gospels is, broadly speaking, the same. His supplementary information has indeed enabled St. Luke to correct Mark's *mise-en-scène* of Simon Peter and his partners. Their call to accompany our Lord continuously was preceded by some earlier acquaintance; and this, with the consequent rearrangement of a few incidents at the beginning of our Lord's ministry, is confirmed by the author of the Fourth Gospel. Apart from this, however, we have only one knot to untie—the omission by Luke of all that the Second Gospel records between the Feeding of the Five Thousand and St. Peter's confession of faith near Caesarea Philippi.

It is now a good many years since the suggestion was hazarded that this omission was not due to a deliberate selection of material by St. Luke, but was the result of an accident in the handling of the manuscript of the Second Gospel. This suggestion, restated somewhat differently from its original form, I am convinced may be shown to rest on a reasonable foundation.

In the *Expository Times* for May 1933 (vol. XLIV, p. 382f) I sought to show that the perplexities of John xiv–xvi disappeared if the matter were rearranged in the way that was allowed by the assumption that in the archetype it was written on the middle pages of a quire or fascicule of paper. Had these central pages come loose and fallen out and had they been replaced in another order, what was an ordered discourse would have become what our MSS. now give.

The hypothesis rests of course on the fact, not established forty years ago, that there were codices of inexpensive format in the first century. Subsequently in a paper privately printed I sought to show that the Fourth Gospel must have been written on two quires of paper, that the amount of matter on each sheet was on the average what in Nestle's small edition is printed to cover 32 lines. Later it occurred to me to test whether Mark's Gospel had been written out in a similar way. The section omitted by St. Luke would have been on a bundle of pages in the middle of a quire, which had fallen out bodily leaving no troublesome fragments of sentences. I observed that pericope after pericope was not only of a length reflected in the Gospels appointed for the eucharistic services of the Church, but harmonizing with the general character of the pages I had determined for the Fourth Gospel.

The publication of the Rylands Library fragment (P.: Ryl.; GK457) showed that it had come from a codex similar to what I had postulated, with pages containing about half the matter in John i. 1–18 and just about what I calculated for Mark's pages, the MS. being written on both recto and verso.

With this encouragement I have plotted out the Second Gospel. It would cover, written in this way, 98 pages, each containing about 14 lines of Westcott and Hort's smaller volume. In a codex written as described page 36 would end with Mark vi. 46 and page 48 with Mark viii. verse 27 in the middle, page 49, beginning with "And by the way He asked" in the middle of the verse. In St. Luke's copy if pages 37–48 fell out it is readily intelligible that he should write as he does (ix. 18): "And it came to pass, as He was alone praying, His disciples were with Him, and He asked them saying, Whom say the people that I am?" It will be observed that these 12 pages would take three complete sheets, and if these fell out St. Luke would have no reason to suspect their loss.[1] For this accident to be likely we must suppose that these sheets were in the middle of a quire, and it follows that the entire manuscript was made up of three fascicules. The first

---

[1] This hypothesis is in an eminent degree superior to Streeter's. It not only explains why Luke does not name Caesarea Philippi as near the scene of St. Peter's confession, but, what is much more striking, it explains the origin of Luke's curious statement, the contradictory nature of which, as it must appear at first sight, is most intelligibly accounted for by our suggestion that St. Luke's copy of Mark passed from the words "when He had sent them away, He departed into a mountain to pray" to "and by the way He asked His disciples."

two containing seven sheets or 28 pages each and the last
11 sheets. If we may suppose that the recto of the first page
showed merely the title of the work (perhaps the words ἀρχὴ
τοῦ εὐαγγελίου Ἰησοῦ Χριστοῦ, which are generally printed as
the first verse of the Gospel) we shall have on the verso of
page 98, Mark xvi. 1–8 and on the recto of the last leaf the
missing conclusion of the Gospel. The last leaf presumably was
lost before St. Luke saw the Second Gospel.[1]

At this point it will be of convenience to the reader if he has
before him in tabular form the pages and their contents
according to this conjectural restoration.

Page	Chapter	Topic
1	i. 1	Title
2	i. 2–7	The Baptist
3	i. 7–13	The Baptism
4	i. 14–20	The call of Simon
5	i. 21–28	The demoniac
6	i. 29–38	Simon's mother-in-law
7	i. 39–end	The leper
8	ii. 1–8	Sins forgiven
9	ii. 8–13	Forgiveness
10	ii. 14–17	Levi called
11	ii. 18–22	Fasting
12	ii. 23–iii. 1	Cornfields
13	iii. 1–7	Withered hand
14	iii. 7–13	Crowds
15	iii. 13–20	The Twelve called
16	iii. 20–27	Satan expels Satan?
17	iii. 27–35	Who is my mother?
18	iv. 1–7	The sower
19	iv. 8–14	To you it is given
20	iv. 15–20	The parable explained
21	iv. 21–28	Lamps under bushel

[1] In Luke xvii we have some incidents and teaching which Mark groups
before his record of our Lord's sojourn in Peraea, and it might be argued
that St. Luke has mistakenly introduced them as previous to our Lord's
journey to Jerusalem not for the Feast of Tabernacles in the autumn of
A.D. 32 but for the Passover in the spring of A.D. 33. We shall, however, be
inclined to accept Luke's dating, believing that our Lord's retirement to
Ephraim took him to a sparsely populated district on the borders of Galilee.
Mark would seem to have no secure knowledge of the exact order of events
between the setting out for the Feast of Tabernacles and the last journey to
Jerusalem.

6   THE GOSPELS

The last page we may suppose contained the Marcan equivalent of Matthew's last chapter. I have long felt that in view of the faithful testimony given by the First Gospel to the contents of the Second, some notion of the lost Marcan conclusion might be derived from the First Gospel.

A systematic attempt to explain Matthew's divergencies of order from St. Mark by postulating similar accidents to his copy of the Second Gospel has failed, and as will be shown later these divergencies are attributable to other causes.

Since no copy of Mark exists or is recorded to have existed (except that Matthew may be believed to have used such a one) which has preserved the conclusion of the Gospel, we must suppose that the archetype suffered this loss before any copies of it had been made. Is it too bold to suppose that Matthew had access to the archetype before it was injured, that copies were afterwards made from the truncated original, and that St. Luke worked with either the archetype or one of these copies when the pages we have named had disappeared? It can at least be said that such a theory seems to reconcile all the phenomena observable in the three synoptists. Be that as it may, our reconstruction of the history of the text will enable us to arrange a diatessaron of the Gospel narratives, and this will be found in an Appendix to Chapter VI.

Chapter Two

THE SECOND GOSPEL

PARTICULAR attention must here be given to the effects upon the arrangement of the Gospel which were produced by the circumstances of its origin. St. Mark, we are told, at last put on paper what he had previously taught by word of mouth to Christian catechumens. He had memorized and made the catechumens memorize the teaching that St. Peter, guided by the exigencies of his work, had put together as most valuable for the instruction of converts. This was in fact what we should call ana of our Lord. To assist the memory they were grouped together to some extent by similarity of subject. While the last week of our Lord's ministry is recorded almost entirely in datal order, and while we find no reason to deny the general correctness of chronology in what precedes (for we find, in the main, a consistent development in the story), there emerge upon careful examination certain signs of the grouping of episodes so as to assist the memory. One example will suffice. The mention that our Lord's friends thought Him "beside Himself" is the cue for introducing the Jerusalem scribes' libel that He was in league with Beelzebub.

For convenience sake it will be well here to tabulate the sections of the Gospel, disengaged from their mnemonic collocation and arranged in historical order in accordance with such warning hints as they themselves provide. A comparison with Luke's order will afterwards go some way to substantiate the claim that our arrangement is historically sound.

i. 1–13. John's mission; our Lord's Baptism and forty days retirement.
    21–39. A sabbath in Capernaum; sabbath preaching in synagogues.
    14–20. The four fishermen partners called.[1]

---

1 It must be left a matter for further consideration whether verse 14 should be attached as a mark of time to the partners' call or to the events on the sabbath in Capernaum.

1*

i. 40–45. A leper healed; preaching principally in wild, open country.

ii. 1–17. The paralytic's sins forgiven; Matthew's call; sinners welcomed.
23–iii. 19. The sabbath question in the cornfields and as to healing a withered hand; retirement to the sea and to the hills; the Twelve chosen.

iii. 20, 21,[1] 31–35. Crowds throng His house; His friends fear for His sanity.

iv. 1–v. 21. Parable used; storm on the sea; Legion exorcized.

vi. 14–29. John's martyrdom.[2]

ii. 18–22. John's disciples ask why the Lord's disciples do not fast.[3]

v. 22–vi. 13. Jairus' daughter; visit to His own country; Twelve sent out.

vi. 30–ix. 27. The five thousand fed; scribes from Jerusalem; retirement to Phoenicia; four thousand fed; Peter's confession; the Transfiguration; the lunatic healed.

iii. 22–30. The Scribes from Jerusalem (see pp. xiv and 12).

ix. 30–33A. Return to His house in Capernaum.

ix. 28–29. The reason for the nine apostles' failure.[4]

ix. 33B–x. 52. The Ministry down to the eve of Palm Sunday.

xiv. 3–9. Feast at Bethany.[5]

xi. 1–xiv. 2. Palm Sunday and the following Monday and Tuesday.

xiv. 10–xvi. 8. The rest of Holy Week and Easter Day.

It will be well here to collect some of the certainties which emerge on a careful consideration of St. Mark's narrative.

(1) The call of St. Peter and his friends occurred after the Baptist was thrown into prison. We may be sure that in the apostles' memory this sequence of events was indelibly fixed.

(2) Although we may be able from a comparison with other Gospels to interpose additional incidents, Mark's order may be accepted for the following events, or in some instances for the sequence, at any rate, of incidents collected within a single group, although it must be understood that not all the incidents in each group are anterior to what appears in a later group.

---

[1] It is not clear whether the whole of this section (or perhaps verses 20, 21 alone) should follow the next section. Luke gives us the former alternative.

[2] It is possible that this should be dated somewhat earlier; in any case it will be after the Twelve were chosen but before they were sent out on their mission.

[3] Had John still been alive, the question would have been put to him, if we may judge by John iii. 25.

[4] The apostles' question may have preceded our Lord's enquiry into their quarrel, but in any case both episodes are said to have occurred in our Lord's house.

[5] This section is plainly brought in where it is to explain why Judas decided to offer his services to the chief priests.

At times Mark has evidently been guided, by the similarity of subject, to group incidents together:

(a) Demoniac healed in the synagogue at Capernaum; Simon's mother-in-law cured of fever; many healed after sunset; preaching in many synagogues afterwards.

(b) A leper cleansed.

(c) A paralytic assured of forgiveness and healed in our Lord's home at Capernaum.

(d) St. Matthew called. Justification of association with publicans.

(e) Walk through the cornfields on the Sabbath day.

(f) The withered hand restored in the synagogue on the Sabbath.

(g) Somewhere among the hills He selects the Twelve.

(3) At this point we may say that in St. Peter's memory the events of one particular day stood out clear and connected: we can tabulate them as follows:

(a) Sitting in a boat, while crowds stood on the lake side, our Lord uttered the first of His parables that His hearers could not understand till they had His elucidation.

(b) Entering His home He gave that elucidation to the Twelve and others.

(c) His friends were disturbed when they saw the crowds about him and were still more troubled when the people pressed into His home. Fearing for his sanity or apprehensive of a nervous collapse, perhaps after hearing of the parable, they wished to arrest him.

In the evening He went away with the Twelve by ship.

(4) (a) After landing on the other side, he was met by the man possessed by the demon Legion.

(b) On crossing the lake he healed Jairus' daughter.

(5) (a) He revisits His own country.

(b) He sends out two by two the apostles.

(c) When they had all returned he crossed with them to some spot of open country where he fed the five thousand who had followed Him, and again returned to Capernaum.

(6) (*a*) A commission of Pharisees and scribes arrived from Jerusalem and criticized the disregard by some of the disciples of the traditional rules for ceremonial cleanliness.

(*b*) After retiring into His house our Lord elucidated the matter further, and later withdrew to the neighbourhood of Tyre and Sidon.

(*c*) Making His way through Decapolis He reached the eastern end of the lake, healed a deaf-and-dumb man, fed the four thousand, and eventually crossed to Dalmanutha.

(*d*) Challenged here by the Pharisees to show a sign in the sky, He bluntly refused and with His disciples hurriedly recrossed to near Bethsaida.

(*e*) After restoring a blind man's sight, He moved on to the neighbourhood of Caesarea–Philippi and presently received St. Peter's avowal that the Twelve believed Him to be the Christ.

(*f*) A week later followed the Transfiguration, after which He foretold to the apostles His death and resurrection.

(*g*) After He had rejoined the other nine apostles He healed the paranoiac youth.

(*h*) He made His way as secretly as possible to Capernaum and into His own house. On the way He told all the Twelve of His coming death "at the hands of men"—a preparatory euphemism for Gentiles.

In the house he corrected their ambition and any desire to monopolize for themselves the right to work for Him.

(7) Mark next states that our Lord was teaching on the other side of the Jordan opposite Judea. Here he relates that our Lord boldly or bluntly pronounced that a man who got rid of his wife in order to marry another was guilty of adultery.

(8) Mark next relates how our Lord blessed young children that were brought to him, and then tells that as He was on His way to Jerusalem, as it appears, a rich young man ran to Him asking for spiritual counsel.

(9) Farther along the road our Lord walked in advance, and to His frightened disciples foretold yet more plainly that He would be crucified and then rise again. Upon this James and John asked that they might have the highest posts at His court.

(10) By a sudden transition Mark next brings us to Jericho, and after it was passed through, relates the healing of Bartimaeus.

(11) With another rapid transition Mark transports us to Bethany on Palm Sunday morning.

Since the rest of the Gospel is concerned with the events of Holy Week, where such problems as arise fall within narrower compass, we may pause here to take stock of the conclusions which suggest themselves from consideration of Mark's framework. In general it would seem that the episodes as we have tabulated them are in chronological order, though it is plain that at certain points there is room to be allowed for much that happened, but which Mark did not record, presumably because St. Peter had not drawn upon these omitted incidents to fill out his picture of our Lord's ministry for His catechumens.

It is right here to draw attention to a feature in Mark's narrative which has frequently been brushed aside as of no particular value for historical purposes. At point after point in the story we get general statements about our Lord's activities. These have been regarded as unimportant editorial links. If, however, we examine them as chronological indications that some interval of time separated the various groups of incidents which, as we have suggested, stood out in St. Peter's memory as focal points, we are able to say that in historical fact some interval of time passed between the following outstanding episodes:

(1) Between the Sunday after St. Peter's mother-in-law was cured and the healing of the leper.

(2) Between that healing and the declaration that the paralytic's sins had been forgiven.

(3) Between this declaration of forgiveness and the call of St. Matthew to discipleship.

(4) Between the healing of a man's withered right hand and the selection of the Twelve for apostleship.

(5) Between the selection of the Twelve and the utterance of the Parable of the Sower.

(6) Between the exorcism of Legion and Jairus' appeal for his daughter.

(7) Between the healing of Jairus' daughter and the visit to His own country.

(8) Between this visit and the mission of the Twelve (previously to which the Baptist had been killed).

(9) After the feeding of the five thousand a commission of scribes was found to have arrived from Jerusalem, who criticized the neglect by some of the disciples to observe the rules for ceremonial cleanliness.

(10) Between the return from Sidon by way of Decapolis (which was followed by the healing of a deaf man) and the feeding of the four thousand.

(11) Between the last visit to His home at Capernaum and the Pharisees' encounter with Him in Peraea.

It will be observed that when allowance is made for these gaps or intervals in the narrative we find that both Luke and John present us with additional matter, which falls aptly in place within the chronological scheme afforded by Mark. There is then no contradiction between the historical order unfolded by Luke and that which is seen to underlie the Marcan Gospel.

In this way we can resolve the apparent discord between the Second and Third Gospels in the matter of chronological sequence and we are released from the necessity of choosing one and rejecting the other. It is also to be observed that when allowance is made, as we have seen, for such explanatory trajections of episodes, whether by way of anticipation or of subsequent explanation, Papias' comment on St. Mark's work is fully justified, but nevertheless does not warrant us in dismissing Mark's order as valueless.

That Matthew groups together teaching and incidents of different dates is generally recognized. That Mark does the same, though undoubtedly to a less extent, is not so generally acknowledged. Yet at certain points in his narrative the conclusion cannot be resisted that he has done so. After relating the utterance of the Parable of the Sower, he gives several other examples of parables designed to illustrate the principles of God's Kingdom. After doing this, he continues with the words "and on that day when evening was come," by which it is manifest that he intends us to understand that the episode that follows came at the end of the same day in which the first parable was spoken. This is as much as to say that it is St. Mark himself who has grouped together the parables he gives without intending us to suppose that they were all spoken on the same day.

Another example is to be seen in the way that he attaches to the story of the healing of the paranoiac youth our Lord's explanation of the failure of the nine apostles to effect a permanent cure. Yet another example is the grouping together of the Lord's defence of His association with publicans and His reply to the calumny that He was Beelzebub's ally. We are probably to see another instance in the utterances found at the end of chapter ix, although the Rev. R. O. P. Taylor supplied the suggestion of a nexus of thought between what at first sight may seem disjointed sayings (see p. 97). Yet, when we have recognized this propensity of Mark, to group incidents and sayings irrespectively of their chronological position, we must observe that he not infrequently indicates what that order is by inserting some note of time or place. Thus, Mark makes it clear that the episode of the scribes denouncing our Lord as Beelzebub's agent is chronologically an intrusion or parenthesis. He resumes his account of our Lord's friends coming to arrest him and picks up the story in a fashion which shows that it has been marking time during the parenthesis.

Matthew treated Mark's account of our Lord's use of parables as a whole, detachable from the chronological order of events, and, having himself told of the storm on the lake in an earlier chapter, he passes straight from Mark's account of our Lord's friends coming to his account of the parables, thus transposing the order. Luke makes the coming of the friends follow the first parable and relates the voyage after the declaration that the Lord's mother and brethren were those who hear the word of God and do it. He recognizes that Mark has grouped together parables spoken on several occasions, and cautiously dates the storm as following one of these parables.[1]

1 It is worthy of consideration whether Luke's words do not carry a meaning other than the English translators have given them. Instead of "on one of the days" we should perhaps translate "on the first of the days" with which we are concerned, i.e. on the day on which Mark's first parable (the only one here reported by Luke) was uttered. Similarly the leper (Luke v. 12) came near "the first of the towns" visited by our Lord, and the

Upon a careful scrutiny of the arrangement which Mark has made of St. Peter's *chreiai* and a scrupulous comparison of the setting Mark has thus given to the various episodes and themes with that in which they appear in Luke and John, certain facts reveal themselves and certain conclusions become inevitable. In the first place it is clear that Mark did not follow an annalistic order in his marshalling of his material. He has planned the whole in a way that will make it intelligible to a reader who is unacquainted with the story, but has heard something of the Christians' claim that they have a happy announcement to make to the world that a divine epiphany long predicted among the Jews has taken place. Twelve men were selected and trained to understand and were commissioned to propagate the New Divine Self-disclosure. To make the selection of the Twelve intelligible, Mark introduces the first four as we have seen, without regard to strict chronology. He moreover ignores all incidents in the Ministry outside Galilee and neighbouring northern districts until a few months before the Crucifixion. To fit in with this scheme of his narrative, he transposes the expulsion of the traders from the Temple and the Scribe's question as to the Greatest Commandment, introducing both these episodes into his account of Holy Week. A similar disregard of dates is to be seen when he has to speak of our Lord's friends' anxiety as to His sanity: Mark attaches to this the Scribes' imputation of alliance with Beelzebub. In view of this we are prepared to understand how Mark throws together some words of our Saviour spoken before His going up to the Feast of Tabernacles and others before His final journey to face His Passion. In the same way we see several parables strung together because they all were of the type adopted by our Lord to reveal while yet concealing the nature of God's Kingdom. Of events after the

Temple (Luke xx. 1) was cleared on "the first day" on which He entered it. This is reconcilable with the Fourth Gospel. Matthew, who like Luke rejects Mark's dating of the incident on Monday, places it on Palm Sunday (but see p. 56, note), as Luke has generally been supposed to do. This correction of the meaning to be attached to the Greek expression is supported by a comparison of the use in Matt. xxviii. 1, Mark xvi. 2, Luke xxiv. 1, John xx. 1, 19, Acts xx. 7, 1 Cor. xvi. 2. This favours the interpretation of πρῶτος as "prior" in Mark xiv. 12 and John i. 15, 30, and obelises Mark xvi. 9 as of later date.

Feast of Tabernacles Mark notices the Pronouncement as to Divorce spoken in Peraea. For the rest Mark devotes the second moiety of his work to the story of Holy Week. He marks with precision what occurred on each day, but in doing so we may be grateful to him that he convicts himself of having in view another aim than simple chronology. He refutes the idea that Christ at once on Palm Sunday drove out the money-makers, and he introduces Mary's anointing of our Lord only at the point when on Wednesday Judas struck his bargain with the priests—a bargain which Mark, presumably following St. Peter's implication, traced to what happened at the Bethany supper. To add one final and subsidiary point, just as Mark brought into Holy Week from its proper place the question put by the Scribe during the Feast of the Dedication, so he has added to our Lord's prophecy as to the End of the Age words which were spoken some while earlier about the Spirit's assistance when believers had to answer for their faith.

Matthew accepts Mark without criticism or question, using its material as it fitted into his argument. Luke subjected it to the most searching examination possible for him, but till John's evidence is called there remain occasionally in Luke misconceptions derived from Mark. In some instances he has omitted what he has judged to be a misdated account of something which he has recorded elsewhere, e.g. he tells of only one Anointing of our Lord and he omits the second revisiting of Nazareth. But he does not omit incidents merely on the ground that they are similar to others already related. We shall therefore believe that Mark's account of the fig-tree's withering is no doubtlet[1] of Luke's parable of the unfruitful fig-tree and that Mark has appended to what was then said to Peter to encourage faith in prayer, teaching about forgiving others when we pray, which was given to the same apostle when he asked how often he should forgive his brother.

[1] Some may hazard the guess that St. Luke's copy of Mark had lost also the pages we have numbered 65 to 76.

Chapter Three

MATTHEW

(1) *General*

DEROGATORY verdicts have sometimes been pronounced on the
First Gospel because its arrangement was not easily reconcilable
with that of Mark. In particular it has been said that the First
Gospel exhibited a succession of apparently aimless crossings
and recrossings of the Sea of Galilee. It may be asserted unhesitatingly that these unfavourable estimates of the Gospel are
consequent upon an insufficient regard for its individual
method. When the evangelist's system of digesting his material
has been accepted, and the reader does not look for the chronological order of Luke yet welcomes the amplification of Mark's
more slender work, we find the whole Gospel not only intelligible in arrangement but most carefully marked with signposts of time and place. This is why the Sea of Galilee is so often
said to have been crossed. As each incident takes its place in the
framework adopted by the evangelist, he takes the trouble
faithfully to mark if the scene is changed from that of the
preceding incident. This can be seen in his account of the Ten
Miracles, which he records before the Baptist sends his two
disciples. Each miracle will be found to be staged in the environment appearing in the other Gospels. In the same way an
attentive reader who notices the evangelist's time-marks finds
him agreeing with the other Gospels, although his grouping of
events may have caused them to stand next to something of a
different date.

It has long been recognized that the First Gospel is, roughly
speaking, a combination of Mark's Gospel and another work.
This second work was used also by Luke, so that almost identical
passages are to be read in Matthew and in Luke. A statement
of Papias quoted by Eusebius has often been treated as authority
for believing that this work comes ultimately from the hand of
St. Matthew. We are told that that apostle arranged on a

systematic plan (later, it may be, writing them out) "the Oracles" in Hebrew, i.e. perhaps in Aramaic, and that they were "interpreted" or translated by others as well as each was able.

Josephus states that he wrote his work on the Jewish Wall first in Aramaic for the benefit of "Parthians, Babylonians and the most remote tribes of Arabia with our countrymen (ὁμόφυλον) beyond the Euphrates and the inhabitants of Adiabene in the Upper Tigris region." St. Matthew, according to tradition, made these regions his sphere of apostolic activity, so that Aramaic, as Josephus shows, would be the natural language to be employed. Elsewhere Greek would be the appropriate vehicle of expression. Josephus for this reason translated his work. The translation of St. Matthew's work, whatever that work was, becomes intelligible as similarly making it more useful amongst the rest of Jewry. It is not clear whether "the Oracles" were a collection of our Lord's words, such as we find in the Sermon on the Mount and in the Parables, or a collection of Old Testament prophecies in which the Christians found our Lord's mission to the world had been pre-figured and prepared. Our First Gospel contains many such prophecies, which are expressly stated to have found fulfilment in our Saviour's mission, and the way in which prophecy and fulfilment are intertwined suggests that, if we have here the "Oracles" of St. Matthew, he did not simply make a list of Old Testament texts, but imbedded them in some sort of narrative. This may incline us further to believe that St. Matthew's "Oracles" included both masses of our Lord's teaching and Old Testament prophecies illustrated by narrative. In other words, just as the prophetic books of the Old Testament contain narrative, homily and prediction, so St. Matthew's work contained all three elements.

So far we have spoken of St. Matthew's work, but we have to reckon with the possibility that the "interpreter" is responsible for some part of these elements. It would be out of place to discuss here at length the meaning of "interpretation." For the moment it will be sufficient to say that we cannot safely attempt to distinguish between what St. Matthew may have written in Aramaic and what the "interpreter" wrote in Greek. All that we can do is to expiscate some of the characteristics in the Greek "interpretation" of St. Matthew. For convenience this Greek work is commonly designated as Q and it is it which we must suppose St. Luke also to have been able to use.

At this point, however, we must notice how in the last twenty years form-criticism has somewhat modified the position. Experience showed the early preachers of the Gospel what episodes in our Lord's ministry and what lessons that he gave to his disciples were most effective in converting unbelievers and directing believers. Amongst the Jews the instruction of the great Rabbis was mediated to the laity by more humble Khazans, who memorized the instruction and repeated it from memory to their pupils, making them also learn it by heart.

St. Mark would appear to have done this more humble work for St. Paul and St. Barnabas on their first missionary journey. Luke in his preface states that he had derived information not only from eyewitnesses but also from such humble assistants. When Papias tells us that St. Mark had acted as "interpreter" for St. Peter and finally reduced to writing what he had before memorized from St. Peter's teaching, we cannot doubt that by "interpreter" he intends us to understand one who fulfilled the role of a Christian Khazan.[1] If this be a true view of the way that converts were instructed, we must allow for some margin of error in our strict analysis of the reactions between the synoptists. Sometimes what seems to be taken from Mark's written record may come from the remembrance of his oral repetition of St. Peter's teaching. Sometimes what may be thought to come from Q may be the remembrance of an oral version of Matthew or Mark.

These considerations become of special importance when, to prosecute the method of analysis currently applied to Matthew,

---

[1] It is conceivable, however, that St. Peter's pronunciation was so crudely Galilean that St. Mark had to repeat the Apostle's words with a less provincial pronunciation. It is possible to use one and the same written language and yet for speakers to be scarcely intelligible to one another, e.g. a Northumbrian and a Devonian, a Californian and an East Anglian. In that case Papias may have intended us to regard St. Mark as the oral translator of St. Peter's uncouth speech, and St. Matthew's written "oracles" to have been translated from Aramaic into Greek spoken or written.

we come to deal with the work of the final editor or compiler of our First Gospel. In large sections we find this compiler following closely the order of Mark, but at the same time abbreviating on the one hand and adding on the other. These additions sometimes are no more than small details.[1] At other times episodes of more or less importance are inserted.[2] We can only tentatively formulate theories as to the sources of these additions and as to the purpose with which the compiler introduced them, and we are treading on perilous ground whenever we argue that particular additions come from the final compiler rather than from St. Matthew himself or his "interpreter," who may have given at the particular point under consideration a parallel account to Mark's. Nevertheless a cautious and unprejudiced analysis of the First Gospel would appear to yield some results which warrant probable, though not incontrovertible, inferences as to the respective sources of particular statements.

With this in mind we may proceed to analyse the contents of our present Gospel and to notice certain outstanding features.

(1) We have first a genealogical record to show that St. Joseph was the heir-at-law to the Davidic Throne and a brief narrative to justify the claim that our Lord was his acknowledged heir. The reader should observe that the angel is represented as addressing St. Joseph by the title "Son of David."[3] Further, the narrative is plainly intended to prove to the Jewish mind that Isaiah's prophecy regarding Immanuel found its fulfilment in the birth of Jesus.

(2) The second chapter plainly is intended to convince the Jewish mind that at last the heir of David was the foretold Messiah. He was born at Bethlehem, not elsewhere as perhaps in other generations the heir had been, and moreover his sojourn in Egypt had fulfilled the prophecy that God would call His Son out of that land. This would meet the objection that Jesus was not David's heir by physical descent. Incidentally the massacre of the Holy Innocents fulfilled the prophecy of Rachel's weeping.

---

[1] Such a detail is, e.g., that our Lord "looked up to heaven" before He blessed and brake the bread for the Five Thousand (Matt. xiv. 19).

[2] E.g. St. Peter's walking over the sea: Matt. xiv. 28–31.

[3] The significance of this title is discussed below (p. 251).

(3) The return of the Holy Family to Nazareth is stressed as a secondary verification of what was currently believed to have been prophetically foretold, viz. that the Christ should be named N.Z.R. Matthew is concerned to show that Jesus rightly bore this name rather than St. Joseph's nephew, James, although he too was a Nazarite.

(4) Next follows an account of the Baptist's ministry, itself a fulfilment of Isaiah's prophecy regarding the voice crying "in the wilderness prepare ye the way of the Lord."

Since the Jewish masses accepted the Baptist as a prophet, his testimony to our Lord was of specially important evidential value to the Jew. Hence Matthew or Q gives some space to St. John's preaching. One feature in particular must be noticed. The Evangelist has thrown together various excerpts from that preaching and, as we may infer from John's more systematic record, has grouped his excerpts without regard to the chronological moment at which they were uttered. This is a valuable indication of Matthew's method of arranging his material.

(5) Our Lord's baptism is next related, and not only does Matthew insist on it as falling in with the Baptist's pre-vision, but he sees in it the complete realization of the words in the coronation psalm in which the new King is said to be God's Son, i.e. his Vicegerent on earth, "begotten" at his hallowing.

(6) Matthew next gives an account of the three crucial temptations, in which, as he explained to the Jews, our Lord refused to subserve their nationalistic hopes. At the same time he exhibits our Lord as finding in the Old Testament the weapons with which to defeat the Tempter.

(7) Matthew then states that our Lord transferred his home to Capernaum after the Baptist's imprisonment, and in this finds a fulfilment of a prophecy of Isaiah. It is reasonable therefore to claim the apostle's authority for this mark of time, even though we should suppose that the editor has mistakenly or unconcernedly followed Mark's unchronological order in antedating the call of St. Peter and his partners and placing it at the very beginning of our Lord's Galilean ministry. It should be noticed that a Judean previous ministry is implied.

(8) In illustration of the way in which "great light" was now come to Galilee, Matthew now gives a long discourse, uttered,

he says, by our Lord to great multitudes gathered about Him among the hills. He may have intended this to be regarded as the counterpart to the theophany on Mount Sinai, but it is clear that here again he has grouped together without regard to chronology utterances of our Lord dealing with various aspects of His message for humanity.

(9) Next follows evidence of what is itself claimed to be a fulfilment of prophecy, our Lord's power to heal.

When we have said that, we are still left to ask on what principle the evangelist has selected these acts, and how they come to be arranged in their present order. Two noteworthy points present themselves to our notice: first, none of these miracles takes place in a synagogue: all are either in the open or in a private house. Secondly, no miracle (of the first five recorded) was the occasion of a controversy with the religious authorities of the day; we know that at first the authorities suspended judgment, and therefore incidents which were the occasions of contention are reserved to a later point.

Further we may notice that no two miracles are of the same kind. The illness of the centurion's servant had brought him, Luke says, to the point of death; the paralytic borne of four could not walk, so that he exemplifies the healing of the lame. The officer's son in John iv. was sick of a fever, which distinguishes him from the centurion's servant; and Matthew mentions Peter's mother-in-law as his instance of a fever cured.

Bearing these principles in mind we find that the miracles arrange themselves intelligibly as follows:

GROUP A

(i) A leper is healed.

Since, according to Matthew, our Lord is on His way from the mountain range to Capernaum, he naturally records first the earliest miracle he remembers as taking place away from Capernaum.

(ii) The Centurion's paralysed servant is healed.

Luke's parallel narrative shows that Matthew or the Interpreter, i.e. Q, is the authority for placing this miracle at the end of the Sermon on the mountain plateau: hence it follows next.

(iii) Simon Peter's mother-in-law is healed.

This is the first miracle given by both Mark and Luke as taking place in Capernaum outside the synagogue.

In connexion with all these three miracles we must notice that Matthew emphasizes our Lord's respect for the Law: the leper must be seen by the priest, our Lord does not enter the Centurion's house, and the sick are healed when the Sabbath is passed.

(iv) The stilling of the storm.

This again is the next miracle recorded by Mark when we exclude, as suggested above, any that took place in a synagogue or that occasioned controversy with the authorities.

Luke also gives it next after the Centurion's servant, except that he interposes the raising of the dead youth at Nain.

(v) The demon Legion is exorcised.[1]

Here again Matthew agrees with Mark and Luke in the order of these miracles.

The remaining five miracles exhibit features of particular interest. In connexion with each one we find the importance of faith insisted on, and it seems clear that it was on the basis of this common trait that they were selected for mention at this point in the narrative. Since, however, Matthew does not in his relation of them emphasize this feature in two cases, we may reasonably suppose that it was either St. Matthew himself or his Greek interpreter who assembled these five miracles as all alike enforcing faith, as a pre-requisite for our Lord's help. The list is as follows:

GROUP B

(i) In our Lord's house at Capernaum a paralytic[2] is assured that his sins are forgiven and is restored to health.

As in Mark and Luke, this incident is followed by the call of St. Matthew and the scribes' censure of social intercourse with publicans.

(ii) Jairus asks for his daughter's healing.

[1] Matthew does not name Legion: he speaks of two demoniacs, as to which see below, p. 50.

[2] Matthew speaks of the centurion's servant also as paralytic: Luke, the physician, distinguishes their maladies.

Matthew shows that this followed immediately on the defence by our Lord of His disciples' omission to fast. Luke agrees with Mark that Jairus made his request after the Lord's return from Gadara. Matthew follows Mark's grouping of incidents which led to controversies with the scribes. Mark followed by Luke preserves the saying "fear not: only believe."

(iii) The woman with an issue of blood is told "daughter . . . thy faith hath made thee whole."

(iv) Two blind men follow our Lord into a house and are healed after answering the question "Believe ye that I am able to do this?"

This miracle would appear to come from St. Matthew's narrative. It would be precarious to regard it as a variant form of the Marcan story about the man who at first saw men as trees walking, but nevertheless if the connecting words in ix. 32 may be understood to mean "As the two blind men journeyed about the country" we shall have them healed near Bethsaida and a little later the paranoiac youth brought by his father while our Lord was away on the Mount of Transfiguration.

(v) A mute, stated to be the victim of an evil spirit, is healed, whereupon the Pharisees declare that our Lord is in league with the most powerful of evil spirits.

This brief notice is of particular importance. Later in the Gospel Matthew, following Mark's grouping of material, refers to this miracle again. There he represents it as the occasion for our Lord's argument that a kingdom divided against itself is doomed to destruction.

The parallel account in Luke shows that St. Matthew or his Interpreter is the authority for connecting this miracle with the Lord's discourse. Yet none of the Gospels specifically states when the miracle occurred, and we are compelled to scrutinize the records further. It may be said at once that the evidence suggests that the sufferer was the one healed on the morrow after the Transfiguration.

The following points deserve attention:

    (a) The scribes were already arguing with the other nine disciples before our Lord and the chosen three came to the spot.

(b) In no case do we find either blindness or deafness and consequent inability to speak intelligibly attributed to demonic agency. The man's son[1] suffered from intermittent paroxysms of paranoia.

(c) Matthew alone speaks of blindness, and this may well be what the father conceived to be the explanation of his son's falling into the fire or the water.

(d) Faith is emphasized in our Lord's words to the father, and this will have been the ground for the miracle to have been included in this group.

(e) This identification of the miracle will supply an explanation of the otherwise strange exclamation of the woman standing by.

(f) Matthew (xvii. 15) makes the man's son a lunatic. If we are right in supposing the Transfiguration to have occurred near the full moon, we may believe the sufferer to have become particularly violent at that time.

(g) Luke's order now becomes explicable. Being without the long-missing section of Mark vi. 46 to viii. 27 he was at a loss where to insert the challenge by the Pharisees that our Lord would give a sign from heaven. Yet the order in Q led him to suppose that the charge that our Lord was in league with Beelzebub preceded the demand for a sign, and since both subjects implied controversy with the Pharisees he found the most apt position for them just before his own story of our Lord's countering of His Pharisee host's surprise at His neglect of ceremonial washing.

---

[1] It is usual to speak of "the lunatic boy," but apart from Luke ix. 42, there is nothing to compel us to suppose the sufferer to have been a mere child, and Mark's record that the father dated the onset of the malady from childhood (Mark ix. 21) might be thought to suggest that the boy had at least reached adolescence. The English version of Matt. ix. 32 has imported the word " man," while the original offers no obstacle to the notion that the mute was young. The word in Luke ix. 42 may conceivably be a pathetic diminutive ("his poor son") just as in Mark vii. 28 the diminutive implies "house-dogs" or "pet-dogs."

Matthew (xvi. 1) rightly follows Mark in placing the demand for a sign after the feeding of the four thousand, although like Luke he has, in an earlier chapter, been led by Q to group our Lord's controversies with the authorities without regard to their chronological dating. This duplication in Matthew is precisely similar to his duplication of the healing of the mute.

Before we pass on, we may remark that while this grouping of the ten miracles appears to come from St. Matthew himself or his Interpreter, its agreement in order at various points with Mark's arrangement lends support to the conclusions we have drawn as to the historical succession of events. That this order is to be found also in Luke supplies strong evidence in corroboration of our conclusions.

(10) After a recapitulatory statement that Jesus went about teaching, preaching and healing, and an explanation that He was moved to compassion towards the uninstructed multitudes, we have an account of the commissioning of the twelve apostles. Luke makes it clear that the Sermon on the Mount was in fact given after the Twelve were selected, and both Mark and Luke relate their sending out after some considerable period of preparatory instruction. Matthew having given the Sermon already as a specimen of our Lord's teaching now antedates the charge to the Twelve, making it follow immediately on their selection. In this charge we again observe that material is amassed from utterances of our Lord given on various later occasions. In particular we may notice the reference to the accusation that He was in league with Beelzebub, although this is only given at length in a subsequent chapter.

(11) After another brief summary of our Lord's work we have the story of the Baptist's message from prison. It would appear that Matthew is now grouping together the evidence that our Lord's mission so challenged the preconceptions of the Jews that it divided them into two classes. On the one hand religious formalists and those with whom material prosperity was the complement of devotion refused a hearing both to the Baptist and to Christ. On the other hand, spiritual babes might learn from Him a simpler way of serving God than by any

elaborate rules of religious duty. Thus Matthew follows his record of the Baptist's message with our Lord's attestation of St. John's high office, fulfilling the prophecy that Elijah should come; next with a condemnation of the places where the most of Christ's miracles were wrought; then with an acknowledgment that it was the Father's will that simple souls should best understand the principles of the Kingdom; and lastly with examples of how our Lord would supersede the detailed regulations which, for example, prescribed what might and what might not be done on the sabbath. Matthew gives two examples of our Lord's supersession of the rabbinic rules. He justified His disciples when, to satisfy their hunger, they plucked and rubbed ears of corn,[1] and He healed a man with a withered hand. When a council was held to plot His destruction, He withdrew, thus, as Matthew says, fulfilling a prophecy of Isaiah. This is followed by three more examples of opposition or misunderstanding:

(a) The exorcism of an evil spirit excites the Pharisees, as Matthew has mentioned before, to attribute our Lord's power to Beelzebub.

(b) The demand for a sign is met with refusal.

(c) Our Lord's putative kinsmen suppose Him to need restraint.

(12) Matthew now gives a collection of parables which exhibit a new character. They are enigmas for the casual hearer, and they are interpreted for the inner circle of disciples. Matthew notes that the first of these parables was uttered on the same day as our Lord's family sought to arrest Him. It is to be noticed too that these parables supply an explanation of the apparent failure which the evangelist has just recorded among the religious leaders of the time. This explanation would be a valuable weapon in the Christian arguments addressed to the Jews.

Moreover Matthew finds in these parables, meaningless to some, illuminating to others, an evidential correspondence with Jehovah's words to Isaiah, so that the prophet was the type and our Lord the antitype.

---

[1] It is perhaps not without significance that our Lord, the legal heir to the Davidic throne, appeals to the example of David and his attendants when He asserts the legitimacy of His own attendants' action.

It may not be superfluous at this stage to state clearly that a candid and unbiassed examination of all these facts forces us to the adoption of one or other of two hypotheses.

(a) On the one hand it may be held that the present order in the First Gospel comes from a final editor or compiler, who had before him either Mark or the oral teaching communicated by St. Mark to catechumens as embodying St. Peter's teaching and afterwards reduced to writing by St. Mark. In this case we have to ask the reason for such variations from Mark as we occasionally find, and we must specially weigh any indications of time and place which a comparison with Luke shows to be anterior to the compiler's work and therefore presumably derived from St. Matthew's logia or his Greek Interpreter.

(b) On the other hand it may be held that the present arrangement of material in Matthew comes from the apostle himself or his Greek Interpreter, in which case when the arrangement agrees with that of Mark it acquires a double authority as resting upon the testimony of both St. Matthew and St. Peter, and where there is disagreement we have to ask whether Matthew's methods of composition explain the disagreement or whether his evidence requires us to reconsider the order in Mark.

One or two instances may be noticed :

(a) In the account of the three temptations after our Lord's baptism, Luke's order appears to be the more consonant with our Lord's consciousness of His royal dignity. Since Matthew also is concerned to insist on His Davidic claim, we must suppose that the Matthean order is due to a feeling that the words "Get thee hence, Satan" should be followed by the Devil's departure and defeat. We ask, then, whether this stylistic effort should be attributed to the compiler or to his Greek source.

(b) The list of the twelve apostles must either come from Mark or from the oral instruction given by St. Mark following on St. Peter's teaching. If we are right in identifying Thaddaeus with Matthias, Luke's list is manifestly the more correct, and we can hardly assign to Matthew (unless he has here unconcernedly

reproduced Mark) what is contradicted by both
Luke and John.

(c) The parallelism of Luke shows that the section in
Matt. xii. which speaks of the exorcism of a
demoniac, the charge of an alliance with Beelzebub,
its refutation and the refusal of "a sign" comes from
St. Matthew himself or his Greek Interpreter. Mark
relates the last incident after the feeding of the four
thousand, and Matthew repeats it in that position
in chapter xvi.

Moreover, Mark shows that he has interposed the controversy
about Beelzebub's assistance in the middle of his narrative in
regard to our Lord's family seeking to restrain Him. If we are
right in identifying the healing of this demoniac with the healing
of the paranoiac youth, we get added significance for the warning
about the possible return of an evil spirit when we observe our
Lord's command "Thou dumb and deaf spirit, I charge thee,
come out of him, *and enter no more into him.*"

It is to be observed that when Matthew introduces the
family's interruption of our Lord with the words "While He
was yet speaking" we need not suppose that what immediately
precedes was what our Lord was saying (contrast Matt. ix. 18
with Matt. xii. 46). In this case there is no disagreement among
the synoptists in regard to the order of these episodes.

There now follow seven chapters in which there is nothing of
which the evangelist observes that it was a fulfilment of ancient
prophecy. Apart from small variations, these chapters reproduce
what is to be read in Mark from vi. 1 to x. 52. We shall probably
be right in regarding this section as the work of the evangelist,
drawing on the Marcan record to supplement the more limited
collection of prophetic words which St. Matthew had put together. He has been under the necessity of making some slight
adjustments at the beginning of the section.

Mark gives first a visit to Nazareth, then the sending out of
the Twelve and presently the picture of how Herod's mind (apparently owing to the increased notice which the apostles'
mission caused) was much disturbed because he had now killed
the Baptist.

We are now in a position to formulate certain conclusions as to the respective characteristics of Q and of the final editor's work.

(a) Q afforded no narrative parallel to Mark vi. 47–viii. 27. as we can see from the fact that St. Luke was unable to detect the omission from his copy of Mark or to repair the deficiency. Taking full account of this, we are led to believe that Q had nothing in the way of an ordered narrative. It consisted of material grouped into masses in the way that we have noticed, and we are led therefore to believe that such further aggregates of teaching as we find in the second half of the First Gospel were similarly put together in Q and that such framework of narrative as has been built around them is derived by the author from Mark.

(b) A comparison of Matthew with Luke shows that although there was in Q no long consecutive narrative, yet there were little introductory notes at certain points, such as, for example, the note that the charge of deriving help from Beelzebub followed on the healing of a mute. [1]

It has been common to brush aside these notes as mere connectives supplied by the final editor, yet this, honestly regarded, is merely subjective criticism, and may be the throwing away of valuable historical evidence. Until we have attempted to extract whatever of value for historical purposes these introductory notes can supply, we have no warrant to dismiss them with arbitrary indifference. On the contrary, they deserve to be weighed, and unless they are proved to contradict known facts, they may be used to fill out our story. A few examples may be given:

(i) Matthew introduces Jairus' appeal for help with the words "While he was yet speaking" and this follows our Lord's reply to St. John's disciples on the subject of fasting. We may conclude that we should place the question of John's disciples immediately before the arrival of Jairus, and this leads to the further conclusion that the Baptist was murdered before our Lord returned to Capernaum from Gadara.

[1] Another instance of such narrative material attached in Q to some utterance of our Lord is to be seen in the story of the healing of the centurion's servant.

(ii) Matthew introduces his account of our Lord's earliest
use of elaborate parables to indicate the nature of
God's Kingdom with the words: "The same day
went[1] Jesus out of the house, and sat by the seaside."
The evangelist thus identifies the day when the first
parable was spoken with the day when our Lord's
mother and brethren attempted to restrain His
actions. Luke makes it clear that this attempt on the
part of His family followed upon the delivery of the
first parables, but Matthew's words are a valuable
confirmation of the fact that all happened on the
one day. When to this is added Mark's explicit
statement after his account of the parables that "The
same day when evening was come" He took ship
and the storm followed, we can clearly follow the
story of that day: first the multitudes at the seaside,
the first parable, the return into His home, where
He expounded this parable, the coming of His
family to lead Him away from the crowd, the going
again to the sea with His disciples and their departure by boat.

We have seen that Q prefixed, to some at least of the episodes
he recorded, little notes describing the circumstances in which
they occurred, and as we have said one such note seems to
deserve special attention. Jairus' application to our Lord
follows the question of John's disciples about fasting. Historically
this is eminently satisfactory. Luke makes it clear that Jairus
came to our Lord some time after the parable of the sower had
been spoken and the demon Legion had been exorcized. Thus
the Baptist will have been dead by this time, and his disciples
now naturally turned to our Lord for instruction. Yet the
evangelist or editor following Mark's grouping of our Lord's
teaching about eating with publicans and about fasting brought
the healing of Jairus' daughter forward in date, a transference
which, however, though historically incorrect, fitted in with his
mention of the raising of the dead when he recounted our
Lord's answer to the Baptist's two messengers. Luke, it will be

---

[1] The pluperfect would better represent in English the true sense of the
Greek (see p. 48, note).

observed, is without this note of time which connected the teaching about fasting with Jairus' appeal. He followed Mark's arrangement. He grouped our Lord's teaching after the call of St. Matthew and he also followed Mark's dating of Jairus' application.

It is, of course, a similar grouping of material by Mark which has led Matthew to give our Lord's refutation of the charge that Beelzebub assisted Him just before the mention of our Lord's brethren coming to take charge of him.

Luke was aware that this arrangement was out of harmony with the chronological order of events, and he has therefore transferred it to a later point in his narrative. From Q he derived another arrangement by which the Beelzebub controversy had conjoined to it the challenge that our Lord would give a sign from Heaven. It is clear that Q here is in turn grouping topics unchronologically, and we have to thank the final author of the First Gospel for supplying guiding clues which may help us to unravel some at least of the perplexing contradictions of chronology. As we have said, the First Gospel has embodied in its pages matter from Q, mainly grouped according to subject-matter, and a narrative, in the main chronological, drawn from Mark. The author has been at pains to indicate by what may be called key-words the points at which Q and Mark touched on identical episodes. Thus, following Q, he attaches the demand for a sign to the Beelzebub issue; but elsewhere, following Mark, he briefly points out the historical circumstances in which the demand for a sign was made.

Again, following Q, he mentions in a list of miracles the exorcism which occasioned the charge of help from Beelzebub, but, following Mark, he relates this healing and its sequel at considerable length before the Parable of the Sower. Yet again he follows Q in detailing our Lord's reply to the demand for a sign, but subsequently he summarizes this when, following Mark, he places the incident after the feeding of the four thousand.

In view of these considerations it is reasonable instead of dismissing as mechanical connexions the notes of time and circumstance which we find in Matthew, to examine and weigh them with patient attention. That we are right in doing so is further demonstrated by the fact that the results we thus obtain harmonize with the conclusions to be drawn from the Third and the Fourth Gospels.

A word must be given to two other features observed in the First Gospel. We have seen that the author and, it would appear, the Apostle St. Matthew himself are concerned to insist on the one hand that our Lord was the Davidic heir and King and on the other that His ministers of state were the apostles. Jesus, it is insisted, was legally the King. This is the point of the story about St. Peter being asked whether our Lord would pay the Temple shekel: to refuse could have been interpreted as an overt claim to the throne, a claim our Lord refused to make.

The earliest believers accepted our Lord as their King and as that special King whom the prophets had prefigured as destined to accomplish a pre-eminent mission in the world. Yet they were slow to assimilate the true significance of the Messianic kingship. In consequence many of them clung to nationalistic hopes which resulted in a rigid assertion of the Mosaic obligations and an inveterate adherence to the nominal kindred of our Lord. Matthew has preserved words of our Lord which disposed of such earthly considerations. Not James, the Lord's brother, nor any other of His family, but the twelve apostles were to sit on thrones judging the twelve tribes of Israel. Not James' lineage but Peter's spiritual insight was the rock on which the Church was to be built.

After this middle section in the Gospel, drawn almost exclusively from Mark, we proceed to a narrative of the final scenes in the Lord's ministry. It is hard to determine with any approach to certainty whether this concluding section is to be regarded as the Marcan narrative supplemented with material from Q or as an independent narrative of St. Matthew himself. In the latter case we shall see here an example of the general method adopted by all the early Christian teachers for the presentation of the story of the Passion and the Resurrection. This would account still for the resemblances between Mark and Matthew. On either theory we observe that from Q must pretty certainly be derived the parables in these chapters which are not found in any other Gospel and some notes of prophecies fulfilled. Such a prophecy is that quoted from Zechariah, which spoke of thirty pieces of silver (the price at which the prophet was valued by his contemporaries) being cast into the Temple. Another prophecy is found in Psalm xxii. 18, which spoke of enemies parting their victim's garments amongst them and casting lots upon his vesture.

Again it is reasonable to refer to St. Matthew the record of our Lord's quotation from the Eighth Psalm, "Out of the mouth of babes and sucklings thou hast perfected praise."

One characteristic of the final editor's work is his practice of condensing or telescoping the source which he is using. This feature continually appears in his treatment of the Marcan narrative, but it is perhaps also discernible in regard to Q when we compare Matthew's syncopated account of the centurion's appeal to our Lord on behalf of the sick servant with Luke's fuller story.

So far we have followed the current fashion of speech in referring to the final editor or compiler of the First Gospel. The reader, however, who forgets for a moment the methods of the comptometer and the test-tube and exercises his faculty of literary taste, is likely to appreciate so highly the artistic skill shown in the arrangement of the Gospel that he will prefer to speak of the author. Be it admitted that that author used, as Luke did, both Mark and Q: nevertheless the genius and literary finesse of the author are so remarkable that they deserve particular consideration. One or two points can at once be stated.

(1) The author's candour and trustworthiness are not to be judged without due regard to his manifest purpose. Hence, if at any point he appears to date an incident otherwise than another Gospel dates it, our author must not be reprobated, but his purpose in re-arranging the order must be explored.

(2) Within the pattern prescribed by his purpose in writing, the author is punctilious in faithfully reproducing the substance of his authorities, while deftly and duly weaving the stuff of their material into the texture of his work.

(3) His method can be seen by comparing his reproduction of Mark's narrative with his original. This shows that he does not scruple to compress on the one hand and to expand on the

other, if expansion will clarify the significance of what is related. He does not, however, correct or amend, but is satisfied that the Marcan record and its Petrine testimony are authentic.

(4) We are justified in believing that the author's handling of his other authority, the Greek Q, is equally scrupulous. On the one hand he is less concerned than Luke was to preserve the precise grammar of his authority: for the sake of literary finish he recasts the Beatitudes into statements in the third person. On the other hand he does not modify, if he explains, the sense of what he found in Q. He adds "in spirit" to elucidate the blessing of "the poor" and he makes clear the point of the question "is it lawful for a man to put away his wife for any and every cause" by inserting in our Lord's reply the words "Apart from any charge of actual infidelity."

(5) Since we have no copy of Q we cannot categorically deny that some phrases, statements and even incidents found in Matthew but not in Luke may come from Q. But, however this may be, our study of the First Gospel warrants the conclusion that when the author introduces additional details which have no precise parallel in another Gospel, his evidence is not to be dismissed as an editorial and unauthentic insertion,[1] but is to be studied for the contribution it can make for the completion of the picture. One such detail indeed might have been thought to carry its own refutation. After the Baptist's disciples had taken up his body and buried it, our English texts continue "and went and told Jesus." Were this Matthew's actual statement, we should find it hard to escape the conclusion that he supposed the Feeding of the Five Thousand to follow a few days after our Lord heard of St. John's murder. The truth, however, is that Matthew, like Mark, has nothing to say about the arrival of that news. Both evangelists are clear that the return of the Twelve[2] led to a retirement which was followed by the feeding of the five thousand.

Armed with these considerations, we may feel some confidence in using the First Gospel, even in its variations from the

---

[1] More than this. Even if the source of such additions is not traceable, our author's verifiable fidelity justifies us in attributing such additions to some other trustworthy source.

[2] See my note in *Expository Times*, vol. LV, No. 4, p. 110.

Second and the Third, to extract additional facts for our reconstruction of the actual course of history.

Such in outline is the substance of the First Gospel, but it remains that this would seem to make it a mere catalogue of disparate materials rather than a methodical arrangement directed by an intelligible purpose. Yet it is manifest that we should be better satisfied that we had understood the Gospel if we could define, however imperfectly, the author's intention in writing it. We could then test the correctness of our definition by reviewing the details with special reference to their contribution and aptness for our author's supposed intention.

Let us then put into a few words what seems to emerge from our study. The book may be said to be an apologetic for the belief held by Jewish Christians, and specially those who spoke Greek, that Jesus was the Messiah, although He was of a type very different from what most of the Jews in His day had expected. The author begins then by indicating certain points in which Jesus entirely answered to those expectations where they were founded upon ancient prophecy.

St. Joseph was the heir to the throne of David. His acknowledgment of Jesus as his Son and heir transferred the presumptive succession from James to our Lord.[1] Besides this Isaiah's prophecy that Emmanuel should be born to a virgin goes to confirm the Christian belief that this adopted son is the Messiah. The prophecy would be left stripped of its startling significance if the Messiah had been born legitimately. Again, the narrative of the Magi's coming adds another point. After the casual and

---

[1] An argument of St. Paul's in his Epistle to the Galatians receives an interesting illumination from this. Critics have sometimes depreciated the apostle's argument from the use of the singular number in the promise to Abraham, but when it is recognized that "seed" is often the equivalent of son, St. Paul's point becomes justifiable that the promise was defined as heritable not by Ishmael, for fourteen years regarded as Abraham's son and heir, but by Isaac. In the same way James, for twenty years regarded as St. Joseph's heir, was displaced by Jesus. St. Paul was rebutting the claim of men who asserted that James was with them and who desired to draw their authority from the law given on Sinai. The apostle's reply is that that law has been superseded by the law of liberty. Hagar, the bondwoman, gave place to Sarah, the free woman; Sinai to the spiritual Jerusalem; Ishmael to Isaac; James the righteous in the Jewish and ceremonial sense to Jesus the righteous in the Christian and spiritual sense.

incidental remark that Jesus was born at Bethlehem, the author draws from the lips of the chief priests and scribes themselves the reference to Micah's prophecy, as warranting the belief that the Messiah should be born in that town. Once more the author quotes from Hosea words that declare that God's Son was called out of Egypt, and admittedly the Messiah was styled God's Son. Thus the Jewish Christian might rest satisfied that the facts of our Lord's birth and infancy corresponded with Messianic prophecies. If more were needed, it was noticeable that the settlement of the Holy Family at Nazareth afforded a paronomasia on a surname constantly associated with our Lord's name. He was called popularly Jesus the Nazoraean or Nazarite, i.e. the Holy One, and indeed the author has previously pointed out that Jesus was Mary's first-born Son and first-born sons were consecrated to God.

So far the author has rested his argument upon the correspondence between the facts and ancient prophecies. He now produces the testimony of John the Baptist, whom the masses of the Jewish people recognized to have been a prophet. John's testimony is important in several respects.

In the first place he repudiates the claim of the Pharisees to be sure of acceptance with God. Descent from Abraham is no sufficient guarantee. The whole outlook of the nation must be changed. Moreover, he is but a slave running to announce the coming of One superlatively great, and this One will bestow upon others God's Holy Spirit. The author quotes words of Isaiah which imply that God will presently be coming, and it can at least be said that when God's Son, the Messiah, mounts the throne, God's sovereignty will have begun. This brings us to a principal part in our author's argument. The popular conceptions of the Messianic rule must be shown to be inadequate; they were nationalistic, materialistic, mundane. Jesus must be shown to have amplified, sublimated, spiritualized what was adumbrated in the Old Testament. The author then tells that Jesus was recognized by this prophet-forerunner as his Superior, and at the same time declared—and the words deserve to be noticed for the progress of his apologetic—that it was His duty to "fulfil all righteousness." Then not only does the Holy Spirit descend to rest upon Him, but the Voice from Heaven pronounces Jesus to be God's Son as the Davidic Messiah and also Jahveh's "Boy" (whether errand boy or son) upon whom Isaiah prophesied that God would put His Spirit. Thus the author asserts that our Lord's Messiahship will bear the character of the "suffering servant." It is in conformity with this that our Lord in the wilderness is taught the alphabet of the spiritual reading of His office. Ceremonial defilement is etherealized into interior purity, imperial command into spiritual attraction, and immediate action on His own initiative for the spectacular inauguration of God's reign must be rejected in favour of patient waiting-upon God for Him to work out His purposes. Next, it is noted that our Lord removed to Capernaum and a prophecy of Isaiah is cited which promised that in that region, designated "Galilee of the Gentiles," great light should be seen. This accords with the declaration that in the name of Jahveh's "Boy" the Gentiles should trust.

The author now proceeds to unfold the way in which Jesus exhibited this spiritual conception of Messiahship. His procedure was unhurried and at times tentative. First we have an assemblage of our Lord's utterances, in which He tells His followers that their "Righteousness" must exceed that of the Scribes and Pharisees. Moreover, for them a generous spirit of humanity towards all men must be linked to an absolute dependence upon God's fatherly care. Then we are told of those acts of healing which illustrate the claim that Jesus fulfilled the prophecy that the "Suffering Servant" should Himself take our infirmities. A leper was touched and cleansed, a centurion's servant was healed, Peter's mother-in-law was rid of a fever.[1] It should be noticed that in none of these cases was there any break with the traditional regulations. The leper was instructed to obtain from "the priest" the sentence of release from quarantine: the centurion's house is not entered: the exorcism in the synagogue before the visit to Simon's house is omitted. Thus, our Lord's disregard of the defilement from contact with a leper and from entering a Gentile's house is obviated and the disregard of the Sabbath is pretermitted. It should be noticed too that the author even thus early emphasizes the point that

[1] These three healings are arranged geographically: the first some way off from Capernaum, the second near it, the third inside the city.

Israel's lack of faith would exclude them from the acceptance of God's sovereignty.

There follows a section which brings into clear light the steps by which our Lord's Messiahship was shown to be at variance with the popular anticipation and the dogmatic theology of the day. Our Lord's calm trust in God through the raging storm and its sudden cessation at His word heightened the disciples reverence for Him. His exorcism of the demons who then destroyed the swine still further strengthened the disciples' feeling, but it is to be observed that here we have the first definite rejection of our Lord: "the whole city . . . besought Him that He would depart out of their coasts." Then the paralytic was both forgiven and cured, and this occasioned an open clash with the religious authorities. Two or three observations must be made. The Jews of that age associated sin and disease so closely that the healing of the one went, in their minds, with the pardon of the other.[1] The author notes that this act of pardoning sin was a first cause of offence to the Pharisees.

Further, he notices that our Lord used the title "the Son of Man" as a succinct expression for the Messiah, whose character and function, He was concerned to teach them, was not what they assumed, but who was a Messiah who loved men of all nations and classes, who brought forgiveness to the sinner and healing to the sick, who attracted men by love instead of compelling them by force, who was comrade and commander of humanity, who personified, interpenetrated, inspired and incorporated in Himself all who trusted Him and depended on Him.

To exhibit the way in which Jesus revealed His Messiahship as of this kind, and in consequence estranged more and more those who clung to their conventional views, the author now proceeds to enumerate a series of incidents recorded by Mark. Jesus invited the customs officer, Matthew, to join His circle. He sat at dinner with friends of Matthew who, like him, were classed as "sinners," and defended His doing so with the words

[1] The first readers of the Gospel would remember that of the "suffering servant" it was said not only that "He bore our sicknesses" but also that "He bare the sins of many and made intercession for the transgressors."

"I am not come to call the righteous but sinners to repentance." He justified His non-inclusion of fasting in His precepts for His disciples on the ground that the conception of religious duty which He was concerned to convey to them was so novel that it was better imbibed by men who were not habituated to the quite alien religious discipline of the Pharisees.

Down to this point the author follows Mark, but here he appends two acts of healing, recorded much later in the other two synoptists, but known by our author to have followed immediately on the discussion of the fasting obligation. In both cases our Lord again shows that as the Messianic Healer He is supreme over all rules as to ceremonial defilement. Our evangelist appends two more examples of our Lord's healing, which could not in themselves give a handle for any charge that He aimed at destroying the Law: two blind men recovered their sight; a mute demoniac was heard to speak. The author adds in regard to this last miracle that while most people saw in it an unparalleled exertion of beneficent power, the Pharisees ascribed that power to Beelzebub. This terrible misrepresentation is taken by Matthew to mark a point at which his argument should pause while he gathers up some other facts as to our Lord's Ministry.

Remarking that our Lord "went about all the cities and villages, teaching in their synagogues, and preaching" the Good News of God's reign beginning, and that "He was moved with compassion" because the people were like sheep who needed a shepherd to fetch them home,[1] our author relates how the Twelve were sent out as itinerant healers and heralds of His reign. He proceeds to group together instruction given by our Lord at various times to His ministers or stewards. It is beside Matthew's purpose to indicate the chronological provenance of his material, and he therefore gives words from the charge to the Twelve, others from the charge to the Seventy, and yet others uttered in the Upper Room on Maundy

---

[1] Attention may be drawn to two titles applied to our Lord, which would subserve the evangelist's purpose of demonstrating that Jesus was what Christians believed. He was the "bridegroom" then present with the "children of the bridechamber." God, said Isaiah (lxii. 5), should marry Israel. If Israel is like a flock of lost sheep, God was the shepherd of Israel (Psalm lxxx. 1). Thus Jesus the Messiah in both aspects is God's Vicegerent.

2*

Thursday evening. This is entirely appropriate to His purpose of building up a true and lively representation of Jesus's messianic function. A few features of the instruction deserve special mention. The propagation and extension of the Gospel is to be achieved by persuasion, even though it be supported by miracles of power. It is to be expected that some will reject the invitation to become Christ's subjects. Obloquy and persecution will fall upon the disciples: if the Master has been called Beelzebub, how much more will His servants be so called. It would seem that Matthew here intends to direct his readers' attention to our Lord's character as a prophet, a purpose which reappears in later chapters. Besides this, he shows that, on the one hand, our Lord declares that open adherence to His service will assure rewards from His Father and, on the other hand, He throws His protection around the humblest and weakest who in any way serve their fellow men. Thus the evangelist emphasizes that the idea of Messiah was fused into the idea of the Son of Man.

Next we have teaching which demonstrates yet further how the prepossessions of those who professed and practised religion, no less than the indifference of the worldly, led to God's revelation being rejected. The Baptist himself was perplexed by what seemed to be unduly slow progress made by our Lord. That John was a great prophet is insisted on, yet men averred that he was possessed by a devil. Despite marvellous acts of healing, Capernaum refused our Lord's call. It was the Father's will that simple hearts alone should accept the new teaching about the character of God's service. All this contributes to the author's thesis that Jesus was the true Messiah sent from God. Our author now introduces the Sabbath controversy, recording, as Mark does, the condemnation of the disciples for eating corn in the fields on the Sabbath and the healing of the withered hand. Our Lord's withdrawal from the angry dispute is claimed by Matthew to have "fulfilled" Isaiah's words, which, as we have seen, were echoed by the voice from heaven at the Baptism. Then, after quoting that prophecy, the author tells again, but this time more fully, the act of healing which was seized upon by our Lord's enemies as an occasion for declaring that He was in league with Beelzebub.

This is followed by our Lord's solemn denunciation of such obstinate rejection of new truth, rejection leading even to the calling of goodness evil. Appended to this is an episode in which some scribes and Pharisees asked for a sign to be given them.[1] The evangelist then continues his account of the acrimonious calumnies of the Pharisees with what Mark also adds, that our Lord's mother and brethren on a certain day confessed to a doubt whether His mind had not become unbalanced. Following upon this is an account of the Lord's method of teaching by parables some of the aspects of the character required in citizens of the new Kingdom. The author is at pains to point out that this method of teaching was in harmony with words from a Psalm in which God's mighty deliverance from Egypt was remembered and His establishment of the Davidic throne. Thus the contention is again enforced that, however unlike men's expectations, Jesus' Messiahship was according to God's everlasting purpose. Moreover, the parables bore testimony to our Lord's prophetic insight, for they anticipated partial failure and insisted on a slow and gradual progress in the propagation of God's rule.

At this point we may say that Matthew is preparing to follow Mark's narrative, without arranging his material for logical argument, but leaving the story, as it developed chronologically, to show what manner of Messiah Jesus was. Before taking up the Marcan text consecutively, he mentions two incidents which Mark has recorded earlier and which Matthew has not incorporated in his previous pragmatic chapters. Thus, he now mentions a final visit of our Lord to Nazareth about the time when He was sending out the Twelve, and the murder of the Baptist, preceding by an unspecified interval this mission of the Twelve. Now, taking up the thread of the Marcan story from the return of the Twelve, he consistently keeps that story before him, as his main source of information, merely spatchcocking into it at intervals material he has derived from some other source. Two such instances may be indicated. On our Lord's

[1] Luke's arrangement shows that this collocation of incidents is not primarily due to Matthew, but comes from some source to which both he and St. Luke had access. Matthew in chapter xvi sets the episode in its proper position, when he is following Mark.

final return to Capernaum, the agents who were collecting the
Temple-money asked Peter if our Lord was in the habit of
paying. When Peter came indoors, our Lord in His comments
upon the matter took it as common ground between Himself
and the apostle that He was the Son of God. Again, Matthew
cites words of our Lord which declared that where two or three
Christians met in His Spirit, He would always be present
amongst them. Here the evangelist emphasizes once more that
the Son of Man is the nerve-centre of the Christian Body,
sensitive to all that its members do or suffer.

A few further words should be added by way of indicating
how the final chapters conform to the general pattern of the
author's purpose. In confirmation of his contention that Jesus
was the true antitype of David's Son, the Jehovah's Christ, he
introduces the parable in which the Son of Man sits to pronounce ultimate sentence upon all mankind. He takes over
from Mark the predictions of Jerusalem's fall and the warnings
that it and the coming of the Son of Man would be sudden
and, for many, unexpected. In this he emphasizes once again
our Lord's greatness as a prophet. That the prophecies were still
unfulfilled when the author wrote will be argued on another
page. Here we pass on to observe how the final chapter
explodes the Jewish fable that the disciples stole away the Lord's
body, and insists again on the supreme position of Jesus in the
universe. When the eleven apostles and, as we shall believe,
five hundred others met by Christ's appointment on a hill in
Galilee, some hesitated[1] to worship Him, and He met their
hesitation by declaring that all power had been given to Him
in heaven and in earth. Then, following his custom of assembling
utterances of our Lord spoken at different times, the evangelist
continues with what we shall believe to be words spoken at the
Ascension. When we grasp the meaning in Jewish speech which
the word "name" conveys, we shall find no reason for doubting
that the author gives an authentic record of our Lord's final
words. Converts were to be baptized and therewith admitted
into the family of God, in which they were to learn, to reverence
and to love the character and Being of Him whom, under the
name of Jahveh, Israel had owned as their God for 1,500 years,

[1] See *Expository Times*, vol. xxxvii, No. 7, p. 335.

and whom the converts were to worship as the Father of His people : whose fatherly love towards mankind He Himself had known and revealed, being the divinely attested inheritor of David's throne, Jahveh's Anointed Vicegerent, God's Son and Holy One, His Unique Interlocutor, the stereoscopic Mirror of His character of universal love and therefore displayed to men as the representative Son of Man, exalted above all creation to judge and rule hereafter; and whose Spirit the disciples had witnessed and known to be dwelling in their Lord throughout His Ministry and were bidden to expect would be sent forth to dwell in them. Thus for the new Israel God's character would be revealed not only, as to the old Israel, through what the Old Testament exhibits, but also through what the Gospels exhibit, and further through the unintermitting illumination and limitless eternity of divine communion and interpenetration.

When it is realized that the words do not express the doctrine of the Blessed Trinity, all reason for rejecting their authenticity appears to vanish. They are the very words of Jesus, waiting to be elucidated by the Holy Spirit to the divinely guided Christian Church.

(2) *Some Particular Features*

Commentators by detailed analysis of the First Gospel have elaborated explanations and interpretations of its arrangement. We need not attempt a discussion or examination of these exhaustive studies. Our last chapter has pointed to the conclusion that the work is in intention an argument or apologia, but it may assist the reader in following our investigations if a few points are here brought to his attention.

(*a*) When the Baptist dispatched two of his disciples to elucidate the apparent procrastination in the Kingdom's advent, our Lord's reply throws light on the evangelist's selection of his previous material. He has left his readers in no doubt that the glad tidings of the Kingdom are brought to the ears of the poor.

(*b*) One of the would-be followers spoken of by Luke (ix. 57) was a scribe.

(c) Matthew is careful to note that when he proceeds to relate the healing of the paralytic after that of the Gadarene demoniacs, he is passing back to Capernaum so far as locality is concerned.

(d) The account of St. Matthew's call and of the disciples' disregard of the Pharisaic rule to fast twice in the week serves as a preparatory explanation of the subsequent words of our Lord as to the libel upon Him that He was addicted to sumptuous living.

(e) The healing of the two blind men it is difficult to equate with any similar healing in the other Gospels. Despite Matthew's meticulous fidelity in detailing the circumstances, and indeed because of it, we cannot find sufficient resemblances to identify it with any other narrative.

(f) The first time that the healing of the dumb man is mentioned, it is enumerated—and only in a bald brevity—so as to make up to ten the number of "signs," perhaps as an antitype to the Ten Plagues in Egypt. The healing is not here related with any fulness, but the postscript that our Lord's power was thereupon attributed to Beelzebub is Matthew's careful note to guide the reader to understand that the incident is the same as that which he describes more fully later. It must be clearly kept in mind that the evangelist does not intend us to date the event at this point in the Ministry: indeed, as we shall see, his subsequent recording of it is placed not in its chronological order but in the grouping of cognate matter in which Mark had set it.

(g) Particular attention must be paid to the evangelist's note (ix. 18) that, while our Lord was yet speaking of the impropriety of using old wineskins for new wine, Jairus came to Him. Since we may view this as historically exact, we shall have to jettison our acceptance of the chronological arrangement of Mark at this point although Luke has followed it and in that measure confirmed it. If, on the other hand, we persist in reading the First Gospel as a work not designed to furnish a chronological narrative but to present the facts grouped according to a systematic plan, it might be thought that our reliance on the evangelist's notes of place and time was unjustifiable. This, however, we have no occasion to do. The note is often regarded as merely inserted to bridge the passage from the teaching as to fasting to the story of Jairus, but it is reasonable to hold that Matthew is not introducing an otiose note nor an unwarrantable addition. On the contrary it will be a sound and necessary connecting link between the incidents which he found recorded in his copy of the Second Gospel. It should be added that a scrupulous comparison of the three synoptists at this point leaves no room for any theory that Matthew found in Q evidence enabling him to correct mistaken chronology in Mark's narrative.

(*h*) Down to the end of chapter x Matthew has handled his material so as to leave the impression, in itself entirely historical, of success and popularity attending our Lord's Ministry. Thus: (1) The antedated healing of the dumb man has been lightly passed over and no prominence given to the charge that our Lord had demonic assistance. (2) To complete the setting for supporting Christ's reply to the disciples sent by the Baptist, the evangelist needed also to show how the Good News was disseminated among the poor, and therefore before telling the story of St. John's message he introduces the Mission of the Twelve. (Mark's narrative may be taken to indicate that in point of chronology this mission followed the Baptist's martyrdom and made so much stir that Herod argued that the saint was risen from the dead. Matthew deftly introduces the subject by premising from Q what Luke has given as our Lord's address to the Seventy.[1])

(*i*) The evangelist now introduces the episode of the Baptist's sending of two disciples to elicit an open avowal or repudiation of our Lord's unique and supreme mission. It is here that Matthew explicitly asserts that the gloom of apparent and partial failure began to gather about a Ministry which until then might have been represented as radiant with the sunshine of success and welcome acceptance. He assembles at this point utterances of our Lord which demonstrate that He was taken by surprise but had in Himself the assurance that authentic

---

[1] Jacob's twelve sons and seventy souls in his family when he migrated to Egypt are perhaps echoed in the twelve springs and seventy palm-trees at Elim (Exodus xv. 27) and may perhaps have suggested to the Lord the number both of the apostles and of the others.

though His mission from the Father was, it carried with it for that very reason the possibility of men's refusal of its call.

(j) Mark appears to make our Lord's Parable of the Sower to be followed the same day by the attempt of His mother and brethren to withdraw Him into seclusion. Luke corroborates this sequence of events. Matthew [1] subscribes to the same arrangement, for after recording the attempt of our Lord's friends to secure and arrest Him, he continues his narrative with the words "the same day" and proceeds to give the first parable of the new type.

(k) The evangelist appends to his mention of the Pharisees' insinuation that our Lord was helped by Beelzebub His brethren's design to take Him into seclusion. This collocation supports the view that the reason for Mark also mentioning the Pharisees' calumny at the moment he does is that it was the natural complement to the Brethren's and the Blessed Virgin's anxieties.

(l) Most important of all is the general corroboration which Matthew gives to our reconstruction of our Lord's Ministry. Disregarding for the moment the chronology of single incidents, we can see clearly enough that at first our Lord was generally if not universally welcomed and His beneficent dismissal of disease roused enthusiasm and expectation. Presently His super-session of religious rules in favour of a spiritual and generous spontaneity awakened animosity, opposition and hesitancy. There followed a new type of teaching which developed spiritual understanding in those who were at pains to learn and which in some instances reconciled the authority of His mission with its appearance of partial failure. This which is the broad chronological course of events deducible from the other Gospels has guided Matthew in the selection and arrangement of his material, though he has made not chronology but topics the basis of his narrative.

(m) By particularly noting that it was spoken on the day when the relatives sought to withdraw Him into seclusion,

---

[1] In Matt. xiii. 1 we may better render the Greek ἐξελθὼν ἐκάθητο by an English pluperfect, as in Matt. ii. 1 and Luke xxii. 15. Cf. *Expository Times*, vol. L, No. 9, p. 420.

Matthew introduces the Parable of the Sower as our Lord's explanation to the apostles of the partial failure which His teaching must have. He shows how it was that, though the Seed was God's word, there were hearts in which it could not grow to perfection. By first stating that our Lord's mother and brethren accepted the view that He was demented the evangelist has prepared his readers for the lesson of the parable, and has accordingly inverted the order of events on this day. The parable, in fact, preceded and occasioned the Blessed Virgin's alarm. Then further he has followed Mark in associating the Pharisees' interpretation of our Lord's enthusiasm (as they regarded it) with His mother's, but Matthew has mentioned the Pharisaic calumny first since it harmonizes with his scheme of arrangements. But we must notice that just as Mark duplicated his reference to the Blessed Virgin's fears, resuming his story after the parenthetic account of the Pharisees, so Matthew gives here the briefest and baldest account of the Pharisees (which is sufficient for his immediate purpose of giving the premises preceding the parables) and relates them again more fully at a later point in his story. This feature in his narrative needs to be emphasized, since it rids us of an apparent recurrence of incidents.

(n) In his account of the Crucifixion Matthew relates the Saviour's cry about the ninth hour, and in doing so makes the words from the Twenty-second Psalm appear in the form HĒLI, HĒLI. This corroborates and explains what Matthew further adds, that some said that our Lord was calling for Elijah to save Him. Mark gives the word in the form ELOI, which could afford no ground for the bystanders' suggestion. Luke confirms the authenticity of Matthew by his manifest misunderstanding of the word as the Greek HĒLI(E), i.e. O Sun. If St. John was away from the Cross at this hour, having for a little while made his way with the Lord's mother to his home, it would not be he who supplied this part of the narrative to Luke, and, since investigators deprecate our referring to Q the story of the Passion, we must claim that we have here two independent authorities for attributing to our Lord the very form of words recorded by Matthew rather than by Mark.

(*o*) Political speakers and religious preachers often repeat an apt illustration, giving it on each occasion the form and setting most appropriate to the situation with which they are concerned to deal. The Parable of the Ten Pounds and that of the Talents have often been recognized as variants, but the significance of their order has not been noticed. The jealousy of the disciples and their rivalry for precedence may explain our Lord's utterance of the former as He passed on from Jericho towards Jerusalem. Preparing the disciples for the impending close of His earthly Ministry, our Lord urged diligence by the Parable of the Pounds. After He had noticed the widow's two mites He recast the parable at the point where Matthew dates it, to impress on anyone—shall we say one of the apostles who was not in the inner circle of the three at the Transfiguration or the four on the Mount of Olives?—who might be ready to excuse himself because he was unimportant, that even the least gifted was called upon to contribute what he could.

Finally, a word may be given to a small incidental point. One distinctive feature of the First Gospel has been frequently noticed. Where Mark relates how one man, Bartimaeus, had his sight restored, and that one madman, possessed by the demon Legion, was recovered to sanity, the First Gospel in each case makes two men healed. It seems clear that in the same way where the Fourth Gospel[1] relates the individual appearance of our Lord to the Magdalene, the First Gospel describes the same appearance as made to two women. We may here find the key to all these divergences. Matthew, possibly guided in this by Q or some other source, recorded the actual fact[2]; John confined himself to what the more prominent witness said. Similarly the more prominent of the two maniacs and of the two blind men lived distinctively in St. Peter's story which Mark recorded.

[1] *Expository Times*, vol. LI, No. 10, p. 478.
[2] Matthew, it must be mentioned, states that the disciples brought two donkeys for the Lord's entry into Jerusalem, and, what escapes the reader of the English version when they say that they set Him *thereon* (unless indeed by "on them" the garments are meant), prepared both animals for our Lord to ride upon them. The evangelist apparently is concerned to have the old prophecy fulfilled in every particular and therefore adapts his language to harmonize with the words "upon an ass . . . and on the foal of an ass." Elsewhere we may believe that he is completing the records as suggested above.

(3) *The Authorship of the First Gospel*

The habitual nomenclature of the Church claims St. Matthew, i.e. Levi, the customs officer at Capernaum, as the author who has given us the Gospel which is regularly placed first in our Bibles. The critical scepticism of the last hundred years has deprecated this attribution. It has fastened on the fact that the work appears incontrovertibly to be built in part on Mark and has pronounced it inconceivable that an apostle should have written in dependence on another evangelist. Long and learned treatises embodying results of patient detailed and statistical investigations have asserted elaborate conclusions which have left little room for any personal connexion between St. Matthew and the Gospel which bears his name. It would be out of place to attempt an elaborate examination or dissipation of these theories: what is proper and desirable is to state an alternative view which, it may be claimed, cannot be shown to contradict any of the available evidence[1] nor to be inherently improbable. Setting matters in chronological order, we shall suggest :

(1) The first written work connected with the Christian movement was a collection of O.T. passages or "oracles" which St. Matthew put together, quoting them in Hebrew, and which, he judged, pointed to Jesus as the long-anticipated heir of David, and as Jahveh's Christ. To validate his appeal to the Scriptures he quoted not from the wider Bible (a Greek collection in common use among non-Palestinian and the less rigorist Jews), but from the smaller Hebrew collection accepted by the most strict Rabbis of Jerusalem. This work of his he left his fellow Christians to use as a promptuary for apologetic teaching, each, as he best could, translating the texts and divining in what way they had found fulfilment in the Saviour's story.

Two comments must here be made. In the first place it is fair to say that the whole monstrous mass of Babel-like theories which have risen one upon another in the last half century is

[1] Except for one detail, the uncritical and inconsiderate repetition of Mark's omission of Judas (not Iscariot) from the list of the Twelve and his inclusion of Matthias.

built upon Papias' statement of this fact, that St. Matthew was
an author of a work which was not written in Greek. On this
we shall say more presently. In the second place we must
observe that since Papias was an erudite and well-read scholar,
as we shall see in a moment, versed in literary and rhetorical
studies, we are compelled to give full weight and exact precision
to his word "oracles." In Greek use two words occur which
express and define the idea suggested by our English word
"oracles." Where a man consulted an oracular voice, the
medium or spokesman-prophet of some god, the answer given
to the enquirer's question was a *Chrēsmos*. But apart from such
direct interrogatory responses, there were in circulation *logia*
or general prophecies dealing with the destined future of the
world's history. Just as in the darkest days of Egyptian fortune
forecasts of deliverance were drawn from the memories of a
corresponding period in the great Sothic cycles, so in other
communities recourse was had for encouragement and hope to
Sibylline or Orphic oracles. They may have been little more
in the main than the vague optimism, the longings of the human
heart and its trust that somehow in spite of present misery
Providence must design something happier for the future. These
oracles were felt to speak with the authority of wisdom that is
more than human. They were like the rune of "Old Nixon,"
long current in Cheshire, that "clubs and clouted shoes will
win the day." When St. Paul spoke of the oracles of God, we
can see that he is not giving a variant title to the Scriptures or
Old Testament, but is speaking of them as the divine prevision
of the providential plan of cosmic and more particularly human
history. Thus they explain the Call of Israel in preparation for
the redemption of humanity. So for St. Stephen they are the
revelations made to Moses for the guidance of Israel so that
the people should understand their high calling. Similarly the
author of the Epistle to the Hebrews takes it to be axiomatic
that a rudimentary grasp of the principles underlying the
oracles of God will include a capacity to recognize in Jesus the
fulfilment of the words "a Priest for ever after the order of
Melchizedek." We shall insist then that so learned a literary
critic as Papias meant what we have said when he spoke of the
oracles assembled by St. Matthew. In spite of all that has some-

times been argued, they were neither words, i.e. discourses or addresses (*logoi*), nor sayings, i.e. mots (*rhemata*) of Jesus.

(2) From the first Whitsunday the Christian believers continued steadfastly in the apostles' teaching. The teaching would infallibly follow the pattern of the lessons given in that age among the Jews, oral lessons learnt by rote. Here Papias assists us. He tells us that St. Peter used to give his lessons in a form which he defines by a name well known in the literary academies of the Hellenistic period. *Chreiai* were concise, pointed mots uttered by some famous character whose authority carried weight, and these mots were introduced by a brief recital of the circumstances in which they were spoken.[1] The lessons given by St. Peter were particularly valued,[2] so that after a while St. Mark wrote them out and the apostle gave the manuscript his approbation. Here again some points need to be stressed. First it may be doubted whether any of the apostles except St. Matthew and perhaps the two sons of Zebedee were capable of composing a volume of reminiscences of their Lord. St. Matthew, as we have seen, had written a book of oracles and was a civil servant in the Customs and Excise. His education therefore may be assumed to have fitted him more than the others to give permanent and written form to the teaching which was otherwise oral. Next we have no warrant for supposing that Eusebius' quotation from Papias is exhaustive and that the only writing that St. Matthew did was what has just been mentioned. We shall return to this in a moment.

(3) While St. Peter's lessons were still circulating by oral repetition, there appeared another written record of Apostolic memories, the Greek work known as Q. This contained not isolated mots of our Lord but continuous discourses, which underlie parts both of Matthew and of Luke. These memories no doubt for some time had been handed on word for word by rote, as St. Peter's *chreiai* were, but comparison of the forms in which they are seen in the First and the Third Gospels suggests they were already written before either of those Gospels was composed. Two comments must be made. The evidence of this document establishes what we should otherwise regard as

---

1 See R. O. P. Taylor, *The Groundwork of the Gospels.*
2 This nullifies the objection that no apostle would draw on Mark.

almost certain, viz. that the form chosen by St. Peter for his lessons must not be taken to delimit the style and method of our Lord's teaching. This consideration may satisfy us that He not only enunciated pithy maxims such as Mark has habituated us to assume as characteristic of His teaching, but also long, ordered discourses or addresses like the Great Sermon and the Charge to the Apostles and the addresses in the Fourth Gospel. Further, St. Matthew's initiative in preparing a promptuary of oracles suggests that we may attribute to him the first writing out of the apostolic teaching. But this is pure conjecture and of no serious significance for our enquiry.

(4) Somewhere before A.D. 67 two written Gospels appeared, but we are not in a position to pronounce which was the earlier. (i) Matthew wrote an apologetic, its general form most effectively arranged for the development of its argument and the particular grouping of its long discourses exhibiting a fine literary sense. In it are incorporated large sections of material drawn from Mark (or perhaps the unwritten record of St. Peter's lessons) and from Q, the volume just referred to of extended addresses given by our Lord. No proof can be given to negative the contention that this Gospel is from the pen of St. Matthew the Apostle. If this contention may be accepted, the little circumstantial notes which appear at various points will rest on his testimony, e.g. that Peter's second denial was provoked by a challenge from a manservant following a maid's assertion, and again the note that "let be, let us see whether Elijah will come to save Him" was in criticism on a soldier's giving relief to the Saviour's thirst. This view of the Gospel will explain its unquestioned title and we may date its writing as perhaps anterior to Mark. It will have drawn on the memorized substance of St. Peter's lessons and the written or memorized volume of Christ's addresses, but Matthew's purpose of presenting an argument of apologetic led to his handling these sources with freedom as regards their order and exact language. Neither Papias' single remark nor any feature in the Gospel contradicts or disproves our hypothesis, and we shall go on also to assert that the work appeared early enough for the Christians in Judaea to act upon the warning to flee when the Roman armies approached Jerusalem.

(ii) About the same time Mark wrote from memory St. Peter's *chreiai*.[1] Luke made use of this written record and also of Q, the volume of Addresses, either memorized or written. With the same accuracy of literary description as we have noticed as to *chreiai* and *logia*, Luke styles his work a *diēgēsis*.

Christ's sermon at Nazareth and St. Paul's at Antioch show the type of Christian preaching. For such preaching neither St. Matthew's Oracles nor St. Peter's *chreiai* nor Q would suit as Scriptures to be read as part of the Church service : they would serve well as promptuaries for the preachers.

As a conjectural reconstruction of the history we might suggest :

A.D. 33 Pentecost.
St. Peter taught, St. Mark memorized, *chreiai* about Jesus.
36 St. Matthew put together his Oracles.
43 St. Matthew put together Q.
47 Mark went with Barnabas and Paul, and later with Peter to Rome.
49 Mark wrote his Gospel.
55 Matthew wrote his Gospel.
59 St. Luke met St. John.
60 St. Luke wrote his Gospel.
63 St. Luke wrote the Acts.

The reader may find it of advantage to calibrate these dates with those set out in Part V, Chap. 3, pp. 361 to 364.

Three comments seem justifiable by way of epilogue.

(1) In the prediction of the fall of Jerusalem Mark inserts after the words "The abomination of desolation," quoted from Daniel, the injunction "let him that readest understand." An unbiassed reader can have no doubt that these words are intended to urge any who learnt of our Lord's prophecy to perpend their meaning, and so to take warning against the time

---

[1] This is not to say that Peter or Mark had had a training in the "rhetoric" of Hellenistic education. Papias, however, manifestly had, and, versed as he was in the categories of the rhetoricians, classified Mark's Gospel as a volume of *chreiai*.

when the Roman army should invest Jerusalem, after which the warning would be useless.

(2) Matthew,[1] we might suppose, if we wished, though writing after A.D. 70, to have repeated the warning, while concentrating his attention on his purpose of establishing our Lord's authority as a prophet. It is, however, more natural to regard the warning as one felt by the author to be still in place. In this case we shall date the writing of the First Gospel also before A.D. 70.

(3) Since Luke omits the enigmatic warning of Daniel's language it might be supposed that he wrote after A.D. 70. We may indeed believe that that obscure language, used by our Lord Himself, was deliberately continued by the first two evangelists to veil from possible spies and informers what the instructed understood, and with the fall of Jerusalem the veil could be lifted. Luke describes unequivocally the Roman siege works, and some critics, in their anxiety not to date the book earlier than a sceptic would allow, have treated this as evidence that St. Luke re-worded our Lord's prediction in the light of the event. For this there is no justification. The evangelist's habitual care to reproduce the Lord's very words makes against this theory, and, as we have seen elsewhere, Christ had drunk deep of the thought and language of Jeremiah. That prophet (vi. 6) makes Jahveh say to the Chaldeans, "Hew ye down trees and cast a mount against Jerusalem," and it cannot be supposed that the methods of siege used by Pompey in 63 B.C. had been forgotten. We conclude that Luke, writing for Gentile Christians, omits the allusive obscurity, but duly preserves the clear warning, as being still needed, so that believers may escape the Roman armies.

---

[1] We need not scruple to accept the apostle as the author, even though we suppose him to have mis-dated Christ's cleansing of the Temple. Matthew had not become a disciple when it occurred, and Mark (who has transposed the date) would seem to him to be writing with Peter's authority behind him.

Chapter Four

LUKE

IT is an accepted truism that Luke has derived his material from at least three sources. Like Matthew he has used the second Gospel and Q, but, besides, he has masses of matter derived from some other source or sources. How he has used Mark we have already considered and something will be said presently about the way in which we may suppose he had been assisted by Q. Here it will be convenient and desirable to say something about the other portions of his work, but before doing so it will be well to dispose of an alternative view of his Gospel.

Some writers have found an explanation of the absence from Luke of certain Marcan sections in a supposed unwillingness on his part to relate two incidents which bore much resemblance to one another.[1] Thus the feeding of the Four Thousand, it is thought, was omitted because it was much like that of the Five Thousand, and in the same way the answer to the Scribe as to the greatest commandment might be regarded as too similar to the sections about the Good Samaritan and the rich young ruler. This notion, however, is not altogether satisfactory when we remember that Luke relates the instructions both to the Twelve and to the Seventy. A simpler explanation might seem to be that the loss from Mark of yet more leaves than the great lacuna left St. Luke dependent on Q at certain points. This might seem to be confirmed by the fact that the statement that no man durst ask any more questions is made by Mark to follow the Scribe's hearty acceptance of our Lord's summary of man's duty; by Matthew to follow His argument that the Christ must be more than David's son; and by Luke to follow His refutation of the Sadducees. It is natural therefore to infer that

---

[1] Two omissions seem to be due to misunderstanding: the visit to Nazareth about the time the Twelve were sent out and the Anointing on the eve of Palm Sunday.

St. Luke was without Mark's pages 73–74, so that he had not before him the Scribe's question and drew the argument with the Sadducees from Q. The loss of this leaf may be thought to be confirmed when we observe that the other half of the sheet, pp. 67–68, is hardly reflected in Luke's narrative. There the sentence on the pretentious but barren fig-tree is absent, and Q may well be the source for what Luke has in common with those pages. In the same way, pp. 57–58 and 83–84, which would be written on one and the same sheet, find so little reflexion in Luke that it may well be thought that the third Gospel was without these pages, and that the parallels which it offers to them come from some other source or sources, whether Q or some unnamed informant to whom he had access.

To summarize and present at once the conclusion to which a scrupulous examination of the evidence would seem to point, it may be said that all seems to suggest that St. Luke, at some time or other, had the opportunity of learning many facts about our Lord's life from St. John, who was the younger son of Zebedee and Salome, the sister of the Blessed Virgin, and who was eventually after the Crucifixion the adopted son and guardian of our Lord's mother.

This theory will explain how it is that Luke can give the facts recorded in his first two chapters, which, as is generally recognized, tell the story from the side of our Lord's mother, while Matthew may be thought to have the story from the side of St. Joseph and his kinsmen. In the subsequent narrative at several points Luke has details which may naturally be thought to have come from one of the chief three apostles, yet are not mentioned by Mark as remembered by St. Peter, nor can very well come from St. James, because he was martyred before St. Luke came into the Christian movement. It will be of interest to enumerate some of these distinctive details.

(1) In Luke's account of the Transfiguration, as will be shown in a later chapter, there are details not found in Mark, for which no authority can be suggested that is as likely as St. John, and if he is the source of Luke's account, we have to our hand a sufficient reason for John's giving no word to it afterwards. Luke and Luke alone records the topic of discussion between our Lord and the spectral prophets, and he names

here John the younger brother before James, presumably because John gave him the story.

(2) Luke has facts additional to Mark in his story of Judas' bargain with the priests, the preparation for the Last Supper and the Supper itself. When Peter and John are named as the two Apostles who made the preparations, it is in Luke's manner to indicate in this way that John was his informant. Mark, Peter's mouthpiece, omitted the names. The saying of our Lord that he had desired to eat the Passover with His disciples before He suffered, harmonizes with John's statement that the Last Supper was not on the Passover night.[1] If Luke's account of the institution of the Eucharist comes from St. John, we have again ready to our hand the reason for John not recording it.

(3) In Luke's story of the agony in Gethsemane there are again details which may most reasonably be supposed to come from St. John, the survivor of the two apostles who, with St. Peter, were near Jesus in the garden. Luke alone mentions that Jesus was withdrawn from them about a stone's cast. He alone tells that there appeared an angel unto Him from heaven, strengthening Him. Luke alone says that, being in an agony, He prayed more earnestly: and His sweat was, as it were, great drops of blood falling down to the ground.

(4) In the account of the Crucifixion, we have three Words from the Cross which, we shall believe, were heard by the Lord's mother and by St. John, while Mark has only the loud cry which was audible at some distance from the Cross. John records three more words uttered after the loud cry, and we shall best reconcile all the evidence if we take it that St. John is the authority for all six of the more private sayings, and that here again the Fourth Gospel supplements the Third.

In all these major instances the features to which attention has been drawn may fairly be considered to have been derived by Luke from a source which is narrowed down to one person and one person only, viz. that one of the three chief apostles who was neither Peter nor St. James the Martyr. This identification of Luke's informant as St. John harmonizes with a number of slighter indications, which by themselves might not have

---

[1] The reader may be referred on this point to F. L. Circot, *The Early Eucharist,* reviewed in *J.T.S.,* January 1940.

been equally definite, but, as confirmations of what has already
been said, may be held to have some value.

(i) Mark, followed by Matthew, states that James and John
were mending their nets, but uses the general expression
"casting their nets into the sea" with reference to Peter and
Andrew. Luke is able to say that they were all washing their
nets at the time Jesus came to them.

(ii) In Luke vii. 9 we are told that the Lord turned Him
about and spoke to the people that followed and in xxii. 61 he
turned and looked upon Peter, a vivid detail which is not
derived from Mark's recollections of St. Peter's words.

(iii) In Luke xxii. 3 we read "Then entered Satan into
Judas," and in John xiii. 27 "after the sop Satan entered into
him," a coincidence in language which is certainly worthy of
attention.

(iv) In Luke xvii. 5 and 6 we find "the apostles said unto
the Lord . . . and the Lord said"; in xxii. 31, "the Lord said
Simon, Simon"; in xxii. 61, "the Lord turned and looked upon
Peter." This unusual nomenclature in the narrative finds its
parallel in the equally unusual "It is the Lord" of John xxi. 7.
That these are the only examples of the use in all four Gospels
is remarkable, and the conclusion suggested by the coincidence
is confirmed when we observe that all four Lucan passages can
be seen to betray, as for other reasons we have already argued,
an origin from some other source than Mark or Q.

If some of the more striking variations from Mark which are
found in Luke came from St. John, we can well understand
why the Fourth Gospel so admirably dovetails into the story,
one Gospel explaining, confirming and correcting the other. To
mention a few such variations, we may note:

(a) We learn that on a certain Sabbath our Lord with
James and John went to the house of Simon and Andrew after
leaving the synagogue at Capernaum. Luke dates this some
considerable time before these four apostles became Christ's
constant companions. John relates that Jesus after His forty
days of solitude returned to where the Baptist was and that
Andrew and Peter and two other disciples of John accepted the
Baptist's witness to our Lord. This illuminates Luke's story and
shows it to be more correct than what Mark would lead us to

suppose to have been the way that these apostles came to be called.

(*b*) Mark, who is followed by Matthew, gives an account of a visit made by Christ to His old home about the time when He sent out the Twelve. Luke speaks of such a visit before the Sabbath on which the demoniac was healed in the synagogue at Capernaum. He interposes between the forty days after the Baptism and His visit a period of indeterminate length during which our Lord was teaching in the synagogue of Galilee. This fits in well with John's statement that Jesus left Judea and healed the son of the king's officer at Capernaum. It is easy to frame a picture of this period which will satisfy the words "whatsoever we have heard done in Capernaum, do also here in thy country."

(*c*) As has been implied on a previous page, St. John may be regarded as responsible for the information which has led Luke to distinguish as he does three separate approaches to Jerusalem during the last six months of the Ministry, and the Fourth Gospel makes clear the occasions of these approaches, viz. the going up to the Feast of Tabernacles, to the Feast of Dedication, to Bethany after Lazarus' death, and for the last Passover.

(*d*) Luke tells of Martha and Mary in a certain village; John has the fuller account of their life at Bethany.

It is right to mention two other signposts, trivial in themselves and such as some readers may dismiss as figments of the imagination. Luke tells that on Simon the Cyrenian "they laid the cross *that he might bear it after Jesus*." This detail is not derived from either Mark or Q, and, as we have argued, may come from St. John. The reader will not forget that it is in John's manner to remark any correspondence between prediction and fulfilment, word and action, symbol and reality. Here Simon is seen as the typical disciple according to the Lord's words spoken after Peter's confession (Luke ix. 23; cf. xiv. 27). Again Luke baldly states that the soldiers divided Christ's garments and cast lots. This cryptic brevity John amplifies and makes intelligible. Since Mark's account also is full and clear it can hardly be doubted that we are right in supposing John to have in view not the Second but the Third Gospel as the one

in vogue which he was concerned to supplement. We must at
the same time notice how here again Luke refuses any
meticulous recital of scriptural passages which others felt had
found a verbal fulfilment in the events of our Lord's ministry.
For his Gentile readers such fulfilments were irrelevant and
negligible.

Whether this be accepted or not as the way in which these
additional facts came to the evangelist's knowledge, the accurate
honesty of St. Luke's historical method may be gauged by one
detail. On at least three occasions he gives a plain hint that he
has not been able fully to satisfy himself as to the date of an
incident. Each time he gives his reader warning by using an
indefinite expression.

(1) The leper came for healing in "one of the cities." St. Luke
could not satisfy himself that Mark's narrative could be followed
when it seemed to place the healing near Capernaum.

(2) In the section before he relates the events of the evening
when our Lord slept unperturbed on board the storm-racked
ship Mark throws together without regard to chronological
order various episodes whose succession to one another seem to
have been suggested by some resemblance in their character.
He mentions that such crowds beset our Lord that it was impossible to eat a meal, that His friends believing Him to be
overwrought, attempted to take Him into protective custody,
that scribes lately come from Jerusalem attributed to alliance
with Beelzebub His exorcism of demoniacs, and this adverse
criticism He exploded as self-contradictory. Mark then repeats
his statement that our Lord's friends came to take Him away
while a multitude of disciples surrounded Him; he next represents Christ as so beset by crowds anxious to hear Him that
He taught them as He sat in a boat, and this is followed by the
Parable of the Sower, with its explanation in private to His
disciples, and two other parables which were undeniably spoken
at a later date. Then, says Mark, the same day when even was
come they took ship and crossed the lake. Matthew with some
alterations gives the same confused picture. He states that after
a blind and dumb demoniac had been healed the Pharisees
launched their attack on Jesus, alleging that Beelzebub was the
source of His powers. This slander Jesus refuted, and while He

was still speaking to the people His friends came to arrest Him. Then, says Matthew, the same day Jesus went out of the house and uttered the Parable of the Sower, which He afterwards explained, and six other parables. The storm on the sea Matthew relates several chapters earlier. Luke was aware that the true order told of crowds pressing around the Lord, His Parable of the Sower spoken from the boat, His return home where He explained the parable, while a multitude surrounded the house, His friends' attempt to get to Him, and finally His taking ship to secure rest and quiet. Yet Luke, in view of the ambiguity which might seem to result from Mark inserting other parables between that of the Sower and our Lord taking ship "on the same day," is so honest as to write "it came to pass on one of the days that He went into a ship."

(3) Again Luke was clear that Mark's interposition of the Cleansing of the Temple at the point where he has placed it was somehow erroneous—as Matthew also has judged it to be and has accordingly antedated it. Luke more prudently con nted himself with saying that it was on "one of the days."

Chapter Five

Q: SOME FACTS AND CONJECTURES

SOME twenty-five years ago a writer in the *Church Quarterly Review* developed the argument that St. Luke in virtue of his profession was both qualified and constrained to reproduce with expert accuracy the exact utterances of our Lord as he had them reported to him. The Greek physicians were neither amateur nor perfunctorily trained. Part of that training was in the faithful repetition of prescriptions, and thus St. Luke must have acquired the habit of giving close attention to formulae and of writing them down from memory. The inference is that where he and Matthew give parallel records of our Lord's sayings, St. Luke's record may be taken to be the closer to the original common source, and an examination of a few examples of this goes to confirm St. Luke's superiority in this regard.

In the Beatitudes St. Luke starts with "Blessed are ye poor for yours is the kingdom of God." Matthew has "Blessed are the poor in spirit, for theirs is the kingdom of Heaven." We conclude, therefore, that Matthew has added the words "in spirit" so as to elucidate what our Lord said, because it might be misunderstood, and has substituted "heaven" for God out of reverence. Again St. Luke gives "Blessed are ye that hunger now, for ye shall be filled." Matthew, evidently for the same reason as before, writes, "Blessed are they that hunger and thirst after righteousness, for they shall be filled."

This is enough to indicate one characteristic feature in Matthew's work. He is at no pains to reproduce with literal fidelity our Lord's utterances. He is concerned to give a true interpretation of those utterances. Another interesting example will illustrate this. After the Baptist's messengers had left our Lord, both evangelists tell of Jesus commenting on the failure both of St. John and of Himself to satisfy the Pharisees. St. Luke ends these comments with the words "Wisdom is justified of all her children." Matthew interprets the last word by substituting "works" for it. A supreme example illustrating the verbal fidelity of Luke and the interpretative additions of Matthew is to be seen in their presentation of the Lord's Prayer. A comparison of Matt. vi. 9–13 and Luke xi. 2–4 shows that Matthew has added, in his usual way: "Our; which art in heaven; thy will be done in earth as it is in heaven; but deliver us from the Evil One." Each of these additions, it will be seen, is explanatory and helps to define the significance of the petitions as recorded by Luke.

Accepting, then, this view of the two evangelists—that St. Luke may be trusted to give us the exact words found in Q, while Matthew interprets them[1]—we may consider a curious divergence which is to be found in another passage. St. Luke records our Lord as saying that "the Law and the prophets were until John. From that time the kingdom of God is preached and every man presses into it." Matthew recasts the whole, and has "the kingdom of heaven suffereth violence and violent men take it by force." The last clause we shall, in accordance with our hypothesis, regard as an interpretative comment to explain the curious passive use of βιάζεται. But the passage suggests something more. The reader may be inclined at the first suggestion to view what follows with suspicion, but he is asked to give it his unbiassed and dispassionate consideration. Copies of Q may be presumed to have been multiplied, in the way that secular works were multiplied, by slave copyists, such as Atticus employed. These copies when not written to dictation would show almost exactly the same number of letters in each line as in the original. Matthew, apparently working from a copy of Q,[2] passed from ἡ βασιλεία τοῦ θεοῦ to βιάζεται, omitting εὐαγγελίζεται καὶ πᾶς εἰς αὐτὴν. We need not suppose that Matthew missed a line. On the contrary we shall suppose the copyist to have done so. In either case it is reasonable to reckon that this gives the length of the lines in Q, viz. 27 letters.

---

1 While Luke xi. 20 has "if I with the finger of God cast out devils," Matt. xii. 28, writes "by the Spirit of God." This has been cited as final proof that Jesus' speech was Aramaic, variously translated, but the explanation given above remains unaffected (see further, p. 318, note 2.).

2 If St. Matthew wrote both Q and the Gospel, the oversight will be like the inattentive reproduction of Mark's Matthias for Judas in the list of the Twelve.

That this is not fanciful may be deduced from the further fact that the previous two lines, if St. Luke may again be trusted to be faithfully repeating Q, contained together 53 letters and possibly a space for a stop.[1]

We shall pursue this argument further presently, but one or two points first require attention. In the first place it is to be observed that St. Luke regularly gives the divine title as God: Matthew follows the reverential habit of substituting "heaven." Secondly we may fairly insist that St. Luke is shown to be faithful to his authority in using the second person in the Beatitudes, writing "yours is the Kingdom of God" where Matthew rewrites the sentence as "theirs is the Kingdom of heaven" to fit in with his change from "Ye poor" to "the poor in spirit." Confirmatory of this belief is the fact that after eight Beatitudes in the third person, Matthew writes "Blessed are ye when men shall revile you" and continues in the second person to the end of his Sermon on the Mount.

Lastly, if we allow for Θυ being written in place of the full Θεοῦ, κ for καὶ and αὐν for αὐτην, our line of 27 letters may well contain 23 letters. In that case, we must notice that the first Beatitude would cover two lines, or 45 letters. But a sober judgment must realize that we are in danger of indulging in mere conjecture and we must return to more solid evidence.

In the account of the Crucifixion Matthew tells us of our Lord's recital of the Twenty-second Psalm, and it is to be noticed that if two lines, or 46 letters with one or two stops, be omitted, we have the basis for St. Luke's statement that the sun failed. He would have had before him ἠλει ἐγκατέλιπες. He or his copyist may have passed over the Hebrew and the statement about its translation, and this will explain how it comes about that he has omitted here words of our Lord which were in Q, and has what is not stated in any other Gospel, that the darkness was ἡλίου ἐκλιπόντος. St. Luke plainly took the first Hebrew word to be ἥλιε. It should be added that the words as given by Q were a truer record of the Lord's

---

[1] I give these probable or possible stops in deference to a pronouncement of my friend the Rev. D. P. Buckle. On microscopic examination he found in an early codex, at the points where clauses end, slightly wider spaces between the terminal letters. This method of indicating the breaks between clauses is anterior to the later notation of punctuation.

utterance than is Mark's, since the form in Q alone explains why bystanders believed that Our Lord was calling upon Elijah, Ἡλείαν.[1]

In view of these facts, the reader must be asked to lay aside any theories which he has been taught to regard as established as to the character of Q. Although much that has been said on the subject has now been repeated so long and so persistently that many are under the impression that it is proved beyond question, it must be insisted that we have no irrefragable knowledge and that all we have is theory which may require to be modified in the light of fresh facts. We may therefore correlate the evidence we have been considering into a few statements, which the reader is invited to examine, since they would appear to be reconcilable with the substantial basis of current theories and also satisfactory as according with the new facts we have just noted. Briefly, then, we may say that Q was a Greek document known to St. Luke and to the author of the First Gospel. St. Luke copied it exactly, so far at any rate as our Lord's words are concerned. Matthew handled Q with freedom, aiming at removing what might be misunderstood. Q was partly narrative, but how far it was chronologically arranged it is impossible to determine, though some of its sequences seem to reflect the historical order of events. If Matthew derived his prophetic quotations from Q and did not himself supply them, St. Luke omitted them as irrelevancies for his Gentile readers. In either case they are Greek translations from the Massoretic Hebrew text, not quotations from the Septuagint, so that they may be thought to be carefully selected to satisfy readers who desired Old Testament confirmation of the Christian faith, based on the Palestinian and not the Alexandrian scriptures.

Two more passages deserve attention. In Mark xiv. 72 we read that Peter ἐπιβαλὼν ἔκλαιεν. Had the other two synoptists here been following Mark, we should be tempted to conjecture that the former word was in the original text ἐκβαλὼν and that the meaning was that he "dashed out of

---

[1] It is simpler to attribute the form HĒLI to Q with both Matthew and Luke deriving from it, although it has been doubted whether Q gave the story of the Passion.

doors." Such a conjecture would be an unwarrantable defiance
of our MSS. tradition, and, understanding the words to mean
"he went at it with a will and began to weep," i.e. "he sobbed
and sobbed his heart out," we are driven to the conclusion that
we have a quotation from Q in the words, identically reproduced in Matthew and Luke ἐξελθὼν ἔξω ἔκλαυσεν πικρῶς.
It will be observed that this confirms the suggestion that Q
contained a certain amount of narrative and possibly that the
story of Peter's denials was lost from St. Luke's copy of Mark.[1]

The second passage has to do with our Lord's words assuring
us that the Father will be liberal in His answer to our prayers.
Luke says that He will give πνεῦμα ἅγιον to them that ask.
Matthew says ἀγαθά. It may not be presumptuous to suggest
that Q had ΑΓΠΝΑ. This would exhibit the natural abbrevia-
tion of the Lucan text and might be misread by Matthew.[2]

Down to this point nothing has been said in this chapter in
regard to what Papias tells us about St. Matthew's literary
activities. Critics have in the main concerned themselves to
fashion some explanation of Papias' words into which they
could fit what they have inferred as to the character of Q.
Without attempting to discuss the various theories that have
been most popular, we may, in a few words, state what seems
to harmonize all the evidence before us.

(1) As is explained in another chapter, those who engage in
argument in defence of their belief are constrained to rest their
case upon what is common ground between them and their
opponents. St. Matthew, aiming to bring conviction to his
fellow countrymen and co-religionists who lived outside the
Greek-speaking world, or looked for guidance to the Rabbis of
Jerusalem, limited his choice of scriptural passages which he
believed our Lord to have fulfilled to those which were to be
found in the Hebrew original. Although the Rabbinic synod
which settled the Hebrew canon was still in the future, the
necessities of his argument drove him to doing what St. Jerome

[1] In that case we might suppose that pages 89–96 or 91–94 were lost from
St. Luke's copy.
[2] A copyist's dittography from the first part of the verse is a simpler
explanation. Pneuma hagion is the regular order of words. If Q was
written by Matthew, we shall here have an inadvertence like the one noted
above on p. 65, note 2.

did later. Hence it is that, as we have already noted, the prophetic quotations found in Matthew do not reflect the Greek Bible of Alexandria and the Church, but the Hebrew Bible of the intransigent pundits of the narrower Judaism.

(2) Q, as we have said, was a Greek document, largely a collection of what the Baptist and our Lord had said, but partly also a narrative. There is no incontestible necessity that we should suppose that it was a translation of St. Matthew's work or, indeed, that it had any connexion with it.[1]

(3) The first evangelist made use of Mark and Q, and in pursuance of his apologetic purpose introduced into his work much or perhaps all of St. Matthew's promptuary of prophetic quotations, which he translated. Hence the First Gospel would be pre-eminently regarded as based upon St. Matthew's testimony, but the unvarying tradition as to its title encourages us to go further and to reject all the speculations which have sprung from Papias' remark.

(4) St. Luke used Mark and Q, but not St. Matthew's Oracles. This agrees with our suspicion that he did not know Hebrew and explains why the quotations found in Matthew are absent in Luke.

One example of the historical evidence which a narrow scrutiny of Q may be thought to yield deserves a word of comment.

A comparison of Matt. ix. 32–34 and Luke xi. 14, 15 is evidence that Q recorded that our Lord's healing of a dumb man was the occasion for the libel that Beelzebub enabled Him to effect such cures. Luke apparently places this episode about three months before the Crucifixion; Mark, as already explained later, mentions the odious charge much earlier, and Matt. xii. 22 ff. punctually reproduces the Marcan collocation.

It would appear from a comparison of Matt. xii. 38 ff. and Luke xi. 16 ff., that Q associated with the above episode and its sequel the Pharisees' demand for a sign from heaven in

---

[1] Papias, to quote his words once again, states that Matthew wrote in neo-Hebrew the "oracles" and everyone translated them as well as he was able. That Q was a written record of one of these translations has for a long time been an unchallenged assumption. It is, however, neither a strictly logical nor a legitimate inference from Papias' statement. It is, indeed, a mere conjecture, however obvious and ready to hand.

contradistinction to acts which might be thought to fall within the sphere of sublunary spirits. Mark viii. 11 shows that although this may be a correct indication of the course of thought in the Pharisees, their request for a sign was made before St. Peter's confession near Caesarea Philippi. As we have seen, St. Luke was without this part of the Marcan gospel, and consequently without that means of detecting or correcting any mistake in the location of this incident. It is possible that the secret motives for the Pharisees' request in the summer found open and explicit expression in the following winter. Thus, perhaps the first request, which might seem as innocent as that made in John ii. 18, was met by a flat refusal; the second, which was coupled with monstrous allegation of Satanic assistance, was countered by the offer of Jonah as a sign.

It remains a possibility that there was but one express demand for a sign from heaven and that the reference to Jonah was part of our Lord's answer, though omitted by Mark. We must then suppose that St. Luke, not having the Second Gospel to guide him to the true date of this demand, was misled by Q's conjunction of our Lord's reply to it with His criticism of the allegation that He had aid from Beelzebub. The evangelist perhaps found a suitable occasion for inserting this teaching about the machinations of evil spirits when he had just related our Lord's words about the Father's gift of Holy Spirit. Finally we must notice that, in spite of the collocation in Mark and in Matthew of the words about blasphemy against the Holy Ghost, Luke has deliberately postponed those words to a point a little later still, i.e. not long before March, A.D. 33.[1]

---

[1] See Part IV, Chap. 4, Excursus III (p. 341).

Chapter Six

THE FOURTH GOSPEL: ITS HISTORICITY AND ITS AUTHORSHIP

(1)

THE vivid details in the Second Gospel are commonly adduced as significant touches which only an eyewitness could have supplied. An unprejudiced reader cannot but recognize the same vividness of dispensable detail in the Fourth Gospel, and, if he sets aside for a while and ignores other burning issues, must conclude that there too is to be found the testimony of an eye-witness. To take but a few examples, we have, as will be presently shown, notes of the exact hour, place, weather and precise statements as to the motives of actions recorded.

All this must weigh with a dispassionate reader and incline him to re-examine the narrative, however different the portrait it presents may, as he has been taught, appear to be from that of the synoptists. He will remember how the Socrates of Plato's dialogues is not precisely the same as the Socrates of Xenophon's *Memorabilia*.

Reading the Gospel again with this consideration in mind and without allowing ourselves to be diverted to the contemplation of possible incompatibilities between the picture in this Gospel and that in the synoptists, we are forced to the conviction that the author has it in purpose to give such memories as he does give, in chronological order. Of the synoptists Luke alone makes chronological arrangement his deliberate aim. It is therefore a strong confirmation of our estimate that we can spatchcock either of the Third and Fourth Gospels into the other without difficulty and discover their narratives to be mutually corroborative. It does not perhaps necessarily follow that the Fourth Gospel has set out to correct or to supplement or even to support the Third; but both these Gospels being constructed on a chronological basis, they dovetail into one

another and illustrate one another as historical records.
Incidentally it is to be observed that the Fourth Gospel makes
no effort to relate all that happened: it assumes, without
narrating, the Baptism and the Institution of the Eucharist, no
less than the selection of the Twelve, the martyrdom of the
Baptist, the Ascension and probably the Virgin Birth. If the
synoptists betray no knowledge of the raising of Lazarus, John
betrays no knowledge of the Transfiguration. An unprejudiced
and balanced judgment must subscribe to the contention that
John is concerned to give in chronological sequence a number of
incidents which lived in his memory and which preserved or
illuminated teaching of our Lord that he regarded as important
and valuable for the Church. This teaching, as I have attempted
to show elsewhere, although it has been commonly regarded as
dissimilar in tone to the synoptic, exhibits when chronologically
interlaced with the other tradition an intelligible development,
harmonizing with a progressive growth in our Lord's human
consciousness of His mission.

In all that has just been said no assumption has been made
as to the identity of the author. It is nevertheless proper at this
point that I should confess my belief that Dr. Philip Carrington
is right in declaring for the traditional view that the younger
son of Zebedee wrote both the Gospel and the Apocalypse
which bears his name. Dr. Carrington's literary taste, his flair
for appreciating the mental characteristics of an author, seems
to have guided him more surely than linguistic tests and
stylistic arithmetic have guided the grammarian commentators.
Besides the common features noted by him in all the writings
avowed to be Johannine, three signs seem to converge suggesting
that one and the same person gave birth to all.

(1) In the first place we detect, it may be thought, a sensuous
appreciation of the physical circumstances which formed the
setting of particular incidents. The Gospel notes that the whole
house was filled with the odour of the ointment and also makes
Martha say of Lazarus' corpse "by this time he stinketh." The
Apocalypse speaks of the saints' prayers as a bowl full of odours.
The Apocalypse represents the most terrible of all its horrors
as having the faces of men and the hair of women, which
suggests that the writer has felt the physical and seductive

attraction of female beauty. It is noticeable that in the First Epistle "the lust of the eye" is specially named and the Fourth Gospel suggests that the woman of Sychar was of a desirable personableness.

(2) The author possessed quick power of observation so that he was vividly and acutely impressed by the surroundings which supplied the setting of particular events. The data we shall presently enumerate in respect of time and place will serve to illustrate this so far as the Gospel is concerned. The sharpness of outline in the symbolic visions of the Apocalypse may be held to betray the same characteristic of mental equipment.

(3) To this acuteness of observation was wedded a retentive memory, the repository and treasure-house of these vivid impressions. In further illustration one curious possibility may be suggested. In the Apocalypse, vi. 13, we are told that the stars of heaven fell unto the earth "even as a fig-tree sheddeth her untimely figs when she is shaken of a mighty wind." This in itself is remarkable for its vivacious vigour, but we are reminded of the fig-tree with leaves only, on Monday in Holy Week, when Mark tells us "the time for figs was not yet." Did St. John remember how a mighty wind that day had blown off the figs, leaving the tree to wither away? It is at least noticeable that it was on the following day that our Lord in His prophecy of the fall of Jerusalem declared that "the stars shall fall from heaven." This matter of memory is of some importance to our view of the Gospel's historicity, as will be seen in a later section.

Be these detailed suggestions correct or not—and it would be irrelevant to our purpose to pursue their discussion at length —it would seem that common mental characteristics traceable in the two works point to a common author. This, it may be added, might throw light on what some readers have observed with regretful yearning, the pretermission in the Gospel of the Transfiguration. We shall see the memory of that stupendous scene in the tremendous vision of the Ascended Lord described in the opening chapter of the Apocalypse. Yet we must not misunderstand that remembrance. At the Transfiguration and on the night after the five thousand were fed, when the Lord was seen by His disciples as they rowed, St. Peter translated his

3*

physical impressions into terms of the miraculous. In regard to
the earlier event St. John with the same abjuration of the supernatural, as popularly understood, that he manifests in the
Apocalypse, relates with scientific exactness what he saw in
sober and unalarming reality. In regard to the Transfiguration
he repaints with a poet's artistry in yet more majestic colours
the Figure he had seen on "the holy mount," but, by tacitly
passing the episode by in his Gospel, he avoids the lending of
support to the notion that on this occasion at least our Lord's
humanity was dissolved or temporarily abrogated.[1]

Another illustration may be given of the author's method,
his economy in the selection of his material and perhaps his
consistent exclusion of anything that an unspiritual or credulous
reader might confuse with unmoral magic. To explain
St. Peter's treble denial of his discipleship, the evangelist finally
introduces Malchus' kinsman as challenging the apostle. In
preparation therefore for this the incident of the injury to
Malchus has to be told. It is not, however, necessary for his
purpose to relate our Lord's healing of the injury, and this
therefore the evangelist omits. Yet it may be surmised that not
only was the healing superfluous for the author's purpose but
also that the omission conforms to a general conception of the
spiritual instruction which the believer should draw from the
Saviour's acts. Throughout the Fourth Gospel healing and
other "signs" are effected without tactual treatment or manipulation. Our Lord speaks the word and the result follows, and
this is so even though at Cana the servants perform manual
acts and though the Twelve distribute to the five thousand.
When the Lord Himself anointed the blind man's eyes with
clay, the cure followed the washing at Siloam, as ordered by
Him. We may believe that Luke's account of the healing of
Malchus' ear was derived from St. John: the agreement in
details is remarkable; but the later Gospel, it will be noticed,
does not magnify but reduces the "wonder."

It has been commonly held that John records a trial of our
Lord before Annas besides the trial before Caiaphas which the

[1] St. Ambrose too, it may be claimed, takes the same spiritual view (see
on his use of "transfigure": F. R. Montgomery Hitchcock in *Church Quarterly Review*, No. 280, pp. 127 ff.).

synoptists describe. A careful and unprejudiced reading will show that there was no trial before Annas. John emphasizes that Caiaphas was the high priest and although the Lord was taken first to Annas' house,[1] He was sent on, still bound, for trial to Caiaphas. When this is recognized, all difficulties evaporate. John and Peter, who had at first fled with the other apostles, went to Caiaphas' house; nothing is said of their going to Annas'.

(2)

For the representation and interpretation of events, poetry, as Aristotle said, is a more philosophical medium than history. This valuation may be applied for the comparison of the methods of secular annalists and historians with the records left by the priests, prophets and religious teachers of Israel. The sacred writers threw into prominence the providential control of human affairs and refused to be content with a simple catalogue of casual incidents.

Our four Gospels were all written for Christian believers. All are concerned to show that God had uniquely intervened in human affairs. The synoptists, however, portray the Saviour's mission, His life-work, teaching, death and triumph, as His contemporary disciples had seen and known them. The Fourth Gospel, written sixty years after the events, reviewed them *sub specie aeternitatis*. The writer saw the divine ordering of these events which the synoptists had known in their human development. But this by no means makes the later record likely to be less historic than the earlier. Indeed, experience shows that an old man's memory is prodigiously faithful in regard to incidents in his early life. Middle-aged critics have sometimes forgotten this, and in consequence have airily dismissed as unhistorical what they could not immediately fit in with the synoptists' story. Those who wished to claim attention for the Johannine Gospel explained its different character by supposing that in old age the apostle, under the guidance of the Holy Spirit, re-interpreted in his own words what he remembered in outline only. This, however, it must be repeated, is not true to the facts

---

[1] It is of course possible that Annas still occupied some rooms in the high priest's palace, but that does not affect our understanding of the story.

of human experience. Old age normally bores with the monotonous repetition of the exact circumstances and words of earlier scenes, and we shall, therefore, be on surer ground if we regard the Fourth Gospel as preserving for us the veritable words spoken by our Lord sixty years before.

Readers have sometimes confessed to a feeling that the long discourses and discussions which are contained in the central chapters of John are so different in character from what we find in the synoptists that they can hardly be authentic records. Yet an unprejudiced judgment must find in them a marvellous force of logic and apt applicability to the immediate situation. It becomes difficult to doubt the authentic fidelity with which the writer has portrayed actual scenes and doctrinal encounters. It is not that the genius of the author has constructed arguments appropriate to a remembered situation. His story fits astonishingly well into the course of events as we recover them from the synoptists. We can hardly hesitate to conclude that the former obscure hints of His impending Passion, Resurrection and Ascension and of the coming of the Holy Ghost were, in sober fact, clarified and explicitly expressed by our Lord in His Last Discourse on Maundy Thursday evening.

The historical fidelity of the Fourth Gospel is corroborated both by the progressive education of the disciples, as is shown in our resultant Harmony, and by the psychological development in our Lord's humanity as it appears in this Gospel. There first we find the Baptist announcing that some at present unknown Successor and Superior of his will baptize men with Holy Spirit. Next he testifies that this Superior Successor has been pointed out to him by a visible sign showing that the Spirit has invisibly come to rest in this Superior. Six weeks later the Baptist recognizes in Jesus the Lamb of God's providing, and Andrew accepts Him as the Christ and Nathanael hails Him as the Davidic King. He Himself exhibits a prophetic insight into Nathanael's character and thoughts and reveals a consciousness of constant intercommunication between Himself and God. Presently He finds Himself authorized to supply more wine for the wedding feast, and His experience of the new Power now directing, controlling and suggesting all His thoughts, words and actions is seen in the instruction He gives

Nicodemus. In His words to the Samaritan woman He shows that He has in mind the prophetic word that He is destined to baptize with Holy Spirit, the living water of eternal life. Soon after He learns that His healing powers may operate at a distance in Capernaum and some while later He is well assured that His messianic powers extend to the revival of physical life where He receives the Spirit's impulse.

We shall not pursue the story of the other Gospels. In them we find a sketch from Isaiah lxi of the purposes with which Jahveh's Spirit had anointed Him, and an account of the various ways in which He exercised His messianic office. He expelled evil spirits; He pronounced absolution; He corrected nervous and functional disorders; He trained the Twelve so that they understood somewhat the extent to which, under the Spirit's guidance, He had learnt that His messianic powers were authorized by God to intervene in physical nature. He then commissioned them to act as His legates.

On their return, John, like the other evangelists, shows Him moved to multiply a modicum of food so as to satisfy the needs of over five thousand men. He turned away from the thought of a political sovereignty and directed His followers' minds to the need of spiritual food. He was to sustain all mankind with heavenly nourishment. Passover supplied illustrative language. If He was the Lamb of God, the Paschal meal must in spiritual antitype be His flesh, and His blood must be the spiritual Paschal charm against moral ruin. Abraham trusted God and God honoured his trust by substituting a lamb for Isaac. Jesus trusted God and God would in His chosen time honour that trust. The disciples should trust the Messiah of God and He would honour their trust. For love of Israel God accepted the Paschal Lamb's life-blood in redemption of their first-born sons. The Lamb of God would shed His life-blood for love of man. His disciples should imbibe the spiritual drink of His life-blood, the refreshing draughts of love and charity towards God and their fellow-men.

So far John tells us the disciples were convinced of no more than that Jesus was God's Nazoraean, whose words were indeed "words of eternal life," revelations of God's truth. The other Gospels tell us next how the Lord was brought to exert His power over evil for a non-Jewish girl at a distance and later was stirred to rebuff the disingenuous request of the Pharisees for a sign to demonstrate that He was not in collusion with Satan. Peter's avowal that He was the Christ was used by the Spirit, we may believe, to confirm the Saviour's own faith in His mission. The Transfiguration aptly lent an added strength to His confidence in His vocation, when it was the more called for in face of the nearer apprehension of the manner in which death was to come to Him.

John passes on to show Jesus on the one hand preconizing His offer of supplying to anyone who believes in Him a never-ceasing stream of Holy Spirit, and His opponents, on the other hand, now openly sneering and disparaging His work and teaching. Their attempt to entrap Him into what might be represented as an attack on the Mosaic Law fails. While their opposition grows more bitter, there is a changed tone in the Lord's assertion of His divine Sonship. Before, He claimed as the messianic Vicegerent to reflect His Father's activities; now He speaks of such an intimacy of communion between Himself and the Father that His words are indeed the words of God.

This confidence in His essential fidelity to the Father's truth follows, as Luke shows us, the return of the Seventy and Christ's exultation in the Holy Spirit. Simple novices, He rejoiced to know, could in His power defeat the spirits of evil; while He could reveal the Father to whom He would, His own absolute nature and personal position in ultimate reality was a secret known only to the Father Himself. It would seem that as He was led under the Spirit's guidance to learn the vastness of the mission on which He had been sent into the world, He had arising in His mind ambiguous questionings and what might seem unholy imaginations about Himself. These, it may be thought, are reflected in some part of His arguments with the Jews who criticized His claim that God was His Father. A few weeks later John tells of Lazarus. His revival was a greater "sign" of the Messiah's control of physical life than that of the youth at Nain or that of Jairus' daughter a few hours after death. Yet faith, inspired by the Spirit, was necessary for bravely facing the prospect of Crucifixion. Such a death might be more certain annihilation than any brought about by sickness. The thunder-voice in the Temple served to reinforce His faith; but faith it was, and not knowledge, which supported Him in the last hour.

In the Fourth Gospel, then, no less than in Mark nor less than in Luke even—Matthew, as we have shown, had another aim than that of historical narration—we find an intelligible and orderly progression and development. This is seen not only in the course of events and in the education and instruction of the disciples so that their pedestrian and nationalistic hopes were transmuted into a spiritual and universal charity, but also in our Lord's reactions to the events, His response to His experience and His growing understanding of His mission and of the Father's will. If at first He spoke to the Samaritan woman of giving living water, He later, at the feast of Tabernacles, invited all to come to Him as the Rock-fountain. While He first said He would give bread from heaven, He afterwards styled Himself the Bread of Life. In a sentence, it is to be noted that our Lord in the last twelve months of His Ministry and with an increasingly insistent directness spoke of Himself as the personal and essential Author of those spiritual blessings which His Incarnation was designed to bring about for man. We read, for example, that He urged men to walk in the light, and at the same time He declared Himself the Light of the World. The Psalmist had addressed Jahveh as his Shepherd; Jesus declared Himself the Good Shepherd. At one time He asserted that God had authorized Him to give physical life to whom He would; a few weeks before the Crucifixion He comforted Martha by the avowal "I am the Resurrection and the Life," and He continued with words which make it clear that for Him that man alone truly lives who puts his trust in Him, and that such life is eternal. This confident assurance of His Person and prerogative is paralleled by the words on the night before the Passion: "I am the Way, the Truth and the Life."

But not only does the history reveal a growing realization of the unthinkable majesty that His messiahship involves, but He manifestly becomes more and more aware of what the Holy Spirit was achieving for man by interpenetrating His human spirit. Luke shows us our Lord some three months before the Crucifixion assuring His disciples that their heavenly Father

would give a holy spirit to those who asked Him, but, a month
perhaps later, speaking of the Holy Spirit as a Person. Our
Lord's own words and actions might be maligned: being con-
ditioned by His humanity, they might be misunderstood; those,
therefore, who traduced Him might be pardoned. But dishonest
and malevolent misrepresentation of the Spirit's activities was
obstinate antagonism to God, and such impenitence must be
unpardonable. Moreover, our Lord continued, the Holy Spirit
would so possess their personalities that when they were
arraigned for their Christian discipleship He would teach them
in the same hour what they should say. A few days before the
Crucifixion Mark testifies that the Saviour again promised this
inspiration and guidance of the Holy Spirit. This change in our
Lord's language is strikingly in agreement with the Johannine
record. In that we read that on the last night before His Passion
our Lord spoke yet more plainly of the Spirit as a Spiritual
Counsel who would continue for the disciples the office the
Messiah had exercised during His Ministry on earth.

(3)

Prominent among the mental characteristics of the writer of
the Fourth Gospel is a sensitive consciousness of the precise
circumstances of the events he witnesses. It was night when
Judas left the Upper Room. It was the sixth hour when our
Lord was taken to stand before Pilate. It was winter when the
Feast of Dedication fell. It was cold when Peter stood and
warmed himself in Caiaphas' palace. That quick sense of detail
is to be noticed not less in the Apocalypse. The vivid descrip-
tions exhibit it, and the terse notes of the Gospel are paralleled
by the Apocalyptic "there was silence in Heaven" and the
poetic imaginativeness which describes the Voice as like the
sound of many waters, and, to quote the words again, the falling
of the stars as when the fig-tree casteth her untimely figs when
she is shaken by a mighty wind.

Yet more significant for our purpose is the close interest and
belief, common to both Gospel and Apocalypse, in the predictive power and introspective faculty of the prophet. Throughout
the Gospel our Lord is portrayed as reading men's innermost

motives. It is so when after His Baptism He meets Simon
Bar-jona. It is so when he sees Nathanael approaching; when
He alludes to Judas as a carping critic; when He reads Judas'
treacherous intention; when He elicits St. Peter's final confession of devotion with its meek avoidance of self-confidence.
The prophetic perception of what is occurring away from the
immediate range of sense and propinquity is brought into
notice when Nathanael is shown to have been observed under
the fig-tree; when the woman of Sychar's life history is dis-
closed; when the officer's son is pronounced to have passed the
crisis of his illness; when Lazarus' death is announced; when
Judas is bidden to act quickly; when St. Thomas is invited to
verify the reality of our Lord's presence. His predictive power
is insisted on when He challenged the Jews to destroy the
Temple of His body; when He told the Samaritan woman that
neither in Jerusalem nor on Mount Gerizim exclusively should
the Father be worshipped; when He foretold the coming of the
Holy Ghost; the manner of His own death; the union of Jew
and Gentile in one Communion; the death of St. Peter; and
the long life of St. John. The Saviour's prophetic power of
intuition, it may be pointed out, is attested by his enemies: they
blindfolded him, we are told, and derisively cried "Prophesy
unto us, thou Christ, who is he that smote thee?"

If the writer of the Gospel was indeed the Apostle St. John,
we can understand how, with these mental qualities, he should
at first expect a speedy and material Advent of the Kingdom,
such as St. Peter and his three colleagues expected, according
to Mark's record of St. Peter's teaching. The death of the elder
son of Zebedee would doubtless favour the notion that the
Transfiguration was the actual fulfilment of the Lord's promise
that some then at His side should see the Kingdom. Yet this
interpretation made the promise almost otiose if it were thus
realized after only a week. St. John then readjusted his perspective and saw in the fall of Jerusalem, so worldly minded that it
was veritably Babylon, the Advent of the King. By that time
St. Peter too had tasted death and the Lord's words took on a
sharper edge. The Apocalypse corresponds to this understanding of Christ's prophecy. Would, then, a further final
Advent come before St. John's death? It is to the correction of

this notion that the last chapter of the Gospel is addressed. St. John had not once nor twice found his understanding of the Lord's words too gross and materialistic. A circumspect scrutiny of the exact wording of the prophecy warned him and his brother Christians that it might well be that his death would come and the Advent yet be far later.

(4)

In the structure and arrangement of the Fourth Gospel one feature can scarcely escape notice. The author at times interposes comments, reflections and meditations of his own in the middle of his narrative. Sometimes he directs attention to this procedure by resuming his narrative after the interruption and marking the resumption by repeating or re-echoing his earlier words. An example of this practice is to be seen in his account of the Baptist's testimony. In i. 15 we read "John bare witness of Him, and cried, saying, This was He of whom I spake, He that cometh after me is preferred before me: for He was before me. . . ." There follows the reflection that "of his fulness have all we received, and grace for grace . . . the only begotten Son, which is in the bosom of the Father, He hath declared *Him*." Then at verse 19 the narrative is resumed and amplified, till in verse 27 we have again the testimony that "He it is who coming after me, is preferred before me." Other examples are to be seen in chapter iii, where from verse 13 to 21 would seem, as has often been suggested, to be the evangelist's reflections on our Lord's reference to heavenly things of which he would speak, and again verses 35 and 36 similarly are the evangelist's comments, after which he resumes his narrative with words which echo what has preceded. Previously we are told that, following some dispute with a Jew, John's disciples told the Baptist that our Lord also was baptizing and that all men came to Him. Now the story is resumed with the more definite statement that "the Pharisees had heard that Jesus made and baptized more disciples than John" and the corrective note is added "though Jesus himself baptized not, but his disciples."

This technique of construction is remarkably similar to what

THE FOURTH GOSPEL 83

we have noticed at least once in Mark, where, after the intervention of our Lord's family, other matter is interposed and then the narrative is resumed by re-stating in more detail this intervention of the family. We are tempted to play with the fancy that it is the same author whose handiwork we thus detect in both Gospels. In support of such a conjecture we might point to the way that Mark opens with the words "the beginning of the Gospel . . . was John." The Fourth Gospel opens "in the beginning was the Word." Mark, after giving our Lord's plain teaching that nothing from without can defile a man, appends his own comment, "making all meats clean." This is not unlike John's appending of comments. Furthermore, such an identification of the author of the Fourth Gospel with John Mark would supply an immediate explanation of the curious note discovered by Dr. Mingana in a Syriac manuscript which appears to attribute the Fourth Gospel to John the younger. We might then suppose John Mark not only to have written the Second Gospel to preserve St. Peter's memories, but to have written the Fourth Gospel from the mouth of John the Elder, the son of Zebedee. We might then go on to imagine that we had discovered the foundation for Eusebius' statement that two Johns were buried at Ephesus. Here too, it might be thought, would be the reason for what has often been said to appear in these Gospels that the writer of the Fourth seems to take notice of what is recorded in the Second.

Yet, despite these alluring fancies, we must return to the more sober view to which we have been led that the Fourth Gospel takes account not of Mark so much as of Luke, and it will be well to add a few words on this head even at the risk of repeating in some measure what has been said in a previous chapter. Accepting John son of Zebedee as the author of the Fourth Gospel, we have to remember that he was a son of the Blessed Virgin's sister and therefore a cousin of our Lord and a relative of the Baptist. Further, he had the entry of Caiaphas' palace; after St. Peter's death he was the sole surviving witness of the Transfiguration; he alone with the women stood near the Cross, and he had the care of the Lord's mother after the Crucifixion. It is remarkable to observe how much of Luke's

Gospel may reasonably be traced to or through St. John as the source of information.

All the matter in the first two chapters—Zacharias' vision, the Annunciation, the birth of both infants, the Benedictus, the Magnificat, the Nunc Dimittis after the presentation in the Temple, and the Lord's first Passover at Jerusalem—may reasonably be thought to have been derived by St. Luke in this way. Luke's genealogy, as has been shown, bears the same marks upon it. The account of the sermon in the synagogue at Nazareth would naturally come from the Blessed Virgin, and the arrangement of subsequent incidents in accordance with the actual order of their occurrence may well be ascribed to her recollection. The raising to life of the dead youth at Nain perhaps bears witness to the same source when we remember the words "the only son of his mother and she was a widow," a poignant touch we may believe due to the Virgin's sympathy. The Lord's anointing in Simon the Pharisee's house would seem to come from St. John, and it is because he knew that Luke had recorded it that he writes in xi. 2 : "It was that Mary which anointed the Lord with ointment, and wiped His feet with her hair, whose brother Lazarus was sick." This explanation of John's note is, as Trench has remarked, more natural than to suppose it to refer to what John is going to relate in chapter xii. At the Transfiguration, as will be shown later, Luke specifies the subject which Moses, Elijah and our Lord discussed together, and he mentions that a cloud came over the scene. Since Mark presumably has St. Peter's recollections, these details would appear to be derived from St. John, and if Luke has given that apostle's story we find in this a reason for the Fourth Gospel giving no account of the Transfiguration. At the Crucifixion it is to be noticed that we owe to Luke and John all the words from the Cross except the loud cry repeating the Twenty-second Psalm. That cry was heard by others than the little group of friends who stood near, the other six words might be heard by St. John, who seems to have led away our Lord's mother after she was entrusted to his care and then returned to hear the last two words "I thirst" and "It is finished." Thus understood the two records depend upon the testimony of the Lord's mother and St. John. Further confirmation of our view that the Fourth Gospel has been written by one who had in view St. Luke's work may be found in the fact that John explains by his account of the healing of the officer's son at Capernaum what is meant by Luke iv. 23, where our Lord says, "Ye will surely say to me . . . whatsoever we have heard done in Capernaum, do also here in thy country." In the same way, John's account of Jesus' attachment to Himself of Peter and other disciples of the Baptist explains our Lord's going as a guest to Peter's house in Luke iv. 38, although the call to become a follower is placed in chapter v. Again, after the un-named feast of John v. our Lord did not re-visit Jerusalem for the great feasts of the next twelve months. About Passover He fed the five thousand and taught at Capernaum, and this is evidently the meaning of John vii. 1, where "after these things" is the connective to link on the events of the Feast of Tabernacles to what has preceded, but "He did not walk in Judea" is not to be taken with the connecting words but as a parenthetic explanation of the remarks made by the brethren. Thus the sense may be paraphrased as "After these things Jesus continued to walk in Galilee, as He had been doing since the unnamed feast," and this fits in perfectly with Luke's narrative and with the actual history.

(5)

That the reader may have before him as far as possible all that suggests itself as relevant, it will be desirable to note some other disjointed observations.

(1) Dionysius, the Bishop of Alexandria about A.D. 250, mentions that some writers contended that the Apocalypse was the work not of St. John the son of Zebedee, but of his "heretical" antagonist Cerinthus. Him they characterized as sensuous, if not sensual, and they drew attention to features in the book which they considered to bear the stamp of a sensualist's disposition. It speaks of the Bride and the marriage of the Lamb; it uses the figure of eating and drinking. No one today would think there is any occasion to take this attribution seriously, but it will be noticed how it corroborates our estimate of one of the characteristics of the author's mind. It is clear that the figurative images just mentioned were used by our Lord

Himself, but it may still be urged that St. John dwelt on them more perhaps than others did. His Gospel shows the Baptist first calling Christ the Bridegroom. It records the wedding feast at Cana, the supper at Bethany ,and the breakfast on the Galilean shore. It shows the Lord speaking of the Living Water, of the Bread from Heaven, of His Flesh and His Blood. Yet more noteworthy as regards our suggestion about Luke's source of information is the presence in that Gospel of frequent remarks that it was at some meal that an incident occurred : Simon the Pharisee was entertaining Jesus ; Martha was cumbered about much serving ; Zacchaeus gave a dinner ; an unnamed Pharisee asked Jesus to eat bread. Luke records the first cup at the Last Supper. These are special peculiarities of these two Gospels : we have no concern with what is common to all the evangelists.

(2) Both the Third and the Fourth Gospels are particularly interested in numbers, a feature noticeable in the Apocalypse also. John remembers the point that the Temple was built 46 years, the paralytic at Bethzatha had lain there 38 years, the fishes netted were 153 in number. Luke gives the years of Anna's married life and widowhood, of the haemorrhage of the woman on the way to Jairus's house, and of the other's bowed back. Two numbers, 12 and 7, we may pass by, since all Jews perhaps respect them, but the figures we have mentioned are of a different order.

(3) Luke relates how Peter saw the linen clothes lying in the Tomb : John tells the full story of the two apostles' visit. In these instances we have the same relation between the two Gospels that we have noted before.

(4) Clopas' companion is unnamed and this, as an earlier writer has remarked, suggests that she was a woman, Oriental propriety demanding that her name should not be emphasized. If she were his daughter who had seen the Risen Lord, the two would have much to discuss, for Clopas might doubt his daughter's evidence. The Saviour, we know, was not instantly recognized by Mary Magdalene, or by Clopas and his companion, or by the seven disciples at the lakeside. The father, therefore, whilst welcoming his daughter's story, might be cautious and hesitant.

APPENDIX I

The Two Anointings

IN his *The Groundwork of the Gospels*, Mr. R. O. P. Taylor effectively marshalled considerable and convincing arguments for the assertion that Mark has preserved for us the exact wording of Peter's vivid and yet stereotyped recollections of scenes in our Lord's Ministry. Papias has put it on record that (to give due value to the tense and voice of his verb and the connotation of his noun *chreia* when used in rhetorical treatises or literary studies) "Peter used to give his lessons in a form fitted for his Ana" of Jesus, and we have thus good warrant for taking each short scene sketched in Mark as the verbatim record of Peter. This leads at once to certain interesting results.

(1) At the supper on the eve of Palm Sunday in the house of Simon the leper—it is not made clear whether this was the home of Lazarus, Mary and Martha—an unnamed woman broke an alabaster box of perfume and poured it over the Lord's head. There is nothing to suggest that she anointed His feet or wiped them with her hair. This record is reproduced by Matthew without any but slight verbal alterations, and may be taken to be Peter's "lesson" word for word, relating the scene as it had printed itself on his memory.

(2) Luke tells us that some days after John had sent his two pupils to ask about our Lord's Ministry a Pharisee named Simon invited Jesus to his house. During the meal a woman, a sinner in the city, came behind Him, wept over His feet, wiped them with her hair and then anointed them with perfume from an alabaster box. The precise order of these actions is confirmed by our Lord's words when He contrasted the woman's loving devotion with Simon's cold inattentions. Diligent readers have long noticed that it is immediately after this incident that Luke introduces the name of Mary Magdalene as one of those women who accompanied Jesus as He journeyed about Galilee. In consequence she has been supposed to have been the sinner of this anointing. Her thankfulness, it has been thought, expressed itself in her ministering from her purse to the needs of the Saviour's travel. With His pupils she waited upon His words and doings. Her fidelity at and after the Crucifixion was rewarded by her being chosen to see and to address before all others the Risen Lord.

(3) John goes out of his way to tell us that Lazarus' sister, Mary, was she who had anointed the Lord and had wiped His feet with her hair. Trench contended that such a note of identification was not natural if it was to be referred to the episode on the eve of Palm Sunday, which John relates in the following chapter. We might indeed explain it as referable to the story which, in accordance with Jesus' declaration and promise, was generally current among Christians. In that case we shall be tempted to suppose that John has intended his narrative to be a correction of Mark, with which many have thought—though, we shall suggest, mistakenly—that he was

acquainted. We should then have to ask whether our confidence in Peter's vivid and detailed recountal was well-founded or again our confidence in Mark's faithful and competent recording of it. An alternative reconciliation of the facts claims consideration and would seem to be more acceptable. John, we may believe, is at pains to tell us that the sister of Lazarus was the sinner who, as Luke relates, wept over Christ's feet, wiped them and anointed them. Subsequently, as Mark and Matthew say, she poured the second box of perfume over His head at the Bethany supper. This second anointing John himself describes in order to give the setting for his clear and positive imputation of cupidity as the motive which impelled Judas to deliver his Master into His enemies' hands. It might then be said that John has been betrayed by his previous reference to the earlier anointing into a confusion in respect of the details. He has lost Peter's photographic re-creation of the scene and, intent on its historical interpretation of motives, repeats the story of the previous anointing. Mark faithfully recites Peter's exact portrayal of the scene. That scene Peter had, as usual with him, acutely and consciously remarked at the time, and afterwards livelily described. But a more acceptable reconcilement of the two narratives offers itself for consideration. From the streaming flood of perfume, which Mark shows us that Peter so vividly remembered Mary pouring over the Lord's head, she took a little and anointed His feet and then, as John relates, wiped it away and dried his feet with her hair. Thus there is no contradiction or correction of Mark's record or Peter's impression. The attention of the robust and solid Peter was concentrated on the main incident—the prodigal profusion of the scent, which John confirms by speaking of the pound weight of the essence and the filling of the house with the odour—while the more sensitive and susceptible John noticed particularly the secondary actions and the beautiful tresses of Mary.

Three comments suggest themselves : (1) Confirmation, it may be claimed, is here to be seen of our belief that John has written with an eye not on Mark but on Luke. (2) He had it in purpose to repair the absence from Luke of the supper at Bethany. (3) Luke has derived his story from John and in both narratives we may see that sensuous sensitiveness to feminine charms which it has been suggested is to be detected in the writings of St. John.

Appendix II

The Archetype of the Fourth Gospel

In *The Expository Times* for May 1933 (vol. XLIV, p. 382f.), I developed the theory that it was possible by assuming a purely mechanical dislocation of the pages in the archetype to explain how the order of the chapters xiv, xv and xvi in John's Gospel might have received their present order and might be rearranged in an order which gave a satisfactory development of teaching. I stated that an examination of the passages in question and of the entire length of the Gospel favoured the view that the archetype had been written on two fascicles of folded paper, and that in the middle of the second fascicle six pages on which these chapters had been written fell out and were put back in their place so that the present order was obtained. The following table will show exactly what I suggested:

Page A1	chapter xv. 1–16	Page C2	chapter xvi. 4–20
„ B1	„ xiv. 1–17	„ B2	„ xvi. 20–end
„ C1	„ xv. 17–xvi. 4	„ A2	„ xiv. 18–31

where I have postulated that three sheets were used, indicated by the letters A, B, C, and that each sheet was folded to give two pages which were actually written on. Thus A1 and A2 are the two pages of the folded A sheet. The three sheets having come loose, I argued that they were put back so that the pages were in the order B1, A2, A1, C1, C2, B2 : that is to say, B was inserted as the outermost of the three sheets, and between its pages the A sheet was inserted first with its pages in reversed order, and after it C with its pages in the right order.

Since that article was written, and, indeed, since it was published, my friend the Rev. D. P. Buckle brought to my notice some observations of Sir F. G. Kenyon, which deserve to be quoted : "The method was to use sheets twice the width of the page required, and to fold them once, thus producing two leaves or four pages. Several sheets could, however, be laid one upon the other before folding, thus producing quires of 2, 4, 6, 8, or any other number of leaves in some series of multiples of 2" (Chester Beatty, *Bib. Pap.*, London, 1933).

It is perhaps superfluous to point out that were the pages in question to have come in any other position in the archetype this rearrangement would have been impossible. It is just because they come in the middle of the fascicle that the reconstruction can be made. To make the matter clear it may be well here to indicate precisely how, as I believe, the pages of the original archetype were made up.[1]

FASCICLE I

Leaf	Accepted numeration	Number of printed lines in Nestle's text, 1932
1	Title of the Gospel	
2	Chapter i. 1–18	31½
3	„ i. 19–34	34½

[1] I owe to the Rev. T. Cottam's *A Rearrangement of the Fourth Gospel*, which I have been privileged to read in manuscript, the conviction that both the pericope in chapter viii and chapter xxi were integral parts of the archetype. I had previously regarded the pericope as an unoriginal addition and had thus made the first fascicle contain leaves 2–32 and the second leaves 33–60, with chapter xxi appended as an afterthought.

FASCICLE 1—*continued*

Leaf	Accepted numeration	Number of printed lines in Nestle's text, 1932
4	Chapter i. 35–48	33½
5	,, i. 49–ii. 11	32
6	,, ii. 12–end	32
7	,, iii. 1–15	33½
8	,, iii. 16–28	32½
9	,, iii. 29–iv. 9	34½
10	,, iv. 10–24	35
11	,, iv. 25–40	33
12	,, iv. 41–end	33
13	,, v. 1–17	32
14	,, v. 18–30	34
15	,, v. 31–end	33½
16	,, vi. 1–14	31½
17	,, vi. 15–27	32
18	,, vi. 28–41	31
19	,, vi. 42–56	31½
20	,, vi. 57–end	31
21	,, vii. 1–16	32½
22	,, vii. 17–31	34
23	,, vii. 32–45	32½
24	,, vii. 46–viii. 9	29
25	,, viii. 9–20	29
26	,, viii. 21–35	33½
27	,, viii. 36–47	31
28	,, viii. 48–ix. 3	33
29	,, ix. 4–17	33
30	,, ix. 18–31	33

FASCICLE 2

31	Chapter ix. 32–x. 6	33½
32	,, x. 7–21	34
33	,, x. 22–39	34½
34	,, x. 40–xi. 13	30
35	,, xi. 14–30	31
36	,, xi. 31–44	32½
37	,, xi. 45–end	31
38	,, xii. 1–15	32
39	,, xii. 16–29	34
40	,, xii. 30–43	30½
41	,, xii. 44–xiii. 7	32½

FASCICLE 2—*continued*

Leaf	Accepted numeration	Number of printed lines in Nestle's text, 1932
42	Chapter xiii. 8–22	32
43	,, xiii. 23–end	34
44	,, xv. 1–16	36
45	,, xiv. 1–17	36
46	,, xv. 17–xvi. 4	32
47	,, xvi. 4–20	34
48	,, xvi. 20–end	32
49	,, xiv. 18–31	33½
50	,, xvii. 1–13	32
51	,, xvii. 14–xviii. 1	31½
52	,, xviii. 2–15	34
53	,, xviii. 16–29	31½
54	,, xviii. 30–end	32
55	,, xix. 1–12	30½
56	,, xix. 13–24	35
57	,, xix. 25–37	30
58	,, xix. 38–xx. 7	31
59	,, xx. 8–20	35
60	,, xx. 21–xxi. 2	28
61	,, xxi. 2–14	32
62	,, xxi. 15–end	33

If this reconstruction be correct we must reject Fr. Sutcliffe's argument for a two-year public Ministry, to support which chapters v and vi must needs be transposed.

It will be observed that there is here no question of subjective selection of passages for readjustment upon the assumption that the subject-matter calls for transposition. The MS. had pages or half leaves written on the recto and half leaves on the verso of the leaf. There is no room for any wholesale readjustment or alteration in the order. As I have said above, the only point at which dislocation is possible is in the middle sheets in each fascicle.

Other suggestions of dislocation approved by Bernard do not immediately lend themselves to such objective confirmation as has been postulated above. Chapter v, it has been computed, contains 3,630 letters; chapter vii. 15–24, has 763 letters; chapter iii. 22–30, has 730 letters; chapter x. 1–18, has 1,495 letters; chapter xii. 36b–43, has 598 letters. The hypothesis elaborated above gives 1,210 letters to a leaf, or perhaps 605 each to the recto and verso.

Archbishop Temple sought to retain and justify the traditional order of leaves 44–49 by supposing that after the words at the end of chapter xiv our Lord and His apostles left the house, passed by the Temple front and at the beginning of chapter xviii went out of the city over the Kidron. This reading of the narrative furnishes an attractive setting for the opening words of chapter xv. The great golden vine of the Temple screen would supply the image developed in our Lord's discourse. That the prayer of chapter xvii should be offered in the open air would be of a piece with the prayer before the arrival at Lazarus' grave and with the exultant thanksgiving when the Seventy returned.

Yet notwithstanding these considerations there remain six obstacles to our contentment with the conventional order of the text. (1) The plain declaration as to the Spirit's advent makes the language of chapters xv and xvi needlessly allusive and mysterious. (2) The precise and definite statement as to our Lord's return makes the disciples' perplexity hard to understand—not so much because they were slow to grasp its spiritual nature, as because their perplexity was cleared away, it would appear, by statements not less unambiguous. (3) The words "hereafter I shall not speak much with you" are more fitting near the end of the Discourses. (4) The concluding sentences fall on the ear with the accents of a final valediction. (5) The words about "peace" more fitly follow than precede the words near the end of chapter xvi. (6) The words "I will not send you out alone into the world" come most appropriately after the last three or four sentences of chapter xvi.

On the other hand, if the mechanical displacement suggested above be accepted, it may be said that the gradual development of these last spiritual lessons proceeds towards greater and greater clarity, that the copyist who arranged the disturbed sheets was led astray by the repetition of the words "let not your heart be troubled," and that the image of the vine could suggest itself from the description of the winecup as "the fruit of the vine"—not to say that as Israel was the vine planted by Jahveh, so Christ is the true, representative, ideal type of that vine as it was designed in God's purpose for humanity.

Finally it should be noticed that an important spiritual truth may seem to emerge. With the traditional arrangement the "much fruit" of the faithful appears to be prayer in Christ's spirit. Although this thought has its importance, our suggested arrangement yields this: "the Spirit now is dwelling near you, and He shall be in you, in order that (or so that) whatever you ask the Father in My name, He may give you." Here we are reminded that till Pentecost the Holy Ghost is not in the apostles. He is in our Lord, and Christ is present with them. The Father is in Christ through His Spirit. Afterwards the Spirit in the disciples will assist their prayers that they may be according to Christ's will and true to His character. This is the source of St. Paul's teaching that the Spirit helps our infirmity, aiding our prayers and making intercession for us. In a sense the Kingdom of God is the Spirit's indwelling so that the Baptist could proclaim His and its approach, and the apostles on their mission could declare that He or it had come.

It would be irrelevant to our present purpose to enter into the controversies as to whether this archetype exhibits evidence of composite authorship and who the authors may have been who contributed to it. Yet for honesty's sake I should perhaps declare that when allowance has been made for one defect in ancient writers, I find Dr. W. G. Rutherford's theory of interpolations in the work of Thucydides not more unconvincing than these partitions of the Fourth Gospel. The single particular in which allowance must be made is this. The writers of antiquity had not at their command the devices of modern typography. Hence what we put into a footnote —comment, correction or explanation of the text—was anciently incorporated in the text, and if it were in the middle of a speech, was thrown into the form of a part of the speech. On a previous page we have given examples of this, and so far as the Fourth Gospel is concerned, Dr. E. A. Abbott averred that the author gave his readers a sign of such notes of his own by using γάρ in place of ὅτι to introduce a reason for what had just been said.

APPENDIX III

A Skeleton Diatessaron

We are now in a position to suggest a chronological sequence of the matter contained in the four Gospels, so that it is possible to follow the progress of events in any reference Bible exhibiting such parallel narratives as the other Gospels may supply. Our argument favours the following order:

Luke i. 1–38	John v.
Luke ii. 1–3	Luke vii. 36–viii. 3
Luke i. 39–80	Mark vi. 17–29
Matt. i.	Luke viii. 4–40
Luke ii. 4–40	Mark ix. 14–18
Matt. ii.	Luke viii. 41–56
Luke ii. 41–iii. 18, 21–iv. 13	Mark vi. 1–6
John i. 19–iv. 54	Luke ix. 1–11
Luke iv. 14–44	John vi. 1–15
Luke iii. 19, 20 [1]	Matt. xiv. 23–34
Luke v. 1–32	John vi. 22–71
Luke vi. 1–vii. 35	Mark vii. 1–viii. 12

So far it has been simple and easy to trace the course of the history by enumerating a series of pages from the Gospels which could be read consecutively. From this point it will be better to tabulate in parallel columns what a comparative examination of the four evangelists seems to yield as the most probable summary of the various episodes arranged in chronological order. Such an arrangement, we may well believe, would appear as follows:

Luke	Matthew	Mark	John
xi. 16	xvi. 1, 4	viii. 11, 12	
		viii. 13–26	
	ix. 27–31		
		viii. 27	

[1] Perhaps this should come between John iii. 36 and iv. 1.

Luke	Matthew	Mark	John
ix. 18–42	xvi. 13–xvii. 18	viii. 28–ix. 27	
xi. 14, 15, 17–28	ix. 32–34, xii. 22–30, 43–45	iii. 22–30	
ix. 43–45	xvii. 22, 23	ix. 30–32	
	xvii. 24–27		
	xvii. 19–21	ix. 28, 29	
ix. 46–50	xviii. 1–5; x. 42	ix. 33–41	
			vii. 1–13
ix. 51–56			
			vii. 14–viii. 11
ix. 57–60	viii. 19–22		
ix. 61–x. 12	ix. 35–38; x. 12–16		
x. 13–16	xi. 21–23; x. 40		
x. 17–24	x. 25–30; xiii. 16, 17		
x. 25–42	xxii. 35–40	xii. 28b–34a	
	xix. 1, 2	x. 1	viii. 12–x. 42
xi. 1–13	vi. 9–13; vii. 7–11		
xi. 29–32	xii. 38–42		
xi. 33–36	v. 15; vi. 22, 23		
xi. 37–54	xxiii. 13, 15–36		
	xix. 3–12	x. 2–12	
xii. 1–10	x. 26–33; xii. 31, 32	iii. 28, 29	
xii. 13–31	vi. 25–34		
xii. 32–34	vi. 19–21		
xii. 35–53	xxiv. 43–51; x. 34–36		
xii. 54–57	xvi. 2, 3		
xii. 58, 59	v. 25, 26		
xiii. 1–17			
xiii. 18–22	xiii. 31–33	iv. 30–32	
			xi. 1–6[1]
xiii. 23–30	vii. 13, 14, 23; viii. 11–12		
xiii. 31–35	xxiii. 37–39		
xiv. 1–15			
xiv. 16–24	xxii. 2–10		
			xi. 7–16
xiv. 25–35	x. 37, 38; v. 13	ix. 50	
xv. 1–32	xviii. 12–14		
xvi. 1–13	vi. 19, 24		

---

[1] This perhaps should be interposed between Luke xiii. 35 and xiv. 1.

Luke	Matthew	Mark	John
xvi. 14–31	xi. 12, 13; v. 18, 31, 32		
			xi. 17–57
xvii. 1, 2	xviii. 6–9; v. 29, 30	ix. 42–48	
xvii. 3, 4	xviii. 15–17		
	xviii. 21–35	xi. 25, 26	
xvii. 7–10			
xvii. 11–19			
xvii. 20–37	xxiv. 17, 18, 27, 28, 37–41	xiii. 15, 16	
xviii. 1–14			
xviii. 15–30	xix. 13–29	x. 13–30	
	xx. 1–16		
xviii. 31–43	xx. 17–34	x. 32–52	
xix. 1–10			
xix. 11–28			
	xxvi. 6–13	xiv. 3–9	xii. 1–11
xix. 29–38	xxi. 1–11	xi. 1–10	xii. 12–18
	xxi. 14		
xix. 39, 40	xxi. 15, 16		
xix. 41–44			
	xxi. 17	xi. 11	
xix. 47, 48			xii. 19
	xxi. 18–19	xi. 12–14	
			xii. 20–43
		xi. 18	
	xxi. 20	xi. 19–21	
xvii. 5, 6	xxi. 21, 22	xi. 22–24	
xx. 1–8	xxi. 23–27	xi. 27–33	
	xxi. 28–32		
xx. 9–19	xxi. 33–46	xii. 1–12	
	xxii. 1–14		
xx. 20–26	xxii. 15–22	xii. 13–17	
xx. 27–39	xxii. 23–32	xii. 18–27	
xx. 40	xxii. 33, 34, 46	xii. 28a, 34b	
xx. 41–44	xxii. 41–45	xii. 35–37	
			xii. 44–50
xx. 45–47	xxiii. 1–3, 5–7, 14	xii. 38–40	
xxi. 1–4		xii. 41–44	
xxi. 5, 6	xxiv. 1, 2	xiii. 1, 2	
xxi. 7–19	xxiv. 3–14	xiii. 3–13	
xxi. 20–24	xxiv. 15, 16, 19–26	xiii. 14–23	
xxi. 25–28	xxiv. 29–31	xiii. 24–27	

Luke	Matthew	Mark	John
xxi. 29–33	xxiv. 32–35	xiii. 28–31	
xxi. 34–36	xxiv. 36, 42	xiii. 32–37	
	xxv. 1–13		
	xxv. 14–30		
	xxv. 31–46		
xxi. 37, 38			
xxii. 1–6	xxvi. 3–5, 14–16	xiv. 1, 2, 10, 11	
xxii. 7–13	xxvi. 1, 2, 17–19	xiv. 12–16	
xxii. 14	xxvi. 20	xiv. 17	
xxii. 15–18	xxvi. 29	xiv. 25	
xxii. 24–29			xiii. 1–20
xxii. 21–23	xxvi. 21–25	xiv. 18–21	xiii. 21–30
xxii. 19, 20	xxvi. 26–28	xiv. 22–24	
xxii. 31–34	xxvi. 31–35	xiv. 27–31	xiii. 31–38
xxii. 35–38			
			xv. 1–16a
			xiv. 1–17
			xv. 16b–xvi. 33
			xiv. 18–31
			xvii.
xxii. 39	xxvi. 30	xiv. 26	xviii. 1, 2
xxii. 40–46	xxvi. 36–46	xiv. 32–42	
xxii. 47, 48	xxvi. 47–50	xiv. 43–46	xviii. 3–9
xxii. 49–51	xxvi. 51–54	xiv. 47	xviii. 10, 11
xxii. 52, 53	xxvi. 55, 56	xiv. 48–50	
		xiv. 51, 52	
xxii. 54a	xxvi. 57a	xiv. 53a	xviii. 12–14
xxii. 54b, 55	xxvi. 58	xiv. 54	xviii. 15, 16, 18
	xxvi. 57b	xiv. 53b	xviii. 24
			xviii. 19–23
	xxvi. 59–63a	xiv. 55–61a	
xxii. 63–65	xxvi. 67, 68	xiv. 65	
xxii. 56, 57	xxvi. 69, 70	xiv. 66–68	xviii. 17
xxii. 58	xxvi. 71, 72	xiv. 69, 70a	xviii. 25
xxii. 59–62	xxvi. 73–75	xiv. 70b–72	xviii. 26, 27
xxii. 66–68	xxvii. 1	xv. 1a	
xxii. 69–71	xxvi. 63b–66	xiv. 61b–64	
xxiii. 1	xxvii. 2	xv. 1b	xviii. 28
xxiii. 2			xviii. 29–32
xxiii. 3, 4	xxvii. 11	xv. 2	xviii. 33–38
	xxvii. 12–14	xv. 3–5	
xxiii. 5–12			
	xxvii. 19		
xxiii. 13–16			
xxiii. 17–19	xxvii. 15–18, 20, 21	xv. 6–11	xviii. 39, 40

Luke	Matthew	Mark	John
xxiii. 20–22	xxvii. 22, 23	xv. 12–14	xix. 1–6
	xxvii. 24, 25		
			xix. 7–13
xxiii. 23–25	xxvii. 26	xv. 15	xix. 14–16
xxiii. 26–33	xxvii. 27–34	xv. 16–23	
xxiii. 34–43	xxvii. 35–44	xv. 24–32	xix. 17–27
xxiii. 44, 45	xxvii. 45–47	xv. 33–35	
	xxvii. 48, 49	xv. 36	xix. 28–30
xxiii. 46	xxvii. 50	xv. 37	
xxiii. 47–56	xxvii. 51–61	xv. 38–47	xix. 31–42
	xxvii. 3–5		
	xxvii. 62–66		
xxiv. 1–11	xxviii. 1–8	xvi. 1–8	xx. 1, 2
xxiv. 12			xx. 3–10
	xxviii. 9–15	xvi. 9–11	xx. 11–18
xxiv. 34, cf. 1 Cor. xv. 5			
xxiv. 13–35		xvi. 12, 13	
xxiv. 36–49		xvi. 14	xx. 19–29
			xxi. 1–23
	xxviii. 16, 17		
Acts i. 1–5			
xxiv. 50–53;	xxviii. 18–20	xvi. 15–19	
Acts i. 6–14			

Note on John viii. 12–59

Even when we have discarded the reading of the inferior MSS., which make ix. 1, "passed by," echo viii. 59, the continuity of the narrative compels us to acquiesce in Westcott's judgment that the whole section viii. 12–x. 42 is to be dated at the time of the Dedication Festival.

Note on Mark ix. 40–50

It may be thought that our division, distribution and rearrangement of the last eleven verses of Mark ix rests on merely subjective considerations. It is right, therefore, that the following paraphrase should be included in these pages. It is from the pen of my friend Mr. R. O. P. Taylor, written a year or two before his death, and it aims at exhibiting a logical sequence of thought throughout the whole passage as a single entity. He writes:

"Those who are not our opponents are our supporters. Indeed, anyone who does even so little as to give you a drink of water because you are adherents of Christ, shall not fail to be the better off for it. On the other hand, anyone who makes a pitfall for those who are childlike and trusting shall bring troubles, worse than death, on themselves. Take care that you yourselves are wholly on the right side, and that there is no opposition mingled with your support. If some part of you, say your hand, decoys you, it would be better to chop it off. It is preferable to find real life at the price of being maimed than to be thrown away, like the rubbish which they pitch into the Valley of Fires at Jerusalem. If your foot decoys you, get rid of it. You had better find real life, going on one leg, than be flung, with two feet, into destruction. If your eye decoys you, you had better blind it. You will be better off as a one-eyed citizen in God's kingdom than keeping both eyes at the price of being flung into destruction. Do not flatter yourself that, when your turn shall come, the fires will have ceased to destroy. Nor will the worm, which devours what is decayed, have ceased its work. Nor will these forces act on one class only. In everyone there is some pollution or decay which will have to be eaten out. No doubt it is good to be the saving salt of society. But if that which passed for salt had only a portion of salt in it, at the best, and even that has gone, what will give it back its bite? Season your minds, lest they decay, even if the seasoning hurts as it searches. Then there will be a healthy life among you."

PART TWO

HISTORICAL

Chapter One

CHRONOLOGICAL ORDER OF EVENTS

IT is natural now to enquire, when we have thus arranged and combined our Gospel narratives, what sort of story unfolds itself before us. In preparation for an attempt to reconstruct this, one or two matters deserve particular examination, even at the cost of some repetition of what has already been discussed for another purpose.

(1)

In chapters xvii and xxi Luke represents our Lord as warning his disciples against following leaders who would falsely claim to be the Messiah come to save the Jewish nation. He told them that if they were alert they would not fail to know the hour of impending doom. It might be argued that the signs premonitory of the fall of Jerusalem were detailed by our Lord on one occasion only. Luke in that case, with two unrelated sources before him, has given us two alternative accounts of the one single discourse. Yet to this view there are grave objections. Luke, unlike Matthew, manifestly designs, however unsuccessful we may account him, to arrange his material chronologically. He distinguishes the missions of the Twelve and of the Seventy, twice speaks of the purpose for which men light a lamp, and assigns to a precise and definite date the utterance of the parables of the Leaven and of the Mustard Seed. This general practice of Luke is confirmed for the particular instance in question by several considerations. In the first place we have the two occasions of the prophecies clearly marked as different. Again, the disciples' slowness to take in Christ's words and their inability to divest themselves of their conventional conceptions as to Israel's future made it necessary to repeat the novel picture of what it was to be. In the same way the disciples had again and again to be taught that humility and service are the insignia of rank in God's kingdom. It was not otherwise when they had to be prepared for Christ's Crucifixion and Resurrection. Yet more noteworthy is it that even after the two predictions of the approaching catastrophe the apostles asked, "Dost Thou at this time restore the kingdom to Israel?" Plainly we are justified in accepting Luke's dating for these prophecies as correct.

(2)

As regards the story of the last year in our Lord's Ministry two or three points deserve emphasis:

(a) The going up to Jerusalem to which our Lord "steadfastly set His face" was not a local but a spiritual movement. From the time that He chose, as Canon J. J. Scott pointed out, not such a translation to the unseen life as, for example, Elijah and Moses experienced, but the redemption of the world by His death upon the Cross, He was preparing for the Crucifixion.

(b) The journey to Sidon, though of short duration, was to gain a few weeks more for the education of the Twelve, and to prevent arrest or murder before His "hour"—not as yet made known to Him from the Father—"was come."

(c) Anyone who reads the story in the order here suggested will find key-words and cardinal thoughts appearing in John and Luke at the same period in the narrative and not at other periods. Such thoughts as that our Lord is the Shepherd of the flock of disciples (Luke xii. 32; John x. 2–16), that for the selfish rich a message from the dead would do nothing (Luke xvi. 31; John xi), and that Holy Spirit and, as it is finally expressed, the Holy Ghost (see Part IV, Chap. 4, Excursus III) is to be given (Luke xi. 13, xii. 12; John xiv. 16, 26), will be found to show this harmony between the two narratives, read—on independent grounds—in the order we have given.[1]

One other result of our postulates need alone detain us. It has often been said that St. Luke, at a loss as to the Gospel chronology, pieced his narrative together by phrases such as "in

[1] One curious coincidence deserves mention. It is after the parable of the Good Samaritan recorded by Luke x. 30 ff. that John viii. 48 makes "the Jews" say, not as in vii. 20, "Thou hast a devil," but "Thou art a Samaritan and hast a devil."

that very hour" which mean nothing. An alert re-examination of Luke's use shows, however, that this view misses a valuable source of information. In ii. 38 it is clear that the writer uses the words to emphasize the coincidence in time of Anna's entrance into the Temple with our Lord's Presentation. Similarly, just after our Lord had warned the apostles—stewards in God's reconstituted household—that heavier punishment would fall on the more guilty and wilful offender and that the last mite would be exacted, by a coincidence which Luke emphasizes, men were present with the news of the butchering by Pilate of Galileans engaged in the very act of sacrifice being offered for them. It was natural after the teaching just given for the question to arise, Did this terrible punishment, then, mean terrible sin? It must be observed that with our re-reading of the story we can date this incident to the time of the Feast of Purim—always a restless season so far as the relations of Jew and Gentile were concerned. When, soon after, Luke adds that "He was journeying to Jerusalem" (xiii. 22), we may see the point at which to bring in the raising of Lazarus—when our Lord left, but without hurry (Luke xiii. 23–35), the trans-Jordanic domains of Herod. After the miracle we are told that He retired to an uninhabited district, apparently on the border of Samaria and Galilee, where the authority of neither Herod nor of the Jewish Sanhedrin would run, and assassins would have difficulty in getting near to strike (cf. John xi. 54 and Luke xvii. 11).

One final word may be offered. Thucydides' narrative, it has been noticed, exhibits the dramatic qualities of a Greek tragedy, but, notwithstanding this, most scholars believe his story to be authentic and the tragic elements to lie in the facts, not in any manipulation of these by him. In the same way, it may confidently be claimed, the forward march of our Redeemer's mission, from popularity through disappointment and defiance to death, is inherent in the facts, and that this progress is most apparent in the Third Gospel, is not due to the writer's art or management, but is the conclusive proof of his fidelity to the facts that he learnt and to the accuracy of the result from our acceptance of our postulates.

(3)

Matthew, perhaps even more than Luke, has suffered at the
hands of the commentators. His marks of time have been dismissed as valueless because it was clear that they could not be
treated as immediate and certain authority for drawing up a
chronological table of events. Yet patient consideration, it may
be claimed, yields something of value. Just as "on that day" in
xiii. 1 supplies confirmation of our understanding of the events
on the day that the first cryptic parable was uttered, so "at
that time" in xi. 25, xii. 1 and xiv. 1, if narrowly and
sympathetically examined, provides us with a fresh illustration
of the author's methods. The ordinary translation is inadequate.
The author's meaning will be better represented if we translate
or paraphrase, "once during the determining period of crisis
in His Ministry." The words then testify to the evangelist's
knowledge that after a period of popularity there followed a
time when the issue might be thought to have hung in the
balance, after which came, in the result, the apparent failure
that was in reality success and the earnest of His glory. He also
testifies to the fact that to that intermediate period of crisis
belonged: (1) the thanksgiving to the Father because the truths
of the Kingdom were revealed and reserved for babes; (2) the
clash with the Pharisees over the disciples' disregard of the
sabbath regulations in their walk through the cornfields; and
(3) Herod's nervous apprehensions that the Baptist was risen
from the dead. Here again then we find Matthew's method of
grouping similar matter irrespectively of its date, and yet of
giving us, if we have the will to learn, indications of it.

Another instance of Matthew's leaving us the means to arrive
at valuable facts of place and date is to be seen in his record of
the parable of the Tares. This he places later than that of the
Sower and earlier than the Mustard Seed, which Luke shows
to have been spoken a few weeks before the Crucifixion. We
infer, then, that the parable of the Tares was spoken shortly
after our Lord has declared that plants not planted by His
Father should be rooted up, and this gives us as its date the
early summer before the Transfiguration and the neighbourhood of Tyre as the locality (Mark vii. 1 and 24). This inference

ıs confirmed by Matthew himself when he mentions (xiii. 36) that Jesus explained this parable not in His home at Capernaum (as Mark vii. 17 says He explained about unclean meats) but "indoors,"[1] that is to say in some house away from Capernaum.

(4)

It is an undisputed fact that certain matter expressed in almost identical language and often word for word the same has been drawn by the authors of the First and the Third Gospels from a source commonly designated as Q. A consideration of the way that this material from Q is arranged inside the framework of Mark seems to yield certain results which may be regarded as chronological sequences resting on Q's authority.

(1) The healing of the centurion's servant at Capernaum followed the Sermon on the Tableland among the hills. The First Evangelist, having antedated the Sermon so as to give it as an example of our Lord's teaching, interposed before the centurion's application the healing of the leper which, Mark showed, took place away from Capernaum.

(2) It would seem that Q introduced the mission of the Baptist's two disciples early after the selection (not the mission) of the Twelve, and before our Lord's first use of cryptic parables. The First Gospel apparently inserts chapters x and xi where they are because the raising of Jairus' daughter (which it has wrongly antedated) supplies an example of the raising of the dead spoken of in the message to the Baptist. But the conjoining of the mission of the Twelve to their selection is shown to be an error by the words about the Master of the house being called Beelzebub, a calumny which, as we have seen, came later. In the same way the declaration that the Son of Man hath not where to lay His head is misplaced in Matthew and belongs to the period in which Luke places it.

(3) Perhaps it may be inferred also that Q made the selection of the Twelve to be followed by a discourse from our Lord. The

---

[1] For the distinction between ὄικος "home" or "room" and οἰκία "house" see my article in the *Expository Times*, Sept. 1938, pp. 566ff. My friend the late R. O. P. Taylor verified throughout the Septuagint the invariable observance of this distinction.

4*

First Gospel having combined this into what might serve as an example of our Lord's teaching, brought forward the mission of the Twelve and accordingly gave at this point the instructions that were given to the Seventy. Luke rightly retained the original order confirmed by Mark in regard to the instructions to the Twelve. Their selection had been followed by our Lord's exposition of the ideals towards which the subjects in God's kingdom were to aspire.

(5)

Yet another inference can be drawn from a comparison of the First and Third Gospels as to the historical occasion of an incident. Before a journey to Jerusalem St. Peter asked our Lord how often he should forgive his brother. Matthew who, like Mark, transports his narrative finally from Galilee to Peraea and then to the last Passover Week, mentions this incident at the point where our Lord is preparing to leave Galilee. Luke records it at the point where our Lord is commencing His final journey to face crucifixion. We may infer that this is historically correct and that it is due to Matthew's method of grouping topics and his acceptance of the literary framework of Mark that has caused any appearance of contradiction between the First and Third Gospels.

To return to our prime enquiry we may next consider parenthetic or trajected passages in our Gospels.

The writer who purposes to give his readers more than a catalogue of events, dated or undated, and to survey them with a philosophic insight into their causes and consequences, cannot arrange his material in a purely annalistic system. His narrative may in its broad outlines be chronological, but at certain points he is constrained to explain the origin or motives of some occurrences: he must go back to trace from an earlier date what at last issued in something precise and definitive. At other times he naturally rounds off his account of some event by stating at once its ultimate sequel. An example of this procedure is pretty certainly to be seen in the way Acts xii follows the mention of the mission of Barnabas and Paul to carry to Jerusalem the proceeds of the Antioch effort to mitigate the famine predicted by Agabus.

In Mark's Gospel the account of the Lord's anointing at the Bethany dinner is parenthetically interposed to explain why Judas decided to bargain with the priests. The date of the dinner is not to be supposed to follow Judas' bargain. Earlier in the Gospel when the narrative has duly recorded that after the parable of the Sower our Lord's mother and brethren feared for His sanity, St. Mark parenthetically mentions what in reality occurred later, that the Pharisees asserted his possession by a demon.

These trajections of matter have been understood and corrected by Luke, and in the same way he has made it clear that Mark's narrative of the call of the first four apostles is an anticipation in date of the actual event.

As to the time of the Pharisees' slander that the prince of demons possessed and assisted our Lord, we can see that Luke rightly places part of what our Lord said, by way of rejoinder, subsequent to the last autumn of His life and after the Transfiguration. That he is right is confirmed by the fact that shortly before the five thousand were fed, it was the Baptist who was declared by the Pharisees to be a demoniac, our Lord was characterized by them as a glutton and heavy drinker. Our Lord's relatives seem to have first surmised that his sanity was in danger when they observed the intense pressure upon Him made by the crowds coming to Him for curative treatment. After His first elaborate parable they attempted action to withdraw Him into seclusion. Matthew, unlike Luke, shows again that he is indifferent to the chronology of the Ministry.

Yet another example of the rounding off of a subject the conclusion being thus antedated is to be seen in Mark ix. 28 ff. The nine apostles, who had failed to heal the paranoiac youth, asked the reason of their failure after the return to Capernaum,[1] but quite intelligibly the author narrates the conversation immediately after his account of the boy's cure.

Another trajection (as I believe it to be) is to be seen in Mark's account of our Lord's "cleansing the Temple" in Holy Week. The course of his story had not brought the Lord previously to Jerusalem; he therefore inserted it at the first point

---

[1] The use of οἶκος in Mark ix. 28 ff. shows that the enquiry was made in our Lord's home at Capernaum. (Contrast the use of οἰκία in x. 10.)

possible, viz. on the morrow of Palm Sunday. Matthew and Luke, working on Mark's Gospel as a framework, could not place it in its true connexion and have indeed gone further by assigning it to Palm Sunday itself. The Fourth Gospel supplied the correction that was needed. Christ's indignation befits His fresh consciousness of His mission: if it were in Holy Week it would not be equally intelligible, even after His open acceptance of the role of Messiah, when we remember that He had been in the Temple at the previous feast of Tabernacles and of Dedication.[1]

The parenthetic habit is further exemplified in John xviii. 24. The writer has been at pains to correct the mistaken notion which the synoptic record might seem to favour that our Lord was taken direct to Caiaphas. This misconception once corrected, he hastens to resume his story with an account of Peter's denials, and then feels it desirable to explain parenthetically how Peter came to be in Caiaphas' palace.[2]

Finally, we may cite one noteworthy example of an author concluding his treatment of a particular theme by appending what in point of time did not immediately happen. Luke delineates with the utmost care the date and circumstances of the Baptist's presenting himself to the Jewish people: he gives specimens of his teaching and mentions various classes of enquirers who came to him for instruction. He then rounds off his account of John's activities by relating what did not at once follow—his imprisonment by Herod.

(6)

One ultimate puzzle remains, the successful solution of which might satisfy us that our schedule of episodes and instructions is

---

[1] It is right, however, to enter a caveat against the assumption that where two somewhat similar incidents are narrated, one must be an unhistorical doublet of the other. This remark applies to the two stories of the "cleansing of the Temple," the two anointings of our Lord and the feeding of the five and of the four thousand.

[2] Fr. Sutcliffe's suggestion that verses 13–23 fell out, being written on one sheet which was afterwards wrongly inserted before, instead of after, verse 24, would not explain how the archetype placed that verse so as to allow this.

in general correct, even though a few subsidiary details are liable on further examination to be pronounced to require some slight rearrangement. The puzzle is this: why did Luke place at that point in his narrative where he has placed it, the Scribes' ascription of Jesus' exorcisms to Beelzebub and their demand for a "sign"? Our first and hasty answer might be that both of these encounters actually occurred at the time suggested by Luke's narrative. In that case we have to suppose either that Mark has misplaced the demand for a sign or that our Lord twice made his reply about Jonah; and we may distinguish the first blunt answer from the second more ample explanation. Further consideration, however, shows two objections. Mark has plainly misplaced the imputation of help from Beelzebub, so that we may accept it that Luke has purposely altered Mark's arrangement in this regard. On the other hand Mark's account of this demand bears every evidence of being authentic history. Further, Luke reveals that his account of the odious charge of alliance with Beelzebub is drawn from Q. At the same time we know that Luke was without that portion of Mark in which is related the demand for a sign. The parallel section in Matthew discloses that Q grouped the two clashes together, but supplied no clear guidance as to when they occurred. Matthew attached this section of Q to his account of the Pharisees' censure of the disciples' plucking the ears of corn on the Sabbath. He here, as elsewhere, is grouping incidents not chronologically but because of their similarity of subject. This is not Luke's method. On the contrary, he is concerned to place the section, so far as he can, at the proper point in the story. Plainly these charges must have come earlier than our Lord's stern arraignment of the Pharisees and Scribes, and accordingly Luke inserts what he had here drawn from Q just before his account of the dinner at which Christ's indignant rebukes were uttered.

(7)

It will be apposite to refer, if in the barest and briefest manner, to some other words and incidents in the Gospel records which strengthen the presumption that our harmony and interlacing of those records is substantially correct and historical.

(1) The first and third evangelists report, evidently deriving them from Q, words of our Lord, declaring that "the Son of Man hath not where to lay His head." It is clear that this utterance belongs to the period where, following Luke, we have placed it, when the Lord's enemies were hunting Him for His life.

(2) On the mount of Transfiguration St. Peter babbled of building there three Tabernacle-booths. In our arrangement this occurred shortly before the Feast of Tabernacles which appears in the Fourth Gospel.

(3) In our arrangement the parable of the rich man and the beggar Lazarus, which concludes with the words "if they hear not Moses and the prophets, neither will they be persuaded, though one rose from the dead," was spoken while at Bethany Lazarus lay "sleeping," whom our Lord had it in purpose to call back to life.

(4) As my friend, the Rev. F. E. Barker has pointed out, following up an observation of Professor Manson, our Lord begins to speak openly and freely of the Fatherhood of God only after St. Peter's declaration that He was the Christ. Our arrangement reveals that St. Luke and St. John are in accord in this regard.

In the same way it will be found that our arrangement reveals development in the use and content of the title "the Son of Man," a development, we may add, obscured in the ordinary reading of the Gospels.

Further examples of the way in which trains of thought or particular expressions are found in close propinquity may be seen on a careful reading. "The disciple is not above his master" appears in Luke's report of the sermon among the hills and in Matthew's charge to the Twelve, but the application of the saying is quite different. The parables of the Ten Pounds and the Talents come at the same period in the two Gospels, but again there are differences. Warnings against avarice, dishonesty and the love of riches sound incessantly in the Lord's teaching in the last weeks before the young ruler—St. Paul, as we may believe—went away downcast and Judas sold his Master. Our Lord's understanding of the two men's fundamental characters appears, we shall think, in His declaration that "the last shall be first."

Again, the fierce hostility of some Pharisees at Jerusalem, consequent upon the healing of a paralytic on the Sabbath, leads on naturally to the parable which explains how the seed of God's word does or does not bear fruit according to the nature of the soil on which it falls. Then presently our Lord speaks of those whom the Father has given Him that they should come to Him, and this is emphasized not once nor twice. Yet again, we may perhaps find in His talk with Moses and Elijah the ground for still greater assurance that Lazarus was not dead but sleeping and for the conclusive argument against the Sadducees drawn from the knowledge that Abraham, Isaac and Jacob were still alive. True to this tenet, the parable represents Abraham, Lazarus and the plutocrat alive in Hades.

The propriety of our view that Luke should be made the foundation of our chronology is confirmed by a consideration of two other passages where that Gospel has substituted vague expressions for definite time-notes in Mark. The second evangelist states expressly that the storm on the lake occurred in the night following the first elaborate parable. St. Luke, presumably observing the apparent confusion in his authority, the parenthetic trajection of the argument about Beelzebub's self-destruction and the assemblage at this point of parables spoken at different times, writes "on one of the days." A similar caution as regards date has been noted in his account of the cleansing of the Temple. It is fair to infer, therefore, that when he does give an exact dating he has satisfied himself that it is precisely correct.

For a historical view then of the course of events and a clear comprehension of the progress and development of our Lord's redemptive mission, we must concentrate our attention on the Gospels of Luke and John. But that is not to say that they do not abound in much picturesque and vivid detail. On the contrary, they often supply touches which kindle the imagination and warm our spirits, as, for example, when Luke tells us that on the way to Emmaus Cleopas and his companion stopped short in the road with sour looks on their faces because the stranger had pried into their private talk. Nevertheless, to rest content with these two Gospels would be to shut ourselves off from a precious treasure of vital interest to any who would recapture the scenes in which our Lord figured. Thus it remains that within the framework deducible from the Third and Fourth Gospels we can fill in priceless additional matter by making full use of Mark. Here we have the memories of an eye-witness whose attitude was unscientific and unsophisticated. The reader who has habituated himself to the non-modernized and mechanical language of the Revised Version will be electrified and transported if he turns again to the Authorized Version of Mark. We may concede that some expressions in the A.V. may mislead us, as, for example, when the Baptist is said to have a girdle of a skin, but the general effect is both arresting and stimulating. Matthew will always be read not only for the additional matter which he alone has preserved but for the invaluable collections he has made of utterances given by our Lord at different times and for the literary skill with which he has interwoven these utterances into impressive and attractive sermons or addresses. Nevertheless, it remains true that while we use the first two Gospels in the manner we have suggested, yet when we endeavour to reconstruct the actual course and development of our Lord's mission and teaching we must build upon the foundation of the Third and Fourth Gospels.

These preliminary observations made, we may now proceed to review in its probable chronological sequence the story unfolded by our four Gospels. For the most part it will not be necessary to do more than indicate the broad course of history, but at certain points it will be desirable to dwell at some length on aspects of the story which might otherwise pass almost unnoticed. We find, then, the following order of events:

(1) The priest Zacharias received divine assurance that a son should be born to him.

(2) Six months later the Blessed Virgin received a similar assurance, and thereupon went on a three months' visit to her cousin Elizabeth.

(3) John was duly born according to the promise, and afterwards in spite of her pregnancy the Blessed Virgin was married by St. Joseph.

(4) Jesus was born at Bethlehem six months later than the Baptist, and after forty days was presented in the Temple and seen by Simeon and Anna.

(5) When He was no longer a babe at the breast but a young child [1] three Magi came to do Him homage, and St. Joseph removed Him for safety to Egypt.

(6) After Herod's death St. Joseph brought Him to Nazareth.

(7) When twelve years old Jesus was taken to Jerusalem for His first Passover.

(8) In Tiberius' fifteenth year John began to announce that God's Kingdom was at hand, and presently to baptize, expecting that by this means he would be shown who it was that should baptize others with "Holy Spirit" (John i. 33; see Part IV, Excursus III, p. 341).

(9) Jesus was shown at His baptism to be the King of Israel and the Lamb of God.

(10) After forty days of solitude, He returned to John and four of John's disciples gave Jesus their allegiance.

(11) He returned to Galilee with Philip and on the third day was at Cana for a marriage feast, after which for a short time He and His putative brethren visited Capernaum.

(12) Thence He went up to Jerusalem for the Passover, where Nicodemus came to see Him by night.

(13) He then spent some indeterminate time teaching in Judaea, where His disciples baptized many neophytes.

(14) The Pharisees' concern led Him to return to Galilee (cf. Matt. iv. 12), passing Sychar on the way, and presently, while at Cana,[2] healed the son of Herod's officer from Capernaum, to which city Jesus himself now removed His home (cf. Matt. iv. 13).

(15) After some time spent in teaching in the synagogues near Capernaum, He revisited Nazareth.

(16) Escaping murder there, He permanently settled at Capernaum.

---

[1] In Matt. ii. 1 we should translate "after Jesus was born." A comparison of Luke ii. 16 with Matt. ii. 11 demonstrates that some interval of time divided the Nativity from the Magi's visit.

[2] If John iv. 35 should be understood to indicate that the journey took place in December, it may not be fanciful to suppose a child was now born to the couple whose marriage is related in John ii. 1–11, and this might give the clue to our Lord's knowledge of the circumstances of a birth (John xvi. 21).

(17) One Sabbath in the synagogue He exorcized a demon, and afterwards the same day healed many sick persons, going out the next morning to preach in other towns.

Later, it would seem, came John's arrest.

(18) The crowds attending Him[1] were so great that He asked Simon Peter that He might use his boat and presently invited him and his brother and Zebedee's sons to accompany Him henceforward on His preaching tours.

(19) Next He cured a leper, and after a period of work in country districts returned home, where He healed a paralytic, whose sins He pronounced to have been forgiven.

(20) On His way from His home to the seaside, He invited Matthew to join His retinue and attended Matthew's dinner-party, publicans though the other guests were.

(21) The scandal of this association with "sinners" was aggravated by His justifying His disciples when they disregarded, as they walked through the cornfields, the stricter regulations about Sabbath work.

(22) Soon after, Jesus Himself, as the Pharisees held, broke the Sabbath by healing in the synagogue a man's withered hand.

This added fresh fuel to the Pharisees' indignation, and from this point forward the religious authorities[2] began to consider what could be done to suppress the new movement. Jesus sought retirement by the sea, but crowds gathered round Him, and to avoid the press He arranged that a small boat should be at hand to receive Him when He required it. It is not surprising that our Lord should now take a new step.

(23) After a night spent in prayer, He selected the Twelve Apostles.

(24) He then delivered to a great audience the Sermon on the Mount.

In these last two sections Luke begins to march out of step with Mark and there is a pause in their parallel progress. He now interposes several scenes which, when examined, yield invaluable hints as to the ultimate sources from which his

---

[1] Matt. xiii. 1 shows Jesus not coming out from His home but simply out of doors.

[2] Mark iii. 6 states that the Pharisees now concerted plans with the Herodians.

information is derived. We can see that Q gave to both Luke and Matthew the knowledge that the centurion's servant was healed as our Lord was returning to Capernaum after selecting the Twelve and before the parable of the Sower was spoken.

(25) On His way back to Capernaum Jesus healed the centurion's servant.

After this Luke recounts two incidents which come from some other source than Mark or Q, and, as we shall be tempted to say, from St. John.

(26) The next day, He raised from the dead the widow's son at Nain. This miracle was much talked of throughout Jewry and perhaps led to the Baptist sending two disciples to ask about our Lord's Ministry.[1]

(27) A little later Jesus attended a feast at Jerusalem, perhaps Pentecost, on His thirty-eighth birthday. There He healed an impotent man and declared that the dead should hear His voice and should live.[2]

(28) About this time a Pharisee named Simon asked Him to dinner, when He was anointed by a woman who was a sinner.[3]

(29) After this, attended by the Twelve, He made a tour through Galilee, eventually coming again to the sea-shore by

[1] One word of comment may perhaps be added. When the Baptist asked "Art *Thou* He that should come?" he is not doubtful of our Lord's mission from God, but of the character of that mission. Jesus was sent, he believed, to anoint with Holy Spirit, but was the Messiah some other, yet to come and to set up Israel's universal dominion? The insertion of the emphatic pronoun imports a different implication into the question from that in the Devil's "If thou art God's Son." Jesus in the Forty Days purged His idea of Messiahship; John had still to do so.

[2] His words are peculiarly apposite and noticeable in view of the recent miracle at Nain. Nor is this all that suggests St. John's authority for the miracle. In relating it Luke uses a form of expression unusual in the narrative portions of the Gospels. Instead of Jesus he writes "the Lord," and we cannot but remember that it was John who exclaimed "It is the Lord" when Jesus appeared on the lake-side.

[3] The woman "in the city" might naturally be thought to have gravitated to Jerusalem, although she came from Magdala. If we take this story too to have come from St. John, we see why at the outset of the account of Lazarus' resurrection Mary is identified in the way she is, not by reference to the subsequent anointing but to that in Simon's house. On this view John tells of the second anointing in order to supply what Luke had not included in his story.

Capernaum, where He delivered the first of a new kind of parable, revealing and yet concealing the nature of God's rule and the conditions of its extension.

(30) Then, followed by a huge crowd, He returned to His home, where He explained this parable, but His mother and His "brethren" feared for His sanity.

Mark, it is to be noted, describes how a great crowd entered His home so that a meal was impossible, and this, apparently, led to His family's attempt at intervention. Then the evangelist tells of a great crowd again by the sea, gives the parable of the Sower and its explanation and adds two other parables. "The same day when even was come" Jesus, he says, took ship. Matthew states that the parable of the Sower was spoken the same day as His family came. Luke places the parable first, then the coming of the family and then, "on a certain day," the voyage. Plainly he is thus cautious because Mark has given several parables together which Luke recognizes to have been spoken at different times. This example of his carefulness for accuracy justifies us in treating his datings as so trustworthy that they should not lightly be set aside.

(31) In the evening He took ship and crossed the lake to near Gadara, rebuking the storm and afterwards restoring the sanity of a madman, when 2,000 swine were seized with panic and drowned themselves.

(32) After recrossing the lake, He was met by some of John's disciples, who asked why Christ's disciples did not fast, and while He was still answering them (Matt. ix. 18) Jairus came begging Him to save his daughter. On the way to the house, He healed the woman who touched His garment and finally recalled Jairus' daughter to life. Subsequently[1] He resumed His practice of going from village to village to preach.

The Baptist, it would seem, had now been murdered, and this may explain why his disciples had come to Christ with their question and why our Lord took the step that followed.

[1] Mark vi. 1–6, followed by Matt. xiii. 54–58, records a second return to Nazareth. If this is not an unchronological transposition of our paragraph 15, Luke has omitted it, possibly as a doublet. See Part I, Chap. 4, p. 57, note.

(33) He sent out the Twelve with authority to preach and heal. This caused such a stir that Herod heard of it and was convinced that the Baptist had risen from the dead.

(34) When the Twelve were reassembled, He took them across the lake to a solitary place in the hills, and when crowds came to Him, He first taught them and then fed them to the number of five thousand.

The gathering of large enthusiastic crowds in a lonely district was too much like some previous attempts at rebellion to be overlooked by the authorities, whether Pilate, Herod or the priestly families at Jerusalem. Some consequences of this are to be seen in the subsequent actions both of our Lord and of His adversaries.

(35) During the following night, He came to the Twelve as they rowed against the wind. They all landed in Gennesaret, and presently in the synagogue at Capernaum He shocked many by declaring that they must eat His flesh and drink His blood. The Twelve, however, remained His disciples, Peter declaring that they believed Him to be "the Holy One of God."

(36) For some time He was continually healing the sick in the neighbourhood, but at this point the authorities at Jerusalem sent a legation to examine His orthodoxy. The first question asked was why He allowed some of His disciples to eat without ceremonially washing their hands. He met this with strong criticism of the Pharisees' rules and a clear declaration to the multitude that ceremonial purity was entirely distinct from purity of the heart. This gave great offence to the Pharisees,[1] a fact which may have led to Christ's next proceeding.

(37) He withdrew to the district of Tyre and Sidon, where He healed a Gentile woman's daughter.

(38) Making His way through Decapolis, He reached the Lake again, where He healed a deaf man with a word and soon after fed the four thousand who had gathered to hear His instruction.

(39) Crossing the Lake again to Dalmanutha, He was there met by Pharisees who would have tested the authenticity of His mission, but he refused to give them a "sign."

[1] Even the disciples had to have the distinction reinforced by plain teaching after He had re-entered His home (Mark vii. 17).

(40) He at once took ship again and crossed the Lake, warning His disciples against the leaven of the Pharisees and of Herod.

(41) Near Bethsaida He healed a blind man, and then moved on to the neighbourhood of Caesarea Philippi. On the way He received Peter's avowal that He was the Christ, whereupon He warned the Twelve that He would be slain and raised the third day and told all His disciples that they must take up their cross daily and follow Him.

(42) A week after He took the three apostles of His choice to the Mount of Transfiguration, and on the morrow exorcized the paranoiac youth.

(43) He explained to the nine other apostles that their failure to heal was due to want of faith, and slowly made a cautious and private passage back to Capernaum, where Peter was asked if Jesus paid the Temple tax, an important issue in the circumstances. Our Lord sent him to find the money in a fish's mouth, and later rebuked the whole body of apostles for selfish ambition, when they should rather learn to be ready to serve.

(44) He refused to join the company of pilgrims going up to the Feast of Tabernacles, but afterwards went quietly through Samaria, where He was refused entertainment at one village, and entered the Temple in the middle of the feast.

(45) The authorities, angered by His teaching, would have arrested Him, but the officers would not act.

(46) The scribes and Pharisees attempted to incriminate Him by inviting Him to pronounce sentence on a woman taken in adultery.

It has been the vogue among commentators to belittle and accordingly to disregard Luke's chronology. We shall therefore find it worth while to scrutinize systematically his record of the events in the last six months of our Lord's Ministry. It will then appear that with the indications he gives of time and place all the incidents can be dovetailed into the structure of the Fourth Gospel.

In the final section of his ninth chapter, Luke shows us Jesus making His way to Jerusalem, as John tells us for the feast of Tabernacles, where He was met with the sneer "Thou hast a devil; who goeth about to kill Thee." The feast itself Luke omits, and passes on to our Lord's actions after it was ended.

(47) Our Lord sent out a mission of seventy disciples, to whom He gave instructions, similar to but not identical with those given to the Twelve previously.

There is, it has been noticed, a change of tone in these instructions. The plenteous harvest needs more labourers (cf. Matt. ix. 37). The missioners are like lambs among wolves (cf. Matt. x. 16): they are sent not to preach but to prepare men for His own coming, as messengers were sent before Him, when on His way to Jerusalem for the Feast of Tabernacles. It will be more tolerable for Sodom in the Day of Judgment than for those who do not receive these messengers (cf. Matt. x. 15), and more tolerable for Tyre and Sidon (which He had visited only six months before) than for Chorazin and Bethsaida: Capernaum should come to ruin (cf. Matt. xi. 21–24): "he who despises Me," He said, "despises Him that sent Me."

(48) On the return of the Seventy, He said: "I beheld Satan fall from heaven" (cf. John xii. 31). "I give you power to tread on serpents" (cf. Mark xvi. 18). "I thank thee, O Father, that thou hast hid these things from the wise and revealed them unto babes" (cf. Matt. xi. 25). "All things are delivered to Me . . . no man knoweth who the Son is but the Father, and who the Father is but the Son" (cf. Matt. xi. 27).

(49) When a lawyer asked which was the great commandment, He delivered the parable of the Good Samaritan.

(50) He next made His way again to Jerusalem for the feast of Dedication, during which He was entertained by Martha at Bethany. He taught in the temple, in veiled language speaking of God as His Father. An angry altercation followed and His opponents would have stoned Him but He withdrew, and seeing a blind man, healed him. Presently He spoke of Himself as "the door of the sheep" and "the good shepherd," whereupon some again said that He had a devil and was mad, and when He said, "I and my Father are one" they wished to stone Him, but He withdrew to the other side of Jordan, where the Baptist had been at the first.

(51) Subsequently, asked to teach His disciples some form of prayer, He gave them what we know as the Lord's Prayer and followed this with encouragements to pray persistently (cf. Matt. vi. 9 ; vii. 7–11).

(52) Asked by a Pharisee to dine with him, He strongly condemned[1] the legalistic religiosity of the Pharisaic scribes (cf. Matt. xxiii. 4–34). In consequence they pressed Him with many questions.

The next scene depicted by Luke presents, once again, features corresponding with the situation described by John as existing at this stage in our Lord's Ministry. Luke states that "the many thousands of the multitude" were gathered together to Jesus "insomuch that they trod one upon another": John tells us "Many came to Him . . . and many believed on Him."

Luke relates that "He began to say to His disciples first of all, beware of the leaven of the Pharisees (cf. Mark viii. 15; Matt. xvi. 6), which is hypocrisy," and this thought is developed into a warning, as it would appear, to men who, though convinced that His teaching was true, had not the courage to acknowledge it. Here, it appears their "play-acting" showed itself in their unreadiness to confess their adhesion to His cause. Secret talk, He told them, would in the end come to light. They should fear none but God; they were of more value than many sparrows; he only that confessed Him before men would be confessed before the angels of God (cf. Matt. x. 26–33). Slanderous defamation of the manifestations of the Holy Ghost's working would not be forgiven a man. When they were brought up for examination before the authorities the Holy Ghost would teach them what to say. All this falls happily into place at the point we have reached in our scheme of the Gospel history, constructed though it has been on the basis of quite other considerations. John specifically states only a few weeks later that many of the rulers believed on our Lord, but "they did not confess Him lest they should be put out of the synagogue, for they loved the praise of men more than the praise of God." John

[1] The common translation "Woe unto you" would be better replaced by "Alas for you" both here and in all other passages, e.g. Luke xvii. 1.

also represents our Lord as saying, "I will give unto them eternal life and they shall never perish. My Father is greater than all . . . and no one is able to snatch them out of the Father's hand." In Luke it is anticipated that the disciples will be "brought before the synagogues, and the rulers, and the authorities"; in John the blind man is excluded from the synagogue after his second examination before the Pharisees. John again tells us that at the Last Supper Christ assured the Eleven that the Holy Ghost would teach them what to say when put on trial. It is possible that John is here correcting Luke's dating of this promise, which Q had attached to the utterance about blasphemy against the Holy Ghost. If so, we must remark how Q keeps the order, if not the date, of the promise.[1]

(53) Jesus urged His disciples to confess Him openly, saying "Be not afraid of them which kill the body and after that have no more that they can do but . . . Fear Him which after He hath killed hath power to cast into hell."

(54) Next a young man requested our Lord's intervention in a family dispute as to an inheritance, consequent on which Christ warned His disciples against covetousness. "Be not anxious," He said, "about food, drink, clothing: your Father, who feeds the ravens and clothes the lilies, knows that you need these things: seek rather the Kingdom of God" (cf. Matt. vi. 19–21, 25–34) which your Father will give to the "little flock," the "babes" (cf. Matt. xi. 25, 26). Unlike the rich fool, they should make their treasure in heaven and be ready as servants watching for their master. The Son of Man's coming would take men by surprise (cf. Matt. xxiv. 42–xxv. 13). On Peter's asking to whom this warning was addressed, the Lord replied in a way which made it clear that the apostles were charged with a special responsibility. The negligence of the instructed disciple

---

[1] In the last few pages references have been supplied to parallel passages in Matthew and Mark. These go to show: (1) that Matthew rearranges his material without regard to chronology but to suit the literary plan of his work; (2) that where Luke has lost part of Mark he is at a loss to determine the date of some things which he got from Q; and (3) that where, though having Mark before him, he has placed some incident or utterance at a point differing from Mark's order, we should accept Luke's guidance in consideration of his manifest care for chronology.

would entail heavier consequences than would the wrongdoing of the ignorant outsider.

Luke follows this with words which reveal our Lord's marvellously realistic understanding of the effect of His mission. "I am come," He said, "to send fire on the earth" and to send division. The baptism He had before Him would sift men's sentiments about Him and set those who rejected against those who accepted Him.

These words accord with the sad thought expressed in an utterance of our Lord made a few weeks later in the Upper Room. "If I had not come," He said, "they had not had sin, but now they have no cloak for their sin" (John xv. 22).

(55) Then, addressing the people, He deplored their blindness to the signs of the times. They were like men play-acting in a world of unreality; they should at once abandon their thoughts of a Jewish empire, be reconciled to Roman rule in civil matters and understand God's rule to be spiritual, otherwise they would have to pay the very last mite (cf. Matt. xvi. 2, 3; v. 25, 26).

An event which happened only two or three days earlier lent point to this warning. Pilate had butchered some Galileans while their sacrifices were being offered in the temple. The report of this shocking tragedy came pat to Christ's words as to more stripes falling on the wilful offender. It is reasonable to suppose that these Galilean victims had made a disturbance at the feast of Purim, which commemorated a violent uprising of vengeance made by Jews against their enemies. This will date our story for a few days after February 4th. It should be added that the whole of what Luke records in xii. 13–xiii. 9 would seem to be the story of a single day, in the same way that we have the events of other outstanding days related.

(56) Christ declined to pronounce adverse judgment upon Pilate's victims, which their fate, coupled with His previous words, might seem to warrant. Rather than this He gave the blunt and stern monition, "except ye repent ye shall all likewise perish." This declaration He followed up with the parable of the barren fig-tree, which shows how fully He had now learnt the Father's will to be long-suffering with men.

(57) Luke's story moves on to some subsequent sabbath. In some synagogue a woman with a bowed back was healed. The ruler of the synagogue angrily condemned this as a breach of sabbath observance. Christ instanced the watering of ox and ass to show how mistaken was this microscopic codification of sabbath offences. The people welcomed His simplification of the law and our Lord showed in two parables how He saw His teaching was winning its way, like a grain of mustard seed and like leaven.[1]

(58) For some weeks after this Jesus was travelling from village to village and from town to town, teaching and making His way for a brief visit to a suburban district in Greater Jerusalem ('Ιεροσόλυμα). Asked once if few should be saved, He said "strive to enter in at the strait gate" (cf. Matt. vii. 13), the opportunity once gone other than the Jews would be seen entering (cf. Matt. vii. 21, 23 and viii. 11, 12).

(59) On the same day some Pharisees, with whatever motives, warned Him to quit Peraea, saying that Herod would kill Him: He replied that He was not to be deflected from continuing, tranquil and unhurried, His gracious offices of healing and exorcism, and that His Ministry would close at Jerusalem. That city which had so often refused His call, would at last, when again it saw Him, greet Him as coming in the name of the Lord.

It was on this or on the previous day that the message came that Lazarus was ill. For two days Jesus remained where He was, a calmness and deliberateness of action well according with His words to the Pharisees. It is worthy of notice that here again we find in our records a double motive recognized. The Galilean Ministry is traced by Mark to Herod's imprisonment of the Baptist. Luke passes this by without explanation of our Lord's withdrawal from Judaea. John mentions the Pharisees' vigilance and sensitiveness of apprehension as prompting the withdrawal. Now Luke reports Christ's riddling reply to the Pharisees when He repudiates a pusillanimous flight before any threats from Herod. John, interpreting the enigmatic words, definitely states that our Lord made no move towards departure till Lazarus' actual death called Him to Bethany.

[1] It should be noticed how Luke's dating illuminates the order in which Mark lists the parables he records.

(60) On the sabbath[1] before starting His journey to Bethany our Lord dined with a Pharisee of importance. Luke again gives us a cameo picture of what occurred in two or three hours of that day. Jesus healed a man suffering from dropsy, defended His action by citing the universal treatment of an ass or an ox fallen into a pit, puts out the parable about taking the lowest "room," bade men entertain the needy rather than their own equals and in reply to a guest's pious platitude told the parable of the Great Supper invitations slighted by the guests originally asked.

It is to be remarked that our Lord here identifies His own and His Father's will for the Jews' recall to service and salvation. This agrees with John's portraiture of our Lord's consciousness at this time.

(61) The next day, perhaps, He told His disciples that Lazarus was dead and that He should go to Bethany.

(62) As He made His way towards Bethany He told the crowd that followed Him that His disciples' devotion to Him must outclass the claim of family or of life itself (cf. Matt. x. 37): they must follow Him to crucifixion; the cost should be counted beforehand; discipleship demanded the entire abandonment of selfish desires; they were to be the salt that should correct the world's selfishness; if they lost this property they would be useless (cf. Matt. v. 13; Mark ix. 49, 50).[2]

(63) Soon after, when Pharisees and scribes criticize His association with publicans and sinners, He spoke the parables of the lost sheep (cf. Matt. xviii. 12–14), the lost coin and the wild younger and the grudging elder brother.

(64) Next, Luke tells us, the Saviour, perhaps in an effort to wean Judas from his cupidity and peculation, urged His disciples by the parable of the Dishonest Steward to use any money they handled intelligently and intentionally so as to have God's commendation: honesty with the money of this world was evidence of a man's fitness to be trusted with spiritual

[1] The date may provisionally be reckoned as March 7th.

[2] It will be seen that though Matthew habitually and Mark in some cases group Christ's sayings in accordance with their literary schemes, yet where several sayings are grouped in one section, their order generally testifies to the correctness of Luke's dating.

gifts and powers; dishonesty in the matter of trust-money was a bar to all hope of receiving the richer treasure and privilege of increased personal endowments and talents[1]; a divided allegiance made faithful service impossible; they could not devote themselves entirely to money-making and at the same time expect to be able to do God's will (cf. Matt. vi. 24).

(65) Some Pharisees heard this and derided Him, for, says Luke, they were lovers of money. Jesus told them that while they made a show before the world of obeying God's law, God read their inmost heart; what men venerated might be an idol in His sight. John's coming had ushered in the era of God's rule, which ended the preliminary stage of Law and prophets. Now everyone pressed forward to enter God's service (cf. Matt. xi. 12, 13), freed from the burden of learning the endless refinements of Rabbinic casuistry. Yet the broad principles of the Law stood unchangeable (cf. Matt. v. 18). No subtlety of explanation could dispel the sinfulness of breaking the marriage tie (cf. Matt. v. 32; xix. 9; Mark x. 11, 12). Such subtleties, He inferred, lay at the core of the Pharisees' rule of life. How wrongly self-centred this was, He exposed in the parable of the rich man and Lazarus. Its concluding words persuade us that it was spoken before Jesus reached the grave at Bethany, and we need not hesitate to date all these utterances to the time of the journey to raise Lazarus.

(66) Arrived at the outskirts of Bethany He was met first by Martha and then by Mary, and proceeding to the grave He called Lazarus forth so that many who witnessed this resurrection became believers. Others reported the matter to the Pharisees.

(67) Presently a council was held at which Caiaphas recommended that Jesus should be put to death, but our Lord momentarily withdrew to the open country near Ephraim or Samphourein, between Galilee and Samaria.

(68) At this point we have a considerable collection of precepts given by our Lord to His disciples. Offences must come, but alas for him who causes them (cf. Matt. xviii. 6, 7); it is worth while to make any personal sacrifice rather than

---

[1] Judas, says John, had the bag and took its contents. He died before the Holy Ghost descended upon the Church.

injure another (cf. Matt. v. 29, 30 and xviii. 8, 9); such sacrifices will help to purify society and to preserve it from deterioration : offenders are to be rebuked : if they promise and purpose to attempt amendment they are to be forgiven. In reply to Peter, who would have liked a statutory definition of limits to be set to this forgiving, our Lord gave the parable of the king who first forgave the servant that owed him ten thousand talents, but afterwards punished him when he showed no mercy to a fellow servant who owed a hundred pence. The apostles felt that if they were to rise to the height of this summons to the duty of incessant placability, they must rely on God's assistance and therefore needed faith. Jesus assured them that with one grain of faith they would be able to do anything (cf. Matt. xvii. 20; xxi. 21; Mark xi. 23), but by a parable He showed them that we can never finish off all our duty and claim discharge or reward.

The Passover was now approaching: the chief priests and Pharisees had directed that anyone who knew where our Lord was should give information, so that they might arrest Him. As usual many went up early from the country to Jerusalem in order to "purify themselves" in preparation for the feast, and Jesus presently set out on His last journey to the Holy City.

(68) As He journeyed ten lepers met Him outside a village on the frontier of Galilee and Samaria.

(69) Next some Pharisees asked when God's kingdom would be seen: He told them that it was an interior realm of the heart. Then He warned His disciples that the Son of Man's coming would be so sudden (cf. Matt. xxiv. 27) and unexpected (cf. Matt. xxiv. 17, 18, 40, 41), like the flood (cf. Matt. xxiv. 37–39) and the destruction of Sodom, that they should rest unconcerned for temporal possessions and even for life itself (cf. Matt. x. 39). Though they would long for His advent, they should not listen to rumours (cf. Matt. xxiv. 23; Mark xiii. 21); He must be rejected first and then astonish the world by His return; then the carrion birds would find what was rotten in the world (cf. Matt. xxiv. 28). Meanwhile as they waited for His coming they should pray unfalteringly, as He impressed on them by the parable of the Unconscionable Judge. God

would speedily do His chosen ones right. Prayer, however, must be humble like the Publican's.

It is eminently desirable and indeed of much importance that here again we should keep in view the rival claims to chronological authenticity which commentators have made on behalf of each of the three synoptists. In Holy Week Luke records that our Lord, in a private talk, told the four senior apostles that among other signs of the approaching cataclysm they would hear men saying, "Lo, here is Christ." At the present point in the story, i.e. in what we now call Passion Week, speaking openly to critical Pharisees, our Lord uses the non-committal expression "the Son of Man." We cannot escape from the dilemma that either Luke manipulated and adapted the language of his material so as to present a picture in accordance with a theory he had built on *a priori* grounds, that Jesus opened Himself to His disciples tentatively and gradually, or that in point of fact our Lord did so reveal Himself little by little, and that Luke is faithful to the fact, while Matthew and Mark are often indifferent to the chronological order. When we weigh the evidence we find here and in other places there can be no doubt as to which way the scales must be pronounced irreversibly to incline.

At this point Luke's story rejoins that of Matthew and Mark, and there will be no occasion any longer to detail it or to examine every incident and utterance so as to show that Luke's narrative fits chronologically into that of the Fourth Gospel. It will be sufficient to give a schedule of what yet remains to be related.

(70) People brought even their babes for Christ to touch, and He reproved the apostles, when, jealous for His dignity, they objected.

(71) When a young "ruler" asked what he should do and was told to sell all and to join Christ's company, he was vexed and went away. Jesus' comment was that the well-to-do would not accept God's rule without discomposure and reluctance. He added that He was speaking of those who put their trust not in God but in their wealth. On Peter asking what the apostles should have for giving up everything, the Lord

promised them innumerable new friends in His Church and spiritual dignities, if attended by persecutions; but by the parable of the labourers in the vineyard He emphasized that the last might yet be first.

(72) Jesus now told the Twelve that the Son of Man should be delivered to the Gentiles and be put to death and rise again the third day. They could make nothing of His words.

(73) Near Jericho Bartimaeus and another blind man were healed (cf. Matt. xx. 30).

(74) Next Zacchaeus had the honour of entertaining Jesus in his home, and was so touched by this condescension that he gave away half his property to the beggars, so that our Lord declared that the Son of Man was come to seek and to save that which was lost (cf. Matt. xviii. 11).

(75) He was now near the end of His journey to Jerusalem, and to correct His disciples expectation that they would immediately see "God's Kingdom" established, He told the parable of the Ten Pounds. This spoke of a long journey before the nobleman's return to settle accounts with his servants and its concluding words are startling in their suggestion that enemies who were unwilling to accept the nobleman's rule would be slain before him.

(76) He proceeded at last to Bethany again, where He was entertained at a dinner, during which Mary anointed Him, as He said, for His burial, but Judas criticized her action as a waste of money (cf. Mark xiv. 2–11). Many people came to see Him and to see Lazarus.

(77) The next day He set out to enter Jerusalem, riding upon an ass, and at sight of Jerusalem He wept to think of the destruction which was destined to overtake her. After entering the Temple and contemplating everything there, He retired again to Bethany.

(78) On the morrow He sentenced to decay the barren fig-tree, healed the blind and the lame and sanctioned the children's hosannas. As He taught the people that the Temple which was to be a house of prayer for all nations had been made a den of robbers, the scribes and chief priests heard and would have killed Him, but feared the people. Again He retired to Bethany.

(79) The next morning He used the fate of the fig-tree to impress on Peter and the rest that they should trust God to answer their prayers; when Greeks asked for an interview with Him, He recognized in this a sign from the Father that the hour for His death was upon Him; He refused to tell the religious authorities who had commissioned Him for His Ministry, and went on to speak the parable of the Vineyard. This so incensed them that they would have seized Him out of hand, but fearing the populace they sent out agents to trap Him if possible into saying something on which they could frame a charge to lay before Pilate. Their question about tribute money failed. The Sadducees then attempted, with a conundrum about the resurrection, to damage His reputation as a sound religious teacher: they too failed completely. This so impressed one of the scribes that he asked which was the first commandment of all, and when he expressed his adhesion to our Lord's pronouncement, he was told that he was not far from "God's kingdom."[1] After this no one durst ask Jesus any more questions. Then Jesus Himself posed the question "how say they that Christ is David's son," and followed this with a denunciation of the scribes "in the audience of all the people." Presently He commended the widow's mite, and sitting on the mount of Olives told Peter and Andrew, James and John in express terms what signs would presage the fall of Jerusalem before that generation had passed away. These signs would be as clear as the indication given by the fig-tree when spring is at hand, but the date of His royal advent was known to the Father alone[2] (cf. Mark xiii. 1–37; Matt. xxiv. 1–xxv. 46).

(80) The following day Judas went and struck a bargain with the Temple authorities to give them an opportunity of arresting Jesus.

---

[1] Luke either was without this episode in his copy of Mark or deliberately omitted it, considering it a doublet of what we have scheduled in paragraph 49.

[2] Matthew seems to have understood Mark's *that day* to mean the end of the age. Luke rightly equates it with the Lord's coming. All three Gospels regard the fall of Jerusalem and the consequent dissociation of the Church from unbelieving Judaism as Christ's return in power to gather all nations in one communion (see p. 131).

(81) On Thursday Peter and John were sent to make preparations for the Passover supper. In the evening at the Last Supper Christ washed the disciples' feet, instituted the Eucharist, gave a last discourse enjoining mutual love among His followers and prayed that they should be one. In Gethsemane He was arrested and taken bound to Annas first and then to Caiaphas, who presided at His trial.

(82) At daybreak He was handed over to Pilate, who at last ordered His crucifixion, but allowed His burial by Joseph of Arimathaea.[1]

(83) On Easter Day He rose again and was seen by Mary Magdalene and Cleopas' daughter, by Peter, by Cleopas and by all the apostles except Thomas.

(84) The next Sunday He was seen by all the eleven apostles, including Thomas.

(85) Some while later He showed Himself to seven disciples by the lake side, and foretold Peter's martyrdom and John's long life.

(86) Still later He was seen, perhaps by five hundred disciples, on a mountain side in Galilee and accepted their worship (cf. I Cor. xv. 6).

(87) On Ascension Thursday, after telling the Apostles that it was not for them to know what the Father designed to be the future history of the world, but promising them that the Holy Ghost should shortly descend upon them, He withdrew Himself from their sight.

Excursus I

The Date and Purpose of the Transfiguration

(1)

In the Gospel accounts of the Transfiguration there are one or two subsidiary and incidental details which may perhaps on examination yield us, surprisingly enough, valuable information regarding the date of its occurrence. St. Peter's babbling suggestion of making three booths is excused as that of a man not fully awake, yet it has been aptly interpreted as indicating that the Feast of Booths was near. More significant perhaps is the statement

---

[1] Perhaps Judas by now had hanged himself.

that a bright cloud passed over the scene. We can hardly doubt this means that the moon was shining, and this, it may be, should be viewed as the physical means which made our Saviour's face shine as the sun and His clothing appear as "no fuller on earth could whiten them." We should infer from this that the date was near the time of a full moon. Of this conjecture a certain confirmation betrays itself in the First Gospel. The paranoiac boy treated the next morning is there said to be lunatic (σεληνιάζεται). It is a matter of common knowledge that, whatever the cause, the approach of the full moon does synchronize with accessions and paroxysms of mental disturbance. It may therefore be argued with reason that on the night of the Transfiguration the moon was shining and was not far from full. Were this the actual full moon of the Feast of Tabernacles there would seem to be too little time for the journey to Capernaum and later to Jerusalem and for the events recorded during that time. We shall conclude rather that the date was about one lunar month earlier. In A.D. 32 the Feast of Tabernacles would be approximately 9–17 September and the preceding full moon 11 August. In that case the ecclesiastical date for the Transfiguration is at the least not unacceptable.

It should be noticed that besides this lunar date and that of the Baptism, it should, on at any rate one other occasion, be kept in mind that there was a full moon approaching or recently passed. We are specifically told in the Fourth Gospel that when the five thousand were fed the Passover was nigh at hand. Passover falls at the full moon, and it may be thought that it was the moonlight falling on our Lord's figure as He moved that gave Him the spectral appearance which alarmed the disciples in their boat.

To suppose that it was a moonlight night too which our Lord spent in prayer before selecting the Twelve is, though tempting, no more than a fantasy. It was, however, such a night when Nicodemus came to Him secretly, for it was during the Passover week.

It has been soberly observed that St. John was a mystic of genius whose spiritual insight pierced behind the outward appearance to the inward reality. St. Peter was an ordinary *homme sensuel* who accepted at their face value the physical impressions he received, yet interpreted them as manifestations of a divine power, which appealed to the higher impulses in his personality. Hence in Mark we read the record of the plain, average observer who saw, as he supposed, a spirit walking over the water. John flatly corrects and contradicts this materialistic conception of the Lord's manifestation of His glory and concentrates the reader's thought on the spiritual truths regarding man's need to feed upon the true manna. In the same way it may be thought that the omission by John of any reference to the Transfiguration finds its explanation. St. Peter took the "vision" as he saw it, with his eyes and ears; he gave this materialistic significance to our Lord's words a week before, that some should see the Kingdom come with power. St. John apprehended the truth, at any rate in his old age. He saw the "coming" as the Church's victorious progress from Pentecost onwards and specially in its liberation at the Fall of Jerusalem from the antiquated and obsolete swaddling clothes of the Mosaic covenant. Thereafter God's generous and faithful love[1] of humanity stood clearly blazoned before the world. Man's duty to God was shown not to consist in punctual obedience to codified rules of conduct, coupled with the cancellation of omissions or infractions of duty by the making of animal sacrifices. Instead men fulfilled God's requirements by a persevering holding on to improvement in character and conduct through the assistance of Christ's Spirit and in association with the others whom the same Spirit animated, admitted to their one Society by the simple affusion of water and held in mutual union by a customary symbol of a common festive banquet, consequent upon their Divine Leader's self-sacrifice in His war against wrong in the world.

One last point deserves mention. We are told that our Lord oft-times resorted to the Mount of Olives, and this naturally suggests that he had done so before Holy Week. We should look, then, for Him to have done so on the nights of the Feast of Tabernacles, when there would be moonlight as in Holy Week. This seems to confirm the historicity of the pericope in John viii which explicitly states that our Lord went to the Mount of Olives. Ignorance of the fact that at this feast our Lord frequented the place misled the copyist who transferred the section to Luke's account of the final Passover week.

Since the above was written I have read G. H. Boobyer's article in *J.T.S.*, vol. xli, pp. 119–140, "St. Mark and the Transfiguration." He argues that the evangelist, like the prophets who looked for the Parousia in a materialistic fashion, regarded the Transfiguration as a revelation, for the benefit of the three apostles, of the future Parousia glory. Dr. Carrington has shown that the writer of the canonical Apocalypse studiously and strenuously refused these materialistic views, which as I have suggested harmonize with the belief that one and the same author wrote it and the Fourth Gospel.

To regard the Transfiguration as a revelation in advance to assist the three apostles' faith, whether in the Resurrection or in the future Parousia glory, is suspiciously akin to a Docetic view of the subsequent weeks in our Lord's Ministry and of His Crucifixion. Dr. Matthews reasserts orthodoxy when he writes (*Essays in Construction*, p. 119): "Any doctrine of the Incarnation which tries to take seriously the belief that Jesus was truly man must hold that his knowledge of the future was limited. Any other view would deprive the Cross of its heroic quality and would be in contradiction with the data of the New Testament. If Jesus went to Calvary with the certain knowledge of all that would follow and with a clear grasp of the course of history, He could be no example to us of heroic patience, and His victory over death would not have been the victory of faith."

The importance of this issue may be held to justify the reinforcement of our conclusions, even at the cost of some repetition. The three synoptists agree that at a certain point in the Lord's Ministry St. Peter avowed his belief that Jesus was the Christ, the son of the living God. No sooner was this momentous acknowledgement made on behalf of the Twelve than our

---

[1] John i. 14 and 17, "grace and truth."

Lord on the one hand forbade them to communicate to others His acceptance of the title and on the other began to prepare them for His temporary defeat and death. Isaiah's Servant sections foreshadowed His rejections by the religious authorities. The symbol of the dove at His baptism and the story of Abraham's offering of Isaac presaged His death, and the Psalms were warrant for faith that He should not be left long in Hades. Yet while this was the theme of His discourse to the Twelve, He pronounced words still more significant, if mysterious to the generality of His disciples. Each of His followers must take up his cross and follow Him. Was He then, they might wonder, about to lead them against the Romans, and must they be prepared for the possibility that some would be taken prisoner and be crucified? In any case they were given no hint that the Son of Man was the Messiah but were urged to devote themselves entirely to His service. Then He would acknowledge them for His, when His triumph was blazoned to the world, as it would be before that generation was wholly passed away.

About a week later our Lord took with Him Peter, James and John on to a mountain where they had the vision in subsequent ages known as the Transfiguration. Mark and, as we may suppose, his informant, St. Peter, saw in this episode a fulfilment in some measure of the Lord's words "there are some standing here which shall not taste of death till they have seen the Kingdom of God come with power." Most of the believers, as has been shown above, could not at first be drawn out of their materialistic expectations of a messianic Parousia with supernatural catastrophic signs and an ocular demonstration of the Christ's Presence. To them, therefore, the Transfiguration appeared as a foreshadowing of this future event. St. John even may have once understood the vision and the Parousia in this way, but as we know he later came to find a triumphant vindication of the Christ in the fall of Jerusalem, brought about by the divine working out in human history of the Messiah's victory over the sin of the world. St. John would lend no countenance thereafter and, as we may believe, for at least some years before, to the grossly materialistic conceptions which are subsequently traceable in the *Apocalypse of Peter*.[1]

If St. John in his Gospel and in the Apocalypse gave a truer, because a more spiritual, portrait of our Lord and His teaching, we must be careful not to attribute to our Lord Himself the materialistic ideas which St. Peter and the rest could not transcend. To our Lord, then, the Transfiguration was no foreshadowing either of the Resurrection or, as St. Peter thought, of the Parousia. What then was it?

Here we must observe certain features in Luke's narrative which are not derived from Mark. These features, it would appear, were derived from St. John, the only other survivor of the three apostles.

[1] We may again refer to Dr. Carrington, for an account of how the Roman Church all but admitted this work into the Canon. The Second Epistle of Peter betrays a vestige of this debased view of the Parousia which has undoubtedly coloured the popular imagination ever since and therewith the ordinary Christian's meditations upon the Transfiguration.

(1) Luke declares that our Lord's primary purpose in withdrawing to the mountain was to pray. His choice of His companions in that case reminds us of His choice of the same three in Gethsemane.

(2) Luke declares that the Lord discussed with the two ancient saints τὴν ἔξοδον, which He was subsequently to accomplish, as the event showed, in Jerusalem.[1]

Here then, it may be believed, we have the key to the true understanding of the Transfiguration. The apostles' acknowledgment of our Lord's Messiahship was the sign to Him that the time was come for His mission to march onward to its earthly end. Its precise manner and occasion were not yet clear; He must seek in communion with the Father to learn His will. Malachi had foreseen a precursor of His mission and that precursor was to be Elijah. One of the literary prophets would have been unsuitable for that purpose. He knew what they had said and the identity of the authors might in some instances be perplexing. If Elijah could speak he might confirm or correct what He Himself had gathered from the prophets and from life's experiences. Elijah had faced alone the corrupt prophets of his day: He Himself, then, was right in His opposition to the ecclesiastics of the time. Elijah had taken refuge in Tyre; so had He. Elijah had raised to life the widow's son there; He had healed a widow's daughter there. Elijah had played the courier to Ahab; John the Baptist had done so for the Messiah. The King had listened to Elijah's teaching; Herod had listened to the Baptist. The King's wife had sought Elijah's life; Herodias had compassed John's death. Beyond doubt Peter's dissuasion from His anticipated doom was Satan's voice. That John, a second Elijah, had prepared His mission guaranteed John's declaration that He was Jahveh's Lamb for sacrifice and that His inferences from the prophets as to His appointed end were right. Yet if He was destined to be a sacrifice, could not Moses direct the course He ought to take? Moses led Israel out of the land of bondage, Egypt with its wealth and debased religion. He must Himself lead His followers out of the bondage of sin, away from the debased religion of the second Egypt,[2] the wealthy, unspiritual Jerusalem of the day. So it must be in Jerusalem that He must be slain as the new Paschal Lamb. Moses and Elijah had died not by the hand of man and on the eastern side of Jordan, and the Baptist had been slain by Herod; He must die by the hand of man and at the centre of the worship which sprang from the revelation given to Israel.

Thus the place of His sacrifice was now determined, but what of the time when it should be? A recent writer has given reason for us to suppose that at the Feast of Tabernacles there was what may be called a religious drama enacted, in which the representative of Israel's life died symbolically that the nation might live: was Jesus to die at that Feast? Or was He to be slain at the next Passover-tide? He must look still for some signal from the Father to tell Him when the hour was come.

---

[1] For the significance of Luke's Ἱερουσαλήμ, see pp. 61 (c) and 123 (59).
[2] Matt. ii. 15; Rev. xi. 8.

We must be careful not to suppose that departed saints,[1] however great and glorious their achievements, would be qualified to reveal beforehand the Father's purposes for our Lord. Even the angels, we are told, could not anticipate what was to be. Nevertheless it would appear that the life stories of Moses and Elijah could make them witnesses to God's continued vindication of faith and perseverance.

This reading of the Gospel narratives will be found to explain our Lord's subsequent preparations for His Crucifixion, and the Voice commanding the apostles to hear Him (i.e. rather than Moses and Elijah) is reflected in the pronouncement, not previously made, that the Law and the Prophets were until John. We find here also the explanation of Luke's naming of Elijah first and placing John's name before his brother. Further it offers a possible reason for the injunction to observe silence. Peter may have supposed that, though some of the Messiah's followers would be killed, the Messiah Himself might be spared. The Vision to him was merely evidence of coming victory; to him the Crucifixion will have seemed final defeat. John, on the other hand, had heard something of what was said and hence he believed more readily the fact of the Resurrection. To have told the Vision before the Resurrection would have led others besides Peter to expectations that would have added to their despair on Good Friday and also would have made more difficult than ever the weaning of their hope from material to spiritual triumph. Finally, since the Scriptures told apparently of secret "translations" granted to Elijah and Moses, the fact that it should be they who appeared to Jesus might augur that He might be suffered to pass from earth like them and thus pursue the easier course urged by Peter. His task, so unlike the two saints', forbade such a notion and our Lord set His face steadfastly to bear the Cross.

Nor, it may be believed, was this all that the Vision meant to our Lord. Something more might well suggest itself to His mind. If the Forerunner, the second Elijah, had been cut off before God's Kingdom had been shown in power, Moses also had not lived on to enter Israel's Promised Land and Elijah passed away before his faith was vindicated in Elisha's ministry. It was Moses' successor, Joshua, bearing the same name as our Lord, who led Israel into their resting-place. If it were the Father's will that He should die as the Lamb that should take away the world's sinfulness, the record of these ancient servants of God presaged that He should nevertheless also lead the Israel of God into the Kingdom. So, though the exact path might be still

---

[1] Heb. xii. 1, where the cloud of witnesses have been shown in the previous chapter to have had their lives recorded in Holy Writ. Their testimony to the substantial actuality of the Christian hope is given not by ghostly voices but by their life-record (cf. Christ's words in Luke xvi. 27–29). We need not consider the meaning sometimes foisted on to the word witness because of its double use in English resulting in an ambiguity between "spectator" and "deponent." For the Greek the αὐτόπτης is no μάρτυς unless and until he deposes before another to what he has seen. If the departed saints are spectators of our actions they are not μάρτυρες unless they report them to someone.

hidden, He could trust the Father that shortly[1] after His death He should triumph.

Note on Holy Week

The day-to-day arrangement of the events in Holy Week presents some difficulties. In the first place, John—and we have agreed to treat that Gospel as historical—states that it was six days before the Passover that Jesus came at last to Bethany. This makes the time of arrival not earlier than Saturday if we adhere, as we must surely do, to the belief that the Passover was on the evening of Friday (it was possible to suppose the arrival was on Friday when the Last Supper was identified with the Paschal feast). If, however, Jesus came on Saturday, He could have travelled no more than a mile or two on that Sabbath day, and must therefore have stayed the Friday night very near to Bethany. Of this our authorities give no hint, unless Luke's words may be taken to imply a halt at Bethphage before the stay at Bethany. Such a halt would fit in with an arrangement being made by our Lord for an ass to be lent Him and for His messengers to be allowed to collect it on giving the owners a certain pass-word. On this view the ascent from Jericho must have been on Friday and Christ stayed at Zacchaeus' house for Thursday night. Further, on Wednesday in Holy Week the Lord stayed quietly at Bethany while Judas took the opportunity to interview the Chief Priests. An alternative suggestion, however, deserves consideration. Did Jesus stay at Zacchaeus' house for the Sabbath, i.e. from Friday afternoon till Sunday morning, being thus entertained, therefore, by Zacchaeus at the usual festive dinner at the commencement of the Sabbath? If this was so, the journey from Jericho was on Sunday and the dinner at Bethany was on Sunday evening and the entry into Jerusalem on Monday morning. This would accord better with John's dating for the coming to Bethany and would get rid of the quiet seclusion of Wednesday which commentators have conjectured, but of which there is no mention in our Gospels. We are thus faced with a choice to be made between, on the one hand, an arrangement of the days resting on the theory of Alcuin and his circle, with a possible hint in Luke to support it, and on the other hand John's express statements that the Last Supper was not the Passover, that the Passover was on Friday night and that Christ came to Bethany six days before, while no day is left unaccounted for. Once again we shall invoke Gregory's words of encouragement and shall choose as he would bid us.

Note on Pilate's Release of Barabbas

Mark xv. 6 and Matthew xxvii. 15 tell us that at each feast—not, as some commentators will have it, "at *the* feast," but at each of, at any rate, the three great feasts—Pilate was in the habit of releasing a prisoner. With the correct translation made, one or two points of interest seem to emerge.

[1] "In three days" (John ii. 19; Luke ix. 22) defined itself perhaps to our Lord's mind from Jonah i. 17.

It was shortly before the Feast of Tabernacles that our Lord was on the Mount of Transfiguration. In the course of that feast our Lord appeared in the Temple. If we may take it that this feast was the one held six months before the Crucifixion we shall arrange the events of the following months as shown on the preceding pages. In that case it would be during Christ's seclusion after the Feast of Dedication that the Feast of Purim occurred. At this feast, always provocative of Jewish fanaticism against the Gentile foreigner, some Galileans caused disturbance, and of their number some were killed by Pilate, while Barabbas was arrested.

If this is passably correct, the first great feast after Barabbas' arrest would be at the time of the Crucifixion. This would illuminate Pilate's reasons for suggesting the alternative of Jesus or Barabbas as the Galilean who was to be released on this occasion. Moreover, Pilate's summary suppression of the Purim disturbance might appear to Herod as an unwarrantable encroachment upon his jurisdiction, and this would explain why Pilate, by remitting our Lord to Herod for judgment, would be doing something to assuage the king's enmity.

This note in its original form was printed some dozen years ago for private circulation. On reading it my friend Sir Frederick Still, a Cambridge first-class Classic, wrote emphatically endorsing the assertion that no other translation was possible. Professor E. Barker, quoting from Josephus, argued that καθ' εορτὴν means "on the occasion of a festival." He overlooked the fact that with εἰώθει the resultant sense is "it was his custom on the occurrence of a festival" to release a prisoner, and Mark's imperfect ἀπέλυεν yields the same sense.

EXCURSUS II

The Resurrection Appearances

DISAPPOINTMENT is an experience inevitably incidental to humanity. Our Lord, we believe, during His incarnate life was perfectly human. We should therefore feel no surprise if, despite His knowledge of "what was in man," He was at times disappointed by those with whom He came in contact. This is in fact what our records reveal, and do so perhaps in some instances which have not been recognized or understood.

That one of the Twelve failed his Master is a commonplace. The Fourth Gospel seems to reveal two causes of this failure. On the one hand a cynical and carping criticism of the Saviour's open-handed generosity and love revealed him as a slanderer, a calumniator, a "diabolos." On the other hand his avarice led him to seek his private gain out of any success that might come to the new movement. To the last three months of our Lord's Ministry Luke seems to assign several parables and exhortations which warn men against greed and dishonesty. We shall perhaps be right in understanding these as aimed to win Judas from his temptations. Yet they failed,

5*

as in less desolating fashion did the Lord's repeated instructions as to the inescapable death which was the avenue to victorious life.

But it was not only in their dullness and stubbornness in regard to His teaching that men disappointed our Lord. Even what might have been viewed as modest compliances with His wishes were often disregarded. Told to keep silence about an act of healing, men would blazon it abroad.

Is this propensity of men to fail and disappoint the explanation of the apparent contradictions as to where the Risen Lord should be, and was, seen? Sane criticism will recognize that our Gospels preserve fragmentary narratives resting on the individual experience of various persons. Yet without attempting here to co-ordinate these partial records in one complete story we may observe one or two salient points which seem to emerge clearly.

(1) Peter specially and the other disciples in general were instructed to expect to see our Lord in Galilee. The women who first visited the tomb were bidden to say that He was going before the disciples to Galilee.

(2) The disciples, however, made no such move. Even when the younger disciple who outran Peter to the sepulchre was convinced that the Lord had passed through and out of the graveclothes, no action followed. It must be understood that the disciples were not all lodged together and that what one person or one group saw and heard was not instantly brought to the knowledge of all the rest. Yet even so it is evident that if or when Mary Magdalene reported that she had seen the Risen Lord, if or when the other women reported that they had seen Him, had the disciples believed that their Lord was alive and had sent them this instruction, His word, we may be sure, would for them have overridden all consideration of the Paschal festival. But they remained sceptical and cynical and took no step to leave Jerusalem.

(3) Only two disciples, for whatever reason, left the city. Cleopas and his daughter Mary walked away to Emmaus, and to them the Lord appeared. In such wise, too, perhaps He would have shown Himself to the eleven if they had complied with His directions. They did not, and that they might be able afterwards to testify that He rose on the third day, he must needs go and show Himself to them in Jerusalem.

(4) When Cleopas and his daughter reported their indisputable experience they found that St. Peter too had seen the Lord. Had he too, after considering the evidence of the graveclothes and hearing the women's positive statements and the message they brought to himself, set out from Jerusalem and found the reward of his obedience? However this may be, it would seem that our Lord, disappointed in His disciples, showed Himself after all to the ten on Easter evening at Jerusalem.[1] Convinced that the Spiritual Body could pass rapidly from place to place and could enter a locked chamber they seem to have supposed it a sort of phantom. It was to correct this notion that our Lord ate and drank before them.

---

[1] If Mark xvi. 13 is correct that Cleopas' story was not at first accepted, we may gather that the rapid transference from Jerusalem to Emmaus seemed puzzling till the entrance through the closed door demonstrated the novel properties of the Spiritual Body.

(5) One apostle—and he not present in the room that evening—had a mind of an unusually logical cast. He saw the consequences that must follow to the traditional Jewish conception of God if the Jesus whom he had known as Rabbi, as his nation's Messiah and as the supremely representative Man of humanity had indeed risen into a supra-natural life. Before he could agree to be a witness, he must be convinced of the identity of the Being whom the others had seen with the One that had been crucified. As he saw it, therefore, he and the rest ought to remain at Jerusalem till the regular festival obligations were over—they would remain binding unless the new Christian hope were substantiated. When he found this done for him, St. Thomas rose to the height of addressing the Lord as the Jehovah of the Hebrew national history and as the God of the pre-Hebrew worship.

(6) Thus the way was clear to that intercourse in Galilee[1] between the Risen Lord and His disciples which He had from the first designed,[2] that He might complete their training for the work of extending God's infant kingdom, till it had the stature of the universal Christ.

Note on the Marcan Conclusion

A word should perhaps here be given to the concluding verses in Mark. Evidence against their genuine authenticity has been sought in the change of style which is observable when we pass from the rest of the Gospel to the final twelve verses. This argument, however, loses its cogency if we see in the previous narrative the language of St. Peter memorized by Mark. A more serious obstacle to our acceptance of the authenticity of this pericope is the strangeness of the abrupt breaking off of the Petrine narrative. It has indeed been said that the Petrine catechetical instruction dwells on the awe which was inspired by the startling consciousness that God was manifestly intervening in human history. Accordingly it is suggested that the words "for

[1] I cannot find in John xxi the signs that Mr. Gardner-Smith claims to see that this gives an alternative first appearance—and in Galilee—of the Risen Lord. The disciples show no surprise, rather they would seem to be habituated to the conditions of the Spiritual Body and its strangeness, so that on the one hand the Lord was not instantly recognized, yet on the other He had the same capability as two years before to direct their fishing to success. This with His knowledge of them, His eating with them—all seems to require as precedent to it such appearances as are related to have occurred in Jerusalem.

[2] We may perhaps note four other instances of the human frailty which disappointed our Lord: (1) If "the rich young ruler" be Saul of Tarsus, our Lord was disappointed of His first desire to have him for a disciple. (2) St. Peter by his denials made our Lord's prayer for him seem at first to have received no answer. (3) The Christian Church by its divisions has so far made His prayer for its unity seem to be unanswered. (4) How far the three apostles who witnessed the Transfiguration failed our Lord after His Resurrection we have no means to infer, but we hear nothing of their testimony to the others when the women brought the report that He had left the tomb.

they were afraid" make a natural and appropriate conclusion to the record. Nevertheless it is hard to believe that St. Peter did not add some definite account of an actual appearance of the Risen Christ. This is confirmed by the fact that some MSS. which are without the twelve verses have an alternative brief ending. This testifies to the general recognition by readers that something of the sort must round off the record. Yet, when we have agreed that the final section is neither St. Mark's own writing nor his reproduction of Petrine teaching, it must be insisted that we have here a far more accurate narrative than has sometimes been believed. From it we gather that Peter and John visited the sepulchre on hearing the Magdalene's report and that later she herself (as the Fourth Gospel says) was the first to see the Lord. The disciples did not believe her new story. (Then, as we learn from Luke and Paul, our Lord showed Himself to St. Peter.) Next came the walk to Emmaus. This contact with the Risen Saviour and His appearance in the late evening within the Upper Room were rejected by St. Thomas, and perhaps others, as incredible illusions. Then came the appearance a week later when the Lord reproved their stubborn repugnance to the new revelation of God's will. The writer passes without warning from Easter to Low Sunday, in the way that Mark passes from Jericho in Passion week to Palm Sunday and the Mount of Olives.

Chapter Two

CALENDARS: EGYPTIAN, JULIAN, ALEXANDRIAN AND JEWISH

(1) *Calendars*

WHEN Julius Caesar, the Pontifex Maximus, resolved to put an end to the possibility of such machinations as his enemies had employed to shorten his command in Gaul by neglecting to keep the Roman calendar in order, he availed himself of the astronomical science which Alexandria could afford him. The Egyptians had for centuries, and indeed millenniums, used a calendar which reckoned in each year twelve months of thirty days each, with five extra days appended before the New Year began. They were aware that with this calendar the year revolved through the seasons returning to its original place in 1461 years more or less, their criterion being not, as in our Gregorian calendar, the position of the sun, but the heliacal rising of Sirius. Caesar's advisers therefore suggested, in place of the old Roman lunar calendar, a new calendar of 365 days like the Egyptian, but with provision for one day to be repeated every fourth year. The day chosen for this duplication was 24 February, the 23rd having been the last day in the old calendar, celebrated by the festival of Terminalia. In the Latin reckoning 24 February is six days before 1 March and the leap year, as we now call it, was known, even as late as the nineteenth century, as bissextile. It is only in comparatively modern times that we have come to reckon the last day in February in leap year as the 29th. The Romans and we ourselves till recently made it the 28th in all years, and in leap year posited what we may call 24*a* February and 24*b* February as supplying the necessary insertion of an extra day.

With such a calendar in view Caesar intercalated month after month in 46 B.C., and it is of interest to consider what his aim was in fixing 1 January at the point in the year where we find

it. As we shall see, he undoubtedly intended to equate it with
the first day in one of the Egyptian months, so that his calendar
would be running side by side with the Egyptian and could
consequently be continually checked by reference to it. Unfortunately two complications present themselves. One is
notorious. The pontiffs after Caesar's death did not understand
the rule as to leap year. They inserted the bissextile day in
42, 39, 36 and so on until 9 B.C., when the error resulting had
become so glaring that no leap year was inserted till A.D. 8.
For most purposes we need not greatly concern ourselves to
work out the true equivalent date for events which were incorrectly dated during this half century, but, as will be seen
presently, the matter does become important when we have
to compare these dates reckoned by the pontiffs' mistaken
calendar with the Egyptian dates, which, of course, were correctly
reckoned. The second complication is this. Modern chronographers have found it useful to extend backwards the Julian
calendar, and for that purpose have supposed a leap year
to have occurred every four years, so that not only are such
factitious leap years reckoned during the time that the pontiffs
were misdating the calendar, but still further back. Accordingly
the modern chronographer imagines an intercalary bissextile day
in 45 B.C. when in point of fact no such intercalation was made.
Caesar had inserted in 46 B.C. as many days as were needed
to get his calendar into such accord with the Egyptian as would
make the first leap year occur four years after, and it is arguable
that in this case the pontiffs were right in making 42 B.C. a leap
year, but went wrong in following it with 39 B.C. and the rest.

To assist the reader in following and checking what may seem
abstruse and arid figures, it will be well to tabulate some of the
more outstanding dates.

B.C.	Egyptian date	Modern factitious Julian date	Pontiffs' actual Julian date
46	1 Thoth	4 September	
45	1 Tybi	2 January	1 January
	1 Phamenoth	2 March	2 March
	1 Thoth	3 September	3 September
44	1 Tybi	1 January	1 January
and	1 Phamenoth	2 March	2 March
43	1 Thoth	3 September	3 September

B.C.	Egyptian date	Modern factitious Julian date	Pontiffs' actual Julian date
42	1 Tybi	1 January	1 January
	1 Phamenoth	2 March	1 March
	1 Thoth	3 September	2 September
41	1 Tybi	1 January	31 December
	1 Phamenoth	1 March	1 March
	1 Thoth	2 September	2 September
	1 Tybi	31 December	31 December
40	1 Phamenoth	1 March	1 March
	1 Thoth	2 September	2 September
	1 Tybi	31 December	31 December
39 and 38	1 Phamenoth	1 March	28 February [1]
	1 Thoth	2 September	1 September
	1 Tybi	31 December	30 December
37	1 Phamenoth	29 February	28 February
	1 Thoth	1 September	1 September
	1 Tybi	30 December	30 December
36	1 Phamenoth	28 February	27 February [2]
	1 Thoth	1 September	31 August
	1 Tybi	30 December	29 December
35 and 34	1 Phamenoth	28 February	27 February
	1 Thoth	1 September	31 August
	1 Tybi	30 December	29 December
33	1 Phamenoth	28 February	26 February [2]
	1 Thoth	31 August	30 August
	1 Tybi	29 December	28 December
32 and 31	1 Phamenoth	27 February	26 February
	1 Thoth	31 August	30 August
	1 Tybi	29 December	28 December
30	1 Phamenoth	27 February	25 February [2]
	1 Thoth	31 August	29 August
	1 Tybi	29 December	27 December
29	1 Phamenoth	27 February	25 February
	1 Thoth	30 August	29 August
	1 Tybi	28 December	27 December

[1] As explained above, the last day of February, now called 29 in leap year, was formerly numbered 28 in all years.

[2] In 36, 33 and 30 B.C., which the Pontiffs made leap years, the intercalary bissextile day caused the numeration of the days at the end of February to be one less than our modern reckoning would have made it.

B.C.	Egyptian date	Modern factitious Julian date	Pontiffs' actual Julian date
28	1 Phamenoth	26 February	25 February
	1 Thoth	30 August	29 August
	1 Tybi	28 December	27 December
27	1 Phamenoth	26 February	24b February
	1 Thoth	30 August	28 August
	1 Tybi	28 December	26 December
26	1 Phamenoth	26 February	24 February
	1 Thoth	30 August	28 August
	1 Tybi	28 December	26 December

It will be seen that the Pontiffs' mistaken reckoning was gradually estranging their calendar from the stable estimate of the Egyptians. In 26 B.C. an effort was made to stabilize the position. The Egyptians, as we have said, kept a control and check on their vagrant calendar by reference to the great Sothic cycle. This was too remote for the Pontiffs, and accordingly a simpler procedure was attempted. The ordinary Egyptian calendar was reformed for the purpose, and an Alexandrian calendar was introduced side by side with the Egyptian. In the Alexandrian every four years a sixth epagomen day was to be added, so that this Alexandrian calendar, it was hoped, would serve as a control on the Pontiffs' calendar. Since the intercalary day in the two calendars was inserted six months apart from one another, the equating of dates was necessarily affected in the period between the two intercalations. It has generally been supposed that the Alexandrian insertion was made in the August subsequent to the Julian bissextile day. No consideration, however, has been given to the actual working of the two calendars in the next twenty years, and while again this is of no importance for ordinary purposes, it has some significance for our evaluation of the dates given us by the early Christian writers for the events of our Lord's life. It is therefore worth while to tabulate out the resultant dates in these calendars for the next twenty years, but it must be premised that we have no ancient warrant for deciding whether the Alexandrian calendar was correctly computed from the first (nor yet whether its first intercalation was in 26, 25, 24, 23 or 22 B.C.) or whether its intercalations were at first mistakenly made, like the Julian, every three years. Subject to this caveat we may plot out our dates as follows, taking the equation of 1 Phamenoth with 24 February as probably the control used for determining the correctness of the calendar.

B.C.	Egyptian date	Modern fac-titious Julian date	Pontiffs' actual Julian date	Alexandrian date
26	1 Phamenoth	26 February	24 February	24 February
	1 Thoth	30 August	28 August	28 August
	1 Tybi	28 December	26 December	26 December
25	1 Phamenoth	26 February	24 February	24 February
	1 Thoth	29 August	28 August	28 August
	1 Tybi	27 December	26 December	26 December
24	1 Phamenoth	25 February	24 February	24 February
	1 Thoth	29 August	27 August	28 August
	1 Tybi	27 December	25 December	26 December
23	1 Phamenoth	25 February	23 February	24 February
	1 Thoth	29 August	27 August	28 August
	1 Tybi	27 December	25 December	26 December
22	1 Phamenoth	25 February	23 February	24 February
	1 Thoth	29 August	27 August	28 August
	1 Tybi	27 December	25 December	26 December
21	1 Phamenoth	25 February	23 February	24 February
	1 Thoth	28 August	26 August	28 August
	1 Tybi	26 December	24 December	26 December

Thus for the Alexandrian calendar 1 Thoth was for ever synchronized with 28 August of the Julian calendar. Further, 1 Phamenoth was synchronized with 24 February or, as it was styled in the Latin, "a.d. VI Kal. Mart." In what we generally call leap year or, as it was known till the last century, in bissextile years, the day a.d. VI Kal. Mart. was repeated, as we have already seen, and the required day was intercalated in this way, rather than by inserting a 29th day of February. In consequence, in these bissextile years, 1 Phamenoth was equated with 24 February, 2 Phamenoth with its duplicate, 3 Phamenoth with a.d. V Kal. Mart., and so on till 26 August was reached, equated in such a year with 5 Epagomen, the fifth epagomen day. Then in the Alexandrian calendar a sixth epagomen day was intercalated, corresponding to 27 August, so that once more 1 Thoth fell on 28 August. It may not be inapposite to point out that on this reckoning, 1 Phamenoth fell on what we may call in one sense New Year's Day, i.e. the first day after the Feast of Terminalia, the end of the Roman Republican lunar calendar.

For the purpose of the above table we have provisionally, for simplicity's sake, assumed that the Alexandrian intercalated day was brought in at the end of six months after the Julian bissextile day. An examination, however, of Clement's estimate of the length of Gaius', Titus' and Trajan's reigns seems to reveal that he reckoned in an extra day in February for the dating in the years following the Julian bissextile year. It may be asked therefore if the intercalation ought not, somewhat surprisingly, to be placed eighteen months after the Julian. Whether this be correct or not will make little difference and we have therefore some justification for leaving our table as we have made it out, pending the appearance of further evidence.

Omitting from this point forward the Alexandrian datings, and continuing only our comparison of the modern and the Pontiffs' Julian dates with the Egyptian, we have the following table:

B.C.	Egyptian date	Modern factitious Julian date	Pontiffs' actual Julian date
20	1 Phamenoth	24 February	22 February
and	1 Thoth	28 August	26 August
19	1 Tybi	26 December	24 December
18	1 Phamenoth	24 February	22 February
	1 Thoth	28 August	25 August
	1 Tybi	26 December	23 December
17	1 Phamenoth	24 February	21 February
	1 Thoth	27 August	25 August
	1 Tybi	25 December	23 December
16	1 Phamenoth	23 February	21 February
	1 Thoth	27 August	25 August
	1 Tybi	25 December	23 December
15	1 Phamenoth	23 February	21 February
	1 Thoth	27 August	24 August
	1 Tybi	25 December	22 December
14	1 Phamenoth	23 February	20 February
	1 Thoth	27 August	24 August
	1 Tybi	25 December	22 December

B.C.	Egyptian date.	Modern factitious Julian date	Pontiffs' actual Julian date
13	1 Phamenoth	23 February	20 February
	1 Thoth	26 August	24 August
	1 Tybi	24 December	22 December
12	1 Phamenoth	22 February	20 February
	1 Thoth	26 August	23 August
	1 Tybi	24 December	21 December
11 and 10	1 Phamenoth	22 February	19 February
	1 Thoth	26 August	23 August
	1 Tybi	24 December	21 December
9	1 Phamenoth	22 February	19 February
	1 Thoth	25 August	22 August
	1 Tybi	23 December	20 December
8	1 Phamenoth	21 February	18 February
	1 Thoth	25 August	22 August
	1 Tybi	23 December	20 December

We need not follow out further the comparison of the Pontiffs' and the modern Julian calendars. It is enough to remark that by having no intercalation in 5 B.C., 1 B.C. and A.D. 4, the Pontiffs' calendar was brought into accord with what Julius Caesar had intended, so that after this last date the Julian calendar was worked as originally designed without any further adjustments or interferences. The intricacies and obscurities of the subject are reflected in a pathetic confession of Macrobius (Lib. I. 15(B)), upon whose evidence modern scholars have nevertheless found themselves obliged largely to rely: "quae omnia quid sibi velint, scire equidem vellem."

(2) *Astronomical*

Some readers, it is to be hoped, will be at pains to check and, if need be, to correct the calculations and conclusions in these pages. For their guidance it will be of service to give a number of astronomical occurrences partly drawn from the Tables of Ginzel and of Ch. Pauli and partly computed from Neugebauer by my friend and former colleague Dr. S. Verblunsky, mathematical lecturer in the Faculty of Technology at Manchester University, and late Fellow of Magdalene College, Cambridge.

1. Full Moons at Jerusalem

63 B.C.	5 January	2 h. 8 m. a.m.
	25 December	5 h. 30 m. p.m.
37	17 March	12 h. 13 m. a.m.
9	30 October	7 h. 22 m. a.m.
	28 December	9 h. 32 m. a.m.
8	25 February	5 h. 42 m. a.m.
	26 March	2 h. 6 m. p.m.
7	8 October	11 h. 56 m. a.m.
6	5 January	7 h. 22 m. p.m.
4	13 March	3 h. 3 m. a.m.
	11 April	5 h. 13 m. p.m.
2	20 January	1 h. 39 m. p.m.
1	29 December	4 h. 46 m. p.m.
A.D. 5	14 March	5 h. 56 m. p.m.
	13 April	5 h. 27 m. a.m.
6	2 April	1 h. 37 m. p.m.
7	22 March	3 h. 32 m. p.m.
22	7 March	4 h. 18 m. a.m.
	5 April	2 h. 22 m. p.m.
23	26 March	1 h. 22 m. a.m.
25	1 April	10 h. 1 m. p.m.
26	21 March	11 h. 41 m. p.m.
	12 December	10 h. 3 m. p.m.
27	11 March	6 h. 56 m. a.m.
	9 April	6 h. 39 m. p.m.
28	1 January	12 h. 42 m. a.m.
	29 March	5 h. 30 m. a.m.
	20 December	2 h. 27 m. p.m.
29	18 March	9 h. 34 m. p.m.
	17 April	5 h. 17 m. a.m.
	9 December	9 h. 49 m. p.m.
30	8 January	1 h. 54 m. p.m.
	8 March	11 h. 14 m. p.m.
	6 April	10 h. 18 m. p.m.
	28 December	6 h. 25 m. p.m.
31	27 March	1 h. 25 m. p.m.
	17 December	5 h. 30 m. p.m.
32	15 March	10 h. 44 m. p.m.
	14 April	11 h. 6 m. a.m.
	8 September	4 h. 56 m. a.m.
	7 October	3 h. 30 m. p.m.
	5 December	6 h. 56 m. p.m.
33	5 March	12 h. 42 m. a.m.
	3 April	4 h. 39 m. p.m.
	24 December	5 h. 44 m. p.m.

1. FULL MOONS AT JERUSALEM—*continued*

A.D.			
34	23 March	5 h. 15 m. p.m.
35	12 March	8 h. 6 m. p.m.
	11 April	10 h. 30 m. a.m.
36	30 March	4 h. 18 m. p.m.
39	28 March	10 h. 15 m. p.m.
40	15 April	10 h. 15 m. p.m.
41	6 January	7 h. 8 m. a.m.
	26 December	8 h. 6 m. a.m.
42	25 March	12 h. 39 m. p.m.
43	14 March	12 h. 54 m. p.m.
	13 April	5 h. 13 m. p.m.
44	3 January	4 h. 18 m. p.m.
	1 April	6 h. 54 m. a.m.
	23 December	7 h. 25 m. a.m.
45	21 March	2 h. 34 m. p.m.
46	9 April	1 h. 22 m. p.m.
63	1 April	10 h. 1 m. p.m.
64	21 March	12 h. 39 m. p.m.
65	9 April	1 h. 22 m. p.m.
69	26 March	2 h. 49 m. p.m.
70	15 March	3 h. 46 m. p.m.

2. SOME NEW MOONS AT JERUSALEM[1]

9 B.C.	14 October	5 h. 13 m. p.m.
7	23 October	9 h. 18 m. a.m.
A.D. 26	7 March	9 h. 47 m. p.m.
	6 April	6 h. 44 m. a.m.
27	25 February	7 h. 24 m. a.m.
28	15 March	2 h. 38 m. a.m.
29	2 April	7 h. 28 m. p.m.
30	22 March	7 h. 48 m. p.m.
31	12 March	12 h. 36 m. a.m.
32	29 March	10 h. 21 m. p.m.
33	19 March	1 h. 7 m. p.m.

3. SOME PLANETARY POSITIONS

9 B.C.	15 October	Jupiter	275°·75	Longitude
		Saturn	319°·42	,,
		Venus	118°	,,
		Mars	233°	,,
		Moon	220° ±7	,,
		Sun	203°	,,

[1] The new moon may be reckoned as visible immediately after the sunset which occurs not less than thirty hours later than the astronomical new moon.

3. SOME PLANETARY POSITIONS—*continued*

9 B.C.	8 December	Venus	203°	Longitude	
	9 December	Mars	262°	,,	
	22 December	Venus	226°	,,	
7	27 October	Jupiter	354°·16	,,	1°·66 Latitude
		Saturn	354°·77	,,	2°·66 ,,
		Venus	326°·22	,,	4°·88 ,,
		Mars	262°·98	,,	1°·44 ,,
		Sun	213°	,,	
		Moon	265°	,,	

4. SOME ECLIPSES VISIBLE AT JERUSALEM

(*a*) Solar

A.D. 29	24 November: total	10 h. 48 m. a.m.
32	28 April: partial	8 h. 36 m. a.m.
33	12 September: annular	11 h. 16 m. a.m.

(*b*) Lunar

4 B.C.	13 March	
A.D. 29	4 June: total	10 h. 17 m. p.m.
	9 December: partial	10 h. 4 m. p.m.
31	25 April: partial	10 h. 46 m. p.m.
	19 October	5 h. 28 m. a.m.
33	3 April: partial	

(3) *The Jewish Year*

Today we are so habituated to a solar calendar that many
people are unable to understand how a lunar could ever have
been of efficient service. It will perhaps therefore be of advantage to give a brief account of the kind of calendar which the
Jews have used from time immemorial. The moon returns to
the same position in its orbit round the earth after roughly
29 days and a half. Lunar months, therefore, in general are
alternately 29 and 30 days in length. To return to the same
point in the seasonal or solar year we have to count about
eleven days over and beyond twelve lunar months. In order to
adjust these outstanding remainders of solar surplus and lunar
deficiency, an extra month is inserted from time to time:
thrice in eight years and seven times in nineteen years. Yet this
was not enough. The moon's motion, as seen from the earth
apparently suffers from irregularities and inequalities. In early
days this was noticed by observation; later these irregularities

were to some extent reduced to order and allowed for in elaborate tables. In either case the variation of the month from the lunar phenomena was corrected by sometimes lengthening a month of 29 days to a month of 30, sometimes by shortening to 29 days a month of 30. It thus resulted that the lunar year contained now 353, now 354 and now 355 days, and correspondingly a lunar leap year might have 383, 384 or 385 days.[1]

Thus much premised attention may be paid to the probabilities of dates which we can compute in the Jewish calendar.[2] For this calendar the day begins and ends with what we should call the late afternoon. The Crucifixion, then, fell on the day which extended from the late afternoon of Maundy Thursday to the late afternoon of Good Friday. The Passover Feast was celebrated in the evening of Good Friday, i.e. on the Jewish day which ran from Good Friday late afternoon to the late afternoon of Saturday. Now if as we are supposing the Crucifixion was on 3 April, the Passover Feast in the previous year will have been either about 15 April or 15 March. In either case the Passover of A.D. 31 must have been about 26 March, since on the one hand an intercalary Ve-adar, i.e. a repeat of the twelfth month, in A.D. 32 could give 15 April for that year's Passover, or on the other hand, a year of common length could give 15 March. An intercalary Ve-adar before 26 March is forbidden us, if we should then have an intercalation in two successive years, viz. both A.D. 32 and 33. Further, if the Passover of A.D. 31 fell about 26 March, that of A.D. 30 must have been either about 8 March or 7 April, and again in either

1 Tiros in the craft of almanac-making often dismiss a lunar calendar as full of wild and wide discrepancies. It must therefore be emphasized that such a calendar, whether controlled by observation or by the rule of a cycle, never allows a variation of more than a day or two to pass unchecked and uncorrected.

2 Burnaby, v. p. 177, has given tables for determining in accordance with the present Rabbinic rules any date in the Jewish Calendar. Badcock has worked out according to these rules the exact dates of the Passover and of Pentecost from A.D. 27 to 35, and approximate dates from A.D. 36 to 70. Such evidence, however, as we have as to the factual date of Passovers in this period shows that the calendar was not then controlled by these rules, but either by observation or by less accurate tables than are now used, and that the Passover was not then rigidly computed to follow the vernal equinox.

case we are shut up to about 19 March for the Passover of A.D. 29. The date of the investment of Jerusalem in A.D. 70 favours the choice of 15 March for the Passover of A.D. 32, thirty-eight years, i.e. two Metonic cycles earlier, and a consideration of the dates we thus obtain for A.D. 29, 31, 32 and 33 encourages us to reject Clement's preference for 7 April rather than 8 March, in A.D. 30.

Keeping our lunar tables before us, we may submit that the Passover feasts perhaps[1] fell on the Jewish day between the afternoons of the following Julian dates:

A.D. 29	March 18–19		A.D. 32	March 15–16
30	March 8–9		33	April 3–4
31	March 26–27			

The first two dates are separated by 355 days, which shows that no Ve-adar was intercalated in the spring of A.D. 30.

The Egyptian day began and ended with the third hour before dawn. Hence the Egyptian equivalent of a Jewish day which covered from the late afternoon of Thursday to the late afternoon of Friday is a day running from the early hours of Friday morning to the early hours of Saturday. Accordingly the Crucifixion on Friday afternoon, 3 April, would be on 14 Nisan, i.e. between the late afternoon of Thursday, 2 April, and that of Friday, 3 April, but in the Alexandrian calendar on the day (whether 10 or 9 Pharmuthi) extending from the early hours of the morning of Friday to that of Saturday.

A slender thread of support for this reconstruction of the Jewish calendar is to be found in the narrative of our Lord's healing of the beggar blind from birth. He received his sight on a Sabbath, and a little—at most a day or two—later was the Feast of the Dedication. If there was an intercalary month Ve-adar in A.D. 33, that feast would have fallen on 15–16 December, and 13 December in any case was Saturday, the Sabbath. If there was no intercalary month, the feast must have been 15 January, while the Sabbaths were the 10th and the 17th of January. Thus, to satisfy the facts as recorded in the Fourth Gospel we can say that there must have been an intercalary month in A.D. 33.

Philo's observations on the time of the Passover might suggest that our date in A.D. 30 should be brought forward by twenty-four hours.

Chapter Three

GOSPEL DATES

(1)

INFINITE labour has been bestowed on the subject of the true dates of the Gospel story, and innumerable writers have devoted much time and thought to the problem. It is not to be supposed that this meagre volume—and still less a single short chapter—can deal with the matter in a way that will satisfy the reader, but something must be said on the results which seem to emerge from our attempted harmony. The documentary and other evidence will be found discussed at some length later; here it will be for the reader's convenience to present in summary fashion the capital dates that claim attention.

Between August A.D. 28 and August A.D. 29 John received a call from God to preach and, perhaps somewhat later, to baptize. After a while Jesus came to John about the beginning of January. This was not in 29 but in 30, when 15 Tybi in the Alexandrian calendar or 9 January followed the Full Moon. John was thrown into prison about a year later and killed in the late autumn of A.D. 31. In the next spring the five thousand were fed. On Friday, 3 April A.D. 33, the Lord was crucified. Zacharias was on duty from 27 January to 2 February 9 B.C. The Annunciation was about 10 August and John was born about 8 November. The Nativity was about 2 a.m. on 16 May 8 B.C. The visit of the Magi was in October, 7 B.C.

Precipitate readers of Luke made the Nativity exactly thirty years before the Baptism and using the Egyptian calendar arrived at 6 January for the date in 2 B.C. From this naturally followed an equation for the Baptism of 28–29 December. Nor was this the end. For the Alexandrian calendar 5–6 January is Tybi 11, and when once this figure had been evolved, it was used for the supposed correction of the Baptism and Nativity day to 24–25 December.

Some readers may be inclined to revolt against what they may regard as revolutionary and new-fangled datings of our Christian festivals, and it is only right to state that we owe our present chronology to Archbishop Ussher, and greatly as he deserves to be remembered with admiration and respect, his authority cannot outweigh that of a writer of thirteen centuries earlier, the learned St. Epiphanius, Bishop of Salamis, the friend of St. Jerome.

We shall now proceed to examine some part of the evidence preserved to us from the first ages of the Christian Church.

(2)

First it may be permitted to reprint with corrections suggested by further reflection a paper privately printed ten years ago.

The earliest writer outside the New Testament who has left us evidence for the Gospel dates is Clement of Alexandria. In his *Stromateis*,[1] I. xxi, §§ 144–6, he writes:

Now our Lord was born in the 28th year when first they ordered the censuses to take place in the time of Augustus . . . with 15 years, therefore, of Tiberius and 15 of Augustus thus are completed the 30 years until He suffered.[2] And from the time when He suffered until the downfall of Jerusalem[3] there are 42 years, 3 months, and from the downfall of Jerusalem to the death of Commodus, 122 years, 10 months, 23 days.[4] There are in all therefore from the time when the

[1] For a previous discussion of this evidence and references to earlier criticism see the *Journal of Philology*, vol. XXVII, pp. 232 ff., where, however, I misunderstood the significant variations in the months given by Clement for the Nativity and the Crucifixion.

[2] Clement here uses "suffered" for the Lord's ministry, regarded as a single point of time and dated at His baptism. That this is so is shown by what follows. If the argument in the Epistle to the Hebrews, chapters ix and x, be followed, we may call the Baptism the beginning of the rite of Atonement which culminates in the Ascension into the heavenly Holy of Holies.

[3] By this Clement means the beginning of the siege on 14 Xanthicus, not its end on 8 Gorpiaeus, which was the Sabbath, Friday evening, 3 August, to Saturday evening, 4 August. The latter date is irreconcilable with either of Clement's statements. The former date corresponds with the eve of the Passover, i.e. 14 Nisan, or 15 March, A.D. 70, but see below, p. 157.

[4] The MS. reading is 128 years, 10 months, 3 days, which H. Browne emended to 121 years, 10 months, 13 days.

Lord was born to Commodus' death, 194 years, 1 month, 13 days. But there are some who add elaborately not only the year but also the day for the birth of our Saviour, which they say was in the 28th year of Augustus on the 25th day of Pachon. And the followers of Basileides keep as a festival the day of His baptism also, spending the night before in readings. And they say it was the 15th year of Tiberius Caesar, the 15th day of the month Tybi, though some make it the 11th day of the same month. And His passion they work out with exactitude, making it, some of them in the 16th year of Tiberius Caesar, the 25th day of Phamenoth, and others the 25th of Pharmuthi, and others again say that the Saviour suffered on the 19th day of Pharmuthi.

Yes, and some of them say that he was born in Pharmuthi on the 24th or 25th.

A consideration of these figures shows that Clement's statements, or rather the statements of his authorities, cannot be accepted so far as the years are concerned. The year he gives for the Nativity is contradictory of St. Matthew's statement that Herod the Great was alive when our Lord was born. The fifteen months St. Clement gives for our Lord's Ministry are shown to be inadequate if St. John's account is not to be rejected, and indeed unless the synoptists' account of the time of year of the feeding of the five thousand is not to be made inconsistent with what would naturally be inferred from the rest of their story. Granting, however, that so far as the years are concerned Clement's statements cannot be employed, we are still left to ask whether the dates he gives can be made to serve our purpose in so far as months and days go. It will be suggested here that we can make profitable use of the dates he gives.

To begin with, we may examine the statement that from the Nativity to the death of Commodus there was an interval of 194 years, 1 month, 13 days. Commodus we know died on 31 December A.D. 192. It follows that the Nativity, according to this reckoning, would fall by the Julian calendar on 18 November 3 B.C. We have, however, to take account of the fact that Clement is certainly using the Egyptian method of reckoning dates, and therefore this Julian date has to be adjusted to allow for the fact that the Egyptian year contains 365 days only, without any provision for an additional day to be added every four years, as in the Julian calendar. The period of 194 years would, therefore, cause a divergence of 49 days between the Egyptian and the Julian dating, and we have, accordingly, to carry forward the date 18 November to 6 January. Now 5–6 January in the year 2 B.C. was in the Egyptian[1] reckoning 15[2] Tybi, and this, as we have seen, is the accepted date with Clement for the day of the Baptism. We can see that he has worked out these figures by taking as perfectly[3] exact Luke's round figure for our Lord's age at the Baptism. Accordingly we find for the date of the Baptism on this reckoning 28–29 December A.D. 28. How are we to suppose that such a date was arrived at? It has been suggested that the date will be the equivalent, worked out by some investigator, of some Jewish date, and that this Jewish date was preserved by tradition. To this we shall return on a later page.[4]

Meanwhile it will be of advantage to examine certain features in Clement's chronological reckoning.

First we must consider the intervals that Clement gives between the fall of Jerusalem on the one hand and the Crucifixion and Commodus' death on the other. The latter interval

---

[1] See Ginzel, *Handbuch der mathematischen und technischen Chronologie*, Leipzig, 1911, 11. Band, p. 541, and Iwan Meuller in *Handbuch der klassischen Altertumswissenschaft*, vol. I. For a discussion of the fundamental statements of Censorinus and Dionysius see *Classical Review*, vol. XIV, pp. 146ff., and XXII, p. 124. See also my *Studies in Egyptian Chronology*, Part II, pp. 1–14. For the convenience of the reader it may be said that it is known that in A.D. 29 the Egyptian 1 Thoth is to be equated with 16 August.

[2] It must be borne in mind that the Egyptian day began with the third hour after midnight, the Jewish with sunset and the Roman with midnight. This leads occasionally to the appearance of a day's discrepancy. Two statements of Epiphanius will illustrate this. On the one hand he states that the Nativity was πρὸ ὀκτὼ Εἰδῶν Ἰανουαρίων, κατ' Αἰγυπτίους Τυβὶ ἐνδεκάτῃ. On the other hand he also gives πέμπτῃ Ἰανουαρίου ἑσπέρα εἰς ἕκτην ἐπιφώσκουσα. The apparent discrepancy here is removed if we understand these calculators to have reckoned the Nativity to have occurred between midnight and 3 a.m. on the morning of 25 December. This, it may be pointed out incidentally, would explain the origin of the Christmas Midnight Mass.

[3] Pretty certainly this notion if it was not originated was yet corroborated by a misinterpretation of Luke iii. 23 as if he meant that at His Baptism our Lord was beginning His thirty-first year instead of that at the beginning of His ministry he was about thirty years of age.

[4] See below p. 164 and *J.T.S.*, vol. LII, pp. 123 ff.

he makes 122 years, 10 months, and 23 days, and this effectually settles one or two points which would otherwise be moot. In the first place it might be expected that Clement had his figures worked out on the basis of the final demolition of Jerusalem as the *terminus a quo*. But we know otherwise that Jerusalem was closed in on the 14th day of Xanthicus, the equivalent of 14 Nisan in the Jewish calendar, and that it finally fell on 8 Gorpiaeus. It is manifest that Clement's date for the καταστροφή is not that of the final overthrow but that of the beginning of the siege—an interesting parallel in the way of computation to Clement's reckoning the Passion from the date of the Baptism.

Next, assuming that the interval given is that from the investment of Jerusalem to 31 December 192, we notice that the Egyptian calendar in that interval would revolve backwards through 31 days, whether the *terminus a quo* be placed in A.D. 70 or in 71.[1] The first leap year in the Julian nomenclature would be 72 and the last A.D. 192. We thus arrive at 272, 282 or 292 days[2] as the equivalent of Clement's interval of 10 months and 3, 13 or 23 days—to include in one statement not only the MS. reading but the corrections suggested.

What, then, is the date thus resulting for the commencement of the siege? The answer is 3 April, 24 March or 14 March. What of these dates? The Passover would fall, according to the accepted rules of computation, in A.D. 70 on 14 April, in A.D. 71 on 3 April. An interesting choice thus presents itself. If the MS. reading be correct, Clement reckoned the Fall of

[1] Since this paper was written I have seen in the *Journal of Theological Studies*, vol. XXXV, pp. 146 ff., Dr. J. K. Fotheringham's most valuable investigation of the evidence of astronomy and technical chronology for the date of the Crucifixion. Pursuing quite different lines of argument, he arrives at conclusions which converge on and agree with the views expressed in this paper. In particular he offers a possible explanation of variations in regnal datings which may clear up the enigma of the date for the Fall of Jerusalem, and demonstrates that Tiberius' fifteenth year can be nothing but A.D. 28–29.

[2] If Clement took into account the incidence of the five epagomen days in the Egyptian calendar, these sums would be increased by that number of days, but none of them yield any date reconcilable with history. It is to be concluded—and the conclusion again is of importance—that in working out intervals the epagomen days are not considered as falling outside the regular months.

Jerusalem to have occurred on 3 April 71. If he placed it in 70, the Passover must have occurred on 13 March in that year, and the MS. reading must be emended to 23 days. The occurrence of Passover before the equinox is no serious obstacle to our acceptance of the latter hypothesis. As we shall see, some investigators dated the Crucifixion on 8 March, but it is hard to satisfy oneself that the MS. text should be treated in quite so high-handed a fashion. Let it be supposed then that Clement takes 71 for the year in which Jerusalem was taken; what follows? In the first place, his interval from the Passion, i.e. as we have seen, the Baptism, to this date is roughly correct[1] as it stands, i.e. 42 years and 3 months.[2]

It is remarkable that if Clement's 3 months be interpreted strictly, we should arrive at 18 March for the investment of Jerusalem, and this date might be reconciled with the interval to Commodus' death if allowance be made for the epagomen days. We should then, however, have to emend the text with a freedom that seems unwarrantable in view of our uncertainties as to Clement's principles of computation, and— what is still more serious—this date for the Passover is an utter impossibility. It remains to decide how the MS. reading of 128 years for the interval from A.D. 71 to 192 is to be corrected; and β rather than α being more naturally miscopied as η, we shall be inclined to read 122 and to take the view that Clement reckoned his years by counting the number of New Year days intervening. Thus if we reckon 1 Thoth in A.D. 71 as giving 1 year, then 1 Thoth in 192 will give 122 years, the number of months and days being then calculated separately. It will be found that the same method of reckoning will satisfy Clement's interval from 6 January 2 B.C. to 31 December A.D. 192.

It should also be observed that Clement lends no support to

---

[1] We can explain Clement's computation as rigorously exact if we suppose him to have reckoned 25 Chislev to 15 Nisan as 3 months less 10 days and then allowed the 10 days' shift in the Egyptian calendar from A.D. 28 to A.D. 71 as if it were to be set off against the 10 days' deficiency. However this may be, it does not affect our general conclusions.

[2] It is to be observed that Origen also, Homily on Jeremiah xiv. 13, and Contra Celsum iv. 22, and Hippolytus on Daniel iv. 6, 13, 15, 23, estimate the interval from the Passion to the Fall of Jerusalem at 42 years.

the hypothesis favoured by some writers that Luke means by his "15th year of Tiberius" something earlier than August A.D. 28–29.

We come now to the date of the Crucifixion. It has been common of recent years to suppose that the true date may have been 18 March A.D. 29. This was suggested by Professor C. H. Turner, who has been followed by many others. An alternative suggestion has been that the date was 3 April A.D. 33.[1] Neither date, it will be seen, finds any support in Clement's statements as they stand. There can be little doubt that he prefers 7 April A.D. 30, though he notes that alternatively some placed the event on 8 March or on 1 April. A careful consideration of Clement's statements suggests that all these datings are merely derived by calculation on the basis of the assumption that Luke's statement of our Lord's age at his baptism was to be taken as rigorously exact. The investigators from whom Clement quotes took no account of the statement in John's Gospel (we need not here inquire what the reason for this was), and giving special attention to Luke's mention of "the acceptable year of the Lord" worked out a date for the Crucifixion which should not be much more than a year after the Baptism. Thus, having as a fixed point the Baptism of 28–29 December A.D. 28, they arrived at 7 April A.D. 30 as the true date for the Crucifixion. This, as it happens, is a Friday, and so in their view had a strong claim to be regarded as a true calculation. Those who placed the date a month earlier ignored the fact that that date was not a Friday. When we come, however, to consider all the Gospel evidence we are driven to the conclusion that this date must be too early. We have statements which show that there was a Passover some few weeks after the Baptism and that there was also another Passover about the time when the five thousand were fed, and then finally there was the Crucifixion at another Passover. Assuming that our date for the Baptism is correct, we are thus led to look for the date of the Crucifixion not earlier at any rate than A.D. 31.

[1] Since this was written, Dr. J. K. Fotheringham's article (see above, p. 157, note 1) has elaborated the astronomical argument for this date. Ginzel, *op. cit.* (see p. 156, note 1), gave this date as far back as 1911. He further points out that there was a lunar eclipse visible at Jerusalem on the evening of this day.

Here may be mentioned a rather interesting and curious circumstance. At some Feast of the Jews, John tells us, a man who for thirty-eight years had suffered from infirmity was restored to full control of his muscles. If we are right in supposing that our Lord was born at Pentecost 8 B.C., he would attain the age of thirty-eight years at Pentecost A.D. 31. It is at any rate extremely plausible to suppose that the unnamed feast was this feast of Pentecost in that year (as St. Cyril and St. Chrysostom say), for this would lend peculiar significance to the mention of the man's age, a detail in the narrative which the commentators have found no satisfactory reason for the Evangelist to give. If the feast were this Pentecost—or indeed if it fell, whether it were Tabernacles or Passover, or any other, before the following Pentecost—we shall place the Crucifixion in A.D. 33. As we have above said, many scholars have already arrived at this date on other grounds as the most reasonable. If this, then, be correct, we reject St. Clement's favoured date of 7 April A.D. 30 as due to a mistaken idea that our Lord's Ministry lasted but fifteen months. But what of his remaining date corresponding in that year to 1 April? Here an interesting line of thought develops before us. As we have seen, those who supposed that our Lord was exactly thirty years of age at His baptism calculated back that His birth was on 6 January 2 B.C. Now in the Alexandrian calendar 6[1] January is 11 Tybi, and we know that this date is, in later ages when the Alexandrian calendar was in regular use, given as the date of the Nativity. It may, therefore, be suggested, since we have in this way one date in Clement that is of the Alexandrian calendar, that one other date, that is, the third date that he gives for the Crucifixion, 19 Pharmuthi, belongs to this Alexandrian calendar. In that case, the day might be 13–14 April, which might be a possible date for the Passover[2] in A.D. 32. Unfortunately that day in that year fell on Monday, and is therefore unacceptable for the Crucifixion. On the other hand, to exhaust all possibilities, if we accept H. Browne's emendation

---

[1] Epiphanius, haeres. 50, equates 11 Tybi with 6 January and it could only be so equated in the years 25 to 22 B.C. It is noticeable that he carelessly says κατ' Αἰγυπτίους instead of κατ' Ἀλεξανδρέας, the Alexandrian calendar having by his time entirely eclipsed the old Egyptian.

[2] See Dr. Fotheringham's table, loc. cit., p. 162.

of 19 into 9 the date would be 3–4 April and this we may suppose is an approximation by calculation to the date we have already discovered in A.D. 33. This, however, is not all. It will be observed that Clement's favoured date makes the interval between the Baptism and the Crucifixion precisely a period of 1 year and 91 days. When by mistake and by confusion between Tybi 11 and 15 the date of the Baptism was placed at 25 December instead of 29 December, some investigators, allowing the period of 91 days and excising the year between the Baptism and the Crucifixion, arrived at 25 March as the date of the Crucifixion. As is well known, this date is found very commonly in later writers. It is, of course, an impossible date so far as the coincidence of a full moon and a Passover is concerned. Whether for this reason, therefore, or through a mere slip of the pen, we have in one authority, in place of 25 March, 18 March given as the date of the Crucifixion. It was on this that Professor Turner fastened and on this that he built his theory that 18 March A.D. 29 was the true date of the Crucifixion. As has just been shown, however, if that be the year of the Crucifixion, we have Clement's evidence in favour of making the date 15 April and not 18 March.

Before summing up our conclusions we may glance at what appears to be another mistaken guess of some early investigators. While the more careful students placed the Baptism at 28–29 December A.D. 28 and the Nativity thirty years earlier, there were those who allowed only thirty years and three months for the Lord's entire earthly life. They therefore placed the Nativity a year later, bringing it forward from 6 January to 25 December, as if the date were a Jewish lunar date and not an Egyptian. This date fixed in the Julian calendar gave 11 Tybi as its equivalent in A.D. 28. This was of little importance. What is notable is that when 25 December came to challenge 6 January for the Nativity, 25 March, as we have seen, came to dispute with 7 April for the Crucifixion. Not only does Origen mention this, but the *Apostolical Constitutions*, using the Alexandrian calendar, gives for the Nativity 28 Choiak πρὸ ὀκτὼ Καλανδῶν Ἰανουαρίων, for the Baptism, 11 Tybi = 7 January, and for the Passion 29 Phamenoth = 25 March.

It was only a step further for Dionysius Exiguus to deduce

that the Nativity was to be dated 25 December 1 B.C., the Crucifixion falling in 30 and not A.D. 29 as Origen supposed.

All these calculations of later writers are in themselves mere curiosities: they are inconsistent with the statements of Matthew and John. Nevertheless, their eccentricities illuminate at various points what seem to be the correct datings.

We may now claim that we have discovered the sources of the various theories which have been propounded as to the date of the Crucifixion. These explanations seem to clear away as built upon errors the dates 18 March A.D. 29 and also 7 April A.D. 30, and we are left therefore perfectly free to determine the true date of the Crucifixion, taking into account all the Gospel evidence and holding fast to what might be thought the firmly established date of the Baptism on 29 December A.D. 28. It only remains to clear away a doubt which might possibly present itself. Since we have allowed that in regard to two datings Clement without warning may be giving us dates from the Alexandrian calendar, it might be suggested that 6 January A.D. 30 was the true date of the Baptism, and it might be supposed that this date was corroborated by a statement in the *Pistis Sophia*,[1] where 15 Tybi is placed at the time of a full moon. We may, therefore, summarize our conclusions in this way. The Nativity was 16 May 8 B.C. The Crucifixion was 3 April A.D. 33. The Annunciation was 8 August 9 B.C.

Some readers may ask, What of Luke's note that our Lord at His baptism was about thirty years of age? Three answers are possible: (1) That this estimate is so rough that it may be taken to cover the fact that our Lord was then in His thirty-sixth year; (2) that E or F has been dropped out of the text after the Λ; (3) that Luke, assured on the one hand that our Lord was nearly thirty-seven years old and on the other that

[1] It will be well to quote here the relevant words in the *Pistis Sophia*. They run as follows: "When Jesus had risen from the dead He passed eleven years speaking with His disciples (§ 1). It came to pass on the fifteenth day of the month Tobe, the day of the full moon, on that day when the sun had risen" (§ 4). We need not digress into theories as to what, if anything, of historical significance these statements may have. It is enough to note that eleven years after the Ascension, if Clement's authorities be followed in dating it in A.D. 30, will bring us to A.D. 41, that 15 Tybi in that year is 25–26 December and that Ginzel's tables give us the full moon as occurring at 5.46 a.m. on the morning of the 26th.

He was born at the time of the first Census, and knowing that Quirinius held the Census in A.D. 6, and that, if born then, our Lord's age would be twenty-three, took the mean number and made it roughly thirty.[1]

In conclusion it may be useful to give the following summary of Clement's dates as it might be thought that he wished them to be understood:

The Nativity . .	6 January 2 B.C.	15 Tybi.
The Baptism . .	28–29 December A.D. 28.	15 Tybi.
	30 years later.	
The Crucifixion . .	7 April A.D. 30.	14 Nisan.
	1 year 3 months later.	
Siege of Jerusalem began	14 March 70 (or 3 April 71).	14 Nisan.
	42 years, 3 months from the Baptism.	
Commodus' death .	31 December 192.	
	194 years, 1 month, 13 days from the Nativity.	

(3)

It has seemed desirable to lay before the reader the above alternatives and uncertainties so that he may frame his own picture of the fixed and impregnable certainties into which every other suggestion has to be fitted. But it is now time to turn from possibilities to what appear to be the correct solutions of our problems.

Let us look first at Clement's interval from the downfall of Jerusalem to Commodus' death. As we have seen, this must end with 272 days or 10 or 20 days more. This therefore fixes the date as 14 March A.D. 70. Since Clement makes the Passion precede this by an interval ending with three months he must be computing in the first instance with Jewish calendar datings. Hence he, like the *Pistis Sophia*, makes the Baptism take place on the fifteenth day of the Jewish month running more or less currently with the Egyptian Tybi. (He cannot be speaking of the Crucifixion, since that was not three months earlier than March and was itself about Passover time.) It follows that the true date of the Baptism must be at a full moon three months before some Passover. When we come to the date of the

---

[1] Some readers may prefer another solution and suppose Luke's elaborate dating of John Baptist's call to be really the date of the Crucifixion.

Nativity we might think that again Clement was giving a date thirty years before the Baptism by the Jewish calendar, but this is shown to be not so by the fact that 6 January is not the date of a full moon in 2 B.C. nor indeed in any year in its vicinity. It follows that the Nativity date is derived from a mistaken view of the figures, which should have been understood to mean the fifteenth day in a lunar month corresponding more or less with the Egyptian Tybi, but have been treated as an Egyptian date. Nor, unfortunately, was this the end of the confusion. In place of the full moon date for the Baptism the Egyptian date was assumed for the Baptism so that it revolved further and further back in the year. The Alexandrian calendar and the Julian tied down the day's observance to 6 January, which Epiphanius contrives by a slight adjustment to equate with 11 Tybi in the Alexandrian calendar. This equation clears up for us Clement's remark that some dated the Baptism in that way, and this again emboldens us to believe that we are on sure ground when we interpret Clement's third date for the Crucifixion as an Alexandrian date. Meanwhile others performed the opposite operation. They took the Egyptian date 15 Tybi as a fixed point, equating it with 28–29 December, and transferred it to thirty years earlier to make it the date of the Nativity. Then later some caught at the supposed improvement of 11 Tybi and asserted 24–25 December to be the true date for Christmas, while 5–6 January maintained its ground for the dating of the Baptism.

We can, then, carry away with us from Clement the certainty that the Crucifixion was on 3 April, the Baptism at the full moon three months before Passover, and the Nativity on 16 May. For the rest he must be discounted as having misread Luke and misunderstood or confused Jewish, Alexandrian and Egyptian calendar dates. One further point may be hazarded. If, as will be argued presently, the Baptism was in January A.D. 30, when the astronomical full moon occurred about midday on the 8th, so that the Baptism was perhaps on the 7th, it is easy to understand that chronologists might regard the fixed solar date of the Julian 6 January or Alexandrian 11 Tybi as a sufficient approximation to the fifteenth day of the Jewish lunar month Tebet.

(4)

In the *Expository Times*, vol. L, pp. 418ff., it was explained that in the field of New Testament chronology recent investigators had based much of their argument on the papyrological evidence of Egyptian census returns and on astronomical computations. They had thus inferred that the Nativity should be dated in 8 B.C., perhaps on 16–17 May; the Baptism in A.D. 30, perhaps on 6 January; and the Crucifixion in A.D. 33 on 3 April. Those who were addicted to the conventional chronology of the last three centuries could argue that no warrant for these dates was to be found in our primitive authorities, and this lends importance to the statements which we shall adduce below.

Epiphanius despite his learning and manifest honesty has for long been strangely neglected. His encouragement of monasticism, his fervent admiration of the celibate life and his frequent conjoining of mutually contradictory hypotheses [1] have apparently prejudiced modern readers against him. Yet these characteristics do not of themselves invalidate an author's testimony. The last of the three, on the contrary, makes his evidence more trustworthy than if through critical perspicacity and decisiveness he had suppressed awkward facts or attempted to reconcile them. It is right therefore to examine with an open mind his statements of facts.

In *Adv. Haer.*, lib. III, tom II, haer. lxvii, paragraph 1041 fin., he writes:

Ἐν γὰρ τῷ τριακοστῷ τρίτῳ ἔτει τοῦ πρώτου Ἡρῴδου . . . γεννᾶται ὁ Εωτὴρ ἐν Βηθλεὲμ τῆς Ἰουδαίας, ὅπερ ἦν τεσσαρακοστὸν δεύτερον Αὐγούστου Βασιλέως. καὶ ποιήσας ἔτη δύο, λαμβάνεται ὑπο του Ἰωσὴφ εἰς Αἴγυπτον. . . . καὶ τελεῖ ἐκεῖσε ἄλλα δύο ἔτη. Καὶ τελευτᾷ Ἡρῴδης ὁ βασιλεὺς ἔτει τριακοστῷ ἑβδόμῳ. Διαδέχεται δὲ τοῦτον Ἀρχελαος ὁ υἱὸς αυτοῦ ἐπὶ ἔτεσιν ἐννέα. . . . Καὶ . . . παραδίδοται σταυρῷ ὀκτωκαιδεκάτῳ μὲν ἔτει Τιβερίου Καισαρος, τοῦ δὲ Ἀγρίππα ἐπικληθέντος Μεγάλου . . . ἔτος ἦν εἰκοστόν . . . τέταρτον γὰρ ἦν ἔτος τῷ Σωτῆρι· τῷ δὲ Ἰωσὴφ ὑπὲρ ἔτος ὀγδοηκοστὸν τέταρτον, ὅτε ἐκ τῆς Αἰγύπτου χώρας παρεγένετο.

[1] An example of this is to be seen in his statement that at the very first Christians were known as Ἰεσσαῖοι. This word he explains as derived from Ἰησοῦς, but as usual his prolific memory prompts him to hazard, as a possibility, that it points to our Lord's descent from David the son of Jesse.

Epiphanius, it will be observed, makes Herod's first regnal year run from the time of the Senate's grant in his favour to the Attic or Olympiad New Year in July, 40 B.C.[1] He reckons Herod's 37th year to run from July, 5 B.C., to July, 4 B.C., and Archelaus' first year from July, 4 B.C., to July, 3 B.C. Archelaus' reign ended accordingly between July A.D. 5 and July A.D. 6,[2] Augustus' between July A.D. 14 and July A.D. 15, this whole year being regarded as his last year, just as Herod's last year was reckoned as far as the July after his death. Thus Tiberius' first year runs from July A.D. 15 to July A.D. 16 and the Baptism falls between July A.D. 29 and July A.D. 30, and the Crucifixion between July A.D. 32 and July A.D. 33. Further, the Nativity is between July, 9 B.C., and July, 8 B.C., and the Magi's visit between July, 7 B.C., and July, 6 B.C.

The reader will see that all the dates of recent investigators agree with Epiphanius.

Our Lord attained His twelfth birthday in May A.D. 5, so that He attended His first Passover in A.D. 6, i.e. in the 10th[3] year after Herod's death.

All the statements we have so far extracted are clear and consistent. What remains might seem at first sight puzzling, but on examination proves invaluable for the light it throws on our author's methods, his weakness and his strength. Augustus' first year after Julius Caesar's assassination runs from July, 44 B.C., to July, 43 B.C. His forty-second year therefore is from July, 3 B.C., to July, 2 B.C. This agrees with the computation accepted by Clement, which was arrived at by reckoning exactly thirty years back from the date of the Baptism as sometimes computed. Epiphanius has reproduced this dating from some author he had read, but is quite unaware that it is irreconcilable with his previous statements.

As to the last synchronism another passage explains what might otherwise be thought mere fatuity. In *Anacephaleosis*, 1119 (Migne 1), Epiphanius writes:

---

[1] Or just possibly the Seleucid New Year in April.
[2] This agrees with Josephus' statement that he was deposed in his tenth year. Josephus reckons the year from Herod's death in March, 4 B.C.
[3] Petavius' suggested emendation to 12th is otiose and ill founded.

Τῷ γὰρ τριακοστῷ τρίτῳ Ἡρώδου, τεσσαρακοστῷ δὲ δευτέρῳ
Αὐγούστου τοῦ βασιλέως γεννᾶται ὁ Σωτὴρ ἐν Βηθλεὲμ τῆς Ἰουδαίας.
Κάτεισι δὲ εἰς Αἴγυπτον τῷ τριακοστῷ πέμπτῳ Ἡρώδου· ἄνεισι δὲ ἀπ᾽
Αἰγύπτου μετὰ τὴν Ἡρώδου τελευτήν. Δι᾽ ὧν ἐπὶ τριάκοντα ἑπτὰ ἔτεσι τῆς
αὐτῆς τοῦ Ἡρώδου ἀρχῆς ἦν ὁ παῖς τεσσάρων ἐτων, ὅτε Ἡρώδης τριακοστὸν
ἕβδομον πληρώσας κατέστρεψε τὸν βίον. Ἀρχέλαος δὲ ἐννέα ἔτη βασι-
λεύει. . . .

Ἀρχέλαος δὲ γεννᾷ τὸν Ἡρώδην τὸν νεώτερον καὶ Ἡρώδης τῷ ἐννάτῳ
ἔτει τῆς τοῦ πατρὸς Βασιλείας Ἀρχελάου κατὰ διαδοχήν. Καὶ γέγονε
λογιζόμενα δεκατρία ἔτη τῇ ἐνσάρκῳ Χριστοῦ παρουσίᾳ. Ὀκτωκαιδεκάτῳ
δὲ ἔτει Ἡρώδου τοῦ ἐπικληθέντος Ἀγρίππα, ἤρξατο ὁ Ἰησοῦς τοῦ
κηρύγματος. . . .

Ἔπειτα ἀντιλεγόμενος ἐκήρυξεν ἐνιαυτον δεκτόν· καὶ γέγονεν ἐννεα-
καίδεκα ἔτη τῷ αὐτῷ Ἡρώδῃ, τῷ δὲ Σωτῆρι τριακοστὸν δεύτερον. Ἐν
δὲ τῷ εἰκοστῷ ἔτει Ἡρώδου τοῦ τετράρχου καλουμένου γίνεται τὸ σωτήριον
πάθος. . . .

We have here a typical example of Epiphanius' work: he
testifies to two solid facts to which he holds firmly, but his
deductions from them exhibit the confusions of his memory.
The two facts are that our Lord was born between July, 9 B.C.,
and July, 8 B.C., and he was crucified three years after he was
baptised. Unfortunately Epiphanius has remembered Luke's
rough statement that our Lord was about thirty years of age at
his baptism. Consequently he reckons the baptism to have
occurred between July A.D. 22 and July A.D. 23, so that His
preaching in Galilee began after July A.D. 23, and the Passion
between July A.D. 25 and A.D. 26. Remembering also that some
Herod was reigning at this time, Epiphanius has confusedly
made him to be Herod Agrippa, has then supposed him to be
Archelaus' son and to have immediately succeeded his father on
the throne about April A.D. 6. He thus arrives at the astonishing
dates indicated above. It will be noticed that this confirms my
suggestion in the *Expository Times, loc. cit.*, that Irenaeus by a
similar process had arrived at A.D. 23 as the date of the baptism,
and because he knew the true date of the Crucifixion in A.D. 33
supposed the Ministry to have lasted ten years.

(5)

It is now possible to see the source and the course of the
confused and confusing theories which have been proposed as

to the various Gospel dates. It will be simplest summarily to indicate our certainties, after which it may be said that little discussion will be needed.

To begin with, then, the Hebrew Christians knew that the Nativity occurred in 8 B.C., the Baptism in mid-winter, apparently A.D. 29–30, and the Crucifixion in A.D. 33. In all probability they also knew that the Nativity took place at the time of Pentecost, the Baptism about the full moon in Tebet (the 4th Jewish month) and the Crucifixion on the day before the Passover.

When Luke prepared to bring the events of the Gospel into the chronological framework of the Gentile world, he was so far defeated in his purpose that he could not give our Lord's age at His baptism more definitely than by the words "As it were thirty years." Unfortunately Luke's prestige as a trustworthy historian led to his statements being handled with the utmost reverence. This resulted in two opposite conclusions, equally disastrous. Both made Luke affirm that the interval between the Nativity and the Baptism was exactly thirty years. As we have seen, St. Irenaeus therefore placed the Baptism in A.D. 23 (we cannot guess how he made this Tiberius' fifteenth year) and consequently believed that the Lord's public Ministry lasted for ten years.

Tertullian knew that the Hebrew Christian tradition was perfectly correct that our Lord was born in 8 B.C., and without being disturbed by Luke's assertion declared plainly that the census was that directed by Saturninus, i.e. in 9–8 B.C.

Various prominent leaders amongst the Gentile Christians converted the dates preserved from the Jewish calendar into Egyptian dates. Accordingly for the Nativity we have dates corresponding to 15 or 16 April or 16 May (the difference depends upon whether there was in 8 B.C. an intercalary month in the Jewish calendar). They also computed that Passover fell in A.D. 33 on the night of Friday–Saturday, 3–4 April. Most of them, however, were daunted by Luke's statement of our Lord's age at His baptism, and to make things worse, inferred from the Lucan text ("the acceptable year of the Lord") that the Crucifixion took place about fifteen months after the Baptism.

In A.D. 30 Passover may have fallen on Saturday, 7 April[1]; and they consequently concluded that the Baptism was in the mid-winter of A.D. 28–29. They then calculated our Lord's birth to have been about the beginning of 2 B.C., and this Clement of Alexandria follows. Moreover, as the *Pistis Sophia* shows these writers equated the full moon of Tebet with the mid-month of the Egyptian Tybi (the dates coalesced in December A.D. 44, the day when in the *Pistis Sophia* our Lord spoke finally to his apostles). In consequence, as Clement tells us, 15 Tybi became the commonly accepted date for the Baptism and, following upon this, the date for the Nativity. Hence Clement accepts the view that 6 January 2 B.C.[2] is the date of the Nativity. The Alexandrian calendar, like the Julian, taking this date for the Nativity gives the same day and month thirty years later for the Baptism. The Egyptian calendar makes 15 Tybi correspond to 28–29 December in the year of the Baptism, and Clement mentions that alternatively some computers had arrived at 24–25 December for this.

We need not follow further the strange vagaries into which later writers were led. It will suffice to say that owing to the nature of the Egyptian calendar the date 6 January in 2 B.C. becomes, as we have just indicated, 28–29 December in the winter A.D. 29–30, and other calculators chose 24–25 December. The consequences that have followed are plain to see, and to repeat the point, the whole confusion has sprung from an unwarranted attribution of exactitude to Luke's statement, and that despite his express repudiation of such precision. When justice is done to him and to the Hebrew Christian memory, everything falls into place.

By way of corollary it may be of convenience to note, even though they cannot here be discussed, the resulting dates for Josephus.[3] He posits 1 Nisan 40 B.C. as the commencement of Herod's *de jure* reign before the end of the 184th Olympiad in

[1] Uncertain as to possible intercalation in the Jewish calendar for this year, some writers calculated 8 March for the Crucifixion. This is a Wednesday, and Clement accepted the alternative of 7 April.

[2] Clement dates it in Augustus' 28th year, i.e. between 1 Thoth (August) 3 B.C. and 1 Thoth 2 B.C.

[3] The relevant passages with their interpretative and calibrating contexts are to be seen in *B.J.* I: 7, 15–19, 33; II: 1, 7, 8: *Ant.* XIV: 4, 14–16; XV: 1, 5; XVII: 8, 11, 13: *Dion.* XXXVII: 16; XLIX: 22; LV: 25, 27.

6*

July 40, and 1 Nisan 37 B.C. as the commencement of his *de facto*
reign, which he reckons from the time when Herod had compassed Antigonus' death. This death occurred some considerable
time after the Temple was stormed on the day of the Fast in the
third month (perhaps Siwan, as W. Whiston pointed out, which
would make it 24 May, and not the Day of Atonement, as
Turner[1] thought) in 37 B.C., when men were feeling the
scarcity of food following on the sabbatical abstention from
sowing in the previous autumn. Hence Antigonus was murdered
not earlier than in the late autumn of 37 B.C. and Josephus,
taking a legitimist's view, dates Herod's accession from it when
the Consuls of that year were holding office. On the other hand,
Sosius and Herod began the siege at least five months before
the Temple was taken. Dion Cassius states that, towards the end
of 38, Antony appointed Sosius governor of Syria, and that
subsequently he and Herod invested Jerusalem, captured it (as
Josephus tells us) after a long siege and later sent Antigonus to
Antony, who finally killed him. By inclusive reckoning[2]
twenty-seven years to the day elapsed between Pompey's
capture of the Temple in 63 B.C. and Herod's in 37 B.C.
Augustus' victory at Actium in September, 31 B.C., was seven
years after Herod's *de facto* reign began.

Herod's death was in the first fortnight of Nisan 4 B.C., when
he had reigned thirty-seven years *de jure* and thirty-four *de facto*.
His son Archelaus was deposed about May in A.D. 6, in his
tenth year if his reign be reckoned from 1 Nisan 4 B.C. a few
days before his father's death, and in his ninth year if it be
reckoned from 1 Nisan 3 B.C., the first New Year after his father's
death. Herod's work upon the Temple began between 1 Nisan 23
and 1 Nisan 22 B.C., and since it was completed in eight years
ended in 16–15 B.C.[3]

(6)

Confirmation of the belief that the date of the Nativity was
16–17 May 8 B.C. is not far to seek. Obstetric tables[4] show that

[1] See his article "The Chronology of the New Testament" in *Hastings'*
D.B., vol. 1, pp. 403–24.

[2] This illustrates and explains Clement's reckoning the interval from the
Baptism to the investment of Jerusalem as 42 years 3 months.

[3] See Josephus, *Ant.*, xv, 11, § 1 and 5; *B.J.*, 1, 21.

[4] See too Halliday Sutherland, *Laws of Life*.

to satisfy this date the Annunciation must be placed roundly between 8 and 23 August 9 B.C. From this it follows that Zacharias' week of duty in the Temple must be from Saturday morning, 27 January, to Friday evening, 2 February, in the same year, and not one of the earlier or later weeks when he was on duty (it should perhaps be mentioned that these dates have been computed by scholars from Josephus' statement as to the priestly course which had just come on duty when Titus invested Jerusalem in A.D. 70). It results from this, according to our obstetric tables, that the Baptist was born roughly between 25 October and 10 November. These limits we can confirm and perhaps further reduce. The Annunciation was in Elizabeth's sixth month, i.e. roughly 11 to 26 August or more probably 2 to 18 August. Luke states that after the Annunciation Mary went in haste to her cousin and remained with her three months. If we give its precise value to this statement, we have for the date of the end of the visit a range of roughly from 7 to 22 November or perhaps more probably from 1 to 17 November. Using these several computations to check one another we get for the date of the Baptist's birth the same range as was suggested above, i.e. 25 October to 10 November, if, as Luke may be thought to imply, the Virgin's visit ended before the child was born or soon after his circumcision.

So far we have based our calculations on the testimony of Luke, and in pursuance of Clement of Alexandria's statement. Surprisingly enough, however, corroboration of our dates is to be found from another quarter. The Apocryphal Protevangelium of James makes Herod's massacre of the Holy Innocents occur before the Baptist was two years old and a few days before or during another week of duty for Zacharias. Now the Syrian Church has consistently asserted that the visit of the Magi was in our Lord's second year of life, and Epiphanius so dates it that it must be subsequent to July, 7 B.C. Further, Kepler, who was familiar with the old astrological rules, declared that after two significant planetary aspects in previous months the most startling and striking conjunction occurred in October, 7 B.C. More recently Neugebauer has determined with our latest and most improved astronomical tables[1] that the date of this

---

[1] See Neugebauer, *Tafeln für Sonne, Planeten und Mond*, Leipzig, 1914, pp. 18 ff.

occurrence was 27 October 7 B.C. Moreover, in that month Venus began to appear as a morning star, and there can be no doubt that Matthew's "in the east" is to be rightly interpreted to mean that the star's heliacal rising was then visible. Venus would then be in Trine with the three planets Jupiter, Saturn and Mars, which were then in Pisces, the sign which dominates Judea. In marvellous agreement with this is the fact that Zacharias would be on duty from 31 October to 6 November, so that the arrival of the Magi and the Massacre may be placed before 6 November, when, as we have seen above, the Baptist may well be just under two years old. Assuming then that there is some historical foundation for the statements of the Protevangelium we shall be inclined to date the Baptist's birth nearer 10 November than the other limit of 25 October.

Yet another interesting circumstance deserves our attention. The supreme combination of planetary aspects occurred in October, 7 B.C., and, although various suggestive combinations occurred at intervals in previous months, it was in late November, 9 B.C., that Mars and Venus were in anything like a similar relation, and this relation did not recur till October, 7 B.C. We can understand therefore why the Magi gave such an answer to Herod's enquiry about the Star's first appearance as led to him deciding that any child of two years old and under must be got rid of. Accordingly the Baptist's birth was, as we have seen, too near the limit for him to be safe. These converging facts may be taken mutually to confirm one another and to establish the correctness of our chronology.

The following timetable may be suggested:

24 October, The Sabbath.
25   ,,   Sunday.   Herod consults the Scribes.
26   ,,   Monday.   The Magi proceed to Bethlehem.
27   ,,   Tuesday.   Having seen the star [1] they do homage to the Babe.
28   ,,   Wednesday. They return another way.
29   ,,   Thursday. The Holy Family start for Egypt.
30   ,,   Friday.   Herod, disappointed, sends soldiers to Bethlehem.
31   ,,   The Sabbath. Zacharias on duty.

[1] As to the divine condescension to meet men's ignorance, see Bishop Gore's argument in *Belief in God* and *The Holy Spirit*.

1 November, Sunday. Zacharias is interrogated about his son.
2   „   Monday. Zacharias is murdered[1] for denying all knowledge
          of his son's hiding place.

Professor Lauth of Munich (as Canon Peter Green recalls in his *Some Gospel Scenes and Characters*) suggested that the heliacal rising of Sirius on 1 Mesori would be noted in some quarters as the sign that a Great King was born. This gives the date 21 July 9 B.C. and its three following anniversaries.

Confirmatory of this computation is a corollary naturally attaching to an observation of Edersheim. He states that a widow's marriage always took place on a Thursday, a spinster's (and he makes no question that it was a spinster who was married at Cana) on a Wednesday. Accordingly, he makes the deputation from Jerusalem visit the Baptist on the preceding Thursday, and our Lord's return after his fast he assigns to the Friday. If this be correct, our Lord's baptism forty days earlier would have taken place on a Sunday, and 8 January A.D. 30 was on a Sunday. This unexpected concurrence with the evidence from the date of the full moon goes some way to warrant the conclusion that this is the true historical date of the Baptism.

(7)

We must now make our attempt to set out the historical dating of the chief events in the Gospel story.

9 B.C. 27 January (Saturday) to 2 February (Friday). Zacharias on duty in the Temple.

Between 3 August and 31 August. The Annunciation.

Between 1 November and 16 November. John the Baptist born.

8 B.C. 16 May (Friday)[2] before 3 a.m. The Nativity (see note A).

7 B.C. 23–28 October. The Magi's visit.

4 B.C. March. Herod's death: subsequently Archelaus succeeded.

---

[1] On the general question of what historical value is to be attached to the books of the Apocryphal New Testament something has been said on another page (see p. 200). As to Zacharias' murder we must notice that Christ's words, "whom ye slew," which make it the *terminus ad quem* for all the sheddings of righteous blood, are puzzling if they refer, as has been generally thought, to an event of several centuries earlier. They gain arresting force and significance if they are to be understood as the Protevangelium tells the story.

[2] If the day were Saturday, 17 May, the words in John vii. 22 had a special applicability to Christ's own case.

A.D. 6   Christ's first Passover: Archelaus deposed: first Roman census.
A.D. 29 Late summer. John's call to preach and baptize (see note B).
A.D. 30 8 January (Sunday). The Baptism (see note C).
         17 February (Friday). End of the Forty Days' Fast.
         22 February (Wednesday). Marriage at Cana.
         8–9 March. Passover night (see note D).
         Late summer. Journey through Sychar to Cana (see note E).
         December. John imprisoned.
A.D. 31 3 or 10 March. Walk through the cornfields.
         17 March. The withered hand restored (see note F).
         17 May (Saturday), Pentecost. Healing at the pool of Bethzatha.
         John beheaded:
         Parable of the Sower.
A.D. 32 The Twelve sent out as missioners.
         March. Feeding of the Five Thousand.
         August. The Transfiguration.
         9–16 September. Feast of Tabernacles.
         16 December. Feast of Dedication.
A.D. 33 3 February. Feast of Purim.
         21 March. (1 Nisan).
         3 April. The Crucifixion (see note G).
         3–4 April. The Passover.
         5 April. The Resurrection.
         14 May. The Ascension.
         24 May. Whitsunday.

One patent fact demands more attention than it has ordinarily received. It was on the anniversary of the best attested date of the Nativity that the Holy Ghost descended upon the church.

Later and less alert chronographers dated the Baptism (when the Holy Ghost descended upon our Lord) as taking place on the anniversary (in the Egyptian calendar) of the Nativity.

No clearer illustration could be found of the utter dissimilarity between the vague vestiges of tradition in the sense that word connotes for us and the precise and pondered paradosis of the Christian teachers given to their catechumens. Neither Mark in his written collection of *chreiai* repeated by Peter, nor Matthew and Luke in their narratives, nor John in his recollections, mentioned this calendar point, and we see the result at once. Since the Church grafted its religious uses in the first instance on those of Judaism the dates for Passover and Pentecost alone were of special significance and were

calculated according to the Jewish lunar calendar. But the
tradition attaching to the date of the Nativity supplied those
who had command of the Egyptian calendar with a date in
8 B.C. which corresponds with our 17 May or 16 April. This
made against the adoption of any fixed day in any solar calendar
for Christmas. Again for the Baptism the full moon in the
Jewish month Tebet was given some stability by placing it on
15 Tybi, i.e. 28 December in A.D. 29 or 30. Then this, mingling
with an unwarrantable hardening and intensification of Luke's
rough and round numbering, fixed the birthday on that time
in 2 B.C. But the vagrant Egyptian year did not satisfy those
who had now learnt the Julian, and thus instead of 15 Tybi of
the Egyptians 11 Tybi of the Alexandrians was noted and this
once noted gave ground for placing Christmas on the night of
December 24–25.

Note A

Sufficient reason has been given by Professor Ramsay and others to make
it permissible for us to accept the Lucan statement that our Lord was born
at Bethlehem at the time of one of the fourteen-year censuses ordered by
Augustus and to place this not in A.D. 6 but in 9 to 8 B.C., perhaps, the
Professor suggested, when Quirinius was holding a military command in
Syria during Sentius Saturninus' civil governorship. Moreover, Lt.-Col.
Mackinlay has shown that the time of year implied by Luke is somewhere
between April and October, and that the crowded hostelry suggests one of
the great festival times. We know that flocks were sent out of the folds
altogether after Passover but brought in at night from about October before
the "former rain." We also know that a year was allowed for people to
register themselves and we may go further and accept dates given by
Clement of Alexandria as based upon sound tradition. For the Nativity he
gives a day which would be 16–17 May if the year were 8 B.C., and this day
would be, as calculation shows, Pentecost in that year. As we have seen
above, Epiphanius is explicit in dating the Nativity between July, 9 B.C.,
and July, 8 B.C. Clement's date of 6 January 2 B.C. is negatived not only by
Matthew but by Luke, who shows, since Zacharias's vision would seem to
be in Herod's reign, that the Nativity was not later than May, 3 B.C.

Tertullian states that the Nativity fell in the census taken when P. Sentius
Saturninus was proconsul of Syria. In the *Journal of Roman Studies*, vol. XXIV,
(1934), pp. 43 ff., Fr. Corbishley had shown that Quirinius may have been
proconsul for the first time just before Saturninus, so that Quirinius began
the arrangements for the census which Saturninus completed. Thus the
census would be taken presumably between the summer of 9 and the
summer of 8 B.C. (Herod, it may be presumed, appeared as the immediate
authority ordering the census, so that it was not resented as was that of

fourteen years later.) Further, since men had to register at their paternal or ancestral homes (this apparently being the rule as we know it was for registration in Egypt), registration could be most conveniently carried out at one of the great Jewish feasts, when multitudes returned to Palestine from wherever they had settled. The crowds at the inn would be due to the Festival, Bethlehem, like Bethany, being as it were a dormitory village for Jerusalem. A Syrian Chronicle assigned to the seventh century records what is still a tradition in the Syrian Jacobite Church, that after the Nativity the Holy Family returned to Nazareth. There they stayed for two years (i.e. more than a year), when they revisited Bethlehem, where the Magi found them.

Note B

Luke says that ἐν τῷ βαπτισθῆναι ἅπαντα τὸν λαὸν Jesus was baptized. This certainly must mean that the Baptism was some time after the Baptist began his Ministry, and if, as all readers in Clement's time understood Luke to mean, his Ministry began between the end of August, 28 and the end of August, 29, we shall naturally suppose our Lord's Baptism to have taken place not at the end of 28 but at the end of 29 or the beginning of 30, since, even if we boggle at Clement's computation of the year, all the patristic evidence is unanimous in fixing the end of December or the beginning of January for the month and day. In that case we shall suppose the Baptist's mission to have opened towards the end of Tiberius' fifteenth year, i.e. about August A.D. 29. As Dr. Badcock has argued, he would secure the attention of the people as they flocked up to the feast—in this case, of Tabernacles.

Note C

When 15 Tebet was mistakenly treated as 15 Tybi the Nativity was reckoned to be 5–6 January 2 B.C. according to the Egyptian calendar, or 11 Tybi in the Alexandrian. The Egyptian 15 Tybi gave for the Baptism 28–29 December in A.D. 29 or 30, and when 11 Tybi was mistakenly thought to be a correction of the Egyptian 15 Tybi, the Baptism date was fixed as 24–25 December. Some ancient writers accepting 11 Tybi as a true correction, substituted 2 January for Clement's 6 January: Hippolytus at one time adopted the former date, the Cappadocians permanently observed the latter. In the West the mistaken day 25 December was substituted for Clement's mistaken 6 January as the date of the Nativity and was finally carried over to New Rome in St. Chrysostom's time as a truer correction, though its parent 6 January retained its hold as the day of the Epiphany. It was reserved for Hippolytus to make one further venture, and, having learnt in Rome that the Baptism was on 25 December, to place the Crucifixion three solar months later on 25 March.

Note D

Clement dates the Crucifixion on Friday 7 April A.D. 30, but unless the Passover was wrongly celebrated a day later than it should have been [1] this would make the Last Supper identical with the Passover in contradiction of John and, as we have claimed, Luke also. Moreover, in that case the priests must, after all, have put Christ to death on the day of the Feast.

As regards the year of the Baptism, two observations must be made:

(1) Our explanation of Luke's round estimate of Christ's age at His Baptism as about thirty years is strengthened if we are right in believing that Quirinius not only organized the census in A.D. 6 but also made the preliminary arrangements with Herod for the census in 9 B.C. An alternative explanation perhaps deserves to be recorded. In some Greek writing the symbol Z was interposed before a numeral to show that a figure was following. Thus we have *Ζφ for δηνάρια (numbers begin) φ in C.I.G. 1992.3265. If Luke wrote ΖΛ (=37), it might have been misread as "(numbers begin) 30."

(2) The statement in John ii. 20, generally understood to mean that the building of the Temple had taken forty-six years, requires a brief comment. Abbott suggested that the years are reckoned wrongly from the second year of Cyrus' reign over Anshan instead of the second year after his conquest of Babylon. He argued that the Jews would not have been content to regard the Temple as a new erection by Herod. He made the forty-six years run from 559 to 513 B.C. Attempts have been made to use the passage as a means for determining the date of the Passover at which the controversy occurred. To quote words in *The Expository Times*, vol. L, June 1939, p. 421, "Turner reckoned from the time that Herod began his extension of the Second Temple and this he placed in 20–19 B.C. Later investigators [2] have demonstrated that his arguments are untenable and that this date must be 23–22 B.C. Further, Turner disregarded Josephus' clear statement that Herod's building was completed in eight years. Nevertheless the dative case remains a difficulty. It can hardly allow the translation 'the work of building lasted through forty-six years,' nor, again, according to the ordinary use 'forty-six years ago the work was finished.' The uses of the dative are to express: (1) time when, (2) time within which and (3) time before or after some date. The second use is entirely consonant with Abbott's view. The work of building had interruptions, but its commencement and its end were separated by forty-six years. The third use may conceivably be invoked to yield the sense of 'forty-six years ago' if we supply e.g. an unexpressed πρὸ τοῦ νῦν, 'before this present time.' This second interpretation is indeed unsatisfactory from the standpoint of sense. The riposte is so oblique as to be, to most Western minds, inept and pointless. Rabbinic arguments, however,

[1] See Burnaby, *The Jewish and Muhammedan Calendars*. As stated on page 148 above, the moon was full on the night of 6 April at 10 hours 18 minutes p.m. at Jerusalem, and, as Philo tells us, the Jewish day (Thursday evening to Friday evening) would accordingly be 15 Nisan.

[2] Fr. T. Corbishley in *Journal of Theological Studies*, XXXVI, pp. 22–32, Jan. 1935, and Dr. F. J. Badcock in *The Expository Times*, XLVII, p. 40, Oct. 1935. The former has certainly explained the discrepancies in Josephus' statement of Herod's regnal years. They countenanced the feasibility of Abbott's hypothesis.

are not always logical in the Western sense." On this interpretation Herod's building was finished between Nisan, 16 B.C. and Nisan, 15 B.C., and the Passover when the words were spoken was in A.D. 30. It may well be judged mere perversity and temerity to advocate a third and different interpretation. Nevertheless it is right to mention it. In the spring of 63 B.C. Pompey made his way into the Temple and indeed into the Holy of Holies. This, we may be sure, was not without damage to the fabric and fittings. The Jews, we may assume, would work to repair and renovate as they had opportunity. Herod the Great took the work methodically in hand and completed an enlargement and magnificent embellishment of the entire Temple. If the first repairs were attempted in 63–62 B.C., this gives forty-six years as the time within which the rebuilding was done. This suits the dative case, and, however much we may be disappointed to lose the hope of eliciting from the statement the date of its utterance, the reference to the time taken in building gives more point to the Jews' scornful scoff.

Note E

From the second century it has been a matter of discussion whether our Lord's words, "Say not ye that there are yet four months and then cometh harvest," give an indication of the time of year or quote a proverb. In the former case we must extend our Lord's Ministry by the Jordan from June to December. Broadly speaking, in Palestine besides the "former rains" about the end of October, gentle rains fall about the middle of February, after which spring commences, and the corn which is a considerable height in March is cut in May. The lands round the Sea of Galilee, however, have a sub-tropical climate.

In the slough of chronological uncertainty which lies between Nicodemus' clandestine visit and the feeding of the five thousand the appearance of any stepping-stone is welcome which promises to be of help towards the gauging and bridging of the interval. Besides the words, "Yet four months and then cometh harvest" and "the fields . . . are white already to harvest" and the reference to an unnamed feast when the man was healed at Bethzatha, there are two indications of date which deserve exploration. The first is to be found in the Baptist's words, "He must increase but I must decrease." It has been remarked,[1] and the remark would seem to be still more applicable to men of early times than to ourselves, that men of action far more than the sedentary student draw the images for the expression and illustration of their thought from the objects which present themselves immediately to their senses. The student may draw upon his recollections of imagery employed by the authors he has read; the man of action derives his language from what he sees or hears himself. On the lowest estimate, therefore, the

[1] Mackinlay noted this, but under the spell of Turner's pronouncement that the Crucifixion was on 18 March A.D. 29, he dated the period of Venus' appearance as a morning star from October A.D. 26 to July, 27. The other periods about this time are from May, 28 to February, 29, and from August, 31 to May, 32—neither of which is of any service to us.

Baptist's words may be regarded as indicating the possibility that he had for some time been observing the planet Venus ushering in the dawn and fading into obscurity as the day-star rose upon the world. Now it is at least remarkable that the heliacal rising of Venus occurred approximately on 5 January in A.D. 30, and that that planet remained a morning star until the beginning of October. As the reader will remember, we have already from entirely distinct premises arrived at 5 January A.D. 30 as the approximate date of our Lord's Baptism, and if that date be accepted the Baptist's words may naturally be taken to indicate some reflections of his upon the relation between him and our Lord, in which he saw the spiritual equivalent of the astronomical phenomenon he was witnessing at that very time. It is then, it may be submitted, a justifiable conclusion that these words of the Baptist were uttered in the summer or autumn of A.D. 30. The second possible indication of date is to be found in the fact of the Baptist's murder following upon Herod's birthday. It would appear that the imprisonment was consequent upon Herod and Herodias' resentment of the Baptist's condemnation of their union. It may be conjectured, therefore, that John's imprisonment lasted less than twelve months, since it may be guessed that Herodias would not have allowed the opportunity of Herod's birthday to pass without compassing her enemy's murder—in other words, there were not two birthdays of Herod during John's imprisonment. After the murder, when the Twelve were sent out on a mission, the stir they caused throughout the country led Herod to the conviction that John was risen from the dead. The Twelve returned from their mission shortly before the Passover of A.D. 32, and therefore to allow time for their mission and yet for the murder to be near enough to disturb Herod's conscience, we are driven to fix Herod's birthday in the neighbourhood of November, and accordingly the Baptist's imprisonment about December A.D. 30. In this case we shall have here further confirmation of the view that our Lord passed through Samaria in December.

Note F

The remarkable accuracy of what may be called the secondary reading in Acts xxviii. 16 may be thought to justify us in attaching weight to the secondary reading in Luke vi. 1 where "first in a second series" can, in spite of much discussion, hardly mean anything but first in the second half of the year, i.e. the first Sabbath in Nisan—unless, indeed, it might conceivably mean the first Sabbath in the second month, which would make it four weeks later, i.e. 14 April.

Note G

19 Pharmuthi might be acceptable as the day of the Crucifixion in A.D. 32, were it not that it is not a Friday. On the other hand, if we take H. Browne's emendation to 9 Pharmuthi, all becomes harmonious. The Crucifixion was on Friday 3 April A.D. 33. But something more may be added. A scrutiny of Clement's figures for the length of the reigns of the Roman emperors Gaius, Titus and Domitian seems to show, as we have said, that he evaluated his

Roman dates by means of the Alexandrian calendar and that he placed the extra day to equate the Roman bissextile in the year following the Roman leap year. In that case this date for the Crucifixion would in A.D. 33 be 10 Pharmuthi, in the following years 9 Pharmuthi and in A.D. 36 and 37 10 Pharmuthi. This gives an explanation of the manuscript 19. It must be understood to mean that the date was, in the Alexandrian reckoning, now the 10th and now the 9th day of Pharmuthi. Even if this reckoning of the Alexandrian intercalation be rejected, it would still be the case that in the Roman leap year the date was the 10th and in other years the 9th of Pharmuthi. It should be added that in leap years the Alexandrian date 9 Pharmuthi would equate with 2 April, the date chosen by the Cappadocians.

For the date of the Crucifixion one curious piece of undesigned evidence must not be overlooked. On the morning of Pentecost Peter, in his address to the multitude, quoted Joel's words, "The Sun shall be turned into darkness and the Moon into blood before that great and notable day of the Lord come." The cursory reader passes by these words with easy inattention. He regards them as a vague apocalyptic portraiture of catastrophic terrors which the prophet associates with the Lord's ultimate advent. Serious consideration, however, shows that for the apostle and for his audience the words gave an exact and recognizable account of definite and unmistakable occurrences which would usher in the universal outpouring of the divine Spirit. Only because the multitude were convinced that they had recently witnessed phenomena which tallied with the prophet's words would they have adhered, as they did, to the faith that the Jesus who had been crucified was indeed the Christ. Plainly, in their belief there had been a vivid and vital verification of the prophet's presage, so that they saw the rest of his message realized in the tumultuous utterances of the Christian believers. Of the two portents mentioned by Joel the former was seen in the darkness which lay over the land on Good Friday for three hours. This fact is recorded by all the evangelists, and since it occurred in the daytime, it necessarily was a darkening of sunlight and not moonlight. It is to be remarked, however, in passing, that it is some argument for the identification of the author of the Third Gospel with the author of the Acts of the Apostles that this Gospel is at pains to emphasize that the sunlight failed, the author indeed using an expression the habitual meaning of which is that there was a solar eclipse. Following upon this, various questions invite consideration: was the author, as tradition will have it, Luke the Physician? If it was, did not his scientific training include astronomy, at least so far as to make him aware that a solar eclipse occurs at the time of the new moon? If he knew this, was his mind so off its guard that he forgot that the Passover is on the night of the full moon? It would be out of place here to discuss these questions: the essential point for us is that the midday darkness of Good Friday was admittedly susceptible of being regarded as corresponding with Joel's words. Unfortunately for our purpose, since it was not an eclipse, the date of its occurrence cannot be determined. So far as it is concerned, the Crucifixion might have taken place in any year. Very different is the position in regard to the second of Joel's portents. In A.D. 33 on the evening of Friday, 3 April, there was a large eclipse of the moon. If this was the date of the Crucifixion the midday darkness followed a few hours later by this lunar eclipse must have received attention and may unquestionably have supplied to Peter and to his hearers a startling warrant for believing that "the notable day of the Lord" had come. Nothing of the kind is to be found in either 29 or 30, the two years generally advocated as alternative dates to A.D. 33. The conclusion then seems inevitable that the true date is, as we have suggested, 3 April A.D. 33.

Chapter Four

THE UNIQUE CONCEPTION

THE first preachers of the Gospel were concerned to urge that the Resurrection of the crucified Lord was the vindication of His authority and teaching. It was the divine will that men should enter the Jewish congregation or fellowship as reformed by our Lord, to lead a new life within that society; thus exhibiting to the world the working in a macrocosm of the spirit in which our Lord had lived His personal life on earth. Christians, however, almost immediately began to ask for as much information as possible about the Lord in whom they had believed. They welcomed reminiscences of His sayings, His actions, His habits and soon they asked about the way in which He had entered upon His Ministry. He had not, they were assured, appeared suddenly amongst men, a prophet in the prime of life or a demigod. True, the first preachers had begun their history with the Baptist's mission; but in as early an Epistle as that to the Galatians, Paul said, "God sent forth His Son, born of a woman." Some memories, therefore, of our Lord's birth, infancy and early years would be recoverable. Accordingly, two complementary accounts were in circulation within a few years, and certainly soon after the middle of the first century, while many of those who were cognizant of the facts were still alive. One of these accounts would seem to emanate from the family of St. Joseph, the other from that of our Lord's mother. Both accounts agree that our Lord was not the naturally born son of St. Joseph and his wife. In Luke's record there is to be noticed a pregnant saying of the Blessed Virgin, which is best interpreted as implying that St. Joseph was unable or unwilling to consummate her marriage or that she herself was vowed to celibacy, although she was betrothed. The words manifestly cohere with the Catholic belief that the Lord was uniquely born without a human father, and they are at the least consonant with the view that His mother bore no children afterwards and further perhaps that St. Joseph was childless. In the Matthean record two details deserve consideration. When the Magi came to Bethlehem, we may suppose about eighteen months after the Nativity, there is no hint of the expectation or of the presence of any other children of St. Joseph, and after Herod's death when the Holy Family returned to Palestine and then to Nazareth, it is the same. Again when our Lord went up to Jerusalem for His first Passover, there is no suggestion either of younger brothers and sisters or of older members of the household. These three facts, however, point to the conclusion that no later children were born to the Blessed Virgin rather than confirm the belief that St. Joseph was not our Lord's father. There remain two passages in the Fourth Gospel which invite examination:

(*a*) When our Lord told the Jews that Abraham was not their father, they replied, "*We* were not born of fornication," where the emphatic pronoun gets justice done to it if the words be taken to insinuate an innuendo that the Lord was so born.

(*b*) When the Jews asked, "Where is Thy father?" we must, it would appear, regard them either as contemptuously humouring one whom they supposed to be demented or as believing Him to be aware that someone other than St. Joseph was His father.

There are those who are satisfied that the biologist can make as irrefragable assertions as can the mathematician. Yet while it is proper that we should accept in faith the verifiable conclusions drawn by scientists from the observations of phenomena in every department of knowledge, it is also proper to retain an agnostic scepticism as a reserve with which to meet the possibilities of additional observations or interpretations of observations which may be subversive of hitherto accepted conclusions.

We have seen in the last half-century too many examples of fresh observation or facts demolishing rigid assertions for us to accept as infallible the scientific "laws" formulated today. They may presently need to be so modified as to upset entirely conclusions which have been rested upon them. After the eruption of Krakatoa in 1883 physicists denied the possibility of the wonderful sunsets seen in the next three years being the consequences of that event, yet later a Committee of Scientists reported upon the matter that "nothing[1] can be said to be absolutely incredible in science until it has been proved to be absolutely impossible." Thus our faith in the current doctrines of science, whether natural science, literary criticism or historical investigation, should, if we are wise, always be tinctured with a spice of cautious agnosticism. There is, however, one still more important aspect of the matter.

Science, it is sometimes said, furnishes an intellectual certainty because its theories can always be verified by experiment and repetition. What truth is in this statement is subject to considerable limitations. In astronomy, geology and biology, although many accepted theories may be regarded as incontestable, experiment to repeat an event is often impossible. The moon no doubt was ejected from the earth's substance millenniums ago, but we cannot stage a repetition of that happening. Catastrophic earthquakes have plainly occurred at various times, and while we can accept many inferences in regard to their nature and consequences, we cannot demonstrate their truth by experiment on an equal scale. It results that a pyrrhonistic attitude is rational when we are dealing with matters which fall within the province of such physical sciences. Their positive assertions may be in the highest degree probable, but they cannot have mathematical certainty. A new observation may make it necessary for a long-accepted theory to be modified. Quite recently the suggestion has been made that locusts arise by an abnormal mutation under certain conditions from grasshoppers. Such a mutation, if it should prove to be a fact, would necessitate the recasting of some accepted "laws" in ecology and a restatement of our present theories in regard to the inheritance of acquired characters. Marconi's experiments were made in defiance of the unhesitating and positive declarations of the physicists of half a century ago. In the result, the theories of physical science were found to require modification in the light of additional observation. The work of Abbot Mendel similarly necessitated changes in the theories as to genetics. All science is admittedly dependent on observation of the world as it has been and is within the limits of space and

[1] I owe this quotation to Dr. Phythian Adams in his *The Call of Israel*.

time. The Christian who has staked his hopes on the reality of a Person exempt from these limitations can feel assured that the observations of the working of the universe and the deductions from those observations furnish no rigid laws or principles within the limits of which it is inconceivable that the Eternal Person may not perform actions anterior and posterior to the material universe of time. Further, if the Eternal Person has at any time intervened, as Christians believe, in this world of time, the theories of all science are inapplicable as laws defining the mode of intervention. Most Christians, therefore, will hold that the weight of historical or literary evidence examined according to the rules of historical and literary science is such as entirely to neutralize the bare assertion of present-day biology. For them, therefore, the birth of our Lord without a human father is more credible than not.

Nevertheless, we must recognize that minds unhabituated to estimate the weight of historical evidence and long immersed in the researches of natural science are sometimes led to read the balance the other way. For them, faith in the observations and inductions of natural science has become a worship which exalts it to the rank of mathematical certainty. It should perhaps be said that in this view, if justice is to be done to the historical evidence, the conclusion would seem to be not that our Lord was the offspring of St. Joseph and his bride, but, as Celsus asserted in his polemic against Christianity, an illegitimate child of the Blessed Virgin by a Roman soldier. From such a suggestion the ordinary Christian believer will undoubtedly shrink back with utter disbelief, finding the Catholic tradition far more credible and reasonable, awaiting meanwhile further discoveries in comparative biology and genetics.

Nevertheless, it should be observed that it is not for man to assert on *a priori* grounds of sentimental predilection or of logical deduction from his own theological premises what must have been the divine method of providential action. Man steps outside his sphere if he does other than seek to learn and study what has been the actual method chosen. Celsus' story might conceivably be true and so reveal how Redemption came even out of such depths of depravity. This possibility noted, we are left free with unprejudiced minds to accept whatever view the weight of evidence favours, and this, we cannot doubt, is that of the Catholic church.

We have now no means of learning whether Celsus had read Paul's Epistle to the Ephesians, and whether this story invented by him is an obscene travesty of the verse of the second chapter in that epistle. We may be sure, however, that uncharitable and incredulous gossip of neighbours discredited the Blessed Virgin's assertion of her virginity and covertly but shrewdly averred that some stranger[1] must be responsible for her motherhood, and what more natural than to suppose that stranger to have been a Roman soldier?

Is it possible that vestiges of such uncharitable scepticism are to be found in the cry that our Lord was a Samaritan? The Samaritans were stigmatized as of only half-Hebrew stock, and we may ask whether, included in what perhaps was mainly a resentment of apparent laxity towards strict Judaism, was the innuendo that the Lord was but half a Jew, in other words that He was a Gentile. This would, if this view were accepted, be a more precise and pointed formulation of the charge covertly conveyed in the Jews' haughty assertion of their unquestionable descent from Abraham.

If, without bias or prejudice, we combine these strands of evidence, we seem to be compelled to a simple choice between two alternatives and no more. Either our Lord's father was a Gentile (not St. Joseph or any Jew) or the orthodox and Catholic belief must be accepted as the sole possible and adequate solution. Few, we believe, would assent to the supposition that the Gentile rape of a sleeping and unconscious maiden was used of God to bring into the world the human nature which the Second Person of the Trinity integrated with His deity. The common judgment of mankind cannot but acclaim as the truth what the First and Third Gospels and the

[1] It would seem that the priestly registrars in Jerusalem, while unable to disallow St. Joseph's legitimization of Jesus as his heir, remembered the doubts as to His paternity, doubts apparently supported by "the brethren." Our Lord's opponents caught at words of His (John v. 17 ff.) which might be interpreted to imply that He had learnt—whether from revelations of His mother or from the insinuations of others—the identity of His actual father (John viii. 14). Hence when He said that His Father had sent Him (John viii. 16, 18), these objectors asked, "Where is thy father?" (John viii. 19).

Christian creeds uniformly declare. Matthew explicitly avers that the marriage was not consummated before our Lord's birth. Luke indirectly and implicitly corroborates this statement. To give adequate value to his words "Joseph with his espoused wife," we must understand him to mean "the girl who was contracted to be his wife, the betrothal ceremonies having been observed but their union not being consummated."

Three points deserve attention. (a) It may be doubted whether the use of the word "virgin" in the Creeds was intended to assert what is today generally indicated by the words "the Virgin birth." (b) The Gospels and presumably the Creeds seem principally concerned to insist that our Lord was the Blessed Virgin's first-born child and that she had borne no other before Him, in the same way that it is noted that in Joseph of Arimathea's tomb no other body had lain before the Lord. (c) The Virgin's asexual conception is attested by an interesting but apparently unnoticed linguistic peculiarity in both Matthew and Luke. They are in agreement in using a certain word and avoiding another to express the relation of the mother to her babe. The former word signifies *generate*, and used of the father it may be rendered *beget*; when used of the mother it is for most purposes *bring forth* or *bear*, but exactly represented it is *give life to*. The other word, to give it its precise meaning, speaks of the mother as so receiving the sperm of the male that the ovum is fertilized and becomes an embryonic germ of life. This second word is twice said of Elizabeth—she conceived; but it is not used of the Blessed Virgin. On the other hand, the former word is used once of Elizabeth—she shall bear thee a son; but both evangelists speak of our Saviour as *that which is given life* in His mother. The Nicene Creed is faithful to the Gospels in saying "was incarnate (out *or* in consequence) of a holy spirit (out) of the Virgin Mary." The Latin Apostles' Creed has confused what the Gospels and the Nicene Creed have expressed thus carefully and clearly. The Latin has incautiously introduced the word "conceived" and has distinguished this from "born." It has moreover interpreted "holy spirit" as "the Holy Ghost"[1] and this alteration has been inadvertently followed by our English version of the Creed.

---

[1] See pp. 341 ff., Part IV, Chap. 4, Excursus III.

This has given commentators who worked on the Latin or English much trouble to explain and square with an acceptable theology, and for further elucidation of this article in our Faith it will be of advantage to combine in one single paraphrase and to express in the language of today four significant passages in Holy Writ. While the Jews had their material altar on which the Mosaic sacrifice renewed the old covenant and furnished for them the feast of thankful reconciliation, we Christians have a heavenly Altar where the Christ eternally offers, presents and yields up in sacrifice His twofold Nature, to be an unreserved and limitless satisfaction for the sinfulness of the universe. From this Altar no one who rests his confidence of God's reconcilement on his carrying out the services of the Mosaic covenant, has the spiritual capacity, warranted and licensed under divine authority, to enjoy the spiritual feast of thankful recollection that the New Covenant has been sealed with the Blood of the Lamb provided by God Himself. . . . When the incarnate Word came to His own country, His own fellow countrymen received Him not, but as many as received Him to them gave He the spiritual capacity and warrant authorized under licence from Him to become sons of God, which were generated, produced and given the embryonic germ of spiritual life not originating in and derived from some particular racial stocks represented by the parents, nor from any will or resolve of a human mother, nor from any will or resolve of a human father, but originating in and derived from God. . . . The windspirit bloweth where it wills or resolves, and thou hearest the sound thereof, but thou knowest not whence it cometh and where it goeth: so is everyone that hath been generated, produced and given the embryonic germ of spiritual life, originating in and derived from the Spirit, the Holy Ghost. . . . That which has been generated, produced and given life in her womb is from a holy spirit, a spirit of consecrated submission to the Divine Will though it should involve reproach, slander, misjudgment by the world. The regenerated believer is spiritually given the germ of eternal life from God the Holy Ghost mysteriously and invisibly entering and penetrating his being. The human Jesus indissolubly united with the Divine Word is generated and given natural or mortal life within His mother's womb, this generation and giving of life being derived from and originating in a holy spirit which stirred her to resign her will and to accept the will of God.

The language of the Gospels then affords clear evidence that in solid historical fact our Lord was not born to any human father, but drew His earthly and mortal existence entirely and solely from His mother's nature. Before the study of microbes had grown into bacteriology or Darwin had found the origin of species in evolution through natural selection, John Ray in his *Wisdom of God*, like other Fellows of the Royal Society in his day, was satisfied that spontaneous generation still occurred. Biological science and genetics have explained otherwise the observations on which this theory of spontaneous generation was founded. Nevertheless Christian Theists believe that God's creation has been gradual and progressive through countless aeons and is even yet slowly continuing. They believe, therefore, that at a certain stage in the process life was first introduced and that various methods of biological development, evolution, generation and reproduction have successively been employed by the Creator. Scientists have learnt much it is true as to the "laws" or processes which are today and which have apparently been in operation within the more recent millenniums, but they cannot dogmatize as to what may be or may have been possible. They can only say that as things are at present their observations give evidence that this or that is what will happen or presumably has happened. When, therefore, historical evidence is strong that a certain event occurred and the "laws" of science as so far ascertained deny the possibility of the occurrence, judgment must be suspended till wider issues have been reviewed. On the particular point we have here been considering, it is clear that the situation is changed if in truth we are in the presence of the cardinal Recovery of the Universe. This weighs down the scale in favour of history and against the presumptions of biology. One point of interest in respect of psychological reactions affecting social behaviour is too important to be passed over without notice. A bastard, it has been observed, commonly suffers from an uncertainty of himself masked in arrogance. That no such disguised self-distrust is discoverable in any period of our Lord's life is strong warrant for believing that He never entertained a thought that His birth was not honest. Yet all the evidence shows that He never regarded St. Joseph as His father, and the conclusion is inevitable that psychological science here challenges biological, and that both must be silent and refrain from positive and absolute pronouncements until their partial conquest over the facts of nature has been extended to a universal and united dominion.

Chapter Five

THE BRETHREN OF THE LORD

(1)

THE exact meaning of the words "His brethren" in the Gospels has been discussed almost throughout the Christian centuries. It must be insisted that no vital theological issue is involved: it is a matter of historical or literary interest. For nearly four hundred years two rival theories held the field without any strong feeling being stirred by them or against them. When Helvidius broached the view that the brethren were the children of St. Joseph and the Blessed Virgin born subsequently to our Lord, the callow sprightliness of St. Jerome met this with the extreme challenge of asserting the perpetual virginity of both St. Joseph and his wife. More mature reflection led St. Jerome to allow that in this he had perhaps gone beyond the evidence, but, as will be seen on another page, an impartial consideration of all the evidence favours the view that the original contention of his youth was sound. For the moment, however, we may be content merely to insist that the mother of the brethren was not the Blessed Virgin, and to leave their paternity undetermined.

Accepting the Gospel statements as substantially accurate, we must, in attempting to reconstruct the actual history, lay our account with certain noteworthy facts.

(1) The Virgin Mary when betrothed to St. Joseph had no hope that she would be given the opportunity to bear a child. It would seem to follow that St. Joseph was, whether naturally or artificially, sterile (in which case his engaging to marry must seem improbable) or else, for some reason [1] which appeared to him and perhaps to the Blessed Virgin sufficient, he designed that his wife should remain without issue. It must be noted that Numbers xxx. 3–8 makes it clear that the apocryphal assertion

---

[1] For a conjectural suggestion as to this, see p. 252.

that Mary was vowed to virginity must neither be dismissed as
alien to Jewish social usages of that day nor as historically
improbable, much less impossible.

(2) James of Jerusalem [1] was martyred in the seventh decade
of the Christian era. We may therefore place his birth about
30 B.C. He was the eldest and had three brothers and at least
three sisters. It follows that the youngest of the family might
have been born between 20 and 14 B.C. This is conclusive
evidence that these would not be the children of St. Joseph by a
wife who was married in 9 B.C. The Matthean story of the
Magi's visit gives no indication that there were other children
who should be taken to Egypt when the Holy Family fled there.
Neither, on the other hand, does this story nor Luke's of our
Lord's first going up to Jerusalem for the Passover favour the
theory that they were the children of St. Joseph by the Blessed
Virgin. At neither date are we led to picture the presence of
other children in the background.

To this extent, then, St. Jerome's contentions may seem to
harmonize with such evidence as the Gospels supply. We are,
however, on more precarious ground when later writers sought
to identify Clopas, Cleopas and Alphaeus, thus making some of
the brethren to be members of the apostolic company of Twelve.
On this one comment must be made. While James the son of
Alphaeus, Simon the Zealot and Judas are identified by these
writers with the three brethren of the Lord who had these
names, the Fourth Gospel is explicit that as late as six months
before the Crucifixion His brethren did not believe in Him.
Since the Twelve were commissioned at least nine months
earlier still, we should according to this view of the identity of
these three apostles have to suppose John to have meant by
"brethren" the fourth only of the brethren, Joses. Remarkably
enough, some have identified him with Joseph, the rival can-
didate for the vacancy in the apostolate after Judas' suicide.
This Joseph, however, we are told, had accompanied our Lord
throughout His public life, and this again is inconsistent with
John's statement. It is manifest that these apostles, then, are
different persons from the brethren. Accordingly many of the
legendary traditions in regard to them are at best a medley of

[1] See *Church Quarterly Review*, vol. CXLVII, pp. 46 ff.

possibly true facts partly about the apostles, partly about the brethren of the same names.

(2)

It has always been taken for granted that the four brethren of the Lord were in the ordinary sense of the word brothers to one another. A remark of Epiphanius', however, makes it necessary to ask the question whether this supposition is well founded. That writer enumerates the four brethren named by both Mark and Matthew, and holds that they were sons of St. Joseph by a former wife. Yet in his account of James' martyrdom he mentions Simeon, the son of Clopas, the Lord's uncle, and describes this Simeon as a cousin—whether of our Lord or of James he does not make clear. This Simeon, as it would appear, succeeded James as Bishop of Jerusalem, and is generally regarded as one of the Lord's brethren. We are therefore confronted with this dilemma. On the one hand was St. Joseph the actual father of James and possibly one or two other children, while Simeon and perhaps others were children of his brother Clopas? On the other hand were all the brethren actually the children of Clopas and nominally and legally St. Joseph's heirs until our Lord was born? The following points deserve attention

Epiphanius is unmistakably positive as to two facts. James died at the age of ninety-six, and St. Joseph was eighty when our Lord was born.[1] He further states that James died "twenty-four years more or less" after the Ascension. From this, reckoning (mistakenly) our Lord to have been thirty-three years of age at His Crucifixion, he computes James to have been forty years old when our Lord was born, and therefore St. Joseph to have been forty years of age when James was born. These inferences are negatived by other facts which are known to us. James was alive, as we know from Josephus, as late as 63 or 64. It follows that either Epiphanius' twenty-four years is a copyist's error or the author means something different from what his words seem to intend. Eusebius in his *Chronicon* gives the date of James' death as Nero's 7th year, i.e. either between October, 60 and

---

[1] The census records of 9–8 B.C., A.D. 6–7, possibly also of A.D. 20–21 would establish this figure.

October, 61, or perhaps between July, 61 and July, 62 or even between July, 60 and July, 61. St. Jerome dates the death in 63 or 64 and says that James held the see of Jerusalem for thirty years. We shall therefore conclude that both wrongly identified with James' martydom a previous arrest by Ananus.[1] While St. Jerome preserved thirty, Epiphanius made the episcopate twenty-seven years from A.D. 42, when St. Peter withdrew from Jerusalem, but at one point he has taken the Ascension to have occurred in 45 or 46,[2] or twenty-four years before the martyrdom.[3] From this it follows that James was martyred just before the Passover in the spring of 70, and this harmonizes remarkably well with Hegesippus' statement that immediately after the martyrdom Jerusalem was invested. If we may accept this disentangling of Epiphanius' confusions, it follows that James, admittedly the firstborn son, was born in 27 B.C. He is reputed, as we have said, to have had three brothers and at least three sisters, and according to Mark his youngest brother was named Simeon. Now Hegesippus states precisely that Simeon the son of Clopas died in A.D. 107 at the age of a hundred and twenty, so that he was born in 14 B.C. The reader may judge whether the probabilities of the case favour the view that this Simeon is identical with James' youngest brother and that the whole family of at least seven are the actual children of Clopas and the heirs presumptive to such inherited rights as St. Joseph possessed. Obviously, if this view be correct, St. Joseph's recognition of our Lord as his son might well occasion a division in the family. The brethren, as John tells us, did not believe in our Lord. Yet we find Mary, the daughter[4] of Clopas, at the Cross beside the Blessed Virgin, and it is natural to see her father in the Cleopas who walked to Emmaus on Easter afternoon. This lends startling significance to our Lord's words about His mission causing division in a family.

One difficulty, perhaps, may be thought to present itself. If Clopas was St. Joseph's brother, would he be capable of walking

---

[1] See *C.Q.R.*, vol. CXLVII., p. 56.

[2] In support of this we may adduce the statement in the *Pistis-Sophia* that our Lord taught for more than eleven years after his Ascension.

[3] We shall then suppose that ΠII came to be read as IIII (cf. Part V, Chap. 6, p. 371).

[4] See below, p. 196 (note) and p. 253.

to Emmaus and back in A.D. 33? Epiphanius' definite statement about St. Joseph's age compels us to reckon that he would have been a hundred and twenty at the time of the Crucifixion. If, however, there were the same interval between St. Joseph and his brother as between James and Simeon, Clopas would only be a hundred and seven, and the whole family seem to have had extraordinary vigour and vitality if we may judge from the two stories of martyrdom.[1]

(3)

Origen in the first tome or section of his Commentary on St. John's Gospel avows his adherence to the opinion that no other child was born to the Blessed Virgin. This opinion, he declares, was held by the more sober and graver scholars down to his time. He fortifies their judgment by a scrutiny of the exact wording of our Lord's utterance from the Cross, "Woman, behold thy son." Had there been any other child, he observes, we should have had ὁ καὶ υἱός σου.

(4)

This threefold testimony, it is reasonable to feel, outweighs any *a priori* theory such as Dr. T. R. Glover built upon his estimate of marital probabilities. Bishop Lightfoot in his penetrating monograph on the brethren of the Lord has assembled and calibrated the statements made by early writers. The recovery in the last half century of papyri from Egypt has, however, considerably clarified the historical background of the Gospel records and we are in a position to reassess the value of traditions that have come down to us and to estimate the probabilities of alleged events. It is clear that the genealogical records of Jewish families and in particular of the Davidic house were easily accessible and that the priestly rulers at Jerusalem knew the hereditary claims in Joseph's house. Moreover, as we have said, the censuses of A.D. 6 and 20 would establish the pretension of our Lord to be the royal heir. The jealous disbelief of the brethren is intelligible if they were persuaded that our Lord had been illegitimately intruded into the succession and that

1 But see below, p. 196.

Joseph had through senile uxoriousness subscribed to a declaration which had extruded his nephews from the succession.

Hegesippus, as Lightfoot allows, is a trustworthy authority, since he is not only of early date, but by long residence in Palestine had learnt facts familiar to Hebrew Christians. He states that St. James was succeeded as Bishop of Jerusalem by his brother Simeon. The picture of the family which this would suggest is confirmed by Hegesippus' narrative that grandsons of Judas, the brother born next before Simeon, were interviewed by Domitian—we may suppose about A.D. 93.

It follows that Cleopas, whom Hegesippus names as the father of these brethren and brother of St. Joseph, was born roughly between 80 and 50 B.C. Thus if St. Joseph were the elder brother, he might well be born about 89 B.C., conformably to the tradition that he was eighty when he was betrothed to the Blessed Virgin, i.e. in 9 B.C. Hegesippus perhaps styles Mary, whom Luke calls the mother of James and Joses, the daughter, not the wife, of Cleopas.[1] She is therefore a sister of the brethren and her sons had the same names as two of their uncles.

So far Hegesippus' statements are both intelligible and in harmony with historical possibility and with all authentic evidence that has come down to us. Yet at this point two or three features appear in our picture of the Holy Family which must excite surprise if not dubitation. St. Joseph would be eighty-two years of age when he took his wife and her Child down to Egypt. He would be ninety-three years old when he made the pilgrimage to the first Passover that our Lord attended at Jerusalem. If Cleopas was St. Joseph's brother, his age in A.D. 33 would approximate, we should suppose, to a hundred and sixteen years, yet Luke tells us that he walked to Emmaus and back on Easter Day, a distance of 15 miles. In view of the well-attested accounts of St. Simeon's martyrdom at the age of a hundred and twenty, of James's at the age of

---

[1] Hegesippus' words are the same as those in John xix. 25. Although the word *daughter* is not expressed, the regular linguistic usage imports this sense. If we suppose the words to mean *Cleopas' wife*, Mary will have been over seventy years of age at the Crucifixion and her sons will be the Lord's cousins. It is reasonable to suppose that a mistaken identification of her sons James and Joses with their uncles led to the interpretation *wife* being substituted for *daughter*.

ninety-six and of St. Polycarp's after he had been eighty-six years
a Christian, we cannot dismiss as impossibilities these journeys
of St. Joseph and of Clopas at the ages stated. Nevertheless, we
must allow for two conceivable errors. The age assigned to St.
Joseph at the time of his betrothal to the Blessed Virgin does not
rest on Hegesippus' testimony and should perhaps be reduced;
or again, Clopas may have been the nephew and not the
brother of St. Joseph. Electing to adopt the explicit declarations
of Hegesippus, we shall conclude that St. Joseph was born in
89 B.C. and was vowed to a celibate life; Cleopas, the son of a
younger brother of the saint, was born about 50 B.C., married
about 28 B.C. and was about eighty years of age in A.D. 33.
St. Joseph married in 9 B.C., was aged ninety-four at the census
in A.D. 6 and died some time later, perhaps even after the census
in A.D. 20.

Another part of Hegesippus' account of James must now be
examined. He tells us that the boy was dedicated to God before
his birth, that his diet was of austerity similar to the Baptist's,
that he never entered the public baths and that he was allowed
by the Temple authorities to go into the sacred inner court. It
is a reasonable inference that his uncle being childless and his
father perhaps first having a daughter, not a son, born to him,
he was vowed to God if a son he should be. The priests acknowledged him as the legitimate heir to the Davidic throne and his
right of entry to the Temple was conceded for this reason. After
his martyrdom, his brothers Joses and Judas being perhaps
dead, Simeon succeeded him in the peculiar and special esteem
of the Hebrew Christians. This will illuminate the significance
to be attached to the last chapter in the Fourth Gospel, our
Lord's blessing of Peter preserved in the First Gospel, Paul's
attitude to James and the request made by our Lord's maternal
cousins for pre-eminent rank in His Kingdom, while His
reputed paternal cousins still refused to acknowledge His title.[1]
Mary the mother of James and Joses would be about the same
age as the Blessed Virgin, i.e. fifty-five at the time of the Crucifixion. Salome, Zebedee's wife, was perhaps two years younger
than her sister, so that John was perhaps born in 4 B.C. and

---

[1] Cousins on the paternal side might be thought to stand in a closer
relation, and so, though only putative, are called brethren.

died in A.D. 101 at the age of a hundred and four. Since Peter and never his father John appears as partner with Zebedee and his sons, we may suppose him to be fifteen or twenty years older than our Lord.

One last point may be mentioned. If our general estimate of the situation is correct, our Lord's reputed uncle or cousin, Cleopas, and Cleopas' daughter Mary were the only members of the family, with the exception of course of St. Joseph, the Blessed Virgin, her sister Salome and Salome's two sons, who accepted our Lord's Messiahship before the Crucifixion.[1] This illustrates our Lord's words about the divisions in families in regard to His claims.

(5)

Accepting this, then, as the most reasonable conclusion[2] deducible from the patristic evidence, we may consider a few points in the Gospel narratives.

(1) If Mark iii. 19 is accurately translated it tells us that our Lord came home to His house. Presently we find His mother and His brethren coming from outside to arrest Him. The natural conclusion is that His mother, alarmed by what she saw and heard of His unremitting labours and perhaps by the strange character of His novel mystery-parables, went to enlist the assistance of His brethren. It would appear, then, that they did not live in Jesus' house and that either the brothers were all married and had their own establishments, from which our Lord's mother fetched them, or the home of the brethren was not our Lord's home. The sisters, it may be remarked in passing, seem to have been married before this.

(2) The impression we thus get is confirmed by what the Fourth Gospel says as to the position just prior to the final Feast

[1] The way that in the *Acts* the brethren are distinguished from the Twelve confirms the correctness of our rejection of the theory that three of them were included among the apostles.

[2] We should perhaps mention, even though it be only to reject, an alternative hypothesis, viz. that the brethren James, Joseph, Judas and Simon with at least two sisters were St. Joseph's children, while his brother Clopas had at least three sons, named James, Joses and Simeon, the last being, as Hegesippus said, Bishop of Jerusalem after the martyrdom of James "the Just," the Lord's brother. This seems unnecessarily meticulous and cumbrous.

of Tabernacles. Mark and Matthew represent our Lord as returning to His home at Capernaum shortly after the Transfiguration. In John the brethren make their challenge to Him to make a demonstration in Jerusalem, and this challenge, it may be said, reads as if they were not living in the same house with Him.

(3) It has been generally felt that the committal of the Blessed Virgin to the protection of the Beloved Disciple was hard to reconcile with the supposition that the brethren were her own actual sons. Even were they married, one of their homes or that of one of their sisters might have been thought a more natural refuge for their mother than the house of a friend, however close and dear, and that *even if he were a nephew*.

(4) In the parable of the Leaven in the meal it is casually and incidentally said, and as it were taken for granted as the normal amount to be used at one baking,[1] that the woman put the leaven in three measures of meal. The same quantity is named by Abraham when he bids his wife Sarah prepare the cereal part of the dinner for his three visitors. It is conceivable that this was the stock size of a housewife's batch of baking, but it may be suggested that it is the appropriate quantity for three persons, and that its mention in the parable is a natural recollection of the quantity regularly used by our Lord's mother when she was baking for her husband, her Son and herself.

(5) If Mary was Clopas' daughter, her sons James and Joses will be distinct from their mother's brothers, and James ὁ μικρός may mean *the younger* as opposed to James "the Just," his uncle.

(6) If it be right to understand the First Gospel as testifying that the Lord appeared not to Mary Magdalene alone but to 'the other Mary," we may believe that appearance furnished additional matter for discussion between the two travellers to Emmaus.

(7) If both St. Joseph and his heir, James, the eldest son of Clopas, were vowed to celibacy, we may find a special significance in our Lord's words in Matt. xix. 12.

---

[1] I owe this observation and the reference to Genesis to the late Vicar of Ringwood.

(6)

None of the apocryphal Gospels represents the Holy Family
as more in number than Jesus, His mother and her husband.
The only statement that could be construed as lending any support to a contrary opinion is that, when a midwife was needed
at Bethlehem, Simeon, the son of Clopas, was sent out by
St. Joseph to look for one. This might suggest that Clopas'
youngest son was in his uncle's charge, but it would be fatal to
the suggestion that the brethren were younger than our Lord.
In the apocryphal accounts no less than in the canonical
account of the flight to Egypt and the return to Nazareth, there
is no vestige of suggestion that the three pilgrims were accompanied by relatives, so that it is fair to conclude that the
brethren were neither children of the Blessed Virgin born later
than our Lord nor, perhaps we may further infer, children of St.
Joseph by an earlier wife. It is right to add that while the
apocryphal Gospels may be considered to be historical
romances, yet it must be remembered that they will be constructed within the framework of the accepted facts whether of
the canonical Gospels or of still living tradition. We can therefore use them in some measure for controlling the imaginative
reconstructions of the Gospel story made by later writers.
Having regard to this, we may with advantage record certain
statements which seem deserving of notice.

In the *Gospel of the Infancy* we read:

Chapter vii. Some while, but no long time, after the flight
to Egypt, it was winter.

Chapter viii. He abode three years in Egypt. . . . At the
end of three years he returned.

Chapter xiv. James and Joses played with Jesus (presumably these may be the sons of Mary, Cleopas'
daughter). Bartholomew and Judas came from Bethlehem.

In the *Book of James* (which is shown, apart from other
reasons, to be of late date by the fact that it regards the Holy of
Holies as open for entrance at all times):

x. 1. Mary was of the tribe of David.

xii. 3. She abode three months with Elizabeth. . . . And

Mary was afraid and departed unto her house and hid herself. . . . Now she was sixteen years old.

xiii. 1. Now it was the sixth month with her, and behold Joseph came from his building.

xiv. 1. Joseph said, If I hide her sin, I shall be found fighting against the law of the Lord; and if I manifest her unto the children of Israel, I fear lest that which is in her be the seed of an angel, and I shall be found delivering up innocent blood to the judgment of death.

xiv. 2. τὸ ἐν αὐτῇ ὃν ἐκ πνεύματός ἐστιν ἁγίου.

xvii. 1. There went out a decree from Augustus the king that all that were in Bethlehem of Judaea should be recorded. And Joseph said I will record my sons: but this child (or maid) what shall I do with her? how shall I record her? as my wife? nay, I am ashamed. Or as my daughter? but all the children of Israel know that she is not my daughter.

xix. 1. σύλληψιν ἔχει ἐκ πνεύματος ἁγίου.

Gospel of Thomas, Greek text B.

i. 1. Jesus . . . came unto the city of Nazareth in the fifth year of his age.

Latin text.

ii. 1. Jesus was two years old when he entered into Egypt.

History of Joseph the Carpenter (or Builder).

Proem. Whose life was a hundred and eleven years[1] . . . the day of the death was 26th of the month Epep.

x. He lived to be a hundred and eleven.

xiv. He was forty when he married, and was married forty-nine years: a year alone after his wife's death. Two years with Mary before the Nativity.[2]

Coptic Lives of the Virgin.

1. Mary was born on the 15th of Hathor.

[1] If so, he died A.D. 23, so that he (not Jesus) made the census return in A.D. 6 and 20, and the Crucifixion was before the next census (see p. 175).
[2] These statements are reconcilable with our other evidence, if 49 is an error for 39. The two years with Mary will be from the betrothal in the spring of 9 B.C. to the Nativity in May, 8 B.C. We shall suppose Clopas' wife to have died in 10 B.C., being married 49 B.C. at the age of fourteen.

7*

The Gospel of Nicodemus.

Prologue. In the fifteenth (or nineteenth) year of the
governance of Tiberius Caesar . . . and of Herod,
king of Galilee, in the nineteenth year of his rule, on
the eighth of the Kalends of April, which is the 25th
of March . . . in the fourth year of the two hundred
and second Olympiad.[1]

[1] The Olympiad fixes the year as from July A.D. 32 to July A.D. 33. The
reading, therefore, of nineteenth year of Tiberius is correct. The month and
day are of course mistaken calculations.

Chapter Six

THE TWO GENEALOGIES

ATTENTION has, of course, long been drawn to the curious convergencies and divergencies between the genealogies furnished by Matthew and Luke. At times it has been thought that some reconciliation could be found in the notion that in the one case the pedigree given was that of the Blessed Virgin. A social custom followed in North Japan has been quoted in support of a suggestion that if she were without any brother and so were the heiress, St. Joseph might be introduced into the family tree as heir to her father, as soon as the marriage was celebrated. To this explanation one difficulty would seem to present a serious if not fatal obstacle: her sister, Salome, Zebedee's wife, was the mother of two brothers, who, it might be thought, would succeed to any hereditary claim after the Crucifixion, but in point of fact it is clear that the next heir is James, the Lord's "brother." It may be argued that if we are right in regarding Zebedee as a priest, his sons were priests and that thus the succession passed to James, but it seems safer to leave out of account any question of the Blessed Virgin's pedigree.

A happier solution was offered by Mr. E. B. Nicholson. He believed that Luke gives the actual lineal descent from father to son, while Matthew, by his expression "begat" designs to give us the legal succession of the owners of the family property at Bethlehem. This solution has never been disproved and an examination of the records goes some way to lend it countenance. At two points certainly, and in all probability at a third, the genealogies coalesce. David, Zerubbabel and his father and, it may be believed, Matthat or Matthan occur in both lists. Now we know that in Matthew's list Jehoiachin was left without a son to succeed him. It is therefore intelligible that his successor in the property should be physically descended from Nathan, a younger brother of David's son Solomon. This encourages us to believe that similarly the senior line of

Zerubbabel's descendants failed, so that Matthan, who was sprung of the junior line, inherited the property. In both cases it may be left an open question whether the heiress in the senior line was married by the representative of the junior line. Nevertheless, the reader may be interested to remember what we are told of Ruth's marriage to Boaz and the story of Tobias. Finally, with these probabilities before us, we are led to suppose that Jacob of the senior line was followed by St. Joseph of the junior line and perhaps we may dare to place Jacob's death after the Nativity in 8 B.C. and before the visit of the Magi at the end of 7 B.C. This will explain why at the first date, the travellers stayed at the inn, while at the second the Holy Family was in the house at Bethlehem and after Herod's death St. Joseph intended to return to it till the news that Archelaus was king determined him to return to Nazareth.

I have purposely omitted from the discussion the question whether our Lord's mother was herself of Davidic descent, and, if so, whether her genealogical line was senior to that of Cleopas or even of Joseph. I will only observe that in my view the canonical writers rest our Lord's Davidic descent upon the legal title established for our Lord as St. Joseph's son: they show a serene confidence and tranquil independence or unconsciousness of any physiological considerations. Nor is it in my view outside the bounds of probability that our Lord quoted the 110th Psalm to meet this very point of true physical heredity, because the Jewish authorities urged it against His messianic pretensions. When St. Ignatius reckons true blood succession to have come through the Blessed Virgin, he would seem to be introducing a justification not suggested in Holy Scripture for the Davidic Messiahship, and it is noteworthy that in other points he shows a perilous propensity to adventure extra-canonical speculation.

One further point may be noticed. It will be remembered that where a daughter, otherwise an heiress, married outside the tribe (as we may suppose that Salome did when she married Zebedee), the succession of her and her children was barred. Thus James and John, though true cousins of our Lord, had no claim to succeed, but the sons of Cleopas had.

Chapter Seven

THE NAMES OF THE APOSTLES

IT is familiar matter that for the Hebrew tribes thirteen names
are mentioned in the Scriptures, so that when twelve tribes are
enumerated one name is set aside. It is curious to observe a
similar superfluity of names when comparison is made of the
various lists given of the Twelve apostles. We hear of Simon
Peter son of John with his brother Andrew; their partners in a
fishing business, James and John, sons of Zebedee by his wife
Salome, sister of our Lord's mother; Philip; Thomas, a twin;
Levi or Matthew, son of Alphaeus and perhaps therefore a
brother of a second James who is also described as son of
Alphaeus; Simon the Zealot and Judas Iscariot.

Further, we have Nathanael of Cana, whom it is natural to
identify with the son of Ptolemy or Bar-tholomew. There then
remains but one vacant place in the Apostolic College, and for
this Luke names Judas "of James," which is confirmed by the
Fourth Gospel's mention of "Judas, not Iscariot." Mark, however, speaks of Thaddaeus and the First Gospel reproduces this,
though some copies give "Libbaeus Thaddaeus." Perhaps we
may find this variant the clue we need for the solution of the
problem. As we know, B and V become indistinguishable in
sound. Labbaeus therefore may be thought an alternative form
of Levi. In that case Thaddaeus might be thought to conceal
Matthew, and Mark to have mistakenly duplicated this apostle,
the error being copied in the First Gospel. Luke later had a
more correct copy of Mark or amended his list. Judas, if we are
to adhere to the normal usage of the language, must be regarded
as the son (not the brother) of some James whose identity we
cannot positively determine.

It has sometimes been sought to identify Thaddaeus with this
Judas, it being suggested that the name Judas was disliked
because Iscariot also had it or because it contained the sacred
Tetragrammaton at least in part. The names John, Joseph,

Joses nullify this latter suggestion and the former is not very convincing. A more serious objection, however, is that Eusebius expressly notes that Thaddaeus was one of the Seventy sent out about a year later than the Twelve, and this, if a true fact, excludes the possibility of Thaddaeus having been one of the original Twelve. If this information be correct, we need not concern ourselves to debate whether the name Judas could be converted into Thaddaeus, as some have asserted, nor whether by some manuscript error Mark gave Thaddaeus as a variant of Thomas ($M=\Delta\Delta$) or of Matthew.

A simple solution of the problem presents itself. Let us suppose Matthias and Thaddaeus to be one and the same person. Luke then gives the correct list of the original Twelve apostles and relates in the Acts how Matthias took the place of Iscariot. As Eusebius says, he will have been previously sent out as one of the Seventy. Mark remembered him as one of the Twelve as they were after the Ascension. He should have omitted Judas Iscariot, but the course of the story required his name to be included. Mark therefore omitted the other Judas. Matthew does no more than repeat Mark, but the inferior or secondary text has attached to Thaddaeus' name the alternative name of Matthew. Lebbaeus is a thorough Grecising[1] of Levi, Thaddaeus a Grecising of Matthias. We may take it that δδ has the sound that it has in Welsh and the sound that δ has in modern Greek. We may take it, too, that θ is to be pronounced not as in *father* but as in *pot-hook*. The *Ma* at the beginning has been

---

[1] It is to be remarked that the ending αιος seems to occur wherever a thoroughgoing effort was made to give a Greek form to a Hebrew name which in any way lent itself to the change. The native name Mattathias was naturally changed to ματθαῖος for the publican Levi, but Matthias retained the more Hebrew form of his name till he went out into the wider world. Then θαδδαῖος replaced the Hebrew original. Alphaeus, it may be claimed, shows similarly that it was a Grecised form, since Horace bears testimony to its use in Rome in the shape of Alfeius. The copyist who originated the inferior text in Matthew would seem to have supposed Thaddaeus to mean Matthew, not Matthias. This identification is of course impossible, since Matthew has already been given a place in the list of apostles. It is interesting, however, to find Eusebius relating that "Judas who is also called Thomas" sent Thaddaeus to Abgar of Edessa after the Ascension. Since Matthew is always with Thomas in the apostolic roll, it would seem likely that here too Thaddaeus means Matthew. This is perhaps confirmed by the tradition that that apostle laboured in (the Asian) Ethiopia.

dropped as the initial P has been dropped in Bartholomew. Thaddaeus then reflects Mat(h)athias. The names Ματταθίας, Ματθαῖας and Ματθίας we may take to be variant forms of one and the same name.

Legends purporting to record the missionary labours of the apostles, the manner of their deaths and the places where their relics rest give accounts of Thomas, Matthew, Simon, Jude and Matthias, which it is hard to reconcile. So much, however, is plainly hagiographic fabrication that it is unnecessary to attempt the task of sifting these legends in the hope of substantiating or refuting our theory, and it is left to stand or fall on the grounds we have given above.

PART THREE

DOMINICAL TITLES

Chapter One

THE SON OF GOD

FOR more than sixteen centuries the title "the Son of God" has by the vast majority of Christians been treated as a variant for, and virtually equated with, the denomination "God the Son." Yet, when Nathanael exclaimed "thou art the Son of God, thou art King of Israel," it is not to be supposed that he had suddenly been transported from the Jews' unitarian apprehension of God to the Christians' trinitarian re-expression of it. When the centurion, whether Jew or Gentile, pronounced after the crucifixion, "Truly this man was a Son of God" (so Mark records it), Luke, who must have used a copy of our Second Gospel, or at least the memorized matter of which that gospel is a written exemplar, expresses the pronouncement in the form, "Certainly this was a righteous man."

We are driven to ask what did the expression mean to those who used it and to those who heard it? But before attempting the enquiry we must satisfy ourselves on two other matters.

Can we rely on the substantial accuracy of our authorities on what may be thought so trivial a point? May it not be thought that the Evangelists would blur the precise significance of the words at each stage of the story, if they had come to attach deeper meaning to it later?

Our answer must be that when the occurrences of the title are examined after they have been arranged in historical order, they reveal a progression of significance which goes far to establish our authors' fidelity to fact. This becomes more impressive when it is remembered that the basis of our historical arrangement has nothing to do with this investigation of the title "Son of God." With these preliminary observations we may proceed to scrutinize our records, and we shall see how the results of our scrutiny confirm our reliance on our documents and consequently confirm their own trustworthiness.

In the first place we must notice the inadequacy of our

English versions so far as this enquiry is concerned. In the original Greek three forms of expression are used, and these it will be convenient to distinguish typographically.

(1) First we have what may be translated as God's son, or, on heathen lips, a son of deity. This title, it is remarkable to notice, is found in a proclamation of Augustus' adopted grandson, Germanicus, issued in A.D. 19. The relevant words will be quoted below, p. 235. The reader will observe that this title falls far short of what our English translation, "the Son of God," conveys to us. A polytheist might use the words god's son, or a son of a god, with a very meagre significance. A Gentile who was a monotheist might regard a great dynamic personality like Julius Caesar as sent into the world, with transcendent powers, by the One sovereign God. If his creed did not, like the Jewish faith, forbid him to give the title of God to beings inferior to the One God, he might style Caesar a god, and in that case Caesar's son or grandson might legitimately be styled a son of deity. A Jew, again, could, without any apostasy from his faith, call good men sons of God in contradistinction to sons of Belial or of the wicked one. Instances of this modest meaning in the expression are to be seen in Matt. v. 9 (" peace-makers shall be called sons of God "), Luke xx. 36 ("those who are accounted worthy of the resurrection of the dead are sons of God "), and Matt. v. 45 (" sons of your Father which is in heaven "), with Luke vi. 35 (" sons of the Highest "), though these last two instances should perhaps rather appear in our next section.

Outside the Gospels, we may notice the following examples of the expression: Romans i. 4 ("Jesus . . . which was made of the seed of David and declared to be God's son with power, according to the spirit of holiness"); Romans viii. 14 ("As many as are led by the Spirit of God, they are sons of God") ; Rom. ix. 26 ("They shall be called sons of the living God").

(2) In other places we have "GOD's son" or "a son of GOD." Examples of this are to be seen in the Tempter's challenge, "if thou art GOD's son," a challenge repeated by the mockers who passed by the Cross (Matt. iv. 3, 6, Luke iv. 3, 9, Matt. xxvii. 40).

It should be noticed that the common usage is to mark the predicate by giving it no article, whereas the subject has one.

In consequence it will be an over-refinement to distinguish too rigidly between this second form of expression and a third which we shall presently consider. Before doing so we must mention Matt. viii. 29 ("thou son of GOD") with Mark v. 7 and Luke viii. 28—which might perhaps be listed in our third division—and John x. 36 ("I said I was GOD's son"), which again as a predicate has no article.

Some instances outside the Gospels again require attention. Romans viii. 19 has "the earnest expectation of the creature waiteth for the manifestation of GOD's sons"; and in Acts xiii. 33 we read "in the second Psalm, Thou art my son," where the reader will observe on the one hand the predicate without the article and on the other the modest measure of the Psalmist's words in comparison with the voices at the Baptism and at the Transfiguration.

(3) Finally we have in other places "the SON of GOD," which might be strictly interpreted "the one and only Son of the one and only God." To state at once the result to which an alert and frank examination points, it must be said that this exalted title proves to be the equivalent and alternative to "the Christ," and those who used it in the first century understood it in that way. The Gospel instances give clear evidence of this.

In Matt. iii. 17, with Mark i. 11 and Luke iii. 22, the Voice from Heaven pronounced "Thou art my SON, my beloved" (Son). Matt. xvi. 16: Peter declared "Thou art the Christ the SON of the living GOD." Matt. xxvi. 63; Caiaphas adjured our Lord, "Tell us whether thou be the Christ the SON of GOD"; and so Mark xiv. 61; "Art thou the Christ, the SON of the BLESSED?" Luke xxii. 67, 70 has "Art thou the Christ . . . art thou the SON of GOD?" where the context shows that the two questions have the same significance.

Mark iii. 11 ("unclean spirits . . . cried Thou art the SON of GOD") is illuminated by Luke iv. 41 ("Devils came out crying 'Thou art the SON of GOD'"). John i. 34, where the Baptist testifies that Jesus is the SON of GOD, does not of itself make clear what the expression means, but i. 49, Nathanael's words, "thou art the SON of GOD, thou art King of Israel," and xx. 31, "these (things) are written . . . that Jesus is the Christ, the SON of GOD," can leave us in no doubt.

Similarly, John v. 25, "the dead shall hear the voice of the SON of GOD," and xi. 4, "This sickness is not unto death . . . but . . . that the SON of GOD might be glorified thereby," may be taken to be defined by xi. 27 (Martha's confession "Thou art the Christ, the SON of GOD").

Once more to adduce the examples of the title in other parts of the New Testament, we must notice 1 Cor. i. 9, 2 Cor. i. 19, in both of which the titles "SON of GOD" and "Christ" are associated. No such explicit identification of the two titles is to be seen in Acts ix. 20, Romans i. 3, 9, v. 10, viii. 3, 29 and 32, but it is difficult to suppose that the expression "the SON of GOD" in these passages does not carry the sense it has at the beginning of that Epistle. It remains, however, a possibility that we should distinguish the "SON of GOD," as equivalent to the King, from the "Christ." To the Christians our Lord's life, death and resurrection had united both conceptions, but if they were in thought separable, Paul in Phil. ii. 11 means more than is often understood when he avows that every tongue shall confess that Jesus is Christ (and) Lord (i.e. King).

We must add, since the words are in truth a variant of this, the expression "Son of the Most High (God),"[1] which occurs a few times. Besides, we must notice that Our Lord speaks of Himself baldly as "the Son" in contradistinction to "the Father," and this both in the Synoptic records and above all in the Fourth Gospel.

Taking the instances in what we have suggested to be their historical order, we find :

(1) The Angel Gabriel tells the Virgin Mother (Luke i. 32) that her Son "shall be called son of (the) Most High."[2] Plainly here, whatever we may suppose the Angel to have understood (and the words of Peter's first epistle may be thought to suggest that they, no less than men, were unaware

---

[1] It is beside the purpose of this enquiry to consider the original significance of this title, as to which the reader should consult Dr. Aubrey Johnson's article in Professor Hooke's work *The Labyrinth*, vol. II, and Father E. Burrows' posthumous article in *J.T.S.*, vol. XLI., p. 152. For the Jew in our Lord's time "the Most High" is a synonym for God, just as for reverence sake "Heaven" was.

[2] The Greek, giving no article, evidently equates "Most High" with "God." It is, in fact, virtually a proper name.

that God purposed to become incarnate), for Mary the words can have meant no more at the time than that her son should be recognised as a good man, a son of God, while bad men were sons of Belial. Confirmation of this is to be found in our Lord's words in the Sermon on the Mount, where Luke (vi. 35) records that if his followers are generous and gracious they shall be "sons of (the) Most High."

(2) Proceeding to confirm his announcement Gabriel reiterated (Luke i. 35) that, because the "power of the Most High" should engender the child, the consecrated (as to which see p. 253) offspring should be recognized as God's son. The words must in the first instance have borne for the Virgin's ears the sense we have just indicated, though this is not to say that as she pondered further upon them they may not have roused strange questions in her mind. For a Jewess the thought of a demi-god must be inconceivable, and the doctrine of the Sacred Trinity could not have presented itself to her.

(3) When the Child was found in the Temple, He replied to His Mother "Wist ye not that I must be in My Father's house?" In some sense therefore at the age of twelve our Lord understood Himself to be God's Son. The possibility has been suggested that as the Child grew to adolescence some spiteful jeer from a boyish companion may have led to His learning from His mother or her husband the incredible truth. The Nativity occurred at Bethlehem; eighteen months later the family was living there; afterwards for the next three years they lived in Egypt. When they returned to Nazareth memory would have become blurred. Yet in spite of these years of absence we may suspect that some whispers still passed about as to the circumstances of our Lord's birth. Although it is rash to assume that the voice of slander assailed either St. Joseph or his wife, the story can scarcely have been entirely forgotten. This, indeed, may be the explanation of Nathanael's hesitation to accept the Baptist's testimony to our Lord's Person. A native of Cana, he knew the common talk about the Saviour's birth, the assertion of a supernatural conception and the fact that St. Joseph had acknowledged our Lord as his heir and so as the heir of the Davidic hope. The Baptist's homage and testimony compelled the future apostle to confront the issue whether Jesus' claim

was solid or an invention: then our Lord acquainted him with His insight into his mental struggle of hesitation to accept the Baptist's estimate. Nathanael surrendered himself to the conviction that here was reality, however surprising—the Advent of the Messianic promise. This reading of Nathanael's conversion may be felt to confirm the possibility we have just suggested that the boy Jesus had been stung by a companion's taunts into putting questions and so learning about His birth.[1] It is better, however, to look in another direction for the explanation of our Lord's belief that He was the Son of God.

If we may accept the view developed on another page that our Lord had been taught that, like St. Joseph, He was the "Son of David," He may be presumed to have been taught also that as such God had promised to be to Him a Father.

As the story is told in 2 Sam. vii, when David proposed to build a Temple, the prophet Nathan was charged by God to tell the king that He would set up his seed after him, and to add "I will be his father, and he shall be my son," and again "Thine house and thy kingdom shall be established for ever before thee." In the first instance the word "seed" plainly meant son, i.e. Solomon, who in point of fact did build the Temple, but later God's promise was understood to guarantee a perpetual relation between Him and David's successor or heir. If and when the heir was, in God's providence, enabled to ascend the throne, the king was assured that he stood in a filial relation to the Almighty.

Something more must be added. No reason can be found for supposing that the Lord's mother would not have told her Son what the shepherds reported as to their experiences on the night of the Nativity. The herald Angel said to them "I bring you good tidings of great joy which shall be to all the People, for unto you is born this day in the city of David a Saviour which is Christ the Lord." As Kittel has pointed out, "Glad tidings" in the Greek of this period is regularly used for the

---

[1] Besides what is noted in the text we must not overlook another episode which may have contributed to our Lord's apprehension of His unique mission. At the presentation in the Temple Simeon may be supposed to have said that he now beheld Jehovah's Anointed (Luke ii. 26). We are justified in supposing that the Lord's mother would have communicated this also to her son if and when she or St. Joseph told Him something of His nativity.

announcement of the birth of an heir to the throne or of the
accession of a new king. The angelic message therefore if
known (as we believe it was) to our Lord would have conveyed
to Him the thought that He had been born heir to the Davidic
throne.[1]

(4) At His baptism our Lord heard a voice from heaven
which declared Him to be the SON OF GOD. From the first days
of Christianity this Voice has been associated with the words
in the second Psalm "Thou art My Son, this day have I
begotten Thee." That psalm beyond all doubt was used at
coronations. When the new monarch was anointed, God, it
was proclaimed, made him His son and viceroy on earth. Our
Lord was at His baptism anointed with the Holy Spirit. This
was His own experience. It was attested by the Baptist. It was
asserted by our Lord in His sermon in the synagogue at
Nazareth. Remembering that the accession of a new king was
regularly made the matter for "glad tidings," we can see the
startling significance of the words "Glad tidings" or "Gospel"
applied, as they first are after the Baptism, to the proclamation
of the imminent advent of the reign of God. It will be noticed,
however, that the idea of the divine sonship is still, so far as
others are concerned, the same as before. David's heir, now
anointed and appointed to the throne, is, according to the
divine promise, God's son or viceroy.

But more must be added. The Voice, as all three Synoptists
record, pronounced our Lord to be the "beloved Son of God."
This is more than "a Son." We may even hold that it makes
our Lord greater than the generality of David's successors. The
Greek word at times connotes an only son. In a papyrus from
Egypt a man with only one eye remaining calls it his "well-
beloved" eye. It is reasonable to believe that the Voice presented to our Lord's consciousness, if He had never thought of it

[1] It is conceivable, but the point must not be pressed, that our Lord
Himself, knowing that He had as an infant lived in Egypt and that St.
Joseph had been divinely directed to take "the young child and go into the
land of Israel," found in this a reflection of Hosea's words, "I called my son
out of Egypt." If this were so He would have found here again corroboration of the idea that He was the Son of God—not as David's heir, indeed,
but as the typical representative and focal point of Israel's mission to the
world.

before, that He was not only David's legal heir nor even another monarch anointed to sit on David's throne, but the long-expected Messiah. If the herald angel's announcement had come to Him from His mother in the exact form in which Luke reports it, the Voice at the Baptism would confirm the "Glad Tidings" of His birth. That the conviction of His Messiahship had established itself in His mind as a matter of faith soon after this appears in His words to the Samaritan woman. When she avowed her belief, "I know that Messiah cometh (which is called Christ)," He replied "I that speak unto thee am He."

(5) When we pass to the Temptations in the Wilderness it is deserving of notice that the matter is expressed in what we may call the reduced form, "If thou art—as indeed thou art[1]—son of (the true) God." Two points require notice. Satan is not omniscient, and there is no ground for supposing him to have known that Our Lord was God the Son vested in human nature, nor perhaps that he knew anything more than had already been presented to our Lord's human mind. We may therefore see exquisite subtlety in the way in which the challenge is not hinged upon the ampler promise just given in the Voice: it is not "If thou art the Christ" or "If Thou art God's beloved or only Son"; it is rested upon the conception, familiar by then for many years, that He was son of the Most High God.[2]

(6) After the forty days when our Lord returned to the place where John was baptizing, the Baptist proclaimed what he had witnessed. He declared that he had seen the Spirit descending and resting upon our Lord, whom he spoke of as a warrior-hero,[3] and he then summed up his estimate of Jesus in words

[1] The precise effect of the form given to the conditional clause is to make it almost a causal clause, "inasmuch as thou art." By way of contrast we may cite the leper's words—"Lord, if thou wilt thou canst make me clean."

[2] The temptations are invitations to choose His own will and not to seek and obey the Father's will. Satan solicits men to sin, i.e. moral offences, not to doubt or to investigate, i.e. mental enquiry. So long as our Lord firmly trusted the Father, He would not be impatient nor insist on His early ideas of duty, but would be recipient of new thoughts and hopes. A more detailed study of the temptations will be found in another chapter (pp. 284 ff.).

[3] This curious detail of expression is specially interesting because it supplies a parallel in the Gospel to what we find in the Apocalypse. In the Gospel our Lord is called "the (sacrificial) Lamb of God"; in the Apocalypse "the (warrior) Lamb of God" (Rev. v. 6).

which, when they are compared with what is attributed to Satan, attest the voice from heaven. The Baptist says, "I have testified that this is the SON of (the true) GOD." Yet, while we notice this further elevation in the title, we must not inadvertently read into it more than that John recognized Our Lord as the Messiah, who pre-eminently among all David's heirs was the SON of GOD. This is confirmed by St. Andrew's words uttered two days afterwards to his brother Simon, "We have found the Messiah." It is further enforced by the form of Nathanael's outbursts—"Rabbi, Thou art the SON of GOD, Thou art King of Israel."

(7) At the following Passover our Lord is recorded to have said to those who sold doves in the Temple, "Take these things hence, make not my Father's house a house of merchandise," where we have the word regularly used to describe the Temple as God's Home. Yet still there is nothing requiring us to read into the title "the SON of GOD"[1] a transcendental sense other than that of the Messiah of God.

At this point it will be proper to rivet our attention on what is, without question, one of the prominent features in our Lord's Messianic activity. He continually showed Himself possessed of a superlative insight into men's personalities and an internal awareness of events external to Himself. We have all discovered that some persons are more observant than others. Some medical men have greater capacities of diagnosis than others. We constantly discover that some of our friends are, as we say, more understanding than are others. Besides this, there are remarkable instances on record (though it would be beside the point to sift here the evidence adduced for their credibility) of men announcing events at the very moment of their occurrence, long distances from the speakers. Emmanuel Swedenborg spoke of a vast conflagration then raging in a city three hundred miles away. The battle between Pompey and Caesar on the banks of the Pharsalus was known to a wizard

---

[1] In John iii. 16: "For God so loved the world that He gave His unique Son," Dr. Abbott has rightly pointed out that the Greek word translated "for" is reserved by the writer for his own comments, so that the words are not derived verbatim from our Lord. St. John therefore may have meant much more by the words than they could be shown to have meant if they had been spoken to Nicodemus.

in Spain. It is reasonable to expect that these powers of observation, insight and awareness should be found in a superlative degree in our Lord, the unique and representative Man. It is, consequently, no matter of surprise that our Gospels record example after example of His exercising such powers. In Simon, son of John, He read that solid firmness of character which justified the bestowing upon him of his new name Peter. Nathanael's occupation before Philip called him and his simple straightforwardness were recognized in the words "Behold an Israelite indeed, in whom is no guile." At the first Passover after His baptism, many at Jerusalem believed "on His name,"[1] but Jesus realized the instability of their attachment to Him and the strength of their prejudices, which would violently resist any suggestion that the Christ must in the event be crucified. He would not therefore at this stage declare Himself in Jerusalem to be the Messiah. To do so would have prematurely provoked the clash with the Jewish authorities. Facts in the life of the Samaritan woman at Jacob's well were patent to our Lord. Asked for a third time whether he loved his Master, Peter averred, "Lord, Thou knowest all things, Thou knowest that I love Thee." Jesus was aware immediately that the son of the officer in Herod's service had passed happily the crisis of his fever and that Lazarus' illness had ended in his death.

All these examples, it may be said, are found in the Fourth Gospel, though the first may be held to be corroborated by the synoptists. The fact, however, that our Lord was possessed to a superlative degree of such powers of insight and awareness is attested by the other evangelists. All agree that He read the character of the rich young ruler, and if we are right in believing him to be Saul of Tarsus we find here a classical instance of our Lord's gift of insight and of foresight. All again agree that when the direct and crafty question was put to Him, "Is it lawful to pay tribute unto Caesar or no?" He "perceived their craftiness." Luke tells us that the worshippers in the synagogue at Nazareth "wondered at the gracious words" spoken by our

[1] The phrase combines the two ideas of their believing His teaching to be a true revelation from God and their acceptance of His claim to be whatever He declared Himself to be. Impressed by His personality and character, they started to rely upon Him, looking to Him for spiritual instruction and kindly help.

Lord, and, it would appear, desired to claim His marvellous powers as belonging specially to their community. They claimed Him as one of themselves, since He was the son of Joseph whom they knew so well.[1]

The evangelist represents Our Lord as reading these secret thoughts, and in consequence proceeding to say "Ye will surely say unto me, this proverb, Physician, heal thyself. Whatever we have heard done in Capernaum, do also here in thy country." Luke too tells us that when "the woman which was a sinner" came into Simon's house, our Lord read the unexpressed thoughts of His host.

This capacity of our Lord is to be seen further in the perspicacity with which He saw forty years before the event the inevitable destruction of Jerusalem. There is no need to labour this point. The powers of insight, coupled with His miracles of healing and spiritual teaching, convinced many, a year before His Crucifixion, that He was a prophet.

The persecutions which befell the Christians before the destruction of Jerusalem and their arraignment before kings and other authorities, all foretold by our Lord,[2] confirmed them in their belief that His prophecies would be fulfilled. In consequence his predictions of the impending fall of Jerusalem saved Christian believers from sharing in that disastrous ruin.

The evidence of all four Gospels then makes it clear that our Lord had in a singular measure the capacity, found in a more humble fashion in some men, of reading the hearts of others, of entering into their secret feelings and motives, of discovering their past, of discovering events at the moment of

[1] A cursory reading of these words has often led to their being viewed as implying the same contemptuous depreciation as we find in Mark vi. 3, Matt. xiii. 55, and it has even been supposed that the two visits to Nazareth are to be regarded as one and the same. The interpretation given in the text is required if our Lord's words are to be apposite to the occasion.

[2] Luke xxi. 12: "Before these things (i.e. wars and rumours of wars, earthquakes, famines and pestilences) they shall lay their hands on you and persecute you . . . being brought before kings and rulers . . . and it shall turn to you for a testimony." Cf. Mark xiii. 7–9, Matt. x. 17, 18, John xvi. 2. In the same way our Lord's prophecy first vaguely then more definitely speaking of crucifixion, and finally indicating His betrayer, went to confirm the disciples' belief that He was a prophet; above all the fulfilment of the promise that the Holy Spirit should be outpoured confirmed their faith in Him. Cf. John xiv. 28, 29; xvi. 1, 4; xiii. 21

their happening, and of truly anticipating the consequences of men's present actions.

This sensitiveness of percipience, this acute awareness of what lies outside the range of sense perception is revealed in another region of human experience. Our Lord, we notice, had always a vivid realization of God's nearness to man. The lives of the saints tell of those whose communion with God was so intimate and intense that they both perceived their duty and had strength to do it. They lived in an atmosphere of spiritual reality. Some, indeed, are said to have been so wrapt in devotion and transported with the ecstacy of the beatific vision that their very bodies were lifted from earth for a little while. Of our Lord it is related that He resisted Satan's seductions as they presented themselves in what appeared to be visible and audible approaches. He heard a Voice at His Baptism, on the Mount of Transfiguration and at the Temple when the Greeks sought an interview with Him. It is right, however, to emphasize and insist on one vital difference between our Lord and the saints to whom allusion has been made. Long periods of abstinence and a meagre diet resulting in inanition would appear to have preceded the visions seen by the saints. Of our Lord it is constantly mentioned that His critics complained that He unhesitatingly enjoyed the pleasures of the table. We are justified in inferring that if "Heaven lay about" Him, this was not due to a trance following upon debility, but that in full vigour of mind and body He was consciously brought into contact with what for us is the Unseen. Be that as it may, what we are here specially concerned to apprehend is that His habitual communion with God gave Him a deeper understanding of the divine will and a firmer resolve to labour for it than men in general possess.

Moreover, as He realized this fact more and more plainly, He grasped more and more certainly the conviction that His divine Sonship was unique. We shall find this growing perception showing itself with increasing definiteness as we follow the course of the history. We have already noticed instances of our Lord's immediate and intimate acquaintance with the Father's purposes in His secure rejection of the Tempter's invitations to misinterpret the principles of God's reign of love, right and truth, and in his tranquil refusal at the wedding feast in Cana to be hurried into presumptuous impatience or premature haste. We shall see later how He hung upon an intimation desired and awaited of the Father's will as to the raising of Lazarus, and again as to the "hour" when He should suffer crucifixion.

It is manifest that our Lord's habitual communion with the Father gave Him an unparalleled clearness of insight into the Father's will. That He also schooled himself to the acceptance of that will is equally manifest, but it must be understood that this acceptance was at times secured only by determined effort and after an agony of prayer. "He learnt obedience by the things that He" experienced. When the signal came that His Passion was imminent, He said "Now is my soul troubled and what shall I say? (shall I say) 'Father save Me from this hour?', but for this cause came I unto this hour. Father, glorify thy name." In the Garden of Gethsemane Luke tells us that "being in an agony He prayed more earnestly: and His sweat was as it were great drops of blood falling down to the ground." His will thus mastered reluctance, so that He never prayed "Father, forgive Me my trespasses," as He bade us do, but only, "Father, forgive them."

Nevertheless, although He had a growing certainty that in some strange, unique, indeterminate and perhaps incomprehensible sense He was the SON of GOD, it must be insisted that He had no demonstrative proof, no indisputable knowledge. His belief was not founded upon a consciousness of His eternal personality, existing before His Incarnation and continuing through His human life. Nor was His faith the bold and firm resolve to stake the issue of His mission and passion upon the truth of His belief that He was what the converging evidences suggested that He was. His faith was a reliance upon God, a dependence upon Him, a confidence in His power and love, a trust in Him as His Father. Therefore, He could leave all issues to God: the present and the future were for Him secure. Life, death, a future life, could all be safely left to the Father, who had sent Him.

Following what we believe to be the chronological order of events, we next find demoniacs at Capernaum declaring

"Thou art the SON of GOD," where again in the inferior MSS. the title SON of GOD is conjoined with the Messianic.

The next scene is just outside the town of Nain. Two points deserve attention. Our Lord is seen to have completely broken with the Levitical ordinances as to ceremonial cleanness. He does not hesitate to touch the bier. Further He is assured that He is the Master of Death.

Perhaps we may believe Him to have remembered how Elijah and Elisha had recalled children to life, and how contact with Elisha's body revived a dead man whose corpse was hurriedly cast into the prophet's grave. The Messiah must have no less power over death, and indeed that could not but be an understatement. Ezekiel, the "son of man," in the valley of dry bones "prophesied unto the winds" and "they lived and stood up upon their feet an exceeding great army." Unquestionably the Messiah, the true Son of Man, was commissioned by His Father to give life to men.[1] It is imperative for us to remember, however, that as we stated at the outset, men make sallies of imagination, and we must not therefore suppose that our Lord's confidence that He was the resurrection and the life was built upon inferences from the Old Testament. His human life could leap forth towards that conviction and the conviction was verified as solid truth. Yet it is in accord with His attitude as Man towards God that He declares that the Father had given Him whatever powers He exercised, and moreover had commissioned Him to be men's Judge.

Here we must remind ourselves that whatever our Lord at each point of His ministry reveals of Himself is by no means the full measure of His own knowledge. Even His chosen disciples were incapable of at once fully grasping the truths He sought to convey. Yet, notwithstanding this, we must beware of supposing that He deliberately concealed what He knew. This would be to act a part—a procedure which we may perhaps detect that He was particularly unwilling to adopt or to continue further than was necessary. It might be worse: it

[1] Abbott found in the use of the conjunction "for" a test by which to separate our Lord's *ipsissima verba* from the evangelist's interpretative or explanatory additions. If this test may be trusted, we should regard as such comments John iii. 16, 17 and 34 and John v. 26, and perhaps with these we must associate some neighbouring verses.

might involve the pretence of what was not the case, and to assume this to have been done by Him would be to associate ourselves with those mistaken thinkers who would have it that He pretended to suffer and to die, while in reality He remained impassive and alive. We are led, therefore, to be cautious in our conclusions, and to content ourselves with asserting no more than this. Our Lord in His humanity knew and believed what we find Him labouring to impart gradually to others. The effect of this is that, so far, He believed Himself to be the SON OF GOD as God's Davidic vicegerent and Messiah. Further He found Himself constantly gaining deeper insight into God's will and purposes, and He as constantly aligned His will with the Father's. So far we see this insight and alignment in action with regard to two points of the Mosaic law. The observance of the Sabbath was fulfilled when the citizens of God's Kingdom remembered that their time on earth was to be used in order to co-operate with God's purposes. Israel had been trained by the Sabbath of the Lord to remember that they were Jehovah's chosen people, and that God cared for servants like Israel in Egypt as He did for masters. Again, the regulations as to the ceremonially clean and unclean were fulfilled when the citizens of God's Kingdom were pure in heart. Israel had learnt from those regulations that because God was holy and separate from sinners, they must be holy and separate from sin. It will be seen that in both these cases the title "the Son of Man" would seem to contribute something towards our understanding of their significance. More will be said of this in another place, but we may notice here how the words "God so loved the world" strike a more universal note of humanity than the words of the prophet Malachi "Jacob have I loved but Esau have I hated."

The next occasion on which we find the title "Son of the Most High God" addressed to our Lord is that on which the paranoiac whom the demon Legion had possessed came begging that the demon should not be "tormented." It is inconceivable that the man himself or for that matter the demon used the words with any understanding of the mystery of the Blessed Trinity. We are compelled therefore to ask what he meant. That our Lord was a demi-god is not very satisfying,

G.G.—8

even if we suppose that the man had imbibed pagan ideas of the
deity. The rest of the story is more congruous with the belief
that his thought moved within the orbit of Jewish or semi-
Jewish theology. The obvious sense then will be that he
recognizes our Lord as the Messiah. We have seen in all the
previous incidents which we have examined that the "SON of
GOD" continually expresses the relation of the Messiah to God.
Moreover, in this particular case we must observe that the
demon expects our Lord to expel him from his victim and fears
that he will be punished before the hour of destiny. We shall
see later in another instance[1] how it was believed that the
Messiah, when He came, would have power to exorcise demons,
and we may notice the words in Isaiah lxi. 1 : "the Lord hath
anointed me . . . to proclaim the opening of the prison to them
that are bound." If we might suppose that the man or his
companion had previously seen or heard of our Lord, and
recognized Him when he landed with His twelve apostles, the
paranoiac's recalcitrance would be yet more explicable.

Nevertheless another explanation lies ready to our hand. We
saw at the first that sometimes a son of God meant a good man
in contradistinction to a son of Belial. Legion then perhaps
meant by the title that he recognized in our Lord virtue
embodied, and so victorious as to challenge his own wilfulness
and wickedness. This interpretation would be quite intelligible,
and would make it unnecessary to suppose that the man had
any previous knowledge of our Lord. On the other hand, we
need constantly to remind ourselves that our Gospel records
leave much untold. We can see that very often the principal
actors and the bystanders talked together, giving and gathering
information. In this particular case it is clear that much of the
man's past history was communicated to our Lord's attendants
before or after the exorcism. In favour of our last interpretation it may not be utterly fanciful to point out one curious
coincidence. The exalted language of Legion, "Jesus, Thou Son
of the Most High God," might be an echo in the madman's
ears of our Lord's words to His disciples (if we might imagine
the man to have heard or learnt of them) "Love your enemies
and do them good . . . and ye shall be sons of the Most High."

[1] See p. 230.

Before we continue our review of the passages in which the title the SON of GOD occurs one observation requires to be made. Our Lord was fusing into one complete whole a number of distinct foreshadowings of His Person. So it comes about that aspects of His work and mission suggested in the Old Testament by our title modifies and enriches what another title suggested. Thus although the SON of GOD was originally equivalent to the Davidic king or the Messiah, on our Lord's lips it took on a wider sense. God was not the God of the Jews only, and so His Son was not the King of the Jews only nor their national Messiah only : He belonged to humanity. This line of thought will be developed in separate chapters dealing with the various titles applied to our Lord. It is enough that we have here indicated its importance.

Proceeding with the history we come next to the night after the feeding of the five thousand. Astounded at our Lord's boarding the boat and saving Peter amid the tempest and still more at its sudden cessation, the apostles, we read, "worshipped Him[1] saying, 'Of a truth Thou art God's son.'" This, as we have said, was a confession falling far short of what was to come six months later. They were no more than impressed with a sense of having witnessed something beyond the ordinary, a manifestation of a dynamic control over nature. Their emotion, if transient, was at the time sincere and certain of its faith.

In the discourse delivered in the synagogue at Capernaum our Lord again says what He had said at Jerusalem that "this is My Father's will that everyone that beholdeth the Son, and believeth on Him should have eternal life : and I will raise him up at the last day." Put into the language of today this would seem to declare that the Son reveals the truth about God's requirements, that in dependence on the Son men can fulfil those requirements and that while living so as to fulfil them they are already entered upon a life which is eternal, and which therefore will emerge again in full activity. All this is in harmony with what we shall see appears in teaching given by our Lord about His office as the Son of Man. We have then once more here an association of the connotation of two titles SON of GOD and Son of Man.

[1] "Made humble acknowledgment, owned their obligation." See p. 286.

It will be well at this point to refer to the further teaching which our Lord gave on this occasion. "He that eateth my flesh," He said, "and drinketh my blood, hath eternal life: and I will raise him up at the last day." It was close to the Passover time, and every one within the Jewish covenant of necessity ate of the paschal lamb and its accompanying unleavened bread, and also drank of the wine that went with it. At the same time the victim's blood was sprinkled as the law directed. Now a new Covenant was to replace the Jewish. Its chosen people were not a nation but humanity, whose head was our Lord and whose members were those who relied on Him. There was no roast flesh to be eaten nor unleavened bread, there was no blood to be sprinkled, yet if they formed one body of which He was the control-centre and power-station they must eat His flesh and drink His blood. He explained that these violent metaphors were not to be taken literally. He told His hearers, "It is the spirit that quickeneth: the flesh profiteth nothing: the words that I have spoken unto you are spirit and are life"; (John vi. 63). His flesh then is His human nature, the ideal humanity; His blood was His Life, the spirit which animated His flesh. Now the mark of His ideal humanity was its absolute dependence upon God. The note of His life, as it was spent and as it was yielded up in death, was philanthropic love. Thus to feed upon His flesh is to assimilate his dependence upon God, to drink His blood is to imbibe His love of humanity. This is no novel interpretation. The earliest explanation known to us is given by St. Ignatius, who says that the flesh is faith and the blood love.

After several months' absence in the neighbourhood of Tyre and Decapolis, the feeding of the four thousand and our Lord's refusal of an invitation made by a commission of scribes from Jerusalem that He would show them a sign in the sky, we find in Matthew again the title we are considering. According to Mark, Peter's confession was "Thou art the Christ"; Luke makes the confession, "The Christ of God." Matthew expresses it in the words "Thou art the Christ, the SON of the living GOD." The reader will observe how here again, as in Nathanael's earlier protestation, the title is equated with the Davidic king, God's vicegerent. Yet one further point must here be noticed.

As has been continually remarked, the immediate sequel to this confident confession that Jesus is the Messiah is the prophetic declaration that the Son of Man must be killed. At the same time our Lord identifies the Son of Man with the Messiah whose Father is God. He declares that "Whosoever shall be ashamed of me and of my words, of him shall the Son of Man be ashamed, when He cometh in His own glory, and the glory of the Father,[1] and of the holy angels."

Some of the Twelve may have attempted to distinguish between Jesus the Messiah and the Son of Man, but it is plain that our Lord, while avoiding the title Messiah, was endeavouring to teach them by the other title to disengage their conception of the Messianic kingship from the current notions of the time.

At the Transfiguration the Voice from the cloud said, "This is My Son, My chosen: hear ye Him." These words still leave us without any necessarily transcendent signification. They march with the Voice at the Baptism.

Subsequently to this we have, in John viii–x, long controversial arguments between our Lord and the authorities at Jerusalem. In general Jesus speaks of "the Father," which no doubt really means that God is His father, but admits of an interpretation which makes the people of Israel God's children: thus viii. 41. His Jewish opponents said, "We have one Father, even God." At another point our Lord spoke unambiguously "I speak the things which I have seen with My Father." Two comments must here be made. In the first place the pith and marrow of our Lord's argument is that His understanding of moral and religious duty is in exact agreement with God's purposes. It is this which makes Him and the Father to be one, i.e. one in spirit.

Secondly the Pharisaic Wisdom of Solomon gives personality to a Divine attribute, so that Wisdom appears as a consubstantial co-eternal being beside the Almighty. If there be truth in the picture we have sketched elsewhere of our Lord's early manhood, we may well believe that this conception was

[1] Mark viii. 38 and Matt. x. 33 say unambiguously "His Father" and "My Father."

not unknown to Him, and as He meditated on the various pre-figurements of His Ministry it would assist towards the thought which found expression in the words "Before Abraham was (born) I am." But more will be said of this in another chapter. Furthermore we must not forget that in the view of the Jews in that age men existed so really in the mind of God even before their birth that a man might be born blind because of his sins. This apprehension of pre-existence in the divine purpose would obviously contribute to the acceptance of such a belief.

Particularly important is the discussion between our Lord and His opponents at the time of the Feast of Dedication. He persisted in abstaining from claiming openly to be the Christ, yet declared that His will was so consonant with that of God that He was in the Father and the Father in Him. The Jews replied that as a man (they tacitly assume that He is not the Christ, since He does not avow Himself to be so) He is guilty of blasphemy in arrogating to Himself the honorific style of "son of GOD." In the last analysis this means that they laboured to confront our Lord with a dilemma. If He were the Christ, which alone they considered would justify the title the SON of GOD, they would present Him before Pilate as a pretender to the Davidic throne. If on the other hand, He were not the Christ, then as the Son of Man he was blaspheming if He arrogated to Himself a co-partnership with God.

Yet later, when we come to the return of the Seventy from their triumphant mission we find words which reveal in our Lord's mind an exalted sense of His functions. "Even the devils," said the Seventy, "are subject unto us in Thy name," and our Lord expressed His satisfaction in the words "I beheld Satan fallen as lightning from heaven," and declared further "All things have been delivered unto Me of My Father." This moment of exultation Luke ascribes to the working of the Holy Spirit, and we shall wisely be diffident in saying more. Yet while we shall feel ourselves to be treading on holy ground and seek to move in humility and awe, we may for a moment recur to what we said at the outset of this study. The human mind of Jesus, like our own minds, would have flashes of insight, dartings of perception, leaps into fuller truth. He had recognized that the Father had revealed to Peter the fact that the Son of Man was the Christ. He felt now in view of the report made by the Seventy that His power was so great that by His assistance His followers could "tread upon serpents and scorpions, and over all the power of the enemy." What, then, was He? His human mind might ask, and regarded in this way His next words acquire a new and deeper significance "No one," He said, "knoweth who the Son is, save the Father." In conformity with this interpretation are the words that follow "neither who the Father is, save the Son and he to whomsoever the Son willeth to reveal Him." Here the additional words which promise that apt disciples shall learn the Father's nature convey by way of contrast the fact that the Son's nature will remain unrevealed to men while He is among them. This then may be taken to indicate that our Lord Himself in His human consciousness had still no knowledge of His deity, however much imaginative sallies of speculative thought may have raised questions in His breast.

In teaching His disciples to address God as Father, our Lord still more evacuates of doctrinal significance the title Son of God. He associates His followers as brethren with Himself in the family of God.

Next in order we must notice Martha's profession of faith, when Jesus came to call her brother from the grave, "I have been," she said, "and still am convinced that Thou art the Messiah, the SON of GOD, even He that cometh into the world." Here once more we observe the conjunction of the title Messiah with that of SON of GOD, and we again infer that the significance of the second title is that the Davidic king has been pronounced and recognized by God to be His Son. We must reserve to another chapter the consideration of what all this imports: here we are concerned only with what the title Son of God was understood to mean.

After this our records do not introduce the title "Son of God" or betray its influence until in the Temple on the day of questions our Lord uttered the parable of the Vineyard. Here He plainly indicated His consciousness that His mission was of unique significance, that He was greater than the prophets who had preceded Him, that He was in a special sense the SON of GOD. What that sense was He does not define. It is enough that as His teaching preserved in the Fourth Gospel insisted, His position was such that the Father and the Son were, so to say, the two Persons in the universe who were of supreme significance both to the world and to one another. This finds clearest and deepest expression in the Johannine record of our Lord's utterances in the upper room on the night before the Crucifixion. After Judas had gone out and night had fallen Jesus said, "Now is the Son of Man glorified and God is glorified in Him, and God shall glorify Him in Himself and straightway shall he glorify Him." When they had risen from the table Jesus prayed: "Father, the hour is come; glorify Thy Son, that the Son may glorify Thee. . . . the glory which Thou hast given me I have given unto them; that they may be one, even as We are one; I in them and Thou in me, that they may be perfected into one." Here at the climax of our Lord's Ministry He fuses in an unmistakable unity the conception of His office as the Christ who is the Davidic king and SON of GOD with that of the Son of Man who embodied as the paragon of Israel the higher principles of humanity in contradistinction to the lower impulses of bestiality. The same fusion is to be seen in the last parable recorded by Matthew, where the Son of Man sits as King and Judge to pronounce sentence on all mankind.

Our Lord's words in Gethsemane and on the Cross present no new features requiring special comment, but two remarks should be made. The agony and prayers in the garden show us One who, however complete His Trust in God, whom He knows to be indeed a Father, is nevertheless absolutely human. It is the same with six of the seven words from the Cross. The cry "My God, why hast Thou forsaken Me?" is, as has been shown on another page, the beginning of the recitation of the 22nd Psalm, but, if this view be not accepted, it again shows us One absolutely human who recognizes God as the Supreme Being who holds his soul in life. It thus becomes a companion utterance to the Johannine "I ascend to My Father and your Father, to My God and your God." In all this, then, the sense of Sonship does not explicitly demand that we should recognize in it a consciousness of Deity. It is sufficient to say that the words

could be seen afterwards upon reflection to be consistent with
the Trinitarian doctrine when that was found to be the only
adequate metaphyscial explanation of all the facts.

Something more must be said of the trial scenes before
Caiaphas and Pilate. To appreciate these properly we must
keep in mind the design of the Jewish authorities and the
difficulty in which they found themselves. They wished to find
grounds for charging Our Lord with treason against the
Roman emperor. If He would say that He was the Christ or
the SON of GOD, by which was meant that He was the Davidic
king, they could lay an information against Him before Pilate.
Our Lord, however, continued to speak of the Son of Man.
Only to the Twelve had He openly avowed Himself to be the
Christ. True, at various times, others than the Twelve addressed
Him or proclaimed Him as king, and He did not repudiate or
rebuke their enthusiasm. But His public teaching advanced
no claim which the authorities could fasten on as treasonable.
The woman of Samaria might hear that He was the Messiah,
but her evidence was to seek; the last parable just referred to
was heard by the disciples alone. The challenge to destroy the
Temple which He would build again in three days might be
thought to imply that He possessed the magical powers tradi-
tionally ascribed to Solomon, and this might then have been
twisted into an assertion that He was a pretender to Solomon's
throne, but the witnesses could not agree as to what our Lord
had said. Caiaphas therefore adjured Jesus to say whether He
was the Christ, the SON of the Blessed. Thereupon our Lord
accepted the challenge, and identifying the Christ with the
Son of Man, i.e. once more insisting that He was not a nationalistic rebel but the spiritual sovereign of humanity, declared
that they would yet see Him seated at the right hand of God
and coming with the clouds of Heaven. This exaltation of
humanity sounded as blasphemy in the ears of the Sanhedrin,
and we shall have occasion to return to this point later. The
heart of the matter, however, was that they could all now aver
that they had heard Jesus lay claim to be the King of the Jews,
and with this avowal in their hands they went to Pilate. Still
Pilate refused to accept their words at their face value. He soon
discovered that on our Lord's lips the word "King" did not

8*

mean anything that could endanger the emperor's authority. Justice required the dismissal of the case, but fear of Tiberius' uncertain temper drove Pilate to pronounce the unjust sentence which the Jewish authorities desired. In their eagerness to bring this about they had reiterated their charge of treason, using their Jewish phraseology and saying that He made Himself (son or a) Son of GOD.[1] To them the words signified that He claimed to be David's heir;[2] Pilate understood the words to mean something else, which fitted in with our Lord's assurance that He had come into the world to bear witness to the truth. Yet though this had more than ever made Pilate desire to act justly, he yielded to his fears.

Thus, throughout the whole gamut of the Gospel narratives, one only meaning is found to attach in the first instance to the title "the SON of GOD." When Jesus is so styled, it is as much as to say that He is the inheritor of David's throne. Those who address Him in this way are giving Him assurance of their service if and when He takes His stand before the world to be the *de facto* successor, as He is the *de jure* successor, to the sovereignty of Israel. The Fourth Gospel does not differ in this respect from the synoptists. On the contrary, that Gospel, in its narrative portions, adheres perhaps even more faithfully than do the others to the original understanding of the title.[3] The

---

[1] They repeated verbally and truly enough Jesus' avowal that He was GOD's son but subtly insinuated to Pilate that Jesus claimed to be the SON of GOD, the Christ or King, whilst in point of fact He persisted in avoiding this title, saying, as both Matthew and Luke show, that it was the High Priest himself who was putting this interpretation on His words (Mark has condensed what was said into a crude and plain downright affirmation of Messiahship which blurs the historical fact that to the end our Lord declined to accept from those who used the word with a nationalistic and political sense the denomination "Christ").

[2] This may be illustrated by a comparison of Mark (presumably repeating Peter), with Luke writing for Gentiles. Mark (and Luke follows him) says that demoniacs cried "Thou art the SON OF GOD"; Luke adds that they knew or testified that He was the Christ.

[3] It has sometimes been asserted that the synoptists emphasize the humanity, while John emphasizes the deity of our Lord. Yet so far is this from corresponding with the actual facts that it might be held truer to say the opposite. The synoptists represent our Lord as exerting a transcendent power, inherent in Himself, of healing disease and controlling evil spirits. John consistently exhibits our Lord as dependent upon the Father for permission and authority to do His mighty works. At Cana He declared

prologue, the envoy and a few verses which, had modern methods of typography been available nineteen centuries ago, would have appeared in footnotes or in parenthesis, develop that original meaning. They interpret its possible, if latent, meaning in accordance with the theological conceptions to which Christians were led by the Holy Spirit. In its first use, however, the title the SON of GOD carried immediately to the Jewish hearer the significance stated above. Quite exceptional is the centurion's ejaculation at the Cross, "truly this was a son of God," and there can be no doubt that Luke is giving for his Gentile readers the essential meaning of the words when he writes "a righteous man."

Two corollaries deserve to be added. (1) In a papyrus of A.D. 19 we find Germanicus in one of his proclamations styling himself as Σεβαστοῦ υἱὸς Θεοῦ Σεβαστοῦ υἱωνος, "son of Augustus, grandson of the deified Augustus." He then proceeds as follows: "Your acclamations, which for me are invidious and such as are addressed to Gods, I altogether deprecate. For they are appropriate only to him who is actually the saviour and benefactor of the whole human race, my father." We may notice too in A.D. 41 a prefect speaks of τοῦ Θεοῦ ἡμῶν καίσαρος, viz. Claudius.

(2) Eusebius claims to have extracted from the archives at Edessa a letter sent by Abgar, the king of that country, to our Lord, and we may be satisfied to accept it as the reason that the Greeks, mentioned in John's 12th chapter, desired an interview with our Lord. Critics of the last century discredited its authenticity mainly, it would appear, because it was supposed to speak of our Lord as the SON of GOD. It is clear, however, that Abgar's letter goes no further than does the papyrus just quoted, and since Eusebius after all was no credulous or ignorant writer,

that His hour was not yet come. At Lazarus' grave He thanked the Father because He had heard Him. When he realized that the Crucifixion was to take place at Passover time, He prayed, "Father, glorify Thy Name." He constantly insisted that He had been sent into the world to do the works which He was doing. What we have shown to be the immediate factual meaning of the title SON of GOD will be seen to be consonant with this reading of St. John's narrative. It is only when the Johannine interpretations of the facts are used to bring out the implicit significance of the title that we can say that the Fourth Gospel dwells upon our Lord's deity rather than on His humanity.

but himself lived in a critical age, we need not hesitate to use the letter for making intelligible the emotion our Lord showed when He was told of the Greeks' request for an interview.

The reader may like to see for himself what Abgar wrote.

"Abgar, Governor of Edessa to Jesus the Good Saviour (*or* kindly Healer) who has appeared in the City of Jerusalem, Greeting. I have heard about you and your cures, as having been effected by you without drugs and herbs. For as rumour has it, you make blind men see again, lame men walk about, and you cleanse lepers and expel unclean spirits and demons and treat those who are afflicted with disease of long standing and awaken dead men.   And after hearing all these things about you, I made up my mind, that the explanation was one or other of these two, either that you are GOD (ὁ Θεὸς) and having come down from the heaven do these things, or you are GOD's son (υἱὸς τοῦ Θεοῦ) doing these things."

One final fact deserves special consideration. Once and once only is our Lord said to have explained His relation to the Father by using any one of the three forms of phrase distinguished in this chapter. In John x. 36 He defends and justifies His declaration (υἱὸς τοῦ Θεοῦ εἰμι), which the reader will recognize as the second of the expressions we have enumerated. By way of contrast and in illustration of the centurion's words we may quote Wisdom v. 5, κατελογίσθη ἐν υἱοῖς Θεοῦ and ii. 16, ἀλαζονεύεται πατέρα Θεόν, both utterances savouring more of heathen polytheism than of Jewish monotheism.

Chapter Two

THE SON OF MAN

FROM the first Christians have believed that the Incarnation was no sudden or catastrophic incursion by the divine into human history. It was indeed the climax of a long and mounting process of preparation. "In the fullness of time, God sent forth His Son."

In no field, it may be said, is this preparation to be seen more manifestly than in the thought and language which were current amongst the Jewish people when our Lord came. That thought and that language supplied an apt vehicle through which the truth He had to exhibit could be made intelligible. This conception in its general outlines is a familiar theme, and Christian thinkers have found in Greek philosophy too a preliminary training of Gentiles for the reception of the Gospel. The idea, however, would appear to deserve and require a wider extension than has commonly been given to it. It has been recognized that the truths ultimately articulated in the Christian creeds became intelligible to men who had been led onwards towards them by more rudimentary expressions, and patient research has been employed in tracing the origins and developments of these truths. Yet, as will be seen later, this knowledge that truth was revealed by gradual stages has not always been kept in mind when the results of the Incarnation were under examination. To indicate by one example how this thought of the divine preparation must be kept continually in mind, we may notice the way in which the doctrine of a Messiah shows itself in the narrative of our Lord's Ministry. The Jews expected a Messiah : our Lord eventually elicited from St. Peter, as the spokesman of the Twelve, an acknowledgment that they accepted Him for the Messiah. Nevertheless, in order to revolutionize their ideas as to the nature of His rule, He scrupulously refrained from using the title till after His Resurrection. Thus while the thought of a Messiah and the title prepared the way for the Christian comprehension of His messianic mission as the divinely intended fulfilment of divinely given promises, we must, if we would keep a proper historical perspective, never read back into the earlier language the fullness of meaning which was afterwards seen to be implied. At each stage we must try to evaluate the significance of the language as understood at the moment, while at the same time we shall gladly and thankfully believe that the truths thus half-revealed and half-concealed are ultimate truths which in this way God was unfolding to men. In other words, we shall on the one hand be satisfied that the resultant statements of the Creed are true, although they at first appear in an embryonic obscurity. On the other hand, we shall not read into the early adumbrations of the truth the fullness of meaning to which it was later seen that they were to minister.

In Arabic even still the expression "son of man" is used as a variant or periphrasis for "man." Yet our records show us that our Lord frequently used the expression as a title for Himself. Christian thinkers have been at pains to draw out the significance of the title. Admittedly the Old Testament has instances of the use which we have just noted from Arabic. "What is man," says the Psalmist, "that Thou art mindful of him, and the son of man that Thou visitest him?" Balaam in one of his parables declared "God is not a man that He should lie nor the son of man that He should repent." The prophet Ezekiel represents himself as being addressed by God with the title "son of man," and it has been said that the message of that prophet is of more general and even universal significance than are the utterances of other prophets. It has therefore been judged that he is addressed as "son of man" because the truths he has to publish are for men as men rather than for Jews as Jews. In the light of this it may well be held that by choosing the title "Son of Man" in preference to that of "Son of David," our Lord is identifying Himself with humanity, and is seeking to permeate with the idea of a universal mission the Jewish conception of a national king. As will be shown elsewhere, the title "Son of David" would at once have given ground for the belief that He claimed to be the King of the Jewish nation, and possibly the long-expected Messiah who, in the popular view, was to liberate them from both the Roman Government and the alternative sovereignty of the Edomite Herod. In the same way to have spoken of Himself as the Christ would have been still more liable to countenance nationalistic hopes, for it would have suggested that he was not only the heir to the Davidic throne nor yet only a Davidic king, but the supreme and paramount exemplar of Davidic kingship. Under these titles it could hardly be hoped that the disciples could be led out of their narrow conception of His mission to the spiritual idea of a divine Redeemer.

In the event, the disciples came to understand that the title was one chosen by our Lord Himself to designate His person, and it connoted for them the attributes and qualities which He had taught them to be the true characteristics of His messianic spirit. Since then all Christians have recognized that again and again when He spoke of the "Son of Man," He meant Himself, while by using the words He was concerned to insist on some aspect of His mission which any other title might have seemed to contradict. There remains, however, for consideration a question which has hardly received the attention that it requires. It has been held by some that the expression "Son of Man" must, without exception, be used by our Lord in one and the same sense. It is said that, were this not so, we should find some indication in the Syriac versions that the words at one time meant one thing and at another, another—that when no more was meant than "Man" one form of translation would be used, and when our Lord was intended, another. This view, as we shall see, stultifies the purpose with which our Lord chose the title for Himself. We can observe the gradual unfolding of deeper meaning out of a rudimentary simplicity in the case of the titles "Lord" and "Son of God," and we should not, therefore, be surprised to find a similar development in the signification of the title "Son of Man."

Manifestly, therefore, we must examine each occurrence of its use, weighing it in its context. It will be no surprise, indeed it is only what we should expect, if we find the words used at first by our Lord in their ordinary and simple sense, while later there can be no doubt that they bear a deeper significance. Let us begin by considering the examples of its use in Mark's

Gospel. Taking them in the order in which they appear—and, as we shall see, this order would seem to be historically correct— we find the following instances:

(1) When the paralytic was assured of forgiveness, our Lord said "the Son of Man has power on earth to forgive sins." Following the line of thought above suggested, we should expect this to mean that men are authorized to declare God's forgiveness in the way that Nathan assured David that he was forgiven —and this without the prescribed sacrifices of the Temple ritual. It is the first time as far as Mark's Gospel is concerned that our Lord uses the words, and therefore, according to the view we are considering, they should bear their conventional meaning. This judgment is confirmed by Matthew's comment that the multitude "marvelled and glorified God, which had given such power unto men."

(2) In confirmation of His relaxation of the Rabbinic rules as to the Sabbath, our Lord said "the Sabbath was made for man and not man for the Sabbath. Therefore the Son of Man is Lord also of the Sabbath." Logical cogency requires that here the "Son of Man" should be identical in sense with the previous "man." To equate it with "our Lord" cripples the argument. What David did, other men may do, and the episode recorded in the Codex Bezae at Luke vi. 10 substantiates the assertion that man is the arbiter in the matter of Sabbath observance. Here again then, in this early stage of His Ministry, our Lord is seen using the expression "Son of Man" as a variant for "man."

(3) It is after Peter's acknowledgment of Jesus' Messiahship that a deeper and more special significance begins to appear in the words. Yet, it may be said that, for the first two or three times, they may be thought to bear a covert meaning rather than an overt. Immediately after the apostle's confession our Lord, we are told, began to say that "the Son of Man must suffer many things and be rejected of the elders and of the chief priests and scribes, and be killed, and after three days rise again." We can see that this is the first hint of Crucifixion, but it might be understood to be a warning of the fate that would attend all men who accepted the Lord's teaching. Such a more meagre sense would fit in with the further words, "Whosoever

will come after me, let him deny himself, and take up his cross and follow me."

(4) After the Transfiguration our Lord charged His three apostles to say nothing about what they had seen "save when the Son of Man should have risen again from the dead." It is manifest that here the Lord meant by the words Himself, but it is not so clear that His hearers understood the words in that way. Mark tells us that they were in doubt as to what this "resurrection" was to be, and Luke declares that even later the apostles could not understand what their Master was trying to convey to them.

(5) During Holy Week when our Lord was asked what signs would give warning that the Temple should be destroyed, He foretold the disturbances in nature and in the political sphere which would precede the fall of Jerusalem when, as He said, they should see "the Son of Man coming in clouds with great power and glory." Here again plainly the Lord meant Himself, even if we allow that the apostles may have been uncertain whether the Son of Man was to be some other who was thus to appear.

At this point we must pause to mention and consider an interpretation of the words which has been much dwelt upon by many writers. In the book of Daniel a dream-vision shows, under the form of four savage beasts, the pagan empires which preceded the Maccabees' victory. Then the expected rule of right is represented as appearing in the form of a man. This doubtless is intended to convey the assurance that the human dignities of right, justice, truth, freedom of conscience are now to be dominant in the world, and that God's chosen and consecrated people are to exercise such a beneficent dominion over all the brutal and grasping powers of the heathen. We read, "I saw in the night visions, and, behold, there came with the clouds of heaven one like unto a son of man, and he came even to the ancient of days, and they brought him near before him, And there was given him dominion, and glory, and a kingdom, that all the peoples, nations and languages should serve him: his dominion is an everlasting dominion, which shall not be destroyed." This figure then stood for the ideal Israel in contrast with the arrogant selfishness of those who worshipped Baal or

Marduk or Moloch. As has been explained in another chapter, our Lord was brought by the Holy Spirit to view Himself as the embodiment, the keystone, the focus, the supreme typical representative of Israel in regard to the mission to which God had consecrated that people. God brought a vine (Israel) out of Egypt and planted it in the land of Canaan. Our Lord was the true vine. In the same way and by a still easier transfer, He took to Himself the title "the Son of Man" as the supreme embodiment of that ideal for Israel which Daniel's vision had portrayed. The reader will notice how in the vision the Son of Man comes "with the clouds of heaven," and will remember how our Lord repeated the very phrase with reference to Himself.

Assuming, then, that before the end of His Ministry our Lord used the title with all the implications which it bore in Daniel, we must ask at what point in the Ministry we should begin to read into the words this deeper significance. The most satis-factory answer would seem to be that, if we keep in mind the distinction between what our Lord's thought was and what His hearers understood at the moment, He, from the beginning of His Ministry, had in view this ideal of Israel as a part of the Scriptures which He had to fulfil.

Following the order we have accepted as historical, we notice first our Lord's rejoinder to Nathanael. Edersheim observed that in that rejoinder Nathanael's conception of our Lord's per-sonality is tacitly corrected. Instead of "the Son of God . . . King of Israel" he should think rather of "the Son of Man." Edersheim interprets this to mean that the deity of our Lord is to be pretermitted for a while and his humanity to be dwelt upon. In the light of what we have already said we must judge rather that our Lord's purpose is to turn Nathanael's thoughts away from narrow nationalistic hopes and to direct them towards the universal blessings destined for humanity. When we remember the significance of the temptations in the wilder-ness, we shall have no hesitation in believing that our Lord has already attached to the title "the Son of Man" the purpose and hopes of universal redemption. The Baptist, too, whether inspired himself to understand this or learning it from our Lord, had declared the week before that the Lamb of God was taking away the sin of the world and not of Israel alone. We must conclude then that throughout our Lord's Ministry He used the title the "Son of Man" with a wider and deeper significance than the hearer may at first have understood. Yet we shall miss something of its meaning if we suppose that it is to be equated with our Lord's own single person, and it is here that we find the cause of the contradictory interpretations that have been given to some of our Lord's utterances.

We can, perhaps, best express the content of the words if we say that they mean Humanity in the way that Comte and the Positivists have conceived of it, but with a vital Christian modification. It does not mean the totality of human beings, pagan, Jew and Christian, but the whole Christian community, including its monarchical Head and indwelt by His Spirit. Thus understood, we find the words to Nathanael indicate that, as our Lord foresaw, the Church would be the true Bethel, and, the heaven being opened at Pentecost or perhaps rather at the Baptism, the Angels of God would be for ever mininstering to humanity, i.e. to its Head and to His Mystical Body.

We can now see in their proper light the next two utterances of our Lord in which He used the words "the Son of Man." When He declared that the paralytic's sins had been forgiven, some of the hearers doubtless interpreted the words in the pedestrian way described above. Their true significance we can now see is that humanity, animated by Christ's spirit, can pronounce on earth judgments which are in accord with the divine will. That this is the right interpretation of the saying is shown by what John relates of the first Easter night. Jesus, we read, "breathed on them and saith unto them, 'Receive ye holy spirit. Whose soever sins ye remit, they are remitted unto them, and whose soever sins ye retain, they are retained'." In the same way we shall not say that every man may please himself as to what duty, if any, he has as the quintessence of the ancient sabbath obligation. Nor shall we say that our Lord as being God could repeal or reform that obligation. Rather we can see that humanity informed by Christ's Spirit can handle the Sabbath question so that it shall be of benefit to humanity. So Jesus Himself, the Head of the new, consecrated community, acted in accordance with the Eternal Spirit when He healed on the Sabbath without demanding that the sufferer should plead that delay was dangerous or that there was no opportunity on another day. More than this, the words present us with a portrait of our Lord's "divine legation."

In this respect, which is the companion and counterpart of pictures given to us by the same words in regard to other matters, the fulfilment of the law becomes what, if we may borrow and remould the jargon of the psychologists, may be described as its sublimation. In other words its precepts are lifted on to another plane. The negative taboos as to the Sabbath disappear, melting into a positive commandment enjoining philanthropic love at all times as the paramount expression of devotion to God. A similar sublimation is seen in our Lord's treatment of the laws as to ceremonial cleanness.

We have considered the use of the title "the Son of Man" as Mark exhibits it, and we have found, it may be believed, the gradual increase in definiteness of meaning till it appears to be virtually a title of our Lord. When we turn to Matthew the results of our scrutiny become yet more interesting.

Passing over those instances in which Mark offers a parallel already discussed, we have to notice one or two which require comment. In viii. 20 we read "Foxes have holes . . . but the Son of Man hath not where to lay His head." Luke ix. 58 shows that this utterance belongs to the period after the Transfiguration. In x. 23 Matthew represents our Lord as instructing the Twelve when they are persecuted in one city to go to another, adding, "Ye shall not have gone over the cities of Israel till the Son of Man be come." Luke x. 10 shows that this utterance may have been part of the instruction given to the Seventy, in which case it again belongs to the later period. On the other hand, after John's two messengers came and were departed, in our Lord's comparison of the Baptist's austerity with His own sociability, both Luke and Matthew, presumably following Q, give His words in the form: "The Son of Man came eating and drinking," where it is hard to suppose that He intends anything but Himself.[1] This, then, gives us an instance of His using the

---

[1] It is, however, just possible that our Lord intends us to understand that the Christian teacher, no less than his Master, will, unlike the ascetic John, enter into the pleasures of human society.

title specifically limited to meaning Himself at a time prior to the Baptist's murder, i.e. as early as the spring of A.D. 31.

When Matthew (xii. 40) explains the sign of Jonah the prophet by the words, "So shall the Son of Man be three days and three nights in the heart of the earth," we cannot be sure that this was said on our Lord's return from His visit to Tyre and Sidon and after the feeding of the four thousand, as Mark viii. 11 may suggest. It is possible that it should be dated, as Luke xi. 30 might seem to suggest, two or three months before the Crucifixion. In xiii. 37, where it is said, "He that soweth the good seed is the Son of Man," the parable of the Tares may be shown by this very expression to have been uttered some time about the Transfiguration.[1]

In xvi. 13 Matthew unmistakably identifies our Lord with the Son of Man, "Whom do men say that I the Son of Man am?" As for xvi. 27 and its parallels in Mark viii. 38 and Luke ix. 26, a word may perhaps be usefully said. The "Glory of God" is an expression continually used for His operations in the physical and spiritual world, these operations being regarded as magnificent to contemplate and glorious when they are considered. Thus "the heavens declare the glory of God, and the firmament showeth His handywork." The recall of Lazarus to life is a splendid example of God's power to give men life, and He glorifies His Son by countenancing the Son's visibly doing on earth what is continually being done invisibly. At the same time the Son glorifies the Father by exhibiting before men's eyes the kind of life-giving operation which is an attribute of God. When, therefore, our Lord speaks of His coming (Luke ix. 26, "when He shall come in His own glory, and in His Father's, and of the holy angels"), we shall understand him to be describing the manifest successes of His Body, the Church, in the next half century (which will indeed be the clear evidence of His spiritual working in the world, showing forth gloriously His power and the power of the Father), and also the processes of physical nature which are angels of His (Heb. i. 7), e.g. the

---

[1] Alternatively we ought perhaps here again to suppose our Lord to mean that the Christian Church, like her Master, will be sowing the good seed of truth about God, but verse 41 ("in the end of this age . . . the Son of Man shall send forth His angels") favours the view taken in the text.

dearth in Judea about A.D. 42 (earthquakes at various times), the fall of Jerusalem A.D. 70 and the eruption of Vesuvius in A.D. 79. All this our Lord predicts should come about while some still remained who were alive in the autumn of A.D. 32. This interpretation becomes important, as will presently be seen, when we come to our Lord's trial before Caiaphas.

In xxiv. 27 and 30 and its parallel, Luke xvii. 24, the advent of the Son of Man can hardly be anything but His catastrophic vindication when the anti-Christian Jewish authorities were in a few weeks crushed by the power of Rome and the Christians and their Master's teaching were justified.

To turn to Luke, in vi. 22, "Blessed are ye when men shall . . . and cast out your name as evil, for the Son of Man's sake," where Matt. v. 11 gives "for My sake," we seem to find a use of the title "the Son of Man" to summarize, if we may so express it, in that way the content of our Lord's teaching about God's nature and man's duty, as Jesus was revealing it. Something of the same kind is to be seen in the Fourth Gospel, where "the Son" is used at times as a convenient way of epitomizing His revelation in contrast with the Rabbinic exegesis of Scripture. In Luke xii. 8 the Son of Man confesses in the day of judgment those who have been true to Him in this life, and here, as in some passages in Matthew, our Lord echoes the words of Daniel. In Luke xvii. 22 the disciples are told that they would desire to see one of the days of the Son of Man, but should not see it. Here the thought is manifestly of our Lord Himself, not of humanity in general. He would eventually exhibit His power in the control of world history, but men would not be able to watch, as a scientist watches chemical processes taking place, the ferment of social and political processes. Christ's triumphal vindication of His sovereignty would burst suddenly upon men's sight, in the same way that Cyrus' demolition of the Babylonian empire, though foretold by Isaiah, came suddenly and unexpectedly. In Luke xxii. 48 our Lord says to Judas, "Dost thou hand over the Son of Man (to His enemies) with a kiss?" and the reader can see how this passage illustrates the significance, as in vi. 22, of the title.

John iii. 13 is most naturally understood as an explanatory note of the evangelist, but it is to be noticed that in that case we have here an instance of the title being used after the Ascension and not by our Lord Himself, though this comment may be countered by observing that the writer is expressing himself in such a way that his comment appears to be uttered by our Lord Himself. The next verse, on the other hand, may preserve an utterance of the Lord, though perhaps we ought to regard it as belonging in point of historical order to some later date in the Ministry. In v. 27 we have again the thought of the jurisdiction and judgment which the Son of Man, as Daniel foresaw, was in God's purpose to execute. In vi. 27, after the feeding of the five thousand, but before the Transfiguration, the Son of Man is indubitably Jesus alone, and this use recurs again, vi. 53 and 62. In the last passage we have a plain assertion of Christ's existence and sublime dignity before His Incarnation, and a prediction of its resumption after the Ascension. Some would doubtless question the historicity and authenticity of these words, but adhering to the view we have hitherto taken of the Fourth Gospel, we shall rather modify our statement as to the use of the title the Son of Man. We shall be prepared to allow that occasionally at least, even before Peter's avowal that Jesus was the Christ, our Lord spoke of Himself alone, apart from His Body, the Church, as the Son of Man. In viii. 28 and ix. 35 and xii. 34 and xiii. 31 it is the same: all of these passages are subsequent to the Transfiguration.

It remains that we notice the two examples of this title being used outside the Gospels. In Acts vii. 56, St. Stephen, his face lighted up with an angelic ecstacy, said, "Behold, I see the heavens opened, and the Son of Man standing on the right hand of God." To those who denied that Jesus was the Christ this glorification of the Son of Man was blasphemy, and it was at this point that his judges' fury hurried them into murdering him. This is the more noticeable because the story of James the Lord's brother's martyrdom points to the same conclusion. Asked to give guidance to the Passover throng, he said, "Why do you question me about Jesus the Son of Man? It is He who is now sitting in heaven on the right hand of the Great Power, and He is going to come upon the clouds of heaven," whereupon he was martyred. These two examples, it will be noticed, entirely agree with what we have said about our Lord's reply to Caiaphas.

Our examination and discussion of this title, "the Son of Man," has been so lengthy and involved that it may be of advantage to put before the reader in a more concise form the sum and substance of our conclusions. We may put the matter in this way.

Much labour has been devoted to the examination of the use and connotation of the expression "the Son of Man." Dr. Kirsopp Lake in particular, in his *The Beginnings of Christianity*, made a thorough scrutiny of the occurrences of the title in the several gospels and discussed its significance in view of this evidence. No attempt will be made here to retraverse the ground which he and many others have fruitfully explored. It is believed, however, that the scheme presented for the arrangement of the chronological records brings useful light to the elucidation of the matter.

It is common ground with all investigators that Semitic speech uses "the Son of Man" as a variant or periphrasis for "man." When Zion is bidden by Zechariah to expect her King riding upon an ass and on a colt, the foal of an ass, one animal doubly designated is intended. What results are obtained if we accept the authentic testimony of our Gospels and if we read their record in the order we seem to have established?

(1) At the outset we find when Nathanael leapt to the conviction that Jesus of Nazareth was "the Son of God" and "King of Israel," our Lord declared that the disciples would see that the heavens had opened and that the angels of God were ascending and descending upon the Son of Man.

When account is taken of the three temptations after the Baptism and of the fact that we have here the first occurrence of the expression, we are led to interpret the announcement as a promise of the Pentecostal gift. On our Lord Himself the Spirit had descended seven weeks before : now He assures His hearers that on "every mother's son" the gift may and shall be vouchsafed. God's angels include winds and flaming fire (Hebrews i. 7) and we remember that these concomitants are mentioned when the Holy Ghost possessed the Christian community.

(2) A few weeks later John adds to our Lord's words to Nicodemus the prediction that "as Moses lifted up the serpent, so must the Son of Man be lifted up." It is not indisputable even

that this is not a parenthetic note of the evangelist similar to others which have been noted elsewhere. If, however, we may accept the words as coming on this occasion from our Lord's lips, they seem most naturally to be understood in the sense that humanity must be exalted above nationalistic aspirations if the world is to be brought into harmony with the divine purpose. Eternal life is the learning, reverencing and loving of the divine character, and this comes to those who are convinced that God cares for "every mother's son" of us.

Nevertheless, we must not exclude the possibility—perhaps the probability—that within the wide sweep of this assertion, the Son first included the specific magnet of His own exaltation as the focal point of humanity, the magnetic pole of human destiny and at the same time He was conscious that His exaltation must be preceded and prepared for by the humiliating elevation on the Cross. (Cf. St. Ignatius' nomenclature of our Lord Himself as the Cross, the mechanism which engineered our access to God.)

(3) The next instance of the expression is found when our Lord pronounced that the paralytic's sins had been forgiven. Matthew, observing that the people glorified God who had given such power unto men, countenances the view, which it is natural to take, that our Lord asserted that humanity had authority to assure a repentant sinner that forgiveness was his.

(4) In the same way the point of the argument from David's hunger being acknowledged to override the Sabbath law and more, is blunted unless we understand humanity to be superior to the Sabbath commandment.

Thus far our records seem to show that our Lord used the title with the connotation of humanity. Plainly, however, in the last few cases, if not in the earliest, the attitude of some hearers would encourage, if it did not suggest, the identification of humanity's champion with the title used for humanity. It is not surprising, therefore, that now our Lord again employs the phrase as a convenient *nom de guerre* for Himself. It avoided the dangerously nationalistic implication of the title Christ, the challenge imported in the style of son of Joseph or son of David, and still more that of Son of God. It trained and developed the spiritual insight, the personal devotion and the charitable disposition of His hearers and all the while opened the way for the conception of a divine purpose anterior to Creation itself, a purpose for the inter-penetration of humanity by deity, and for a spiritual communion and union between the Father and His offspring, man.

Thus the significance of the title, the Son of Man, merged into that of Son of God, and moreover, it brought with it the implication that humanity might be so united with its capital representative that He could be present in each individual unit. So it was that in the last week a parable told that "inasmuch as ye did it unto one of these, ye did it unto Me." So it was that Paul said that the Christian body should judge angels (1 Cor. vi. 3). Thus ultimately it may be said that the expression "the Son of Man" carries by implication the sense of the Christian body vitally and organically united with its Head and Helmsman. That this sense is to be seen in the final utterance of our Lord and not in the middle of His Ministry is no small confirmation of our arrangement of the Gospel material. In the middle period when the phrase partly revealed and partly cloaked His prediction of His death, listeners, while often understanding Him to be speaking of Himself, if they were yet unprepared for the dark realities of the Crucifixion or the disappointment of national ambitions or the recognition of divine self-sacrifice, could draw a distinction between the Son of Man and the Jesus they knew. The blind man from Siloam put the question as did others in the Dedication week, "Who is this Son of Man?" but the two or three days before the Crucifixion exhibit clearly what we have described as the ultimate significance of the words. That the Synoptists no less than John demonstrate this development in the connotation of the phrase is strong confirmation of our interpretations and of our harmony of the records.

Chapter Three

THE SON OF DAVID

(1)

IF we should pitch at random upon a reader of the Gospels and ask what he understood by the statement that our Lord was the Son of David, we should certainly be told that the Son of David means one of many lineally descended from that monarch. This notion is not one adopted after careful study and much consideration. There can be no doubt that it is no more than a loose, general, hazy interpretation of the title. Yet the evidence, scrutinized and sifted with painstaking attention, would appear to suggest something different.

St. Joseph is addressed by the angel in his dream as "Joseph, thou Son of David," and as the words are commonly understood, this must seem surprising and puzzling. Why should he not be styled in the same sort of fashion in which St. Peter appears as Simon, son of John? At once the thought occurs that the title is equivalent to naming the bearer of it as the heir presumptive or heir apparent to the throne of David. If this is so, all the passages in the Gospels where the title appears are illuminated with a new significance. When the Syro-Phoenician woman cried for help, she testified to the circulation around her of statements that Jesus was the Davidic heir, and doubtless a modern commentator is right in supposing that, in the semi-pagan atmosphere of Tyre, that heir had associated with him memories of the marvellous and magical powers which had come to cling about the memory of David's son Solomon. However that may be, when Bartimaeus raised the same cry, he was protesting his acknowledgment that our Lord was the Davidic king, not one casual member of the Davidic house.

It is unnecessary to pursue the thought through all the instances in the Gospels of the title being used. Suffice it to say that in every case the interpretation here suggested lends fresh and vital force to its occurrence.[1] There is, however, another aspect of the matter which requires mention. Until our Lord was born, St. Joseph's heir would be his brother Cleopas' son James, and James would therefore be the son of David. When he lost his title as heir through St. Joseph acknowledging Jesus as his son, it is intelligible to human nature that James would not be likely immediately to subscribe to our Lord's messianic claim. It will be found that, on this line of interpretation, a great deal becomes clear which on the common interpretation seems to have no special significance.

It is tempting to venture a little into the field of conjecture. We know that Zerubbabel ruled at Jerusalem for some time after Cyrus allowed Jews to return to Jerusalem. The story is obscure, but it leaves room for the following reconstruction of the Davidic family's history in the next five hundred years. In each generation the first-born son was consecrated from his mother's womb in the hope that he might be the expected Messiah. Hence he did not marry and the next heir came from a younger brother. Matthew's genealogy shows the succession of heirs. Luke's gives the lineal descent through the junior brothers. This will account for the number of names in Matthew being no more than fourteen, while in Luke we have twenty-three names. It also harmonizes with Epiphanius' statement that St. Joseph, our Lord, and James his brother were all Nazoraeans, which he adduces as a fact justifying the belief that St. Joseph would understand the perpetual virginity of our Lord's mother. These considerations prompt yet another suggestion. We have seen that the title "the Nazoraean" was habitually given to our Lord by those who were acquainted with his story and that this

---

[1] Some confirmation of our view may be found in the fact that, as we are told, the sons of David and they alone were all buried in the City of David. It is fantastic to suppose that every lineal descendant of David was brought to this ancestral sepulchre. It is understandable that all the kings in general were there buried, and if the unique interment there of Huldah the prophetess must be explained, we need not hesitate to suppose that she was in reality the heiress to the throne, passed over in favour of the next male heir. Exceptions to the rule here suggested are specially noted in the Books of Kings and Chronicles, e.g. Manasseh 2 Kings xxi. 18, 2 Chron. xxxiii. 20 and Amon 2 Kings xxi. 26. Further confirmation may perhaps be found in what we are told by Hegesippus in regard to James, the Lord's brother. He too, after his martyrdom, was buried in the precincts of the Temple.

meant that He was the "Holy One." It is deserving of note that while this is the linguistic sense of the title, that title is found associated with no names other than those of James and St. Joseph. This suggests that among the Jews of that age it was reserved for the Davidic heir and so was equivalent to Son of David, understood in the way we have just explained. This is as much as to say that the title "the Nazoraean" was tantamount to indicating its possessor as the potential King of Israel and even perhaps the king destined to be the Messiah. To hail any-one as king was directly to challenge the position of Herod or of the Roman Emperor; to call him Nazoraean was not equally defiant. Understood in this way, the title seems to throw light on many details of the story.

It will be of advantage here to quote some words of Epi-phanius (*Adv. Haer.*, 1/2/29) which will be felt to acquire a new and special significance in the light of the suggestion we have just made. He writes:

ἀλλὰ καὶ εὑρίσκομεν αὐτὸν ἐκ τοῦ Δαβὶδ ὄντα, διὰ τὸ τὸν υἱὸν εἶναι τοῦ Ἰωσὴφ Ναζωραῖον γενόμενον. ἦν γὰρ πρωτότοκος τῷ Ἰωσὴφ καὶ ἡγιασμένος, ἔτι δὲ καὶ ἱερατεύσαντα αὐτὸν κατὰ τὴν παλαιὰν ἱερωσύνην εὕρομεν, διὸ καὶ ἠφίετο αὐτῷ ἅπαξ του ἐνιαυτοῦ εἰσ τὰ Ἅγια τῶν ἁγίων εἰσιέναί ὡς τοῖς ἀρχιερεῦσιν ἐκέλευσεν ὁ νόμος, κατὰ το γεγραμμένον.

Let us assume that these conclusions are at the least possible and even probable and at the best are in general certain: what new significance do they lend to the Gospel story and what features of that story do they illuminate?

(1) If James, the Lord's brother, had regarded himself and had been regarded by his family as the Davidic heir until our Lord was born we can understand some of the motives which impelled him and his three brothers to disbelieve the validity of the claims of the Blessed Virgin's Son. Cleopas, we may well suppose, accepted his brother Joseph's word for it that he him-self was not the father and also that he was not shielding or conniving at any misconduct of his wife. Thus the father, Cleopas, was divided against his son. Since we find Cleopas' daughter Mary, the mother of James and Joses, at the Cross and greeting the Risen Lord on Easter morning, we may well understand how she too was divided from other members of the family by her belief in Jesus as the Christ.

(2) At Nazareth and the neighbouring Cana, some who heard from the family their disavowal of our Lord's legitimacy would hesitate as to whether St. Joseph was to be regarded as uxorious or the Blessed Virgin as indeed the instrument of a divine redemptive act. Thus it was that Nathanael, apparently after some hesitancy and perhaps a prayer for divine guidance, when impressed by our Lord's prophetic insight exclaimed, "Rabbi, Thou art the Son of God; Thou art the King of Israel."

So far we might seem to be resting the case on the fact that St. Joseph and our Lord are both addressed as "son of David," that both they and James are styled Nazoraeans and that a possible explanation of the two genealogies of St. Joseph may be found in our theory. But the matter does not end there. Jeremiah xxxiii. 21 announces as a word that had come to him from Jahveh that David should always have "a son to reign upon his throne" and it cannot be doubted that this prophecy, coupled with the promise in Psalm lxxxix. 34, kept perpetually alive in Jewish thought the belief that the genealogical line of succession was to be treasured and that in each generation the heir presumptive was to be remarked. Such a belief squares exactly with what we have suggested. Finally, it should be noticed that we can find here the clue to the vocalization of the title Nazoraean. Just as the name Jahveh was given the vowels of Adonai, so Nazarite when it designated the Davidic heir took on the same vowels and became Nazoraios, to use its Greek form.

In conclusion, two minor points may be mentioned:

(1) Where Jesus as a boy questioned the Rabbis in the Temple, they treated him with respect, answering his questions because they knew of his descent; and since there would be various views of his paternity, they would wish to learn what they could about his thoughts and attitude.

(2) When St. Paul writes that we no longer know Christ after the flesh, the point is that originally we knew him as the Davidic heir, but now as something much greater, not depending on physical descent nor even on Jewish nationality.

(2)

Writers of the Liberal School in the nineteenth century regarded our Lord as one who gained adherents primarily as

the preacher of a higher and more spiritual ethic than what the
Jewish Rabbis taught. Later students have seen that this
account does not accord with our records. These make it clear
that Jesus impressed His world as a man with powers superior to
those of ordinary men, and because of this His religious message
was listened to with attention. It is worthy of consideration
whether the Jewish priests did not in some degree fear Him.
What Josephus tells us of the records kept at Jerusalem of
family descents makes it likely that the priests knew, as other
people probably did not, that St. Joseph was not our Lord's
father. That Jesus should nevertheless show Himself possessed of
extraordinary powers must have much exercised their minds.
The guests at the Cana wedding were satisfied that He provided
them with the best of wine and the servants testified that that
wine was drawn from the water-pots. This must have reminded
men of the wonders told of David's son, Solomon. Small wonder
that the priests asked for some sign when Jesus drove the
traffickers from the Temple, and our Lord's reply, speaking of
His quickly re-erecting the Temple, might very well be taken
to point to His assurance that He had powers such as popular
legend associated with the name of David's son, Solomon.
Nicodemus' words again make it evident that people recognized
Jesus to possess extraordinary powers. At Sychar the woman
could have no doubt that He was a prophet, able to read men's
thoughts and life-story. So too the king's officer found that Jesus
both commanded his son's recovery and knew at what moment
the malady took a turn for the better. Not unnaturally, careless
and vicious livers were disturbed and even incensed at the
presence of One with magical thaumaturgy, as they regarded
it, in their midst. So the demented worshipper in the synagogue
at Capernaum reacted and protested, we must suppose, when
he had heard our Lord's teaching. The leper was sure that
Jesus had the power to heal him, and the friends of the sinner
who had become paralysed were equally confident. But it was
when it was known that the dead youth at Nain had been
restored to life that men told one another with absolute conviction that a prophet was risen and Christ by His parable
showed Simon the Pharisee that He could and did read the past
life of the woman who was a sinner. So perhaps scepticism,

hesitation and fear were commingled when the scribes from Jerusalem asked for a sign from heaven and still more when they vilified His works of healing as achieved with the help of Beelzebub. It is consonant with this view that Herod would have liked to see some wonder wrought before him, and we are specially told was not alarmed while he had his soldiers standing by him. When the Syro-Phoenician woman and when Bartimaeus invoked Christ's help with the cry "thou Son of David," they probably looked on Him as Solomon's counterpart. If the priests were indeed afraid of our Lord, we shall ask whether this is not the explanation of His being sent bound to Caiaphas. It goes some way also to explain why Pilate was the more afraid and why the priests were so peculiarly exultant as they looked upon the Crucifixion.

This idea that the priests viewed Jesus as a warlock is further supported by two remarks made by speakers in two of our Gospels. Before the final Passover some declared "He deceiveth the people," according to John. After the Crucifixion, Matthew declares, the priests said to Pilate "that deceiver said." Our Lord used no drugs or words of magical spells. He was not a sorcerer; but He was, if rejected as a prophet, a charlatan wizard, and like Solomon of the legends, a controller of genies.[1]

---

[1] This conception perhaps underlies the words in Mark vi. 2: "From whence hath this man these things? and what wisdom is this which is given unto him, that even such mighty works are wrought by his hands?" To the sceptical amazement of these critics was it partly contributory that, as they understood the situation, He was not physically descended from David?

Chapter Four

NAZARENE AND NAZORAEAN[1]

BOTH "Nazoraean" and "Nazarene" are found in the historical books of the New Testament appended as a denominating title to the name Jesus. As Epiphanius[2] and Jerome state, the former is equivalent to "the Hallowed" or "the Holy," while the latter indicates that our Lord was at one time domiciled in Nazareth.

When we examine the evangelists' individual use in attaching these titles to His name, we discover some interesting and important facts.

(1) Mark never uses "Nazoraean," but has the designation "Nazarene" four times in all. In i. 24 he appears to give the Greek equivalent of "Nazoraean" in "the Holy One of God." The possessed man corrects the surname usually given in Capernaum to the newcomer from Nazareth, "(Jesus) the Nazarene," by substituting "Nazoraean."

(2) Matthew never uses "Nazarene," but twice gives the other title. In ii. 23 he makes use of a paronomasia[3] on it to find

---

[1] For a fuller discussion of the subject the reader may be referred to an article in the *Church Quarterly Review* for July 1945, vol. CXL, pp. 194–207.

[2] Epiph., *Adv. Haer.*, lib. III, tom. II, haer. lxxviii, 1039. (Joseph) ἔσχη μὲν οὖν πρωτότοκον τὸν Ἰάκωβον τὸν ἐπικληθέντα Ὠβλίαν, ἑρμηνευόμενον τεῖχος, καὶ δίκαιον ἐπικληθέντα, Ναζωραῖον δὲ ὄντα, ὅπερ ἑρμηνεύεται ἅγιος.

Lib. I, II, xxix, 5: Γνόντες δὲ αὐτὸν ἐκ Ναζαρὲτ ἐν γαστρὶ ἐγκυμονηθέντα καὶ ἐν οἴκῳ Ἰωσὴφ ἀνατραφέντα, καὶ διὰ τοῦτο ἐν τῷ Εὐαγγελίῳ Ἰησοῦν τὸν Ναζωραῖον καλεῖσθαι, ὡς καὶ οἱ ἀπόστολοι φασιν Ἰησοῦν τὸν Ναζωραῖον ἄνδρα ἀποδεδειγμένον ἔν τε σημείοις καὶ τέρασι, καὶ τὰ ἑξῆς, τοῦτο τὸ ὄνομα ἐπιτιθέασιν αὐτοῖς τὸ καλεῖσθαι Ναζωραίους, οὐχὶ δὲ Ναζιραίους, τὸ ἑρμηνευόμενον ἡγιασμένους. τοῦτο γὰρ τοῖς τὸ παλαιὸν πρωτοτόκοις καὶ θεῷ ἀφιερωθεῖσιν ὑπῆρχε τὸ ἀξίωμα, ὧν εἷς ὑπῆρχεν ὁ Σαμψών, καὶ ἄλλοι μετ' αὐτὸν, καὶ πρὸ αὐτοῦ πολλοί.

[3] Epiphanius mentions that Nazoraean had been connected by some with Nazarene, but he otherwise ignores and rejects the idea. Jerome explicitly contradicts such an interpretation of Matthew's words.

in our Lord's residence at Nazareth a fulfilment of the repeated declarations in the Old Testament that the first-born[1] son "shall be called a Nazoraean." The incident in the Capernaum synagogue where, as we have just said, the possessed man seems to have emphasized the difference between the two words is omitted by Matthew. Where Mark makes the maid assault Peter's self-possession by saying, "You too were with the Nazarene—(you know), Jesus—weren't you?" Matthew avoids the word by writing "With Jesus, the Galilean." At the same time, at the second assault, he writes, "Jesus, the Nazoraean," where Mark merely says "this man is one of them." Where Mark represents the crowd as telling Bartimaeus that Jesus the Nazarene was passing, Matthew merely says Jesus. On the other hand, when our Lord makes His entry into Jerusalem, Matthew gives the reply of the crowds to the question "Who is this?" in the form "This is the prophet Jesus, from Nazareth in Galilee." Once more where Mark records the angel's words to the women on Easter morning as "You are looking for Jesus the Nazarene, the crucified," Matthew avoids the title, writing "You are looking for Jesus, the crucified." It is plain that he deliberately excludes the title "Nazarene," while at the same time he appears to direct attention to the way in which the crowds who attended our Lord on His final journey up to Jerusalem insisted with demonstrative enthusiasm that he was come from Nazareth in Galilee.

(3) Luke presents us with a single certain example of either word and variant readings in a third passage. Reproducing the story of the demoniac at Capernaum, he follows Mark in making the man correct the obvious "Nazarene" as an unworthy account of our Lord and replacing it with the Greek equivalent of "Nazoraean." Where Bartimaeus is told the reason for the crowds surging along the highway, Luke substitutes for Mark's "Nazarene" the title "Jesus the Nazor-

[1] Perhaps in view of the way that, as appears lower down, the title is constantly Grecised, we should see another O.T. anticipation, though the Hebrew is Korban, in Isaiah iv. 2 and 3, our Lord having escaped the massacre of the Holy Innocents. The Levites were hallowed as substitutes for the firstborn sons and in Hebrews xii. 23 "the firstborn" is well explained if we regard the Christians as "Nazoraeans" in the same way as were the firstborn.

aean."[1] On the way to Emmaus, Cleopas, according to the
better text, speaking to a stranger spoke of our Lord as the
Nazarene: the alternative text has "Nazoraean," and this, with
all the evidence we have so far given, suggests that our Lord was
habitually spoken of as Jesus the Nazoraean, i.e. the Hallowed,
and where "Nazarene" or "of Nazareth" occurs, it is a
description to convey the information that Jesus' domicile had
been in Nazareth—a matter of pride with Galileans and of
contempt with others. This conclusion is supported by the other
evidence, which we shall now have to examine.

(4) John never uses "Nazarene," though he makes Philip
say to Nathanael "Him of whom Moses wrote in the law . . .
we have found, Jesus, Joseph's son, (a man) from Nazareth";
and Nathanael answers, "Can there be anything good out of
Nazareth?" On the other hand, he thrice gives "Nazoraean"
as the recognized title regularly appended to the name Jesus. In
the garden of Gethsemane twice the men who have come to
arrest our Lord when asked, "Whom seek ye?" reply, "Jesus,
the Nazoraean." Pilate, writing out the title to be set upon the
Cross, words it as "Jesus the Nazoraean,[2] King of the Jews."
Had it been "the Nazarene" it would have proclaimed that
Pilate had intruded into Herod's jurisdiction.

(5) In the Acts, again, there is no example of Nazarene.
When St. Peter addresses those whom Cornelius had assembled
to hear an account of the Christian movement, he traces its
origin to the early days when God anointed Jesus who came
from Nazareth. Otherwise in the six instances where a title or
description is attached to the name Jesus, the word is Nazoraean.
Besides, we have one passage, xxiv. 5, where Paul is described
as πρωτοστάτην τῆς τῶν Ναζωραίων αἱρεσέως. This is
particularly interesting, since Epiphanius tells us that members
of the Church were known as Nazoraeans[3] before they were

---

[1] Since Bartimaeus hailed our Lord as "Son of David," Nazarene is a
less apt reply for the crowd to have made than Nazoraean. They might be
proud that they had a Galilean prophet with them, but the blind man was
stirred when he heard that the Nazoraean, whose title and, we may believe,
whose legal lineage were known to all, was passing by.

[2] See also above, p. 254.

[3] As a still earlier name for them he gives what may be translated as
"Jesuits"; see above, p. 165 note.

called Christians, and when we remember that the Greek equivalent of the name is "holy, hallows or saints" we cannot but find it in Paul's habitual nomenclature in the addressing of his Epistles. This Grecised form of the name given to the Christian Church in its first days is to be seen in Acts ix. 13, τοῖς ἁγίοις σου; ix. 32, τοὺς ἁγίους τοὺς κατοικοῦντας Λύδδα; and in ix. 41 and xxvi. 10.[1]

[1] It is interesting to notice that Philo, *Alleg. Interpretations*, Book I, Chap. VII (para. 18 in the Loeb edition), dealing with Numbers vi. 9 and 12, speaks of the passage as treating of "him who has vowed the great vow" (ἐπὶ τοῦ τὴν μεγάλην εὐχὴν εὐξαμένου). He does not use the title "Nazirite."

Chapter Five

JESUS: SAVIOUR: HEALER

THE name Joshua or Jesus is explained by Matthew as indicative of our Lord's function. He is to save His people from their sins. Luke tells us that the angel told the shepherds on the night of the Nativity that there had been born "a Saviour." Scholars have remarked that this title was in much use in the Greek-speaking world in this age. Grateful cities often recorded their deliverance from oppression or their liberation from troubles by setting up monuments to those whom they designated as "saviours" or "liberators." Doubtless this connotation must not be forgotten when we try to estimate the import of the title as applied to our Lord. Those who first heard what the shepherds reported might very naturally expect the babe to be one who would deliver them from the rule of the Edomite family of Herod and the paramount influence of Rome. The achievements of Joshua in recovering the land of Canaan for the Israelites may have been thought to be a pattern of what this new-born Joshua was to do.

Christians, however, were weaned from these crude expectations by our Lord's training. They came to see that His sovereignty was a spiritual rule, wholly disentangled from politics. They would subscribe to Matthew's explanation of the title. Yet we have to notice that this does not end the matter. At this time the Jews associated in their minds sin and sickness as alike separating men from God. Disease was so constantly, they believed, God's visitation in reproof of sin that a man born blind presented the dilemma as to whether he had in an ante-natal state sinned or his parents had sinned. It is this deep-rooted conviction of the Jews at this time that led them to accept the physical healing of a paralytic as the concomitant evidence of his spiritual pardon. We are thus led to ask whether our common thought of our Lord as the Saviour from sin adequately represents His office.

We notice first the prominence given throughout our Lord's Ministry to His acts of healing. He Himself in his charge to the Twelve puts in the forefront their commission to heal the sick and to cast out devils. Again, besides the oft-quoted words "Thy faith hath saved thee," addressed to St. Mary Magdalene, we find the same encouragement given to the woman who was healed by our Lord on his way to Jairus' house. Here they are regularly and, we may believe rightly, translated "Thy faith hath made thee whole." It is fair to conclude that the verb means both "save from sin" and "heal of disease," and, correspondingly, that the title means both Saviour and Healer.

Accepting this view, we find a special significance in our Lord's remark in the synagogue at Nazareth, "Physician, heal thyself." The same is true of the mocking words of the priests at Calvary: "He saved others, Himself He cannot save." In both instances the "Saviour" is thought of as the Healer.

It is plain that our modern orthodox conception of our Lord's Person and functions only gradually emerged from a welter of competing narrower ideas. We shall, therefore, be prepared to find that some sections of the Christian community attached greater importance to the physical benefits of a Christian faith than did the majority.[1] Now that we have recovered a truer sense of the relations between the parties which were afterwards labelled as Gnostics and the great body of Christians who became known as Catholics, we can find room for a better understanding of those Christian groups who dwelt especially upon the healing powers of our Lord. We shall be prepared, therefore, to follow Eusebius in regarding the Therapeutai described by Philo as a group of Christians, springing out of the Jewish moiety of the Church. It would take us too far from our immediate purpose to develop this view at length. Suffice it to say that these Jewish Christians withdrew from the heathen environment of the Egyptian cities, lived in the open country,

---

[1] Two passages in the Epistles throw light on this dual aspect of our Lord's Ministry. In Hebrews ix. 14 it is insisted that our Lord was "without spot," an expression reminiscent of the Mosaic requirement that an animal for sacrifice should be without blemish. The language of Ephesians v. 27 suggests the same thought. In Hebrews x. 22 we are bidden to draw near to God "Having our hearts sprinkled from an evil conscience and our bodies washed with pure water."

spent much time in reading, praying, keeping vigils [1] and lying upon the ground. As their name implies, they made much of the Christian gift of healing. Ten years ago a portion of a prayer-book was recovered in the very part of Egypt where these Therapeutai are said to have lived. In these prayers our Lord is specially invoked as Healer. To assist the reader in judging for himself in regard to this suggestion, Philo's description of the Therapeutai and a translation of these prayers will be appended at the end of this chapter. One final word may be added. A fragment of an uncanonical gospel has been found in the same neighbourhood, and it may not be too fanciful to imagine that it was used by these Jewish Christians. It is not without interest that this gospel, in relating the healing of the leper, recorded in the Synoptists, adds details in which the leper explains that he contracted his disease by contact with others when he stayed at an inn in the course of a journey.

That these Therapeutai were a type of Jewish Christian is not only a reasonable inference from Philo and Eusebius, but is lent some support by the insistent recommendation of James v. 14, that "if anyone is sick among you, let him call in the elders of the Church and let them pray over him, anointing him with oil in the name of the Lord."

We need not enter into a discussion of the question whether the Church has been at fault in allowing this side of her mission, as it was at first understood, to fall into desuetude. It is enough to emphasize the fact that the name Jesus implies a deliverance not only from sin but from disease.

Note A

The relevant words quoted by Eusebius from Philo are as follows:

"Like physicians, by removing the evil affections, they healed and cured the minds of those that joined them . . . as soon as they commenced a philosophical life, they divested themselves of their property, giving it up to their relatives [cf. Acts iv. 34, 35]. . . . They not only pass their time in meditation, but compose songs and hymns unto God. . . . For none of them is to bring food or drink before the setting of the Sun . . . there were also females of whom the most are aged maidens . . . in consequence of that zealous desire of wisdom [cf.

---

[1] We must compare with this St. Paul's claim that he had spent much time in such vigils (2 Corinthians xi. 27).

Luke x. 41, 42] in the earnest prosecution of which they disregarded the pleasures of the body . . . they lie on straw spread on the ground." Eusebius further states that Philo describes their "fastings and vigils."

Note B

Quotations from a Liturgical Fragment edited by Bell and Skeat, *Fragments of an Unknown Gospel, etc.*:

"Thou art the only physician of our ailing souls . . . heal us in sickness, cast us not away as unfit to receive Thy healing. The word of Thy mouth is the giver of health. . . . Receive from us . . . these vigils . . . these couchings upon the earth."

Chapter Six

MESSIAH: CHRIST: ANOINTED

IN the Hebrew economy priests and kings were consecrated to their office by a rite of anointing. Thus Aaron and his sons were separated to the priesthood, Saul, David, Solomon to the kingship. Yet by an extension of language the word Messiah, i.e. Anointed, was sometimes used with a more general sense. In Isaiah lxi. we read, "The Spirit of the Lord God is upon me: because the Lord hath anointed me." Modern Rabbinical doctrine will have it also that Israel as a people is to be regarded as anointed or consecrated to a special service of ministering to the world by imparting to all the knowledge of the true God. Of this we shall have more to say presently: for the moment we must dwell upon the significance attaching two thousand years ago to the name "Messiah."

The books of our New Testament canon testify to a widespread expectation at that time that there was shortly to appear in the world one who might be most aptly described as the Messiah. When the Hasmonean dynasty sank into feeble futility and internecine divisions and when the Edomite Herod usurped the throne, discontent was kindled into a flame of hope among those who meditated on words of promise which they read in their Bible. Expectation grew lively that there would shortly appear a leader who would liberate God's people. Especially was it in Galilee that these hopes burnt high, when the Romans took over the administration of Judea after Archelaus was deposed. The ruling class in Jerusalem had petitioned for Rome to take the control of the country, preferring this to the inept despotism of Herod's successor. Yet the machinery of Roman taxation offended national pride. At the previous census which Herod carried through no disturbance had occurred. Opinions were divided as to where the expected liberator was to appear. After the Nativity the chief priests and scribes told Herod unhesitatingly that the Messiah would be born at

9*

Bethlehem. During Holy Week the scribes were equally emphatic that Christ would be the son of David. There was, however, a rival view that he would spring from the tribe of Aaron, not Judah, and it is clear that there was room for aspirants to pose as the promised liberator without possessing any special claim. Thus Judas, perhaps on the strength of his name, headed the revolt against the census, and just before the fall of Jerusalem in A.D. 70 several pretenders secured adherents. In the same way sixty years later Barcochba struck a blow for the recovery of Jewish independence.

All this goes to show that for about a century and a half at the beginning of the Christian era there was a widespread expectation that a leader would arise amongst the Jews who was destined in virtue of an anointing from God to bring deliverance to His people.

While this expectation, as we have said, was widespread, it is important to observe that various and differing ideas were entertained as to the character which the destined leader was to have. In Galilee a military genius and political deliverer was hoped for. In Samaria a prophet or a religious director was expected, who could pronounce authoritatively on the questions at issue between Jerusalem and Gerizim. Among the Pharisees there was no keen desire for the appearance of any new leader: they were content with the religious freedom they enjoyed and were apprehensive of any movement that might disturb the established order. The great priestly families who under the Roman authority exercised a supervision, in the main religious, over the Jews in Palestine and abroad were peculiarly sensitive to any stirring of nationalistic spirit.

Our Lord, as all our records agree, set Himself from the very first to discourage and dissipate any materialistic expectations of His messianic intentions. This attitude, it is plain, was largely the cause of His unacceptability to the more fervid nationalists. They were selfishly isolationistic, and they had accepted a devaluation of Israel's mission and of the divine promises to them. We have followed Christ's anagogical method of reading those promises and in consequence find proofs innumerable that His coming was foreshadowed in the history of Israel and in utterances of Israel's prophets and psalmists. The dogged

adherence of the antichristian Jews to their own literal interpretation of the Scriptures was stultified and those who nevertheless retained a faith in the God of Israel found, as the one
way to reconcile their faith with their rejection of Jesus as the
fulfilment of God's preparatory hints, the new doctrine that not
an individual but the whole nation of Israel was the antitype of
the types outlined in the Scriptures. Yet an alert survey would
seem to show that the development of progressive and growing
hopes set before Israel was rather in the opposite direction. Not
all Abraham's seed but Isaac alone carried the hope forward.
Not both of Isaac's sons, but Jacob only was to be Israel, God's
son. Not all twelve tribes alike were to raise up rulers for Israel,
but Judah was to do so; and out of Judah David's son was to be
God's son. In the same way we Christians are satisfied to narrow
and individualize the figure of the Son of Man. Contrasted with
the savage sub-human tyrannies of Assyria, Babylon, Macedon
and Rome, Israel was typically and representatively human,
but we believe that Jesus was the concentrated quintessence of
Israel and of humanity. Israel was the vine which God brought
out of Egypt, but we accept our Lord's declaration that He was
the true Vine, He being the supreme consummation, the focal
point, the capital specimen of the ideal Israel. Not otherwise we
shall avow it to be with the title "Messiah." Even if it were well
founded that the original thought was of the nation (an
assertion contradicted by all the evidence), it would yet be a
justifiable and a reasonable position to take up that the ultimate
fulfilment of the promise is to be seen in one representative
Person and that Jesus entirely satisfies the description given in
the Scriptures. That the modern Jewish Rabbis have now come
to count the sufferings of their fellows as a sacrifice ordained by
God for them to make for the sake of mankind may, we shall
believe, be regarded as one step towards the possibility of their
coming at last to understand and accept our Lord's Passion as
the classical and sovereign example of Israel's sacrifices for the
whole world. In any event God in His Providence will yet revive
a Jewish Christianity which, if it does not at once assent to the
Catholic Creeds, may hold the faith of James, the Lord's
brother.

Chapter Seven

Boy: Servant or Son

THE Hebrew word *ebed* represented in our English versions by "servant" is rendered in the Septuagint almost as frequently by δοῦλος as by παῖς. Of these two words, the former essentially defines the class of society to which a man belongs: he is a slave, not a free man. The second word indicates rather the man's relation to his master: the slave is his master's page-boy or personal attendant. We must presume that the Septuagint chose now the one now the other of the two words according as the translators felt that the Hebrew suggested or implied the sense thus distinguished in the Greek. In the four sections interwoven in the texture of Isaiah xl–lv and generally distinguished as speaking of the Suffering Servant, the Greek Bible uniformly uses παῖς. Readers who were unacquainted with the Hebrew not unnaturally understood the word sometimes as "son" instead of as "servant." Matthew would seem to have done so. A comparison of iii. 17 with xii. 18 favours this view. His argument that Jesus fulfilled these ancient prophecies would seem to require this if it was to contribute anything solid to his apologia for the Christian faith. In Acts iv. 27 the A.V. understood the Christians to have thought of Jesus as God's son. The Revisers have scrupulously translated "servant," but in view of the considerations we have here in mind we may wonder whether the Greek Bible may not have been understood in a sense incompatible with the Hebrew original. In any case, we may feel that those Christians who knew only the Greek Bible would find less difficulty than readers of the Hebrew in equating the Suffering Servant with the Son of God.

The suggestion has recently been hazarded that the four sections which speak of the Suffering Servant come from the pen of Isaiah and are his meditations upon the unhappy later years of Uzziah. That the prophet was interested in that king is shown by his insistence that it was "in the year that King

Uzziah died" that he had his great vision in the temple. That Uzziah whom the historian declares to have done "that which was right in the sight of the Lord" (2 Kings xv. 3) should in the end be smitten with leprosy must have awakened questionings in the prophet's mind. If the four sections be read attentively with the thought of Uzziah's fate in our minds, the words acquire a new poignancy and a pathetic promise of the victory that may be granted to vicarious suffering. Should there be any truth in this suggested origin of these passages, it is conceivable that some recollection survived to our Lord's day of the fact that Uzziah, God's son as the Davidic king, had become the Lord's servant who suffered to redeem his subjects.

Unexpected support for this theory comes from another quarter. Jeremiah in chapter xxxiii thrice speaks of David as Jahveh's servant, but, in harmony with the language of Psalm lxxxix. 3, the Greek Bible uses the word "slave" to express the thought. That in Isaiah the word "boy" should always have been chosen is significant, and, it may at least be said, lends countenance to the suggestion that the Greek translators were aware that it was not an undistinguished slave that the prophet had in mind but one who, as David's successor, was not only Jahveh's servant but His son. If our contention be well founded, that our Lord was habitually nurtured upon the Greek Bible, it is intelligible that the Voice which spoke to Him at His baptism could awake in His consciousness the recollection of the divine utterance in Isaiah xlii. 1, with the word "boy" changed to "son" in accordance with the language of Psalm ii. 7. His mind, if we may reverently say so, would be unaware that the word was changed, since for Him both words bore the same sense. If we may assume this view to be correct, we shall feel that the revisers were over scrupulous when they substituted "servant" for "child" in Acts iv. 27.

Chapter Eight

LORD

IT is necessary here to pay some little attention to the uses of the Greek word Κύριος often represented in the English by the word "lord." In the first place we must notice that in Hellenistic Greek the word is used as a polite title to a stranger whom a speaker wishes to address with courtesy and respect. Thus the woman of Sychar says to the Lord, "Sir (Κύριε), I perceive that Thou art a prophet." Secondly we must note that the word is used of the master or owner of an animal, vineyard or the like.

When the two disciples set about their errand of taking the ass for the entry into Jerusalem, "the masters" (κύριοι), i.e. presumably the owner and his wife, challenged them for the secret password from our Lord. Far commoner than these uses and of greater importance to us is the use attested by papyri from Egypt that a king or emperor was thus designated. We may believe that those entirely ignorant that St. Joseph was not our Lord's father by physical generation acknowledged the Lord as King of Israel or at least heir to the throne if and when they hailed Him as Son of David. On the other hand, we may venture to affirm that those who knew of the virgin conception accepted His claim to the throne if and when they acclaimed Jesus as Son of God or Lord. Jeremiah xxii. 18 gives as a natural and normal lamentation over a dead king, οἴμοι Κύριε. In Matt. xxv. 37 and 44 at the Great Assize the King is addressed with the title Lord (Κύριε).

At this point we encounter a more intricate problem. Reverence for "the Name" in the literal sense of that word, in place of its signification of nature or character, led the Jews of later ages to avoid the utterance of the incommunicable name "JHVH" and to replace it by "Adonai." The Septuagint gives Κύριος as its equivalent, for the title was given in Egypt to gods there worshipped. Moreover, since "JHVH" was King, what title more suitable than Κύριος when His name was not pronounced? Thus the title not only served to acclaim the earthly vicegerent but also connoted JHVH Himself, and those who read the sacred Scriptures in Greek might and did derive from them theological conceptions which the Hebrew text might not have suggested or sanctioned.

In the Epistle to the Hebrews i. 10, "Thou, Lord, in the beginning hast laid the foundation of the earth," the logic of the argument requires the title to refer not to God the Father but to the Son. Yet in Psalm cii. 25 the words are addressed to JHVH and it is clear that some Christians must have been led to identify Jesus, the Son of God, with JHVH. Theological thought building upon passages of this sort as they appeared in the Greek Bible sometimes strayed into strange imaginings, as when JHVH was regarded as a different god from the supreme God to whom indeed he was inferior. Yet in spite of these Gnostic futilities we can see how the Orthodox and Catholic Church was helped by the language of the Greek Bible towards some understanding of the truth as to our Lord's deity. A modern writer [1] whose orthodoxy none would dispute has given utterance to what will be felt to be a valuable reflection upon the matter. "The Christian Church," he says, "which believes that Yahweh the God of Israel is the true God, the maker of heaven and earth, thereby confesses that the Eternal, willing to make His Name known to men, condescended to take upon Him the form of a tribal God according to the Semitic notion, as in the Incarnation He accepted the limitations of human nature."

Apart from these abstruse speculations we must observe that within the compass of the New Testament Scriptures as a whole, with the exception of so rare a use as that just noted in the Hebrews, the title "Lord" when applied to Jesus appears invariably to mean that He is acknowledged as the King. Thus, by using the title "Lord" the leper hails Him as King, the centurion at Capernaum recognizes Him as King, the aspirants for admission to the company of His followers do the same: Martha and Mary address Him as King, the brigand on the Cross recognizes Him as King, St. Thomas worships Him as his King, St. Peter argues that He is both King and Christ, St. Stephen prays to Him as King or possibly as JHVH the King

---

[1] A. G. Hebert, *The Throne of David*, p. 96.

(cf. Psalm xcix. 1), St. Paul looks forward to the fulfilment of God's purpose that the whole universe shall acknowledge that Jesus is Christ and King.

For completeness' sake mention must be made of another use of the title "Lord." Many departmental gods (as we may call them) were worshipped in our Lord's day. Their votaries hailed them with the style of lord or king. Adonis was such a lord, and we may take it as certain that the deified emperors were both Κύριοι and Θεοί. Their rank was, so to say, not unlike that of the saints in mediaeval thought. Hence Paul allows that there are gods many and lords many. Some writers have sought in this direction for an additional cause which contributed to the early believers adoring Jesus as their Lord. It must, however, appear doubtful whether Jews disciplined by centuries of suffering to worship One God only would have any thought of Jesus as a departmental or subordinate god, however possible such a view might have been among converts from heathenism. Yet it is stalwarts like Peter and Paul whom we find styling Jesus their Lord. Manifestly they did not arrive at their recognition of His right to the title from any such theological tenets as were inconsistent with the pure monotheism of Judaism. On the other hand, when Thomas is recorded to have cried, "My Lord and my God," we shall understand the utterance, as we have already said, to mean that the apostle acknowledges Jesus as his King (perhaps also as JHVH) and now as a theophany of the One true God. Contributory to this perhaps may have been the words of Psalm v. 2 and lxxxiv. 3, where God is addressed as "my King and my God." Another believer of Jewish origin makes plainer how those of a monotheistic faith found a way to reconcile it with their conviction as to Christ's pre-eminence. He was an effluence of the Divine Glory—not, be it remarked, an emanation once for all given an independent existence, but One that was eternally being generated from and yet within the Godhead.

PART FOUR

THE LORD'S HUMANITY

Chapter One

The Silent Years at Nazareth

AFTER our Lord's first attendance at the Passover Festival, our canonical gospels give us no detailed history of His life until His baptism. We are left to recover by the reverent use of reason and imagination some picture of His life and conduct. The circumstances of His home and of the society in which He lived must, if we adhere faithfully to the orthodox belief in His true manhood, have largely determined the cast of His thought and His religious habits.

We have no warrant for supposing that in these years of privacy He rejected any of the common usages of devotion or any of the conventional ideas as to man's duty towards God. We must believe that, like other children, He was taught to pray, that He learnt the basic doctrines of Judaism and the moral obligations defined by the Mosaic Law. He would scrupulously observe the Sabbath, would go to the synagogue, hear the Hebrew text of the Law and of the Prophets and a meticulous rendering of it into the language commonly used in Galilee.

(Absolute certainty on this head may be thought impossible of attainment, but the evidence is strong that our Lord commonly spoke Greek in His public utterances. That He was bi-lingual is shown by His addressing Jairus' daughter with the words "Talitha cumi" and the deaf mute with "Ephphatha." These two instances are recorded in a way that suggest their unusual character. It has sometimes been said that Peter remembers these two words because the occasions had specially impressed him. Yet the healing of the deaf man can hardly be thought of as likely to impress him more than "Peace, be still" amid the storm and "Follow me" at the time of the apostles' call. When Judas approached to greet our Lord in Gethsemane, Jesus in a sorrowful jest repeated three Greek words to be seen on the rim of a wine-cup. Not now was Judas bidden "Enjoy yourself, that's what you're here for," nor yet perhaps "Give the kiss of friendship," but "Hand me to my enemies, that's what you're here for."

Bi-lingual Wales would suggest that Greek was the language of the street, the market-place and public assemblies, while Aramaic was the language of the hearth and the home, of little children and the very old. Moreover, it must not be forgotten that until He was four years of age our Lord lived in Egypt, and, we can hardly doubt, learned as a baby to speak Greek.)

All this our Lord would imbibe as every Jew in that environment must necessarily have done. When we ask further whether the Holy Family adhered to any particular school of religious thought, we have but slender grounds for making any pronouncement. Such evidence as is accessible negatives the idea that they could have been Sadducees. Our Lord certainly referred to the Prophets as supplying authoritative teaching; He took for a text when preaching at Nazareth a passage from Isaiah. He speaks of angels and of spirits in a way that is consonant with Pharisaism. It is possible that the Family were not addicted to the practices of the Pharisees[1] and did no more than humbly observe in a simple fashion the broad rules of the Mosaic Law. Nevertheless we must notice that the Apocryphal Wisdom of Solomon, which was clearly known to Paul, would seem to have left its impress directly or indirectly on our Lord's thought.[2] That work is rightly judged to be the Pharisaic counterpart to the Sadducean Ecclesiasticus, and in view of this it is not to be thought surprising if our Lord should have been brought up to observe the Pharisees' rules of conduct. Undoubtedly He showed Himself thoroughly acquainted with them. But something more must be said.

James, the Lord's brother, went further than the Pharisee in the strict austerity of his life. Like the Baptist he ate no meat,

[1] It is a question worthy of consideration whether this name is to be connected with Persia and Parsee, since Zoroaster taught a doctrine which may be thought to have originated some of the conceptions held by the Pharisees.

[2] Commenting on the contradictory criticisms of the Baptist and Himself our Lord said, "Wisdom is justified of her works one and all." This use of the title Wisdom is at least akin to what we read in the Wisdom of Solomon. If our Lord did know that work it is tempting to go further and to believe that He was familiar with a Greek version of the Scriptures resembling if not identical with the Septuagint.

he drank nothing drawn from the grape, he cut neither hair nor beard, he spent long hours in prayer. For this he was styled the Just or Righteous, i.e. he was regarded as a perfect pattern for any who desired to fulfil "righteousness," the obligations of the Law. It is natural to suppose that the Holy Family regarded James with a respect and reverence equal to that felt by outsiders, and it is to be supposed that our Lord Himself would be brought up to regard His brother in the same way. We are told that James, like our Lord, was popularly known as a Nazoraean, an oblate, a votary or devotee of God, the Holy One of Israel, and this would lead us to expect that our Lord's religious observances would be of a character similar to those of James. We shall see a little later what a startling flood of light this throws on much of the Lord's public utterances after His baptism.

It is to be observed that the Pharisees' rule of life essentially concerned itself with behaviour and external conduct. Yet we need not suppose that this rule of life was mere formalism, and we can hardly imagine that if our Lord did adhere to such a rule of life, He did not understand it to be the outward expression of an inward devotion to duty, as inculcated by the Law. A sincere will to be of service to God and to his neighbour was the ultimate motive of Pharisaism. The just or righteous man was he who set himself to fulfil this duty. Not only was James hailed as a perfect exemplar of such duty, but Matthew pronounces St. Joseph to have been a "just" man when he felt it his duty to repudiate the Blessed Virgin because she was with child, the Law requiring that she must either be stoned to death or divorced on some trivial pretext. His attitude towards religion must have influenced our Lord not less than James's attitude can have done, and to this must be added that the Baptist, the son of the Virgin's cousin, was recognized by Herod as a "just" man and a holy, i.e. a conscientious observer of the Law and a devotee.

Brought up in such a religious atmosphere and habituated to such moral and devotional practices, our Lord went to respond to the Baptist's call that men prepare for the arrival of God's Kingdom. John himself seems to have thought of his baptism as an additional religious rite. His preaching at the first was concerned to enforce a sincere observance of the moral obligations recognized by the Pharisees and perhaps by all Jews. Our Lord too appears to accept this view when He says, "Thus it becometh us to fulfil all righteousness," i.e. religious practices. But the Baptist received a second "word of the Lord" which told him that One upon whom the Spirit would be seen descending should baptize with Holy Spirit and with Fire. The full significance of our Lord's baptism cannot be understood unless we realize that this was the opening of a new chapter in religious experience. Our Lord heard Himself addressed as the newly crowned King of Israel, God's Son. The words of the Second Psalm rang in His ears suggesting that it was true, then, that if He was not physiologically St. Joseph's son, yet He was not a base-born child, he was indeed the Holy One of God, dedicated to God's service. He was David's legal heir, born moreover at Bethlehem and, it must seem, the destined Messiah.

It is here that the Forty Days in the wild open country are found to be the critical turning-point from our Lord's life of seclusion at Nazareth, where He was surrounded and hemmed in by Judaism, to His public Ministry with its universal message. The three temptations of which He spoke to His disciples reveal something of the turbulent upheaval in His religious consciousness. The first may be labelled as an example of the *libido sentiendi.*

In His hunger He saw the small round stones near Him as mimic rolls of bread. God fed Moses' followers with bread from heaven. Elijah and Elisha were recorded to have had meal and oil multiplied to satisfy their needs. Could not He in virtue of His plenary powers (Psalm viii. 6) transmute stone into bread? Yet the Father's Spirit indwelling the Son's humanity convinced Him that the physical laws of the universe expressed God's will and must not be superseded. Scripture [1] too declared that man should not live by bread alone but by any and every creature that God by the word of His mouth provided for food. The physical laws of nature might not be overridden just to avoid a non-observance of the Mosaic Law. The former man

[1] Genesis ix. 3, 4 and Psalm viii. 6–8 might seem to allow such escape from Mosaic limitations to an anterior liberty.

must obey, the second was made for man. Here we find, we may believe, the germ from which grew the positive assertion that repealed the Mosaic Laws about clean and unclean animals for food, and with it all the Pharisaic rules about ceremonial washing of the hands and segregation from Gentiles and sinners—and from lepers and from the dead. It repealed even, we may add, the Sabbath rule.

If we are right in this, we may perhaps see what Mark intended us to understand when he said that our Lord "was with the wild beasts,"[1] i.e. the creatures of the wild, e.g. conies. Though unclean according to the Law, such food was provided by the Father to satisfy the Son's hunger, and this too, perhaps, though strangled or killed without completely draining the blood.

There followed a stirring within our Lord of the *libido dominandi.* Accepting the lesson that His personal and individual satisfaction was to be subordinated to His mission, and that that mission passed outside the limits of the Judaic Law, He had to clarify the purpose of that mission.

Psalm after psalm told how God would subjugate beneath the power of His royal Son His enemies, the heathen, the kings of the earth so that they should be the footstool of His feet (Psalms ii., lxxxix. and cx.). Prophetic vision had shown Jerusalem as the metropolis of the civilized world, with all nations bringing their treasures to adorn the Temple and begging the Jewish people to instruct them in their duty to the one living God. Was this, then, the way in which the mission of the Christ was to be fulfilled? Again the Father's Spirit indwelling the Son's humanity convinced Him that this ambition to rule the world by force of arms was not in harmony with the Father's will. God desired the voluntary obedience of free men. This desire, then, for a world yielding compulsory service originated with the Spirit of Evil. To act upon this thought was to turn aside from the Father's service and to

[1] The word is used particularly for animals that are hunted, game in fact, e.g. the stag, but also for fishes, eels, leeches and other small creatures. Peter's mid-day vision illustrates the point, as does the account in 4 Maccabees of how the Jew was tempted to eat forbidden foods. Cf. Leviticus xi and Aristotle, *Poetics*, 1148, viii. 12: ἃ λυπηρῶς ὁρῶμεν . . . οἷον θηρίων τε μορφὰς τῶν ἀτιμοτάτων καὶ νεκρῶν.

worship a lower ideal. Here again we can see the germ of the teaching which insisted that man's first object should be to labour for the establishment of God's rule of right, that the gathering of costly treasures for the Temple, and the accumulation of wealth were not the supreme ends of life, that civil government was not identical with Spiritual leadership and that Jerusalem eventually would be no metropolis in the economic or political sense.

After this we are told that a third choice presented itself to our Lord's mind. Regarded in one way, this choice may appear as the *libido dominandi* in another guise. If the Christ was not to compel obedience to God by force of arms, should He compel it by demonstrative proof, by convincing the unbeliever against his will, by exhibiting inescapable evidence that God was supreme? If the Gentiles no less than the Jews were to be won to God's service, what better than, at Passover time, when crowds of Jews and foreigners were congregated in the Temple precincts, to throw Himself down from the pediment above the eastern side of the Temple and in sight of the worshippers to be proved to be the Christ by God preserving Him from destruction? Yet once more the Father's Spirit indwelling the Son's humanity convinced Him that such demonstration necessarily excluded the possibility of free obedience. Ocular proof must make faith impossible. The Father's will was that men should walk by faith, not in knowledge. Only so could their obedience be truly voluntary. And here we may detect the *libido sciendi* intruding itself into our Lord's consciousness. Had He acted upon this impulse at the Passover, He would have fixed the time when His victory was to be completed. Now He learnt that times and seasons were reserved within the Father's knowledge and will, and so again and again we find our Lord later waiting for the inward sign from the Father that the hour was come for this or that step to be taken. We may detect in this the germ of the teaching that the Son did not know when the end of the world should be and that the sowing of the seed was not immediately or always followed by the harvest and that the Kingdom of God does not come with observation. Peter's confession that our Lord was the Christ was the sign that the Crucifixion was at last to be expected, the interview with the Greeks in Holy Week was the sign that it was immediately to follow. To wait for such signs was part at any rate of the lesson our Lord learnt from the last temptation. From these spiritual experiences our Lord learnt to understand more intimately and to obey more truly the Father's purpose for the world than He had been taught, whether by the Mosaic ordinances as generally interpreted or by the Pharisees' rule of life or by Nazoraean austerities. He now knew that the aim of religious practice must be orientated afresh. The Father's character could not be reflected or reproduced in men by adding more and more rules of conduct and behaviour. The springs of action must be altered. A new spirit must inform the will. With the King arrived to establish God's sovereignty on earth, men must have a new outlook on life. He had Himself found that the Father's Spirit within Him had changed His view of the means and methods for the achievement of "righteousness." The same spirit He was to impart to others, and in that way the Kingdom of God would arrive and indeed was already arriving.

All this is not to say that our Lord had not yet to learn many lessons. The Spirit transformed the prospect of spiritual life, but that life was not instantaneously and magically full-grown. He learnt obedience from the things that He experienced.[1] Nevertheless we are entitled to say that from the time of His baptism, or at any rate from the time of His retirement into the wild, our Lord consistently regarded religion as necessarily centred in the heart and directed by the Holy Spirit. So it is that within a week from His return to the Baptist He declared that the disciples would see God's angels ascending and descending upon Him and, if we may so understand the words, upon all men who entered the Kingdom. A few weeks later He spoke of His Body as God's Temple, i.e. the shrine in which the Father's Spirit dwelt. Presently too He insisted that men must be born anew, i.e. they must have a completely fresh start for their spiritual life, and that the Spirit came upon men with secrecy comparable to the obscure rise and passage of the wind. But it would be superfluous to pursue the matter further:

[1] The conventional English translation "suffered" (Hebrews v. 8) is inadequate and unjustifiably narrow.

the reader can see how the rest of our Lord's ministry reveals the growing clearness of teaching which has shed the swaddling clothes of Judaism and has entered upon the free life and movement of the Holy Spirit.

One final remark may be offered. The Christian believer came to see that our Lord was a Nazoraean in a higher sense after His baptism than He could be as a mere follower of Mosaic precepts. It is noteworthy that James (v. 6), the Lord's brother, after his acceptance of our Lord's rule recognized that Jesus was indeed "the Just" rather than he himself with all his austere devotions.

In the same way, while Pharisees were scandalized that the life of a Nazoraean, or "religious," should be of so original and unconventional a type and stigmatized Jesus as a glutton and a wine-bibber, Peter, not yet acclaiming our Lord as the Messiah, yet after the feeding of the five thousand, in an embryonic and immature confession avowed the apostles' conviction that our Lord, despite His breach with the Mosaic ordinances, was the Holy One of God more truly than any conventional Nazoraean.

In the same way, too, the Christians were long known to one another as Nazoraeans, not "saints" in its modern sense, but devotees dedicated to the Lord, although they did not observe the traditional regulations for Nazoraeans.

Thus far we have considered the development of our Lord's religious thought in the light of what we may suppose to have been the environment in which He was brought up. There is, however, something more which ought to be said. Can we add to our picture by inferring something as to His individual character?

What characteristic traits of mind and disposition were to be found in our Saviour's youth and early manhood we have no record to tell. There are, however, certain features in the Gospels which may be thought to supply some material for portraying the manner and temper which He exhibited. We shall surmise that His nature was quick and mercurial, prompt to react and respond to every appeal and stimulus which His environment presented. A suggestion or a request from His mother He would, we may believe, instantly obey. The beauty of nature, the changes of the seasons and of the weather passed not unnoticed. He observed the behaviour of His fellow-men, kind and unkind, and the incidents of daily life. His quick reaction to outward circumstances shows itself in the way that He was moved to pity (or according to some texts to anger) when the leper came close to Him in defiance of the law and begged to be cleansed.[1]

The same quickness of temper is seen when His anger was stirred by the murmurs of the scribes when He pronounced the absolution of the paralytic and when He healed on the Sabbath day. It is the same when His Pharisee host marvelled that He had not carried out the customary ceremonial washing before eating. It is in this mercurial readiness to act upon any provocation that we may find one of the principal points in which He had to learn obedience to the Father from His experience during His Ministry. To put the matter in a nutshell we may say that as Man He had to curb His impetuous nature so as to bring it into step with the Father's patient slowness. One aspect of His temptations was that He was naturally impatient of God's long-suffering endurance of man's free will when it chose rebellion against the law of right. We shall examine this view presently when we consider the Three Temptations recorded after the Baptism, but we may notice at once how we have here an explanation of our Lord's words to His mother at the marriage in Cana.

These words have often been felt to be hard and brusque, but when they are viewed in the light of what we have just said, they take on another character. Our Lord has learnt in the wilderness that His quick readiness of temper must be bridled so that it shall not outrun the Father's will and permission. His mother expects that as He had always done before He would immediately help her to meet a difficulty. In His new character of Messiah He will, she expects, not only be able but instantly be ready to provide what is needed. He, however, has learnt that He must not anticipate His Father's directions. He must not be guided by His mother's wish but by His Father's

[1] Told of the centurion's servant, He replied at once, "I will come and heal him." At Nain the sight of the young man's funeral led Him at once to intervene.

Will, and He has not yet received that inward intimation that this miracle should be performed. His mother must understand that He can no longer take orders from her; He is under His Father's orders.

The same understanding that His natural impulsiveness must be made subject to the Father's purpose and permission is to be seen in the story of the raising of Lazarus. The sisters' message that their brother was ill did not lead our Lord to set out for Bethany immediately. Four days after Lazarus' death He thanked His Father that He had heard Him. At last the intimation had come that He should recall Lazarus from the dead.

Three more observations ought here to be made. In the first place it should be noticed how in the very first temptation the Son is taught that the Father's will forbids the impulse to act immediately and to snatch at the quickest and obvious means of resolving a difficulty. It would have been a short cut to the satisfaction of His hunger if He could have transmuted stone into bread, but He learns to wait patiently till He has secured a substitute for bread in the way that the Israelites were fed with manna in place of bread. Again we may see here the origin of our Lord's habit of speaking of Himself as the Son of Man. The temptation presents itself in the guise of an assertion that He is God's Son, but the Scriptural words which recur to His memory declare that God provides a variety of food for man, a reminder that, however truly He is God's Son, nevertheless He is to live His life within the limits of human nature. It is a natural consequence of this thought that our Lord, as we have previously remarked, when Nathanael hailed Him as God's Son, should instantly amend the title into the Son of Man. Further, it would seem to deserve consideration whether by the Father's appointment our Lord was not required to work within certain limits which have not been generally noticed. These limits may be succinctly stated in this way. He might not destroy the physical properties of dead matter, but He might expedite and accelerate the processes of vegetable growth and human industry. He might not change stones into bread, since from a little barley seed more might be grown and be baked. He might multiply two small fishes since fishes can reproduce themselves. In the same way perhaps He might increase the supply of wine, since the vine yields a fresh vintage each year.[1] We may be mistaken in postulating these limitations

[1] Meditation on Deut. xxix. 6, "Ye have not eaten bread, neither have ye drunk wine or strong drink," may lend countenance to what might otherwise be thought a sceptical rationalization of this "sign." At the close of his life Moses recalls the ways in which Jehovah had trained the Israelites. They had been taught that they should not live on bread but on manna in the wilderness. They had been taught also that in their nomad life water from the rock should be their drink, and not the wine of settled rural life, a lesson which the Rechabites refused to forget. The collocation in this passage suggests that just as in the first Temptation our Lord was reminded that manna had been given to Israel, so at Cana He was prompted to teach that wine was not for man to get drunk, but was to make glad the heart of man. The ruler of the feast said that it was usual when men had got drunk (the A.V. has toned this down into "have well drunk") to give them worse wine. If water was now given to the guests, they might drink it with satisfaction and be saved from intoxication. On this view our Lord was instructing men against drunkenness, an instruction the more significant when it is remembered that He was not like the Baptist a total abstainer, but was libelled as a wine-bibber. If this suggestion be accepted we shall say that when the evangelist says, "Water become wine," *become* means transubstantiated in the strict sense of the word as used by the Schoolmen. The water retained all its physical characteristics, but it served as wine for the guests, who did not recognize it for what it was, though the servants of course did. On this interpretation we shall not only accept the sign as setting forth our Lord's glorious instruction for men as to the use of wine, but shall see in it a pointer to the significance of the eucharistic elements. The physicist may demonstrate all the objective properties of the bread and wine, but the Christian is satisfied that to those physical properties there is superadded a subjective significance so that in the scholastic sense the sacred species are transubstantiated.

Since these words were penned I have learnt from *The Church Quarterly Review*, July 1945, pp. 127–153, that St. Ambrose taught this. As the sacred species at the Eucharist are physically unchanged, so, he says, the water was physically unchanged: it was its function that was changed. On the other hand St. Athanasius in his *De Incarnatione* understands the "sign" in the way in which it has usually been understood, and takes it as a proof of Christ's deity. We must, however, view this proof with suspicion since it would seem liable to lead to a Monophysite Christology, which in point of fact was cradled in Alexandria. Ambrose would know the duties of an ἀρχιτρίκλινος or *arbiter bibendi*, settling at each stage of the feast in what proportions the wine and the water should be mixed.

On the other hand if this "functional" view of the "sign" could be supposed to be correct, we might be justified in finding a vital, if cryptic, significance in words attested by St. Paul as part of Christ's eucharistic institution. The bread was perhaps to be broken at all meals in remembrance of Him; the cup *when wine was drunk* was to bring Him to mind. Thus His Presence would safeguard His members from drunkenness when they drank wine, as, unlike Islam, they were left free to do. If this should be the to our Lord's working of such miracles, but the reader may feel that the suggestion deserves to be considered.

The second temptation, if we follow Luke's order, was conveyed in the form of an impulse to achieve a swift acceptance of God's sovereignty by using material force to constrain men to an outward conformity.

One subtlety in the temptation is worthy of note. Our Lord is not invited to abandon His devotion to the true God in favour of a false god of force and tyranny. The suggestion is that He should pay a temporary homage to the god of force. In other words, it is a question whether, to secure the extension of the worship of the true God, use should not be made of such material compulsions as are habitual amongst those who accept gods of a lower nature.

Obviously it is a temptation which has often presented itself to Christ's Body the Church not less than it did to Him in His earthly Ministry. In the power of the Holy Ghost He swept the temptation aside, recognizing it for what it was. He learnt that to the Father man's freedom of conscience and independent power of self-determination were so precious that He was willing that men should still remain outside His sovereignty rather than be forced into an external compliance while internal rebellion persisted. It has often been presumed that the temptation was the lure of military glory or imperial splendour. The truth, however, would seem rather to lie in the direction we have just suggested. If so, we have here again another lesson learnt by our Lord that He must be patient and unhurried. If the Father was willing to leave men free to refuse His rule because He valued free will so highly, the Son must do the same. He must be content to find His teaching rejected, disregarded or opposed. Compulsion was a device of the Devil. As a corollary of this lesson we can understand His acceptance of the rôle of a martyr, which the form chosen for the visible descent of the Holy Ghost prefigured. We must notice further that following upon this rejection of any thought to spread God's

original fashion of the Eucharist, the Latin Churches may plead it as some palliation of their rule of Communion in one kind, although we shall still subscribe and adhere to the Orthodox sentence of excommunication upon their uncatholic and autonomous action.

kingdom by force among the Gentiles, our Lord's deliberate purpose was to confine His Ministry to the Chosen People: "I am not sent," He said, "but to the lost sheep of the House of Israel." In other words He understood it to be the Father's will that He Himself should confine His labours to the fields in which others had laboured so that they were ready for harvest. Mr. C. R. King has shrewdly commented on the fact that our Lord seems never to have entered Tiberias, and because He did visit Tyre and Sidon argues that Tiberias must hardly have been built when Jesus frequented the shores of the Galilean lake. Yet the truth is that the retirement to Tyre and Sidon was for the special reason of avoiding for another twelve months arrest and, it might be, murder on Herod's orders. The hour for the Crucifixion was not yet come, nor, it may be, the perception that it must take place at Jerusalem. He therefore left Palestine and yet did not break away from His rule of ministering exclusively to Jews, for in Tyre and Sidon there were synagogues and a Jewish settlement, just as in Acts xxi. 4 we find Christians there. To visit Tiberias, the deliberately Hellenized city, would have been a very different matter. It is in harmony with this acceptance of a restriction upon His work that our Lord should have recognized in the coming of Greeks to interview Him the Father's sign that the time for the Crucifixion was at hand. He Himself had not sought the interview: it came to Him as a call to prepare Himself to die, like the corn of wheat that is to bear much fruit.

The third temptation according to Luke's numeration springs naturally out of the last.

If our Saviour is not to spread God's Kingdom throughout the whole world by force of arms, why not convince Jews and Gentiles when assembled in the Holy City for the coming Passover by showing to them God's miraculous power?

On the one hand, if He was to die for man's redemption, why not at once sacrifice Himself where all eyes could see His sacrifice? The reader will notice here again the impatient eagerness to act at once, and again our Lord is taught that He must wait till it is shown to Him that the hour is come. On the other hand, would not the Father demonstrate that here was His Holy One by saving Him from death and destruction?

When Israel was brought out of Egypt God showed by mighty miracles that He would redeem His people. With their eyes they saw God's power and mercy. Was not a similar sign to be expected now? But once more our Lord in the power of the Holy Spirit recognized that this too was a suggestion of the Devil. Israel had been taught at Massah that they should not try to test what God would do, if they followed their own impulses instead of waiting upon Him. So now Jesus should not act upon His own impulse, but must wait to learn the Father's will in regard to the manner and the time of His sacrifice. Moreover, man's reason must be left free, not overwhelmed by ocular demonstration. He must walk by faith and not by sight: "Blessed are they who have not seen and yet have believed."

Once again we might read this third temptation in the following way. After our Lord had rejected the lure of earthly sovereignty and had, as the Psalmist said,[1] chosen Jahveh for His habitation, why not verify (He might think) the assertion that He was a Son of God by testing Jahveh's love and power and willingness to save Him if He flung Himself down from the pinnacle of the Temple? Still our Lord stood firm in His persevering resolve to wait upon Jahveh's will, till the truth as to His office should be made plain.

A word may be added as to the occasions when our Lord spoke of these Temptations to His apostles. It is not to be supposed that He related the story in one set narrative as we read it today. Rather we may suppose that when He explained privately to the apostles His declaration which, Mark says, made all food clean, He told them of the first temptation, when He Himself learned that man should live on any and every thing that God had made. After Peter's confession that Jesus was the Christ, when the apostle protested against the idea that the Christ should be martyred, our Lord may well have told of the second temptation, when He Himself learned that His Kingship was not to be exhibited in military triumphs but in sacrifice. Still later when our Lord was waiting for the sign

[1] Psalm xci. 11 would assure Him that though He must not test God in order to verify His Sonship, yet if others slew Him, God would crown His mission with such triumph as the Father designed it to have.

that the hour for the Crucifixion was at hand, He will have told the apostles how He had learnt that He must not hasten His end, and so we find Him refusing at first to go up to the Feast of Tabernacles and after that avoiding death by stoning.

The reader should observe that these threats of stoning are subsequent to the Feast of Tabernacles: they are not scattered promiscuously in the Gospel narrative. This is strong confirmation of our belief that we can rely on the chronological arrangement of the Fourth Gospel, and, further, that Luke's order for the Three Temptations is historically correct.[1]

[1] This suggestion consorts well with what Luke xxii. 28 implies, that "temptations," besides the "trials" of persecution (1 Peter iv. 12), beset our Lord after His Ministry was begun.

Chapter Two

THE GREEK BIBLE

(1)

WHAT language did our Lord habitually use? Was it Greek or Aramaic? It is in an eminent degree desirable that the reader should judge this question for himself [1] untrammelled by any preconceptions or dogmatic pronouncements of modern times. Specialists whose theories are not reviewed by considerable numbers of non-specialists and who are applauded and accepted by a coterie of like-minded specialists easily pursue a mistaken path, and, with their followers, resent and reject any challenge to their conventional doctrines. Yet it remains an imperative duty that what are no more than theories should be treated as theories and not as certainties, and nothing can be more profitable than that the mass of students should periodically re-examine the arguments on which these theories rest. For a good many years now professors and lecturers have repeated that our Lord did not habitually speak Greek but Aramaic or Neo-Hebrew. Anyone who questions this assertion is discredited as an amateur. Yet there are certain facts which are either overlooked or are given an interpretation that is by no means inevitable. Some of the facts have already been mentioned, but some others also deserve attention. It is at least remarkable that of the seven words from the Cross only one is stated to have been expressed in Hebrew, and this one must be regarded as a recitation of a treasured Psalm. No adequate reason can be given for the unanimity of our records in giving our Lord's utterances in Greek with three exceptions unless it was the fact that Greek was the language He used. The exceptions, as we have shown, are susceptible of explanation on either theory. The current view is that the unusual language remained in

[1] For a fuller and freer discussion of the question see R. O. P. Taylor, *The Groundwork of the Gospels.*

Peter's memory because of the emotional strain at the time— a not very convincing view as regards the healing of the deaf man. The alternative is that the language of the home was natural in addressing a young girl and a man who had been deaf for years. Those who have observed the phenomena of bilingual Welshmen will have no difficulty in accepting this alternative. Lloyd George's public utterances found, in the main, English expression; by his domestic hearth Welsh doubt-less was not less common. This argument takes on another complexion when we lay our account with the chronological order of events. The restoring to life of the youth at Nain had preceded that of Jairus' daughter and must have been yet more impressive. Was Peter away at that time and is that how Mark came to omit it? Be that as it may, Luke makes Christ address the dead youth in Greek. The reader will perhaps pardon a momentary digression. An attempt has been made to buttress up still further the current view by claiming that some difficulties in our records are explicable as due to in-competent translation from an Aramaic original. One such example has been regarded as supplying strong justification for this hypothesis. In our Lord's "High Priestly Prayer" John gives (xvii.11) τήρησον αὐτοὺς ἐν τῷ ὀνόματί σου ᾧ δέδωκάς μοι.

It has been said that here the relative pronoun is blunderingly made not to agree with its antecedent. In point of fact, however, this interpretation misses the theological teaching intended by our Lord. He has received from the Father an intimate know-ledge of the Father's character: He has been given the Father's name, the secret of His Nature. The disciples are to be kept safe by retaining a vivid understanding of that Name, which they have been taught by Christ. As someone has well said, the disciples were not won to acceptance of our Lord by admiration for His lofty ideology. They were impressed by His manifest prerogative of power over disorders of conscience and of nature. The impression made them willing to accept His new teachings as to men's duty towards God and man. Those who accepted this entered into eternal life, those who clung to the traditional doctrines as to ceremonial duty were blind. Our Saviour prayed that His disciples should be kept safe in the new knowledge He had imparted to them as to the way by which they could enter into Life.

Here again then we find the Aramaic pundit straining the facts in support of his theory and we may make bold to revert to the old belief that our Lord spoke Greek in public, even though in the family circle He used Aramaic. To make a final point, except on our hypothesis it is hard to explain why, on the one hand, our Lord prayed, "Abba, Father, let this cup pass from me," and on the other gave to the disciples the prayer "Our Father," for which no variant with "Abba" has ever been known. Paul's declaration that Christians learnt to call God "Abba" and his watchword "Mara Natha" give no warrant for the opposite opinion, since we know that in the Christian assemblies "tongues" were to be heard and that the Apostle spoke with tongues more than they all. Two further points deserve mention. When Paul addressed the mob at Jerusalem, they gave him the more attention because he spoke in Hebrew. It is manifest that they had expected to hear Greek: Aramaic surprised them because it was unusual. It is not to be supposed that Pilate had learnt Aramaic in order to discharge his office, so that we infer that our Lord and he spoke to one another in Greek. As for the surnames Cephas, Boanerges, Barnabas and the like, they go no further than to show that the population was bilingual. Cephas was quickly superseded by Peter, Boanerges is never mentioned except in the list of the apostles' names. Barnabas, as the Rev. R. O. P. Taylor has shown, may have replaced the name Joseph for a special reason. Nicknames are perhaps more common where two languages are in use, and Elymas Bar-Jesus is an example. William Rufus, Henry Beauclerc, John Lackland may illustrate the point with their surnames drawn from Latin, Norman-French and Early English. In further confirmation of this view attention must be called to a point which has never, it would appear, received due consideration. It is stated in our authorities that our Lord gave to the Twelve the style or designation of "apostles." There is nothing said of any Aramaic equivalent ever being used. The natural inference from this is that in our Lord's speech the Greek rather than the Aramaic would be heard, and this certainly favours the belief that where Aramaic utterances of our Lord are quoted, it was their rarity which had led to their being remembered.

One final observation must be made. John's practice of prefacing Christ's emphatic utterances with "Amen, amen," has by some been thought to show that He habitually spoke in Aramaic. Due reflection, however, makes it clear that the opposite conclusion is the more justifiable. The word "amen" was carried over into the speech of Greek-speaking Palestinians in the same way that English-speaking Welshmen ejaculate "Dear, dear," almost certainly a development from the genuine Welsh "Duw, duw" which the Welsh speaker is to be heard using. Similarly such speakers may add the tender "bach" in addressing a child. Thus John's evidence is that Jesus essentially spoke Greek but used "amen" as an expletive and, we may add, "abba" from His baby speech (Mark xiv. 36), just as a British child calls to his father with the Celtic word "daddy." Normally, Luke and John agree, our Lord addressed God as Father with the Greek word. Q attests the same form of address in the Lord's Prayer. John shows Him twice as addressing His mother with the Greek title of "lady."

(2)

For a satisfactory understanding of any historical period it is not enough to reproduce the texts and documents which deal with it. Some reconstruction of the social environment must be attempted by the use of the imagination : otherwise the intervals between noticeable events may be passed by, although in reality they were fraught with remarkable consequences. This consideration applies with signal force to the years of our Lord's infancy and of His early manhood. We shall here deal with one aspect of these years.

In another chapter we have seen reason to believe that our Lord spent nearly three of His earliest years in Egypt, i.e. from October, 7 B.C. to the spring perhaps of 4 B.C. Too little attention has been paid to the probable results of this evacuation to Egypt. Anyone acquainted with the way in which children learn to speak knows that from the second to the fifth year the mother-tongue is mastered, and the experience of those who during the war have been transplanted from London to Wales serves to show that the child Jesus must inevitably have acquired some knowledge of Greek, even if—and this itself needs to be established—St. Joseph and the Blessed Virgin were monoglot speakers of Aramaic. We know that as early as the seventh century B.C. there were Greek-speaking Jews in Egypt, and after Alexander founded the city which takes its name from him, one of its three divisions was assigned to Jews, yet Alexandria as a whole was Greek-speaking. We infer that while in the synagogues the Hebrew scriptures were read, a Greek interpretation would be regular in Egypt. More than that, we know that such an interpretation had been written out some centuries before the Christian era. These Greek translations, not being the sacred scriptures themselves, could be written out in inexpensive form. The Hebrew texts, we know, had to be elaborately checked and guaranteed and were seldom seen except in expensive rolls kept in the synagogues. The Greek versions could circulate in cheap codices which could be kept and read at home. We must, therefore, be prepared to accept the possibility—and, it may be thought, the certainty—that at any rate after their stay in Egypt, the Holy Family had in their possession and constantly read some portions of the Bible in a Greek version. It ought at the same time to be noticed that, as the action of St. Joseph shows, movement between Palestine and Egypt must have been common, so that we may expect that considerable numbers of those who lived in Palestine would know something of the Greek used in Egypt.

This possibility of the Scriptures in Greek being known in Palestine receives confirmation from what we are told about Matthew's work. On another page we have seen how the evidence of Papias' remarks about Matthew throw light on the extent to which the Greek language was in vogue amongst Jewish Christians in Palestine. An examination of the Old Testament quotations in the First Gospel shows something more. In xii. 17 a passage is quoted from Isaiah xlii. 1 ff. For this the Septuagint gives an interesting interpretation: Ἰακὼβ ὁ παῖς μου, ἀντιλήψομαι αὐτοῦ. Ἰσραὴλ ὁ ἐκλεκτός μου, προσεδέξατο αὐτὸν ἡ ψυχή μου. The evangelist, however, gives a Greek version which agrees in essential with the Hebrew text. We conclude that these Jewish Christians were familiar with a Greek Bible not the same in every detail as our present Septuagint. Nevertheless, the evidence points to the conclusion that it was from a Greek translation and not from the original Hebrew that they derived their knowledge of the Bible. Three illustrations of this are of interest. As we shall show elsewhere, they had no difficulty in understanding the prophecies of Jehovah's Suffering Servant as descriptive of His Son. Where Jeremiah in his great prophecy of restoration declared that the Lord would "raise up for David a righteous branch," the Septuagint spoke of ἀνατολήν. This word might be understood to mean "the rising of the sun" or "the east," and we cannot but notice how Zacharias in the Benedictus declares that "the dayspring from on high hath visited us," and Matthew dwells upon the appearance of the "Star in the East" or "in its rising." The sacred name "Jahveh" appears in the Greek Bible in the form of the substituted title Κύριος, and, as we have shown in another chapter, this easily admitted of the identification of our Lord with Jehovah.

One word of comment may be admissible. Verbal inspiration, as it was formerly understood, is now discredited. There is, however, room for a belief that the Holy Spirit may so direct, control and suggest the language used by an inspired writer that that language may become the starting-point for truth hardly discerned by that writer. If we may entertain this belief we may even go on to believe that the language of the Greek Bible was so directed and suggested that it prepared the way for Christian truth transcending what the original Hebrew contained and conveyed. A signal instance of this may be seen in the way that the word παρθένος, used in translating Isaiah vii. 14, is felt by Matthew to have been a prophetic anticipation of the eventual fact. The Hebrew in reality speaks of a young woman: Aquila, aiming at exact scholarship and, perhaps, at countering such a Christian argument as Matthew's, renders by νεᾶνις. We may believe that the first Greek translators were guided by the Holy Spirit to adopt the obvious and regular word[1] so that the Greek-speaking Jews, ignorant of the Hebrew, found in it a foreshadowing of what they had learnt to have been a fact. It is not to be thought that they

---

[1] The primary meaning of παρθένος is maiden or girl.

invented the story to bring it into conformity with the prophecy, but, knowing of the story, they could not but see in it a fulfilment of what they read in their Greek Bible.

So far we have urged nothing more than that our Lord was intimately acquainted with some Greek translation of the Hebrew authors included in the Palestinian canon. It is worthy of consideration, however, whether He was familiar with the larger canon recognized in Alexandria. In that were included a number of works which from the first days of Christianity have been read by all Christians except Protestants of the last four centuries as sacred Scriptures. In this they have followed the practice of the Greek-speaking diaspora. St. Jerome, it is true, after intercourse and controversy with Jews in Palestine, pronounced against basing any theological argument on the books which those Jews did not acknowledge to be Holy Scripture. It was not that these books had no Hebrew original; the discovery, fifty years ago, that there was still preserved in a lumber-room attached to an Egyptian synagogue the Hebrew original of the book Ecclesiasticus disposed of that contention once and for all. The Rabbinic synod which determined the Palestinian canon was doubtless influenced by other considerations. Yet it may not be without significance that a study of one at least among the Alexandrian books would seem to lead the reader on to some of the tenets which orthodox Christianity has adopted.

The stark isolation of Jewish monotheism is softened in the Book of Wisdom, where God not only has His Word as an assistant but His Wisdom as an assessor on His throne. This book, believed to be a Pharisaic counterpart to the Sadducean Ecclesiasticus, requires our particular attention. If our Lord, as we have suggested, was brought up, like Paul, a strict Pharisee, and if we are right in supposing that He read the Alexandrian Greek Scriptures, the book may well have been pondered by Him, and its thought will have helped to mould His religious ideas.

It will be of advantage at this point to cite some of the most noteworthy sayings which the writer of this book, the Wisdom of Solomon, was inspired to put down, and which seem directly or indirectly to have affected our Lord's thought and His conception of His personality as the unique Son of God. The reference to chapter and verse is appended to each passage so that the reader can easily satisfy himself as to the context in which it occurs.

"She that is the artificer of all things taught me, even Wisdom" (vii. 22), "She is a breath of the power of God" (vii. 25; cf. Heb. i. 2 and 10); "and a clear effluence of the glory of the Almighty" (cf. Heb. i. 3). "She is an effulgence from everlasting light and an unspotted mirror of the working of God, and an image of his goodness. And she, being one, hath power to do all things" (cf. Heb. i. 3). "It is given her to live with God, and the sovereign Lord of all loved her" (viii. 3; cf. John xvii. 5). "She chooseth out for him his works" (viii. 4). "O God of the fathers, who madest all things by thy word, and by thy wisdom thou formedst man" (ix. 1, 2; cf. Heb. i. 2). "Wisdom that sitteth by thee on thy throne" (ix. 4; cf. John xvii. 5). "And with thee is wisdom, which knoweth thy works, and was present when thou wast making the world" (ix. 9; cf. John xvii. 5 and Heb. i. 5). "And hardly do we divine the things that are on earth, but the things that are in the heavens who ever yet traced out?" (ix. 16; cf. John iii. 12). "Wisdom guarded to the end the first formed father of the world . . . wisdom knew the righteous man, and kept him strong when his heart yearned toward his child" (x. 1, 5; cf. John viii. 56). "Thine all-powerful word leaped from heaven out of the royal throne a stern warrior, into the midst of the doomed land" (xviii. 15; cf. John viii. 23 and 42).

(In confirmation of our belief that in some fashion the book had influenced our Lord's thoughts we may add three other quotations: "And in the time of their visitation they shall shine forth, and as sparks among stubble they shall run to and fro. They shall judge nations, and have dominion over peoples" (iii. 7, 8; cf. Matt. xiii. 43, Luke xxii. 30): "Yea and a disbelieving soul hath a memorial there, a pillar of salt still standing" (x. 7; cf. Luke xvii. 32): "And I chose to have her rather than light, because her bright shining is never laid to sleep, but with her there came to me all good things together" (vii. 10; cf. Matt. vi. 33).

The reader may hesitate to suppose that these statements

10*

about Wisdom could have been even momentarily regarded by our Lord as applying to Himself. There is, however, a significant passage in the Gospels which suggests that the first generation of Christians sometimes expressed their conception of the relation between the Father and the Son by styling the latter the Wisdom (not, as later Christians did, the Word) of God. In His sorrowful declaration that the blood of all the martyred prophets should be required of that generation, our Lord announced that He would send prophets and apostles to them and prophesied that some of them would be slain and persecuted. This utterance of His has been preserved to us through the author of Q, but while Matt. xxiii. 34 appends them without comment to other utterances of our Lord, Luke xi. 49 specifically states that they came from "the Wisdom of God," yet by the form of expression he uses, he identifies this with our Lord. Two other passages may be thought to be tinged and coloured with something of the same conception as we have seen in the book of Wisdom. After the Baptist's two disciples had set out to return to John, our Lord contrasted the circumstances of His mission and those of John's, concluding with the remark that "Wisdom is justified in respect of all her children" (Luke vii. 35). When our Lord re-visited Nazareth the critics remarked, "From whence hath this man these things? and what wisdom is this which is given unto him (Mark vi. 2) that even such mighty works are wrought by his hands?" All this may be held to show that the thought would not be strange which the book of Wisdom has explicitly developed.[1] It is as though the descent of the Holy Spirit upon our Lord was the descent of the Spirit of Wisdom (Isaiah xi. 2), and being possessed by this Spirit He was Himself the Wisdom of God.

Nor is this all. There are yet other pronouncements of the Wisdom of Solomon which merit our attention. Besides their germinal doctrine, the book supplies a picture of cosmic and human origins, a companion picture alternative to the primitive archaeology incorporated in the early chapters of Genesis.

[1] ix. 17: "Who ever gained knowledge of Thy counsel, except Thou gavest wisdom, and sentest Thy holy Spirit from on high?" (See Excursus III, p. 343.)

It is perhaps not without significance that our Lord Himself flatly contradicts the statement in Genesis that God rested from His work. Wisdom represents God with Wisdom's assistance as still continuing His operations in the world. Jesus said, "My Father worketh hitherto and I work." Again, chapters ii–v, whether read by our Lord or by His Greek-speaking disciples, must have seemed a divinely inspired apocalypse, a God-given prevision of the Passion, when He whom His followers had "numbered among sons of God" (v. 5), a "servant of the Lord" (ii. 13), who vaunted that God was His Father (ii. 16), was mocked by His enemies in their hour of transient triumph.

So far we may claim to be keeping to solid and substantial probabilities. We shall now venture for one moment to tread on more precarious and perilous ground. In John vii. 38 our Lord is represented as saying "As the scripture hath said, out of his belly shall flow fountains of living water." Since "the scripture" is in the singular, some one passage must be meant, and the commentators here are sadly to seek. Hoskyn and Davey can do no better than suppose the thought to resemble that of Paul, when he writes "they all drank of the rock that followed them, and that rock was Christ" (1 Cor. x. 4). They suggest that the quotation comes from some Midrash on the Biblical account of Moses drawing water from the rock. Our Lord's words, however, would seem not to refer to Himself as supplying eternal life, but to the believer who has within him an unfailing supply of spiritual energy. Westcott is no better with his reference to Isaiah lviii. 11—where, however, the Greek version is closer to the Johannine passage than is the Hebrew. If we must look further it is not unreasonable according to the argument we are pursuing to conclude that our Lord is quoting from some Greek apocryphal work which is not now accessible to us. We shall then at the least be able to justify our use of the full Greek Bible in preference to the narrower Massoretic, not only by reference to a few passages in the canonical Epistles, but by the example of our Lord Himself. If Jude was our Lord's putative cousin, his use of Enoch is confirmatory of the idea that in their family circle the Greek Bible and some Greek apocryphal books were read to their spiritual profit.

Controversialists must of necessity, if they are in any way to win their opponents over, rest their arguments upon what is common ground between the two parties. Hence it was that St. Jerome, arguing the Christian case against the Jews, defined the canonical Scriptures which he used as the same that had been recognized by the remnant of the Rabbis at their "Rump" Synod in Jamnia after the fall of Jerusalem. He therefore relegated to a secondary position the other Books of our Old Testament, not inferring that for Christians they were not to supply spiritual truth but consenting for the special purpose he had in hand to limit his arguments within the ambit accepted by the Jews. The fathers of the Anglican Reformation repeated Jerome's words, but, perhaps under pressure from others who were impressed by the fundamentalist theories of the Jews, extended the saint's caveat so far as to disclaim the Apocrypha as a source from which Christian truth is to be derived. This unfortunate exclusion has been partly responsible for the mis-understandings of the development of Christological thought and for the contention that the doctrine of the Blessed Trinity originated at Nicaea. If we may believe that our Lord Himself used the full Greek Bible, we shall not hesitate to do the same when shaping our theology, however much we may be ready to follow St. Jerome when arguing with Jews. Support for this proceeding may be found in the fact that St. Athanasius in his treatise *De Incarnatione* does not hesitate to quote the Wisdom of Solomon in confirmation of his theology. He shows no suspicion that he is not quoting authoritative and authentic Scripture, a fact which warrants the conclusion that the ante-Nicene Christian Fathers had no thought of such a curtailment of the Old Testament as St. Jerome accepted later.

Chapter Three

THE DEVELOPMENT OF CHRIST'S HUMAN CONSCIOUSNESS

"JESUS is God," wrote F. W. Faber, making the words the keynote of one of his hymns. That hymn was included in at least one collection of English hymns intended for use by worshippers who were outside the Papal communion. It was valued by some, doubtless, because it sounded a counterblast to such latitudinarian attenuation of our Lord's prerogatives as made Him no more than a great prophet or saint. Yet but little thought is needed to make it clear that Faber's words lend themselves only too easily to a very different and no less dangerous belief. The English and the Latin languages suffer from their incapacity to express with terse precision the distinction between God, meaning the Blessed Trinity and God when used to affirm the deity of each of the Three Hypostases within the Trinity. The Fourth Evangelist is careful in his prologue to distinguish ὁ Θεὸς and Θεὸς, which are blurred into one in the Latin *Deus* and the English *God*. Jesus is Θεὸς, but not ὁ Θεὸς. The difficulty and the danger resulting from such a bald and indiscriminating expression as is contained in the hymn just quoted may be illustrated from the following anecdote.

A little child taught by his mother that Jesus was born on Christmas Day and also that "Jesus is God" presently asked, "What did the world do before God was born?"

We need not here concern ourselves with the problems as to how the rudiments of Christian tradition and experience are to be imparted to our children, nor yet with the subtleties of psychological discussion which developed into Christological controversies—Apollinarian, Nestorian, Eutychian, Monophysite, Monothelite, whose contending theories still persist, albeit the old party labels are mostly forgotten. Orthodox thinkers themselves are often at a loss to conceive how the divine consciousness and the human in our Lord could be so conjoined as to express themselves as they are represented in our

Gospels to have done in incident and in utterance. It will be suggested in these pages that this difficulty has been fashioned for us by our own perfunctory citation and precipitate interpretation of biblical texts. A patient study of the Gospels, if the methods of historical investigation are pursued, not only shows our Lord's followers step by step advancing to a realization of His supreme position but also reveals the human consciousness of the Lord Himself step by step coming to be interpenetrated and fused with the divine. Thus it was, as it would appear, that He "took Manhood into God."

It is such a historical study that this chapter aims at presenting. One caution must be added. When we read the Gospels to inflame our souls' devotion, we rightly read the record as illuminated by its sequel. In this study, on the other hand, we must divest our minds at first of such memories and see everything, so far as possible, as it was seen at the time. We must strip from the language the fullness of meaning which under the guidance of the Holy Spirit we have since learnt to see that the language adopted was providentially adapted to allow. Thus studied, our records will be found to have dissipated the perplexing permutations which have been supposed to appear in our Lord's incarnate life.[1]

The birth of consciousness in an infant and its gradual growth to mature perfection must always be for a reverent observer as amazing a process as the daily miracle of the dawn of "another new day." The Christian holds the conviction that the Second Person in the Holy Trinity lived on earth from the first moment of embryonic existence to the last moment of dissolution a life that in every point and particular was absolutely human. How then, we ask, did His human consciousness not only awake to His own identity as Man, as we ourselves have waked to our identity, but rose to that stupendous and perhaps to us for ever inexplicable consciousness that He, the Man Jesus, was withal God the Son? Can our historical records in any way illuminate this ineffable mystery?

---

[1] I purposely abstain from multiplying references to the works of those who, from varying points of view, have sought to give an orthodox account of our Lord's twofold consciousness. Perhaps, however, mention should be made of Mr. W. McDougal's *The Trinity*.

First, then, what are we told of thoughts and expectations antecedent to our Lord's nativity? The answer is easy to our hand, for there is no valid reason for denying the essential veracity of our Gospels in this regard, and, as we shall see, the painstaking accuracy of phrase particularly exhibited by the scientifically trained Luke frequently illuminates and defines the content of those expectations. It would unduly extend the length of this investigation if we pursued in detail the enquiries suggested by this requirement. They are to be seen discussed at length elsewhere. Here it must suffice to state that where the English versions uniformly write "the Son of God" our original authors distinguish clearly: (1) God's son *or* (a) son of (a) God; (2) God's Son *or* (a) Son of God; and (3) the SON OF GOD. We learn, too, that there was an expectation of an heir to David's throne appearing for the inestimable benefit of the Jewish people. One anointed by Jehovah was looked for to establish a permanent empire, but whether he was to be David's heir was not beyond question. A prophet "like unto Moses" was to arise, and he was spoken of as the prophet. Many hoped that a leader would appear who would liberate the chosen people of Israel: the Galileans longed for liberation from Rome or from the son of the Edomite Herod; others seem to have anticipated liberation from sin or from disease, often regarded as the concomitant or consequence of sin, or again from the frustrating social environment which cramped their desire to offer a pure worship or service to God. Keeping in mind these facts, we can understand the significance of the utterances recorded to have been made before the Nativity and afterwards, by Gabriel to Zacharias and to the Blessed Virgin; by the angel to St. Joseph; by Mary, Zacharias and the angels to the shepherds; by the Scribes to Herod; and by our Lord after his first Passover.

How much of all this was told to our Lord as He grew up we have no means of telling, but we cannot doubt that something of it was known to Him and must have lent point to some passages in the Bible with which He would be familiar. We shall feel little doubt that He pondered on the wording of the second Psalm, which makes Jahveh's Anointed to be told "Thou art My Son: this day have I begotten Thee." In the

Prophets, too, we may well believe that our Lord was led to ruminate on some passages which served to mature His human consciousness of His peculiar functions and to guide Him to an understanding of His unique mission. He had been told that He was God's Son and that for a space of time He had sojourned in Egypt. When Hosea was read, He would be likely to note the words (xi. 1) "When Israel was a child, then I loved him, and called my son out of Egypt." [1] Similarly in Isaiah He heard of a virgin bearing a son, of a Son born on whose shoulder the government should be; who should be hailed as "the mighty God, the everlasting Father, the Prince of Peace."

We can conjecture how two conflicting and alternating tides of confidence and hesitancy, of doubt and conviction would sweep over Him as He heard the covert innuendoes or open scoffs of unkind gossip, or meditated on the bold promises of Holy Scripture which harmonized so aptly with what His mother had said. Nor, it may be believed, were these the only or even perhaps the primary sources from which there flowed into our Lord's human mind the momentary conception, if not the habitual consciousness, of Himself as God's Son. In early Hebrew thought and language cities were accounted as daughters. Regional rulers were styled sons of the overlord. Jair, for example, is said to have had seventy sons who rode upon white asses: they were the provincial or district governors in that dominion. In the view of the nobler Hebrew minds, Jahveh was the real King of Israel. Their true form of government was a theocracy. Nevertheless, when the monarchy was instituted it was accommodated to the theocratic theory by regarding the king as the visible representative or vicegerent of Jahveh, the invisible and real ruler. The king therefore in Hebrew parlance was God's Son and in Psalm ii, a coronation anthem, the King's accession to office is regarded as the generation of the Son. This mode of thought is to be seen again in other passages, as, for example, when it is said that the Son has been anointed with the oil of gladness above his fellows.

---

[1] It is tempting to hazard the surmise that Matthew's Logia was a collection of scriptural passages which our Lord was remembered to have "opened" to His disciples, and had perhaps Himself digested as His human consciousness developed.

With such ideas insinuated into His mind and, as we may suppose, fermenting within Him, He lived the ordinary and orderly life of a Galilean Jew. The years passed, and St. Joseph died. Our Lord, acknowledged by him as his son, was known in the family to be *de jure* King of Israel, and if His brethren resented His intrusion (as they personally regarded it) they were powerless to disturb the settlement of the succession which St. Joseph's action had established. Then Zacharias' son, John, received a charge from God to announce the imminence of a vindication of the Divine Sovereignty. Men were to readjust their outlook on life, to die to their past habits and to enter on a new life of deliverance to God's rule, and to testify this sacramentally by baptism. More than this, they were to be infused with a spirit of consecration to these ends at the hands of One who would be indicated to the Baptist by a visible descending and remaining upon him of God's consecrating Spirit. We can have little doubt that the Baptist and our Lord, before the actual rite, discovered in conversation their family connexion and their past. Thus the Baptist's saying accords with his mother Elizabeth's salutation to the Blessed Virgin: the Neophant is his Lord, by whom indeed he needs to be baptized. Naturally enough he asks then, Dost Thou (my Master) come for baptism? Still our Lord will carry out all rules of religious practice that have been revealed to men. John's call to baptism has come from an instruction given him by Jehovah. It is therefore to be obeyed, though He be not conscious of sins to be remitted. He desires to be ready for the achievement of God's purpose now to set up His unveiled rule over men. Both baptizer and Baptized saw the Holy Dove settle upon our Lord, both perhaps heard the voice which reinforced the old assurances that Jesus was God's Son, but now a word was added which might assert that this Sonship was unique.[1] The Baptist, as we shall see, rose to the height of that assertion. Doubtless he did not understand what the words were, in the event, to be discovered to reveal, but he testified his conviction that Jesus was the Son—not one son among many, but the unique Son of God.

[1] ἀγαπητός in a papyrus is used to indicate the only eye of a one-eyed man.

In His solitude our Lord could review the significance of all that He had heard before and of the stupendous circumstances of His baptism. His office was so exalted that in Isaiah's language He could be hailed as " God with us " men.[1] Not only was He Himself anointed, not with oil but with a spirit of consecration to God's service, but He was, as the Baptist declared, to bestow the same gift on others, thus fitting them to be God's subjects. The sign of the Dove, however, betokened that sacrifice was that for which He was consecrated. The words of a Psalm, however, said clearly God did not desire sacrifice but had prepared a human Body in which God's servant should fulfil His will.[2] Did not this interpret what His mother had told Him of His birth? He was indeed the Temple of Jehovah and in His body would offer a sacrifice better than that of bulls and goats and lambs. But yet again, was this illusion? The cynical spirit of cold rationalism whispered that, assuming that He was God's Son, He should put the matter to a proof by transmuting stones into loaves of bread or by flinging Himself from the pediment of the Temple. His rejection of these promptings led on to a thought of setting out to establish by force God's sovereignty over men. But this thought too was refused as inconsistent with His understanding of what God's service meant. What else in those forty days of retirement our Lord learnt as to the conditions under which He should execute His mission we can only conjecture and infer from His subsequent procedure. He may have then grasped that a rule of life like the Pharisees' was insufficient, unless mercy, justice and humility were enthroned in the heart. He may have felt that no creature made by God could be ceremonially unclean for food and that neither the touch of a leper nor contact with a dead body, a Gentile or a sinner could defile.

Meanwhile it would appear that the Baptist too had meditated on the sign of the Dove. He too recognized the divine message that He whom Jehovah had anointed with the Spirit of consecration was to offer not service only but sacrifice. Then,

[1] Isaiah vii. 14 and ix. 6.
[2] The Massoretic text is different (Psalm xl. 7). Unless the Septuagint text was known to Jesus (xxxix. 6) or records an alternative Targum current in our Lord's day, the above suggestion must be modified.

as Sir John Seeley pointed out, when he marked the thousands
of lambs driven up to Jerusalem to be the Temple victims, his
mind awoke to the typical significance of two passages in
Holy Writ.[1] Jehovah's servant was to be led as a sheep to the
slaughter, dumb as a lamb before the shearer. Moreover,
Jehovah Himself provided the lamb for Abraham when he
prepared to slay his son.

So when our Lord returned from His six weeks of solitude,
the Baptist pointed Him out as the Lamb of God who taketh
away the sinfulness of the world. It is hardly to be doubted
that our Lord and the firm of Zebedee and Co. were mutually
acquainted. Zebedee was His uncle by marriage, his sons[2] were
His cousins; and the partners Simon and Andrew, the sons of
another John, must have known something of Zebedee's sister-
in-law and her Son. The words of these first adherents merit
particular attention. Clearly they accepted the Baptist's pronouncement that our Lord was his infinite superior, destined
to bestow the Holy Spirit and to remove sin from the world,
although they would not have expressed themselves in the
language of the Nicene Fathers. Yet the disciples' words made
this language possible as their full implication emerged. To
our Lord Himself, it would appear, the declarations of those
who were brought in contact with Him and with what He said
and did were one channel through which understanding was
brought to Him of what His Sonship was.

It was as Rabbi and not yet as Lord[3] that these first disciples

[1] Isaiah liii. 7 and Genesis xxii. 8.

[2] We may accept the Rev. T. Cottam's argument from the expression
τὸν ἀδελφὸν τὸν ἴδιον in John i. 41 that Andrew's companion, presumably
John, also had a brother to bring to the Lord.

[3] In this age men often professed themselves the votaries of some demigod
(so to say), a powerful if partial manifestation of the supreme deity. This
selective worship was, we may say, not unlike the veneration of some patron
saint in the Middle Ages or the worship of a Roman Emperor. The Jews
worshipped Jehovah, whose name they would not utter, as their "Lord"
and for a time Christians spoke of our Saviour as their "Lord," a nomenclature which later facilitated under divine providence their understanding
that He was one with Jehovah. All this the commentators have often urged,
but there is reason for adding something more. Careful consideration shows
that a more natural and truer sense is given to the title in many instances if
it is recognized as the equivalent of "the King," "his Majesty," in the
vocative "Your Majesty," the speaker thereby acknowledging our Lord's
claim to the Davidic throne.

addressed Him, but they had already advanced in their appreciation of our Lord far beyond what this word might seem to signify. Andrew spoke of Him to his brother Peter as the Messiah; Philip spoke of Him as "him of whom Moses in the law, and the prophets, did write."[1]

Nathanael, raised to a pitch of enthusiastic reverence by our Lord's reading of his hesitations, hailed Him as "the Son of God" and "King of Israel." Whereupon our Lord addressed to him and Philip words which require particular attention. "Ye shall see that the heaven has been opened and that the angels of God are ascending and descending upon "—not the Son of God—but "the son of man," i.e. the inheritor and embodiment of all men's hopes for the future. This will doubtless signify at the moment, Himself, the Bethel in human flesh, but it holds the promise of such divine indwelling for every believer.[2]

The sign at the marriage feast in Cana need not detain us from our immediate quest. Plainly here was no testing of the truth of His Sonship, but a manifestation of His gracious kindliness when the accession of His disciples to the wedding party threatened to bring shame upon the family.[3] We shall posit some inward monition that such a "sign" would be vouchsafed and approved by God, and we shall be reminded of what we are told of Socrates' mysterious voice.

We must next mention our Lord's unhesitating description of the Temple as His Father's house and of His own Body as a temple, but neither expression adds anything to what we have already noted. They but confirm what has been said.

It is by the well at Sychar that we discover more of our

[1] John i. 41 and 45. It is noteworthy that Nathanael was unaware (as it would appear) that Micah's prophecy of Bethlehem had been fulfilled. Under the fig-tree he perhaps wrestled with doubts, in part suggested by this apparent contradiction of the prophecy, when he was told of what had happened in the Baptist's company.

[2] This illumines John ii. 19, 21 and 1 Corinthians vi. 19. The Humanity of the Positivist is not altogether unlike the Son of Man, thus interpreted. I am indebted to Rev. R. O. P. Taylor for this interpretation. He adds that in the passage so often quoted from Daniel this "hope of Humanity" is viewed as predetermined in God's purpose and therefore pre-existent. Cf. Paul's thought in 1 Cor. x. 4.

[3] His mother's concern at the exhaustion of the cellar and her ordering of the servants point to some special relation with the bride or the bridegroom.

Lord's self-revelation and, we may believe, progressive self-discovery. The Galileans were notoriously restless and turbulent under Roman rule. They were ready to rise in rebellion if any leader offered himself. We are not surprised, therefore, that our Lord steadfastly avoided any word when He was with Galileans that might excite their fanatical hopes. In Samaria it was not so. There men waited for Jehovah's Anointed who would settle the religious controversy between them and the Jews,[1] and our Lord openly avowed Himself to be that Anointed One. Yet still with His Galilean followers He set Himself to convert their thoughts and hopes and ambitions to spiritual aspirations towards consecrated service of God and their fellow men.

At this point it will be well to consider two matters of importance to our understanding of the progress of our Lord's public ministry.

In the first place we must notice His insight into the past and present life of the Samaritan woman. This we may perhaps regard as a manifestation of power of the same order as His knowledge of Nathanael's meditations under his fig-tree. To the same power we shall credit our Lord's knowledge of the crisis in the fever and of the sure recovery of the officer's son at Capernaum.[2]

We must further observe the Lord's confidence in His power to heal this boy, the first example, apparently, of this supremacy over disease. The words of Isaiah lxi. 1, 2, which He used for a text shortly after in the synagogue at Nazareth, would be His warrant for such confidence whenever "the hour was come" for generous kindliness to those who relied on His readiness to help.

Here we must pause to remark that while the disciples still addressed our Lord as Rabbi (but perhaps with its Greek equivalent) both the Samaritan woman when convinced that He was a prophet and also the officer used the title "Lord," though likely enough in its conventional sense of mundane respect, "sir." When the men of Sychar avowed Him to be the Anointed (using the Greek word, Christ, where the woman

---

[1] John iv. 25.
[2] John iv. 52.

said Messiah), but added that He was the Saviour of the world, it is natural to think that the disciples told what the Baptist had said—that He was the Lamb that taketh away the world's sinfulness. We have seen that the Lord already had apprehended that His commission was of wider scope than might be designated by the words "for the Chosen people," and this may have reinforced His choice of the expression "the Son of Man" while He sought to raise His followers' minds to a spiritual conception of the purpose for which he had been sent.

To one scene in this period of the Ministry we must advert for a moment. Caught in the storm on the Galilean lake, the disciples cried "Rabbi, Rabbi, we perish," and yet used no loftier title. Our Lord, we shall believe, nursed the conviction that He was destined to be slain as the Lamb provided by God for sacrifice. As we shall see, His followers were prepared for the event by very gradual disclosures and they were slow to learn. He Himself recognized that His hour was not yet come when death by shipwreck threatened. If God "maketh of winds His angels" and bade all gods (Hebrew *elohim*) or angels (Septuagint) to worship the Son: if God maketh the storm to cease so that the waves thereof are still, then the Father's will was that His hour was come to lay His command upon the angels of the wind and wave, and so they should be brought to the haven where they would be.[1]

It skills not to follow in detail the course of our Lord's subsequent Ministry, nor to recapitulate the acts of healing and the spiritual instruction which revealed His gracious love of mankind. Suffice it to recall two noteworthy sayings only. First, conscious that He was "sent" to call sinners to a change of outlook on life, He declared Himself authorized as the spokesman of humanity and, as it would appear, humanity after Him authorized, to declare to sinners that God had forgiven their sins—this when they relied upon the gracious readiness of our Lord to help them to a new start in life. Again, He answered that He as humanity's representative, and it would appear humanity after Him, was the maker, not the slave, of the rules for the observance of the Sabbath. So far we discover a now settled conviction that He was uniquely God's Son, His legate, His anointed and consecrated One, His Lamb that was

[1] Psalm xcvii. 7; cvii. 29, 30.

removing the world's sinfulness, the Saviour. But of a consciousness of essential Godhead in Himself we so far see nothing.

Particular attention should be paid to our Lord's words when the Baptist sent his two disciples to elicit a statement upon the Lord's mission. We see calm and unhurried confidence that He is fulfilling the purpose with which He has been "sent" and that His commission included, besides the glad blessings enumerated in Isaiah, the authority to raise to life the dead and to proclaim to humble hearts the joyful coming of God's rule. He had accepted it that the Baptist was no more than a courier before His superior Majesty: the Son of God, uniquely born and uniquely qualified, was greater than His "angel" or messenger, though he was himself more than a prophet, i.e. such as had in general received a special instruction ($\dot{\rho}\tilde{\eta}\mu\alpha$) from God. The form too in which Malachi is quoted may perhaps imply that the Son's way was the Father's also.

From this we pass to the episode of the paralysed sinner at Jerusalem. That he was bidden to carry away his bed brought to a clear issue the question of Sabbath observance. The Law therefore, and not the Prophets or the Psalms, is adduced in confirmation of our Lord's unique position of authority. We shall believe that He had meditated on the promises made to Abraham, and that the words of Isaiah and of David had assured Him that the Son of Man who was likewise the Son of God was prepared by His Father before time was to be the Judge of all men at the Great Assize.[1] The Jews' intelligence was not at fault when they divined the loftiness of these claims, but they obstinately refused to consider our Lord's interpretation of "Moses."

To make stones become loaves of bread for His own satisfaction He had recognized would be a failure when His resolution in all ways to do the Father's will was being put to the test. To multiply a scanty modicum of food out of compassion for auditors who welcomed His teaching was a different matter, and He did not hesitate to prove that this fell within the purview of His stupendous authority. By Jacob's well at Sychar He could avow Himself sent to supply spiritual refreshment to souls athirst for righteousness. Now He declared Himself the true food

[1] Genesis xxii. 18; xxvi. 4. Isaiah ix. 6. Daniel vii. 9–14.

for man sent from heaven by His Father. It is to be noted that His hearers asked Him to give them this food, thus (we may say) giving Him parity with God. Yet His words fell on ears dulled by thoughts of material prosperity, and He went on to make the unequivocal statement that His human life and His sacrificial slaughter was to supply the spiritual sustenance of mankind.[1] We may perhaps believe that our Lord about this period took account of the Psalmist's words "Thou art a Priest for ever after the order of Melchizedek" and of the record that that Priest-King "brought forth bread and wine" for Abraham's refreshment.[2] We shall thus have the genesis of the eucharistic rite in which the eternal Priest is also the eternal Victim whose Flesh and Blood are sacramentally[3] made the post-sacrificial feast.

At length the experiences of the Twelve, their close and constant intercourse with our Lord, what they had seen of His mastery of disease and death and wild nature, His generous love of the helpless, the disabled and the weak-willed sinners, brought them to the point when, as their spokesman pronounced, they judged without wavering that Jesus was the Christ, anointed of Jehovah to be King and Prophet and Priest. Perhaps we shall be right to hold that this spontaneous, unprompted and authentic verdict upon their experiences reinforced the Lord's own conviction; it was, as He said, a truth revealed to them by His heavenly Father. Upon this truth, as on a rock, the Church could be built. Accordingly from this time forward we find a more explicit insistence on the Son's unique knowledge of the Father, a knowledge mediated by the Son to those and those alone who were "given" Him by the Father.[4]

[1] St. Peter's profession of faith at this juncture deserves notice. "Lord," he said (not Rabbi, it will be observed), "to whom shall we go? . . . Thou art the Holy One of God, the Consecrated One," but more he does not say (John vi. 68, 69).

[2] Psalm cx. 4; Gen. xiv. 18.

[3] Our Lord's figurative language drawn from physical food was a stumbling-block to the Twelve on a later occasion. The "leaven of the Pharisees and of Herod" was not immediately understood by them to signify hypocrisy and a dread of spiritual enthusiasm which might disturb the established order of society.

[4] This limitation of the number who accepted the truth is to be seen in the parable of the Sower and in our Lord's words to His critics at Capernaum (John vi. 44) and at Jerusalem (John vii. 17; viii. 47).

Yet first the chosen Three were to see what might in reminiscence fortify them against despondency and despair in dark hours that were to follow. Moreover, the Voice exalted the Christ above both Moses and Elijah: "This," it was said, "is My Son, my Chosen: hear *Him*." His utterances then were of such validity as overrode both the Law and the Prophets. His words were God's.

The Three thus confirmed in their reverence for Him, our Lord began to intimate with increasing directness and simplicity what was the appointed issue of His Ministry. Doubtless to Himself also what at first was only seen through a veil of obscurity as a sacrificial slaying grew gradually plainer as a horror of ignominious suffering the most extreme. The human instinct of self-preservation He repudiated as a temptation to disregard the Father's will, and it is noted that from this time forth He set Himself steadfastly to look forward to a prophet's death. In Luke's account of the Transfiguration which we may regard as derived from John, a detail is added to Peter's story as recorded by Mark. Moses and Elijah, we are told, talked with Jesus about his approaching destined departure from this life which was to be at Jerusalem. Hitherto Pharisees, dissatisfied with his religious teaching, had joined Herodians in plotting against him. Herod's dominions of Galilee and Peraea might have been the scene of his murder, as they had been of the Baptist's. Now, Jerusalem, the centre of the Jewish Faith, is chosen, and that choice determines that the Roman authorities are to be the instruments for the Pharisees' attempt to extinguish His Gospel.

Here it will not be out of place to interrupt momentarily the orderly and chronological consideration of our subject and to pause while we notice one particular feature in the story. This illustrates clearly the gradual and increasing apprehension in our Saviour's human mind of what the Father's divine omniscience ordained to be the one, full, perfect and sufficient course which must be taken for the redemption and reclamation of the whole world. The avowal by Peter of his and his fellows' conviction that Jesus was the Christ, the Son of the living God—in less formal language the long-foretold King, the Viceroy in the Israelite theocracy—was recognized by our

Lord as a time-signal. He knew that now two preliminary objects were secured. His mighty signs had demonstrated His extraordinary rank; His teaching had shown men the universal ethical principles which by divine providence and sanction are eternally operative. The moment was come when He should enter upon the second part of His mission in the world. At His baptism His human spirit had been occupied and was henceforth interpenetrated by the Divine Spirit of self-sacrificing love. As the Lamb[1] of God's providing He must pour out His life in the battle against wrong if He was to ascend His throne. He was conscious that now the time was come to prepare Himself and His followers for the mortal crisis. How immediate that crisis was He did not know, but He was assured that it and its instant sequel of triumphant accession would now follow within the lifetime of some at least among His followers. With the nearer approach of the hour determined by the Father we can trace the growing clearness of our Lord's awareness as to its predestined date. In His third temptation He had seen that there must be no reckless audacity on His part—no plunge from the sanctuary pediment to crash on the Temple pavement. He was to trust the Father and leave to Him the time and the manner in which His victorious mission was to be accomplished. His death therefore was not to be brought about by any violence of nature such as a sudden storm on the lake. He was to be overborne by the violence of enemies—the malignity of jealous and doctrinaire ecclesiastics and materialistic nationalists. At the Transfiguration He was taught that Jerusalem was the fittest and most central spot for His universal sacrifice, and since the Roman government reserved for itself the right of capital punishment, He realized that His death must inevitably be at the hands of the foreigner and take the form of crucifixion. As He seems to have thought during His retirement after His baptism, the time should be that of some great festival when Jerusalem was thronged with multitudes of pilgrims. The first feast that now followed was the Feast of Tabernacles, and after some lingering in Galilee He

---

[1] The figure of the Paschal Lamb (*amnos*) in the end proved more generally fruitful than did that of the warrior Ram (*arnion*) in the Apocalypse.

presented Himself in the Temple. Yet He found that the Father did not sanction His death during that feast, although, it has been argued, at that feast there was a dramatic representation of the sacrifice of the king for the welfare of his people throughout the New Year. Three months later He attended the Feast of Dedication—which was perhaps unusual with Him—when Psalm cxviii. is believed to have greeted those who approached the Temple. That Psalm had celebrated the re-dedication in such words as "Open to me the gates of righteousness: I will go into them, and I will praise the Lord: . . . The stone which the builders refused is become the head stone of the corner. . . . Blessed is he that cometh in the name of the Lord." But still the hour was premature. At last, when Greek strangers approached Him, He knew that His sacrifice was thus marked as destined to be of significance to Jew and Gentile alike. Disquieted for a while by the imminence of the crisis, He was reassured by the voice which guaranteed the Father's glorious support in the hour of His death as it had been guaranteed in that of Lazarus' shortly before. Finally at His trial before Caiaphas He could declare that presently upon His condemnation and crucifixion His entry on His spiritual rule over humanity would be made manifest. He would be reigning from the Tree and, yet more indisputably, after His Resurrection, Ascension and Mission of the Holy Ghost.

Once again then in this particular we can see how the circumstances of His environment and the impact of events stirred and stimulated our Lord's human consciousness of His duty if He would fulfil His Father's will. He learnt here as elsewhere obedience through His experiences. But it is time to return to the general survey of the development, as far as we can discover it, in our Lord's human consciousness.

At the Feast of Tabernacles He boldly assumed the office of a Rabbi who taught in the courts of the Temple itself, the status (if we may so describe it) of a university professor. In figurative language He proclaimed Himself the appointed mediator of that Consecrating Spirit which created eternal life in the human soul. He insisted that He had been sent from God and that the acceptance or rejection of His God-given teaching was the touchstone of men's final and eternal quality.

Clearly He had grown to a sense of the transcendent greatness of His commission.

Some while afterwards when the Seventy reported how, vested with His authority, they had found that they could control mankind's malignant enemies both physical and spiritual, He was filled with exultant triumph, more than ever assured that His mission was no illusion, but spelt victory over the powers of evil. When the Feast of Dedication came He again took up the office of a Temple Rabbi. He declared[1] Himself the Light of the World, reiterated that He was uttering God's truth and "before Abraham was born," He said, "I am."[2] In these words we are tempted to find the consciousness of identity between the human and the divine personality, but to do so is suddenly to break the continuity of development otherwise traceable throughout our Lord's incarnate life. The language is sufficiently exalted to provoke those who rejected His claims: they heard in it a blasphemous derogation from the unshared Majesty of the one true God. On the other hand those who accepted our Lord's teaching found His claims compatible with His claim to have come from God and to be about to return to Him.

It is perhaps worthy of attention that our Lord views the affliction of the man born blind and later the fatal illness of Lazarus as designed to make possible a manifestation of God's glory. At the same time He speaks of Himself as the Son of Man when He challenges the blind man to express his feelings after his cure.[3] Yet He knew that His will was so continuously in accord with God's that He declared in plain terms "I and the Father are one."[4] None the less we must remark that He justified the saying by quoting the language of a psalm in which the judges were styled "gods" because through them God's judgments on questions at issue were held to be pronounced. Many who heard our Lord's words vehemently protested, rejecting as blasphemous claims they seemed to imply; some

[1] If we are right in attributing the Matthaean Logia to our Lord's exegesis, we may see the germ of this declaration in Isaiah ix. 2 and xlix. 6.

[2] John viii. 58. This perhaps should be understood as in verse 24, "I am he," i.e. the Christ, existing before all time in the divine purpose.

[3] John ix. 3, 35.

[4] John x. 30.

were so convinced that our Lord had been sent from God that they subscribed to the truth of the claim, interpreting it presumably in the way our Lord suggested. He recurred to His previous recognition of the fact that some only would become His adherents. That was, He knew, the Father's will. Yet He persisted and persevered with His declaration of His claims to be the supreme and unique revealer of the Father's will. Psalmist and prophet had spoken of God as shepherding His people.[1] Now our Lord avows Himself to be the Good Shepherd not of the Jews alone but of the Gentiles. He lays down His life of His own will for His sheep; He resumes life of His own will, such powers has the Father given Him. His coming is of purpose that He may bestow life abundantly upon men. Clearly though He be not as yet conscious of His deity, He is serenely conscious of a rank and authority astoundingly superior to that of ordinary humanity. Inevitably it follows that adhesion to His discipleship is of primary moment to men, and hence His own coming into the world brought with it a crisis in its history. Men could not hold aloof as neutrals in face of His commission. Thus they passed judgment on themselves at once, whether they would enter into eternal life or into condemnation.[2]

A little later, when He was impressing on His followers the certainty that their prayers should be answered, we have a very noticeable saying, uttered, as it were, incidentally and parenthetically. "If ye then, being evil, know how to give good gifts," said our Lord, dissociating Himself in this regard from humanity.[3] The conclusion is inevitable that He knew Himself to be "separate from sinners," but it would be illegitimate to infer that He knew Himself to be God. Only it may be said that we may observe an increasing plainness of portrayal of the Father's character—not so much, now, as manifested in the character He looks for in men as in His own dealings with and disposition towards men. Love and constancy characterize that disposition, and love and trust are to characterize men's disposition towards God and also (and this must be particularly

---

[1] Psalm lxxxii. 6. Psalm xxiii. 1. Isaiah xl. 11. Ezekiel xxxiv. 11, 12. John x. 1, 11–18.

[2] John ix. 39.   [3] Luke xi. 13.

remarked) towards the Son.[1] He is greater than Solomon or Jonah. He can foretell the fall of Jerusalem within a generation. He does not know[2] when the end of the world shall be, and at times he speaks not of "the Father" but of God.[3]

From the narratives of immediately subsequent incidents and teaching nothing new emerges that is apposite to our present enquiry. Nevertheless the reader must not fail to remark how our Lord would appear to become more and more aware that His will to alleviate men's distresses, whether physical or spiritual, was in accord with the Father's will, so that He had an imperturbable confidence that the Father heard His desires.

The mighty works of the Christ are to magnify the glory of God. The Samaritan leper whose trustful obedience to our Lord's command led to his healing "returned to give glory to God." Yet just as trust in the Son is encouraged side by side with trust in God, so the Father's glory is enhanced by the establishment of the Son's glory. It may be that the evangelist has himself appended words of explanation when he records the Lord to have said that Lazarus' sickness was "not unto death, but for the glory of God, that the Son of God might be glorified." Otherwise we have here a solitary example of our Lord speaking of Himself by this title. Yet, however this be, it is manifest that our Lord, though still distinguishing Himself from God in all He said, was utterly confident of the transcendent majesty of His commission and of the unfailing correspondence between His will and the will of the Father. It was no mere subjective belief of His own; others were convinced that it was objective reality. Martha avowed her faith that He was "the Christ, the son of God." He Himself with all the serenity of knowledge and of truth declared "I am the Resurrection and

[1] John xiv. 1, 9, 12; xv. 10.

[2] Matt. xxiii. 35 gives as our Lord's words "Zacharias son of Barachias," where Luke (xi. 51) omits these last three words. It is usually said that the First Gospel has incorrectly added them, but it deserves to be considered whether we have here an example of our Lord's humanity in a liability to a confusion of memory. In that case Luke, we must suppose, has detected and quashed the error. Accepting, however, the view that Luke has more faithfully reported our Lord's words than Matthew did, we shall say that the additional words are a mistaken intrusion.

[3] Luke xi. 50; xii. 6, 8. John x. 18, 30, 34, 35, 38.

the Life." Still, notwithstanding all this, we shall confess that we have here no consciousness of deity, but only of the unique and superhuman powers of the Anointed, the Consecrated, the Everlasting Christ, the Son of God.

For such a being a non-Jewish thinker might find a place in his scheme of ontology by including him in a pantheon, or if he had adopted a monotheistic view of the universe by assigning him the rank of a secondary or subsidiary god created by the One Supreme Deity to subserve some special purpose, as, for example, the Demiurge or Artificer of some particular segment in the universe, or the Mediator through whom the one God communicated His will to some part of His creation. With the Jew the case was different. The Babylonian captivity had extirpated polytheistic conceptions. Unless our Lord's "signs" were regarded as tricks and traps of Beelzebub to bring men to apostasy and destruction, the dilemma was inescapable: either Jesus was a man created by God or in some manner He was God. It is not to be supposed that our Lord did not meet this dilemma Himself. The more stupendous He found the powers the Father willed that He might use, the more insufficient the former alternative must have appeared. We find no clue to guide us as to any way in which He could have held Himself to be one with the Father. Yet we may read again His boldest utterances as indicating on the one hand that He had been led to the conviction that our second alternative was true, and on the other hand that His secret conviction could not be published in unambiguous language. It was not alone a messianic secret that was first hid and only later to be proclaimed: the certainty of deity (however that was to be reconciled with the monotheistic creed) was also at first the secret thought of His own spirit alone. Yet He realized that He had been "sent" to execute His mission within the limitations of human nature. He accepted this limitation as the Father's will and therefore depended continually for guidance upon intimations of that will being conveyed to Him as He inwardly communed in spirit with the Father. He curbed impulses of His individual humanity which He found to be at variance with that Will.[1]

[1] John ii. 4; xi. 42; xii. 27–29; xvii. 19. Luke xxii. 42.

By what stages His human mind gained this conviction of His essential Deity, though its precise articulation remained, as it would appear, veiled in the mystery of the Godhead, we cannot hope to discover. Nevertheless we may say that it is after the Transfiguration that we observe more positive and unequivocal affirmations of His unity with the Father. As before, the words and actions of those about Him seem to contribute towards His confirmation in His innermost conviction. When non-Jews, in Holy Week, asked that they might see Him He felt that God had "glorified" Him. When St. Thomas cried, "My Lord and my God," He did not reject such homage as blasphemous, but declared that they were blessed "who shall not have seen but shall have believed."[1] Meanwhile He still could say, "I ascend unto my Father and your Father, and My God and your God"; and in the days before His ascension though He claimed all sovereignty He disclaimed omniscience. When some of the five hundred hesitated to adore Him as the Eleven Apostles did, He announced that all authority had been given to Him. When the apostles desired to know the future history of the world, He declared that the Father kept such knowledge within His own discretion.[2]

We are led to infer in all reverence that to the very end of His terrestrial life the Son submitted to human limitations even though after His resurrection those limitations were those of man's spiritual body. It was at His ascension that the Lord resumed the consciousness of deity in all its implications and hence it is that that event was no otiose appendage to the Resurrection, but the triumphant conclusion of the divine mission.

Still even in Holy Week when speaking to those who were not His adherents, He abstained from assuming the title of Christ. "The Son of Man," He said, "shall be glorified," and "I, if I be lifted up, will draw all men unto Me." His hearers inferred that He was not the Christ.

---

[1] John xx. 29. A literal translation does not do justice to the aorist as the tense of undefined time.

[2] Acts i. 7. Yet it may be not without significance that here the ignorance of the Son is not emphasized as it is in Mark xiii. 32.

In conclusion it will be proper to say something on our Lord's words from the Cross. The night before, He had in anticipation realized the shame and pain and agony of death by crucifixion. Human nature had instinctively recoiled. Through fervent prayer He had merged His will in the Father's, and retained His trust in the Father's gracious goodness and love. Yet the reality of the agony, the exhaustion, the collapse was more oppressive to human nature than any anticipation. His was no dull insensitiveness, no stoical apathy. Had He had any faint flickering of hope that the Father would rescue Him as Isaac had been rescued by the providing of a lamb, that hope fainted and failed as death drew near: He was Himself to be the Lamb. It may be that an uncertainty invaded His spirit: had His conviction of His exalted mission been a self-deception and were His adversaries after all in the right? It may be that He was only still refreshing His courage and will by recalling the words of a familiar psalm. However this may have been, while the opening cry of Psalm xxii. aptly expressed His horror of loneliness as He went into the valley of the shadow, He presently had serenity and confidence in His Father—it may be as He recalled the later verses of the psalm: "I will declare Thy name unto my brethren: in the midst of the congregation will I praise Thee"; or even perhaps passed on to the psalm that follows in all arrangements of the Psalter. Thus was it that while God cannot die, God the Son, having been made Man, was crucified for us and suffered.

We can detect the rise in men's estimate of the Lord's person if we observe their modes of address to Him. Convinced that He was a prophet [1] the woman of Sychar used the expression which at times was no more than a courteous *sir*, at others betokened a votary's devotion to "a lord." The officer at Capernaum used the same form of address when he begged for His son's healing. Peter, before the astounding catch of fish, substituted "Captain" for "Rabbi," but after it cried out, "I am a sinful man, O Lord."

The Centurion at Capernaum deferentially makes his appeal in the words, "Lord, I am not worthy that thou shouldest come

---

[1] The disciples who had gone to buy food in Sychar addressed Him still as Rabbi (John iv. 31).

under my roof: but only say the word, and my servant shall be healed"; but the discourteous courtesy of Simon the Pharisee shows itself, we shall feel, in his "Rabbi, say on." [1]

Meanwhile it is noticeable that Martha and Mary repeatedly address Christ as "Lord," although Martha speaks of Him to Mary as "the Rabbi." At the Last Supper our Lord declared that His disciples call Him "Rabbi" and "Lord," and it is significant that He adds, "Ye say well, for so I am." Judas, giving the sign to the officers when they came to Gethsemane, hailed our Lord as "Rabbi." Mary Magdalene on Easter morning cried "Rabboni." St. Thomas, the devoted yet logical rationalist, a week later could say nothing less than "My Lord and my God."

Those voices manifestly crystallize the fluid estimates of our Lord's dignity which the speakers had formed. He Himself, it would appear, found in them signposts intended by the Father to guide Him and to confirm His confidence in His own understanding of His mission. When Simon was first brought to Him as a new adherent, He surnamed him Cephas or Peter because He judged his character to be solid rock. So when Peter avowed that He was, in the apostles' view, the Christ, the Son of the living God, He welcomed the declaration as furnishing a foundation firm as rock for the superstructure of the new assembly of the true Israel. Similarly, when certain Greeks during Holy Week presented Abgar's offer from Edessa, our Lord recognized in it the Father's signal that the hour was come when by death and departure from human sight He was to set all believers on an equal footing whether they had or had not seen Him. So it is that the Fourth Evangelist does not hesitate to say that He died that He might bring into one all that believed, and He Himself prayed that they might be one, when He should bring His other sheep which were not of the Jewish fold. Thus the title "the Christ," which might seem to import no more than the fulfilling of the hopes and the fancies of the Jewish people, was transcended by the title "the Son of Man."

That title left room for Abgar's alternatives. The Gentile might believe that the one God of the universe had come to

[1] Matt. viii. 8. Luke vii. 40.

sojourn a while among His human creatures, or he might believe that the one true God had, after His prophets were disregarded, sent amongst us a super-prophet whom, it was to be hoped, they would reverence, one who was indeed a Son of God. Yet our Lord saw that this universal mission of His would be unacceptable to the Jews because of their selfish desire to appropriate and monopolize the Saviour. They would kill Him and so open the gate of eternal life to Jew and Gentile alike. It was for Him by His teaching to fuse into one the thoughts of the Christ, the Son of Man, the Lamb of God. Meanwhile it nevertheless remained for Him by His " decease " to fulfil what both psalmist and prophet had declared, that "the Christ abideth for ever." [1]

In the privacy of intimate converse with the Twelve, however, we find, as we have said, an undisturbed consciousness of His exalted mission, and after the last Supper this reaches its highest. "If," He said, "ye shall ask Me anything in My name, that will I do"; and He told them that it was the Father abiding in Him that did His works. He was in the Father and the Father in Him, and He prayed that His followers should be one as He and His Father were one.[2]

It will be seen that I have not scrupled to cite from the Fourth Gospel words that are there attributed to our Lord. A few words should perhaps be given in defence of this procedure.

It has been contended that the Fourth Gospel cannot be accepted as giving us a veracious and authentic record of our Lord's words. It would be outside the scope of our present investigation to discuss this issue at large. We must be content with one observation. I have elsewhere attempted to co-ordinate the matter in our Four Gospels, spatchcocking John's record into the synoptists' framework. In so doing I had no thought of what we have been considering here. It is therefore remarkable and, it may be claimed, a point of no little importance that we find in the Fourth Gospel evidence of a continuously progressive growth in what bears upon our present subject. It

---

[1] Psalm lxxii. 17; lxxxix. 36; cx. 4. Isaiah ix. 6. Daniel ii. 44; vii. 14. It will be observed that the people are represented in John xii. 34 as referring to "the Law" for this, a use which throws light on our Lord's quoting words of a Psalm as "written in your Law": John x. 34.

[2] John xiv. 14; xiv. 10; xvii. 11.

is fair to infer that either the evangelist was faithfully giving his recollections of our Lord's words at various stages of His Ministry or we should find discontinuity and disorder within the Fourth Gospel itself and contradictory order in the synoptic tradition. Our Lord's apprehension or revelation of His unique authority advances by parallel stages in the synoptic and the Johannine traditions, and it is hard to avoid the conclusion that the Fourth Gospel gives us a historical portrayal of the way that the Lord's teaching developed amid the circumstances of His Ministry.

Yet it is in the High-Priestly Prayer on Maundy Thursday night that we find that height of tranquil certitude which suggests a consciousness of His essential deity. When He asks the Father to glorify Him with the glory He had before the world was, there can be little doubt that the Catholic Creeds have rightly expressed what the prayer implies. Even if the words are not our Lord's *ipsissima verba*, they stress what the evangelist was convinced that the Lord's prayer moulded by the Holy Ghost revealed implicitly, if not explicitly. For the Lord's human mind the thought may conceivably have been derived from the prophetic previsions and anticipations of the Christ's dignity. If His achievement was in the Father's purpose before the foundation of the world, He could forecast His triumph as a return to His supra-terrestrial existence. His sublunary humiliation would be a temporary and temporal interlude in His eternal appointment by the Father to judge and govern all men. Further, if we may believe that our Lord's thought had received some contribution from the theological doctrine found in the Book of Wisdom, we have reason to suppose that what is there said of Wisdom being present as an assessor or assistant of God prior to the Creation of the World gave shape to Christ's conception of premundane existence and dignity. One further remark must be made. Some parts of the prayer would appear to define the "glory" as union with the Father, a glory which His adherents are to exhibit also— unity with one another, unity with their Lord and in Him unity with the Father. We are led, therefore, to interpret even these utterances of the High-Priestly Prayer consonantly with what we have discovered elsewhere, and to regard them as the undefined convictions of the human consciousness, which never-theless contain the truth in germ, ready to develop into the fullness of the Christian doctrine of the Blessed Trinity.

It has indeed been thought that the words disclose in our Lord a consciousness of his deity. In John xvii. 5, our Lord utters the petition: "And now O Father, glorify thou me with thine own self with the glory which I had with thee before the world was." Those who deny that the Fourth Gospel gives us the *ipsissima verba* of our Lord will not hesitate to brush aside this utterance as offering no difficulty to the line of thought we have followed. Accepting, however, as we have done throughout, the substantial accuracy and fidelity of the writer's memory, we have to examine the precise significance of the words and to consider what may have given rise to the thought which underlies them.

In the language of the Jew, "glory" gives in one word an idea which we may perhaps express by a periphrasis, viz. working or operations so splendid as to evoke our admiration and praise. "The heavens," said the psalmist, "declare the glory of God, and the firmament showeth His handiwork." We see in the heavens a masterpiece of contrivance, magnificent artistry, mathematical skill, handiwork, which is indeed a glory. So in another psalm it is said, "O Lord, our Lord, how excellent is thy name in all the earth! Who hast set thy glory upon the heavens." This sense in the Jewish heart that God's working in the universe was a glorious revelation of His name or character is seen again in the first chapter of Genesis. At each point catalogued by the writer in his survey of the universe he declares that "God saw that it was good," i.e. as the Greek translators put it, καλόν, superb in execution, splendid in operation, not, as the English reader often imagines, devoid of any taint of rebellious self-will and innocent of sin. When our Lord was asked whether the man blind from birth owed his misery to his own sin or to that of his parents, our Lord replied, "Neither did this man sin nor his parents; but that the works of God should be made manifest in him." When Lazarus fell ill, Jesus declared, "This sickness is not unto death, but for the glory of God, that the Son of God may be glorified thereby." The two passages illuminate one another. By doing the sort of gloriously kind action which God the Father does in His habitual treatment of men, the Son glorifies the Father and is Himself glorified, for He is shown in these operations of giving sight and restoring life to possess and exercise the same nature and power (though that power is derivative) as the Father exercises. Again, when the Lord realized that His passion was imminent, His human nature momentarily shrank back from the agonies He foresaw, but He prayed not to be delivered from the approaching test, but to be supported so that He could testify, by His behaviour, to the truth of His understanding of the Father's character. "Father," He said, "glorify Thy Name." The heavenly voice replied, "I have both glorified it," i.e. by authorizing the raising of Lazarus from the dead, "and will glorify it again," i.e. by raising Christ Himself from the dead.

These instances make it clear that glory means magnificent working (to express the idea in two words), and that glorify means exhibit for men's admiration some magnificent work or operation. In the light of this the petition in the High-Priestly prayer directs our thoughts to what is said in Proverbs viii and in the Book of Wisdom about the pre-mundane activities of God. As we have shown in a previous chapter, Wisdom has been the eternal companion, assessor or assistant of God, working with Him in the planning, creation and direction of the universe, and we are led to understand our Lord to have conceived the thought that He was the Wisdom of God.

Human nature is so constituted that the mind of man is continually receiving, reacting to and recording impressions made upon him by his physical and social environment. These impressions may awaken impulses, whether to seek some animal satisfaction or to curb and sublimate[1] them to some more distinctively human purpose. Yet this is not all. The mind of man also makes imaginative leaps or darts into an immaterial world of possibilities and probabilities. In the intellectual sphere these sallies of the imagination are seen as hypotheses, theories of cause and effect, laws conjectured to coordinate,

[1] The Christian will recognize in these imaginative sallies part of the technique (so to say) used by the Holy Ghost in His revelation of spiritual truth to men.

interpret and explain phenomena and events observed by ourselves or reported to us by others. Such conjectures do not require us to attribute them to what used to be called spontaneous generation, nor to regard them as mutations, to use the language of modern genetics. It may be doubted whether exhaustive consideration will not show that in every case they are preceded by some suggestive impression, whether made upon the individual thinker or derived from thinkers who have preceded him. Sir Isaac Newton, as we know, conceived the law of gravitation only after he had observed the fall of an apple. Darwin and Wallace thought of the struggle for existence as the means for achieving evolution only after Malthus had called attention to the relation between the price of corn and the size of families. Another point must be noticed in regard to these ventures of the imagination. The seriously minded are provoked by such conjectures or hypotheses to endeavour their demonstration or reputation by the methods of experimental science. Here the adhesion of another person and his confident acceptance of the hypothesis goes far to confirm the conviction of the original thinker. Thus a solitary flicker grows into a great flame of certainty.

With these considerations in mind we are led in all reverence to ask what antecedent impressions left upon our Lord's mind made it possible for Him to believe Himself to be the Son of David, the Son of Man, the King of Israel, the Lord's Christ, the Saviour or Healer, the Son of God, the Resurrection and the Life. We are led also to note how what was at first His own secret belief as to His mission and personality was confirmed by the enthusiastic outbursts of others transported from hesitancy to conviction. Man walks by faith and not by sight. He does not know in this life: he can but trust that his daring hope shall yet be substantiated. So, we shall confess, it must have been with our Lord. In His human life He could not know that He was all that we acknowledge Him to be. Unproven glimpses flashed upon Him; words that He heard, passages of scripture defined and confirmed His understanding of Himself; incidents in His life, the consciousness of intimate communion with God, the miracles which verified experimentally that He possessed the powers anticipated by the prophets—all these corroborated His convictions, and when a plain, blunt, solid character like Peter burst out with the declaration that He was the Christ, our Lord Himself was moved to rejoin that the declaration was a revelation from God.

On a review of all that has been said we are entitled to claim that the general correctness of our historical arrangement is confirmed by the resulting picture of our Lord's Ministry, and we may go on to say that this is still further strengthened by the evidence collected in the chapters that followed. There it has been shown that the subjective or ideological progress of the Ministry runs parallel to the objective or factual progress which we have traced on the basis of textual, linguistic and chronological considerations.

It may be not inappropriate at this stage to pause and consider from the standpoint we have adopted in this enquiry the possible and, as it may appear, the probable origin of our Saviour's language in the sixth chapter of the Fourth Gospel. It has been argued that the whole of what is there recorded as His teaching in the synagogue at Capernaum, which it is generally agreed is to be regarded as John's counterpart to the synoptic account of the Last Supper, is an unchronological or even an unhistorical insertion. In the light of our present conclusions, however, a different estimate will seem justifiable.

The evangelist has been at pains to tell us that a Passover was "nigh at hand," and we have previously learnt that our Saviour at His baptism received a sign that might be interpreted to mean that He was destined to be a sacrifical victim, and, as the Baptist himself pronounced, the Lamb provided by God to give His life that the world's sinfulness might be taken away. It may be supposed that our Lord meditated on the Passover ritual. In that two things stood out as vital. The offering to God and the killing are subsidiary and incidental. What is indispensable is in the first place that the blood should be sprinkled on door-post and lintel and in the second that the roast flesh should be eaten by everyone who would be within the covenant made by God with His people. How should these two cardinal prescriptions of the rite be fulfilled when the divinely provided Lamb took the place of the typical animal of the Exodus?

(1) The flesh and blood of the antitype would replace and dispense with the flesh and blood of the type. Communion with Him, not participation in the Paschal Lamb, would be the guarantee of continual membership in the people of the covenant, in the Israel of God. Such communion with Him, such participation in the Flesh and Blood of the antitypical and true Lamb of God, must of course be after a spiritual manner. As He had already taught, material food could not make anyone unclean: spiritual food and spiritual blood-sprinkling could alone keep the spirit of man clean.

(2) Yet the populace thought in terms of material things. Five thousand looked for a life of plentiful food miraculously provided. Before they could be brought to think of spiritual sustenance, they must be forced to reinterpret the language so lightly repeated amongst them. If they could only say "evermore give us this bread" when they were told of the true bread from heaven, they must be startled and even shocked by hearing that they must eat His flesh instead of the Passover lamb.

(3) To compel, if possible, their materialistic thought to rise to some spiritual understanding, our Lord went further. Clearly the blood of the antitype could not be dashed upon the doorjambs and lintels of His followers. Their bodies were temples and houses of God (Bethels). They were defiled by spiritual evil. Blood which was the life might not be eaten, yet His spiritual life-giving power must enter their spirits. In symbolic language, they must drink His blood. Those who were impercipient were revolted and scandalized: even the plain declaration that the Lord's words were spirit and life could not wean them from their gross materialism. The Twelve alone held to their faith that His teaching would germinate into eternal life and thus they were in training for abandoning the righteousness of the Law rooted in animal sacrifices and for accepting the free gift of grace, and for understanding that the righteousness acceptable to God, that is the entire fulfilment of duty, is a loving trust in the Saviour, a ruminating upon His human life and teaching and an absorption of His spirit.

A year later when His body was on the morrow to be given to death and His blood to be shed, He instituted and initiated a mode of commemorating His passion. The yearly Passover

11*

had commemorated the original lamb-killing, blood safeguard, hasty meal and exodus from Egypt. All who continued that yearly commemoration were kept within the number of the chosen people. But as we have said, the Lamb of the antitype was not an animal: His flesh was not to be eaten materially nor His blood dashed upon things material. His words were to be the spiritual sustenance of His people, His Blood was to support their spiritual life. The Paschal meal could not easily be converted into a means of commemorating something other than the Exodus. The old associations would cling to it too closely. It would be a hindrance rather than a help to the spirituality of the Lord's flesh and blood.

There would be similar obstacles if any other sacrifice were chosen as the vehicle through which a spiritual commemoration should be suggested. Another way was to be found, immune to that particular danger—a thanksgiving meal. On the day before the Passover it was customary to introduce a social thanksgiving (eucharist) which spoke of the manna eaten in the wilderness. "This is the bread your fathers did eat," said he who presided at the feast. The Anointed King was God's provided Lamb, but He was also the Priest who was making Himself an oblation. He was indeed a Priest-King like Melchizedek, and as that ancient gave bread and wine to Abraham, so our Priest-King chose bread and wine to be the material means by which His followers should remind themselves of Him, that so their souls should receive still more of the spiritual nourishment which He had sought to blazon before their thoughts by the figures of eating His flesh and drinking His blood.

It may be thought desirable, if not necessary, to say a few words by way of attempting to illustrate how the contemporary or parallel coexistence of a divine and a human consciousness is to be finally integrated in the eternal Christ, both God and Man. A boxer was knocked unconscious; before time was called he recovered enough to go on boxing, though only semi-conscious. He won the match, but when he regained consciousness entirely, could not remember or tell whether he had won or lost. This surgical case may show how a binary consciousness may come about, to be resolved at last in an integrated double consciousness. It is not of course the same with Christ's Person. For the boxer concussion affected the brain. No physical condition could paralyse the divine consciousness. Yet the human dualism may enable us to imagine the possibility, though we cannot understand the technique, of two natures being so united without confusion that either may be studied as a distinct and detached entity. Either may be studied by itself, just as the physical processes of the brain and the psychology of the mind may be treated as independent subjects for investigation, despite mutual interaction. Understanding in this way our duty as regards the mystery, we shall extend St. Athanasius' argument (see p. 285 f.) and claim that all Jesus' words and actions attest His deity, but we shall not look for that attestation in a few astonishing incidents only, which may seem beyond human capacity. The Son of Man will be intelligible as a specimen of humanity, however superlative : God the Son will be intelligible as the Demiurge in the divine plan of creating and redeeming mankind.

A last perusal of these pages leaves the attentive mind with an anxious feeling that their total intention may be missed or misunderstood. It is right, therefore, to state roundly that throughout the Orthodox and Catholic faith has been unreservedly accepted and maintained as the controlling norm to which every suggestion made is to be humbly submitted. In our Lord's words then, in His thoughts and in His actions we must understand that both a divine and a human nature were present. That that human nature might be truly human, it necessarily functioned within the limitations of the age and place in which His incarnate life was set : it was not blended or blurred with the divine nature. It is manifestly beyond our capacity to understand or even to surmise how the two natures could coexist and function simultaneously or how they even now continue to do so. All that we can do—and this is what alone had been attempted in the foregoing pages—is to study what, as far as we can discover, the Lord's human nature actually thought, said and did. One possibility indeed must not be overlooked. Did the divine nature (so to say) put at the disposal of the human, powers beyond the range of mere humanity? And, if so, were impulses injected into His human consciousness to do what other men could not have done? Such a view of Christ's dual nature would seem to escape the pitfall of Docetism and at the same time would make it intelligible that He should do what all men regard as superhuman. In that case we shall say with St. Athanasius that some acts, e.g. the changing of water into wine, demonstrated that He was not only human but divine. Yet there are serious objections to this view. Even when we have made allowance for our ignorance (which the researches leading to the atomic bomb have shown to be far greater than the scientist tiro assumes), it is manifest that we cannot make incontrovertible statements as to what God can and cannot do. All we can say is that within the range of human observation He always works by slow and gradual evolution, not by sudden and catastrophic mutations. This, as far as we can see, is so even though the crown and consummation of some evolutionary process may be justly called a mutation or a definitely creative act. We shall hesitate therefore, although we regard the Incarnation as a definitely redemptive act, to say further that a series of creative acts supported and reinforced the central and essential act of incarnation.

Without dogmatizing therefore by deduction from *a priori* tenets as to what God in Christ could or could not do, we ask what the Gospel records show that He actually did. Is there anything that humanity cannot do, or at any rate may not be expected eventually to be able to do? If we find nothing of the sort, we shall rest in the Orthodox doctrine of Christ's complete humanity. If on the other hand we find some things which we cannot explain except as superhuman, we shall conclude that, beside and behind the human nature, the divine was achieving its purpose of redeeming the created world. If St. Athanasius may be quoted in support of this latter belief, St. Ambrose may be quoted for the former, and while Alexandrian Monophysitism may have been the offspring of the vanquisher of Arius, no one has yet impugned the orthodoxy of the Bishop of Milan.

One further observation must be made on this theme. Rationalistic criticism has challenged the credibility of nature miracles (to use the current catchword). Such a miracle was the stilling of the storm on the Lake of Galilee and the pronouncement of the fig-tree's sudden wilting. Such were the timely fluctuations in the waters of the Red Sea and of the Jordan when they might have barred the passage of the Israelites, and again the fall of the walls of Jericho. In regard to all such miracles we are bidden to face squarely the plain issue of choosing one or other of these alternatives: that our records are not to be trusted or that the course of cosmic nature was unprecedentedly interrupted and its uniformity disturbed. Yet it may be that this is not the final closing of the matter. There is, it may be suggested, one further possibility which deserves consideration: instead of making them solitary instances of autocratic interruption in the established laws of nature, should we not rather say that God the Holy Ghost inspired in the mind of God's human agent the internal decision that, in confident reliance upon God, he should lay his command on nature at the very instant when God's unaltered laws were on the point of bringing about an external physical change, which men neither could effect nor durst hope to see happen, but thankfully hailed as a God-wrought miracle?

Finally one more observation may perhaps be allowed. If we might restate in our own fashion the substance of an impressive argument developed by Canon Phythian-Adams we shall make bold to say that an unprejudiced study of the Hebrew Scriptures leads to a conviction that Israel's exodus from Egypt was divinely timed to take place when the processes of physical laws were issuing in earthquakes and volcanic eruptions of unusual frequency and violence. It is reasonable to assert similarly that when the focal representative and capital exemplar of Israel in the fulfilment of His individual mission (as in the divine purpose He, the inclusive Christ, is to fulfil Israel's and humanity's destiny) came to achieve His exodus (as Luke calls it), it too was timed to synchronize with celestial and terrestrial phenomena—the day darkened, the moon eclipsed and the earth rocked with repeated tremors.

Chapter Four

DEVELOPMENTS IN OUR LORD'S TEACHING AND TRAINING OF THE DISCIPLES

(1)

IN an earlier chapter it has been attempted to discover what help a historical rearrangement of the Gospel narrative furnishes towards the solution of the dark and perhaps for us men the inscrutable enigma of our Lord's human consciousness. We saw reason to insist that two questions must be distinguished from one another. On the one hand we have to ask at each point of the story what the disciples were intended or expected to understand by what was said to them. On the other hand we may sometimes wonder whether behind the obvious meaning there was in the Lord's mind a deeper meaning which only time and experience could bring out. Yet we may observe in the instruction given to the disciples a development and a change of emphasis as we pass from the first weeks after the Baptism to the last days before the Crucifixion. Edersheim has noticed that whereas at first there was passive opposition on the part of the religious authorities of the day, later there was active opposition. Our historical order shows something more than this, and it is worth while to look at the matter more closely.

In the last parable by Matthew, and assigned by him apparently to Tuesday in Holy Week, our Lord represents the "goats" at the final judgment as condemned for sins of omission. This deserves particular attention. They are pronounced to be cursed not because they have broken the ten commandments, but because they have shut themselves away in a selfish indifference from looking for opportunities to relieve their brother men in their distresses. This climax in our Lord's teaching has a different note from His earliest teaching, and yet it is in entire accord with it. We may perhaps group the cardinal features of His teaching in the following way:

(1) Man, not a building, is God's temple. Nathanael will see the angels of God ascending and descending not upon Bethel but upon the Son of Man. If the Jews destroy the temple of Christ's Body, He will speedily raise it up again.

(2) The current view of religious duty must be superseded and a fresh start must be made. Men must be born again. Ceremonial purity was obsolete: a pure heart was God's requirement. He must be worshipped in spirit and in sincerity, and His true character understood.

(3) The sinner is allowed a fresh chance if only he will trust God to help him. Dependence upon God is the vital attitude for men in all the circumstances of life.

In accord with these lessons is our Lord's disregard of the Law not only as to the touch of a leper, a corpse, a woman and a Gentile, but also as to abstention from work on the Sabbath, and moreover His condemnation of casuistical evasions of broad rules of conduct.

(4) The love of money interferes with spiritual growth. It diminishes man's sense of dependence upon God. It tends to isolate him from the poor and confirms class distinctions in the social sphere. Hence rich men are bidden to feast the waifs and strays of life. The same spirit of selfish materialism has obtruded itself into the worship of God, when the embellishment of the Temple is made the special aim of its custodians.

Springing out of this is the teaching that men must not measure their religious standing by comparison with others: all are sinners, and heaven rejoices when the sinner agrees to try again.

(5) Our Lord's prophetic insight read in the social and religious character of the Jewish people the certainty of a clash with Rome and the destruction of Jerusalem. His disciples must be on the alert to make their escape when there should appear the signs that He foretold, and their habits of life must in the interval be of one piece with His teaching. They could not change suddenly at the last moment.

So it is that philanthropy stands out at the end of our Lord's
teaching as the supreme duty to which He summons His
disciples. National pride, ceremonial purity, rules of behaviour
are gone. Sincerity of spirit, dependence upon God, service to
our brother men are the sum of religion; and as John puts it,
Christ died that He might gather into one the children of God
that are scattered abroad. Hence that His disciples should love
one another was not only our Lord's prayer and the purpose of
His death, but it is the sign by which we must show the world
that we are His disciples, so that others also may know and
believe.

(2)

Dr. Carnegie Simpson has said that Christianity is distinguished by one noteworthy feature from all other religions.
While they instruct their followers as to duties to be performed
and tenets to be believed, our Lord invites His disciples to Himself, declaring that He is, for example, the Way, the Truth and
the Life. This observation opens up a valuable line of thought.
Dr. Simpson, addressing himself to Christian believers, quotes
from the Gospels indiscriminately. When we examine the
records with due regard to chronology and to authorship, we
find some interesting facts. Matthew quotes the invitation,
"Come unto Me all that travail and are heavy laden," but he
does not continue this with any declaration as to our Lord's
Person, but with a call to learn of Him. It is the same with the
other synoptists. The Fourth Gospel alone records utterances
which summarize in key words all that Christ is. Yet it must be
noticed that this was not His manner of speech from the first.
Accepting John's record as historical, we observe that it was
first in the synagogue at Capernaum, after the feeding of the
five thousand, that Jesus under the stimulus of incredulous
opposition was moved to say roundly, "I am the Bread of Life."
At the outset of His Ministry He had said that if He were asked
He would have given the woman of Samaria "living water,"
and at first at Capernaum He said that He would give the meat
which endureth unto everlasting life. But from this point onward He adopts this new turn of speech, a change as clearly
marked as that when He began to use parables to set forth the

mysteries of God's rule. Matthew represents our Lord as declaring quite early in His Ministry that the disciples were the light of the world, but John shows that not more than three months before the Crucifixion our Lord said of Himself, "I am the light of the world." We may note that in the last few months of His Ministry Jesus declared, "I am the door of the sheep," "I am the door" and "I am the good shepherd"—all these about the time of the Feast of Dedication—"I am the Resurrection and the Life," a few weeks later; and on Maundy Thursday night, "I am the Way, the Truth and the Life." That our understanding of the historical order is correct is further confirmed by our noticing that Luke places the parable of the Lost Sheep some few weeks before the Crucifixion. Two further points may be noticed: (1) In the Apocalypse our Lord appears as saying "I am Alpha and Omega," and "I am the root and the offspring of David, and the bright and morning star." This identical fashion of speech may be thought one more small detail confirmatory of the belief that the Gospel and the Apocalypse come from the same hand. (2) Our Lord is shown, when account is taken of the circumstances in which He began to use this form of expression, to have prepared His disciples to understand the sacramental species in the Eucharist. He is not the bread nor the wine; they are His body and His blood. He is the Bread of Life, and the words that He speaks are spirit and life.

(3)

Evidence of development in our Lord's teaching may be detected from another aspect of the story. If we re-examine our records, some facts of interest appear in regard to the reactions and actions of His opponents. At the first the authorities are seen not so much hostile as startled and sceptical. They want a demonstration of His right to reprove and reform the established ordinances of religion. Some hearers of a more receptive temper welcome what they feel to be more spiritual truth mediated to them by Jesus from God Himself. This religious issue would be more quickly precipitated in Judaea, and Jesus withdrew to Galilee. There it was possible to declare God's loving-kindness towards mankind despite their sins and to exhibit that loving-kindness as reversing disease and death and welcoming back the sinner. At the same time He freed men from the burden of a multiplicity of regulations made by the Rabbis for the better observance of the Sabbath, in which, however, the divine desire for mercy was overlooked. This aroused the fiercest anger of the Pharisees who sought to enlist the support of Herod's partisans, since Galilee was under Herod's control. But there was no ground for Herod's interference. Jesus was not reported as denouncing Herod's union with Herodias, and the issue was still the question whether the prestige and dignity of the professional teachers of the Law was to bow before the upstart Nazoraean. No word was said of a claim to the throne of David. He habitually spoke of Himself as the Son of Man, ignoring the occasional outbursts of enthusiasm which hailed Him as the Son of God or as King of Israel. That He was a Nazoraean was manifest to all, and after the miracle at Nain He was generally regarded as a Prophet. Simon the Pharisee, we are specially told, debated that possibility in his thoughts as he sat at table. At the unnamed feast at Jerusalem, however, our Lord defended His view of the Sabbath obligation by asserting His divine Sonship, and the authorities were not slow to take up the challenge by sending a commission of enquiry. The commission met the Saviour as He returned from where the five thousand had been fed. The encounter led to a further discovery of the complete and radical disagreement between the rabbinic doctrine as to God's requirements and Jesus' revelation of them. The Rabbis' rage at the new Prophet's rejection of their rules as to ceremonial uncleanness prompted Him to withdraw from Palestine for several months, yet soon after His return Peter avowed his belief that Jesus was the Christ. Assured that now the apostles had to this extent modified their expectations of what the Christ should do, our Lord began to prepare them for the further and fuller lesson that he was charged with the double role of Messiahship and of suffering service. Convinced that He must achieve His victory by dying at Jerusalem, He resolved to remove from Galilee.

His critics now attempted to damage His reputation by imputing His miracles to an alliance between Him and Beelzebub, but this had no serious success. For six months attempts were made to catch some word which could be construed as a pretender's bid for the throne. Did Jesus pay the Temple money, as He would surely refuse to do, if He aspired to the crown? Would He give sentence on an adulteress, as a king sitting in judgment? Would He refuse the payment of tribute money to Rome? If He evaded these invitations to commit Himself, He might be discredited with the people; if He did not, information could be lodged against Him with the governor. All these attempts to trap Him failed. But the Jewish mode of execution was open to two objections. Although it evaded the commandment which forbad murder, by dividing the responsibility for the killing, it would be unpopular and it would be traceable to its authors. If the Roman governor ordered the execution, the Jewish Council would still elude the sixth Commandment[1] and could not be held responsible by the people.

At the Feast of Tabernacles He stirred His enemies to yet more bitter hatred by still plainer words as to His unique office. They would have stoned Him to death for blasphemy, as they would have done later (for they knew that He was indeed a man), but He was aware that nothing but crucifixion would make Jew and Gentile partners in His death, and He therefore on each occasion retired before their violence. For a few months He avoided arrest; then, three or four days before the Passover, He realized that the hour was come for Him to face the end. His enemies, though resolved on His destruction, wished to avoid the odium of themselves putting Him to death. They looked about for something which would make it inevitable that the Roman governor should sentence Jesus to crucifixion. Still they looked in vain. At last, having arrested Him, His captors tried to find what might be made a charge which would satisfy Pilate. No witness could be found who had heard Him style Himself the Son of God or King or Christ, and He declined to accept such a title when adjured by Caiaphas. Yet, still speaking of the Son of Man, he preconized His ultimate Advent in triumph. This Caiaphas, whether in honest horror or in pretence, treated as blasphemy and set out to secure from Pilate Christ's condemnation with the bare assertion that He had spoken of Himself as

---

[1] In the Gospel of Nicodemus Pilate sees this sense in the words "it is not lawful for us to put any man to death."

King. Pressed for a definite proof of this, Caiaphas could only quote Christ's noncommittal answer to his question, "Art thou the Christ, the Son of God?" It was not in the mere words "the Son of God" that blasphemy was heard: that was contained in the prediction that the Son of Man should be vested with glory which might seem divine. Even yet the Jewish doctrine is insistent on the unbridgeable gulf between deity and humanity. Nevertheless, the words of Psalm viii testify to the existence at one time amongst the chosen people of a knowledge that God was man's Father and visited him. But this faith was lost to the Jewish doctors and Jesus' words shocked them. On the other hand, they understood and used the title the "Son of God" to bolster up their charge that Jesus was challenging the monarchy of Caesar. Pilate did not immediately comprehend this Jewish form of speech and so was the more afraid, says John.

To reduce the issue to its simplest form we may say that our Lord laboured to the very end to transmute into a spiritual and universal faith the hope of a Davidic heir, a king, a Son of God, a Christ: to the Jews that hope either meant some nationalistic and political dominion or it meant nothing. Jesus insisted on His unique divine Sonship in the sense that He by His actions and words exhibited in human terms the character, the will and the conduct of God. He refused the title the Son of God when used in the sense of the Davidic king, who was God's vicegerent on earth. The Jewish authorities rejected the idea that man, God's creature, could reflect the nature of God, the Creator. Jesus controverted the dogmas which successive generations of students and professors of biblical learning had deduced and promulgated as authoritative articles of faith and religious practice: the Jews rejected what He taught as to God's requirements and they resented His commanding independence of tradition. Jesus spoke of an unobservable infiltration and establishment of His sovereignty: they looked for a catastrophic and violent victory, achieved by a superhuman being. Hence while Jesus emphasized that He was veritably man and they were satisfied themselves that He was so, they were too rooted in their preconceptions and prejudices to regard as anything but blasphemy His claim to be the true fulfilment of the messianic expectation. They were therefore ready to snatch at the title the "Son of God" and with astute chicanery to represent it as an assumption of royalty which challenged the Emperor's sovereignty. Thus at length the jealousy of the discomfited Rabbis, the revulsion against novelty and the nervousness of the comfortable contrived to frame a cry which intimidated a subject of the suspicious Tiberius, and so it was that Caiaphas the Jew chose that one man should die rather than the whole nation possibly perish, and Pilate the Gentile chose that an innocent prisoner should be executed rather than that there should be a breach of the peace. The whole world, Jew and Gentile alike, showed its selfishness by preferring a lazy quiet to a costly maintenance of justice.

Excursus III

The Holy Ghost and Holy Spirit

It is now many years since scholars directed attention to the difference between two forms of expression distinguishable in the Greek of the New Testament but continually confused in our English versions. The one is adequately represented by our "the Holy Ghost"; the other, it has been said, is often rather "a manifestation, an outpouring, an activity of the Holy Ghost." More recently some scholars have desired to equate the latter expression in some cases with the former, claiming that in these "Holy Ghost" was, as it were, a proper name so that the omission of the definite article did not ascertainably affect the sense. There is, however, a more serious aspect of the matter which requires our consideration.

Admittedly all our New Testament Books were written subsequently to the outpouring of the Holy Ghost upon the Christian believers on the first Whitsunday. Yet in what is said about events prior to this and events subsequent to it, all our writers agree in expressing themselves with the distinction precisely and clearly marked between the Holy Ghost on the one hand and on the other a supra-sensuous spirit imparting and supporting a consecrated life. Thus both Zacharias and Barnabas are described as full of a holy spirit, not, as the A.V. has it, the Holy Ghost (Luke i. 67, Acts xi. 24), but a spiritual power to lead a life of consecration to God's service. It is worth while to review all the examples of these two forms of expression which are to be found in the Gospels and in the Acts. The results are interesting and may be thus classified.

A. "HOLY SPIRIT" is found.

I. In the narrative portions where the writers are not giving the words of speakers we find:

Luke i. 41.	Elizabeth was filled with . . .
i. 67.	Zacharias was filled with . . .
ii. 25.	Holy Spirit was upon Simeon . . .
iv. 1.	Jesus full of Holy Spirit . . .
Matthew i. 18.	Mary was found with child of . . .
Acts i. 2.	He had given commandment through . . .
ii. 4.	They were all filled with . . .
iv. 8.	Peter filled with . . .
iv. 31.	They were all filled with . . .
vi. 5.	Stephen, a man full of . . .
vii. 55.	Stephen, full of . . .
viii. 15.	They prayed that they might receive . . .
viii. 17.	They received . . .
viii. 19.	That he may receive . . .
ix. 17.	That thou mayest be filled with . . .
xi. 24.	Barnabas was full of . . .
xiii. 9.	Paul filled with . . .
xiii. 52.	The disciples were filled with . . .

It is to be observed in regard to these passages that (*a*) the invariable use is to speak of men as being filled not with the Holy Ghost but with a sanctified spirit—which of course Christians will recognize as the working or an outpouring of the Third Person of the Blessed Trinity; but the language does not say more than we have indicated. (*b*) Various things are done in a consecrated spirit, not in a spirit of selfwill or wantonness or rebellion against God.

II. With these thoughts in our mind we may consider words attributed to various speakers:

St. Gabriel:

Luke i. 15.	(The Baptist) shall be filled with . . .
i. 35.	Holy Spirit shall come upon thee (i.e. Mary).

An Angel:

Matthew i. 20.	That . . . is of Holy Spirit.

The Baptist:

Luke iii. 16.	He shall baptize with . . .
Mark i. 8.	„ „
Matthew iii. 11.	„ „
John i. 33.	„ „

Peter:

Acts xi. 16.	Ye shall be baptized with . . .

Paul:

Acts xix. 2.	Did ye receive . . .

Here again we must remark how all our evangelists agree in making the Baptist's announcement not that the Holy Ghost should come upon men but that our Lord should baptize them with a Holy Spirit. It cannot be by chance that this uniformity of language is found in all our writers.

III. The same precision of expression is to be seen in the records of our Lord's words:

Luke xi. 13.   Your heavenly Father shall give . . .
Mark xii. 36.   David himself said in . . .
John xx. 22.   He breathed on them . . . receive ye . . .
Acts i. 5.   Ye shall be baptized with . . .

B. "THE HOLY GHOST." Let us now turn to the passages in which the Holy Ghost is mentioned. Again classifying the occurrences as before, we have:

I. In the narrative portions:

Luke ii. 26.   It had been revealed to Simeon by the Holy Ghost.
iii. 22.   The Holy Ghost descended in a bodily form.
Acts viii. 18.   Simon saw that the Holy Ghost was given.
ix. 31.   Walking in the comfort of the Holy Ghost.
x. 44.   The Holy Ghost fell on them.
x. 45.   The gift of the Holy Ghost.
xiii. 2.   The Holy Ghost said . . .
xiii. 4.   Sent out by the Holy Ghost.
xvi. 6.   Forbidden by the Holy Ghost.
xix. 6.   The Holy Ghost came on them.

It is noticeable that Luke constantly realized that the Holy Ghost is a Hypostasis or Person, and this has moulded the form of his language. Whitsunday and Christian experience has had its effect upon his thought as upon that of later generations.

II. Peter, according to Luke's record, is no less definite:

Acts i. 16.   The Holy Ghost spake by David.
ii. 33.   The promise of the Holy Ghost.
ii. 38.   The gift of the Holy Ghost.
v. 3.   To lie to the Holy Ghost.
v. 32.   We are witnesses and so is the Holy Ghost.
x. 47.   Which have received the Holy Ghost.
xi. 15.   The Holy Ghost fell on them.
xv. 8.   God giving them the Holy Ghost.

St. Stephen:

Acts vii. 51.   Ye do always resist the Holy Ghost.

The Council letter:

Acts xv. 28.   It seemed good to the Holy Ghost and to us.

Paul:

Acts xx. 23.   The Holy Ghost testifies to me.
xx. 28.   The Holy Ghost hath made you bishops.
xxviii. 25.   Well spake the Holy Ghost.

Agabus:

Acts xxi. 11.   Thus saith the Holy Ghost.

III. Of particular significance is what we find recorded as regards our Lord's own language. He first[1] spoke of the Holy Ghost a few months before His Crucifixion. Luke xii. 10 places just after the Transfiguration our Lord's solemn warning that to "him that blasphemeth against the Holy Ghost it shall not be forgiven." Mark iii. 29 and Matt. xii. 32 confirm the authentic fidelity of this hypostatization.[2]

Furthermore, at the same point in the story Luke has other words uttered by our Lord which infer that the Holy Ghost is a Person. When the disciples were brought to trial for their faith, they were not to be anxious as to the character of their defence: "for the Holy Ghost shall teach you in that very hour what ye ought to say" (Luke xii. 12). Mark xiii. 11 has the same utterance and dates it even later, viz. during Holy Week.

After this we have the plain words of John xiv. 26: "But the Comforter, even the Holy Ghost, whom the Father will send in my name, he shall teach you all things." There remain two other instances of our Lord being said to have spoken of the Holy Ghost. One is in Matt. xxviii. 19, on which something has been said on another page (Part I, p. 45), the other is in Acts i. 8, where, while refusing the curiosity of the apostles as to the future course of the world, He assured them: "Ye shall receive power, when the Holy Ghost is come upon you."

Certain conclusions must inevitably be drawn from these facts.

(a) Till near the close of His earthly Ministry our Lord did not indicate that the Holy Ghost was a person. From Him, however, the disciples learnt to regard a consecrated spirit as an activity of the Holy Ghost within a man's human spirit.

(b) No one is ever said to have been filled with, or full of, the Holy Ghost. The expression invariably is "filled with Holy Spirit."

(c) The Holy Ghost is never given. He is sent, He falls upon men and He is with them.

(d) A spirit of consecration is given and is received and we are led to ask whether "the gift of the Holy Ghost" does not mean the gift bestowed by the Holy Ghost rather than what the language of popular preachers has often suggested.

---

[1] This was, it would appear, a new fashion of speech. Its nearest analogues are to be seen in Psalm li. 11: τὸ πνεῦμα τὸ ἅγιόν σου; Psalm cxliii. 10: τὸ πνεῦμά σου τὸ ἅγιον; Isaiah lxiii. 10: τὸ πνεῦμα τὸ ἅγιον αὐτοῦ; lxiii. 11: ὁ θεὶς ἐν αὐτοῖς τὸ πνεῦμα τὸ ἅγιον; Susannah 45: τὸ πνεῦμα τὸ ἅγιον παιδαρίου; and above all in Wisdom ix. 17: ἔπεμψας τὸ ἅγιόν σου πνεῦμα, where the form of phrase and the use of the verb "sent," which seems to suggest the personification of the Spirit, are strongly corroborative of the notion that that book was familiarly known to our Lord.

[2] It may perhaps be thought that the Lord's human mind reacted in this to the Pharisees' slander. They attributed His exorcisms to an alliance with Beelzebub, the hypostatized Prince of Evil Spirits. Our Lord realized that the divine spirit of love in whose power He wrought His exorcisms was to be recognized as a divine Person, the hypostasis of the Father's love. It would seem that from this time forward He repeatedly spoke of the Holy Ghost.

A word should perhaps be added in regard to the expression so frequently used in the Epistles, "the Spirit." In John i. 32, 33 the sense would appear to be that upon Him who was to baptize with a spirit of consecration that spirit was first to descend visibly. Manifestly this is far from conveying to the world the knowledge that the Holy Ghost, a Person, should come to indwell men. Moreover, while Christ declares that God is Spirit He speaks of the wind (or the spirit) blowing where it listeth, and this may serve to help us to understand something of the significance the expression had for the Christian Church, John iii. 8. After Pentecost they were conscious of living in a new world in which the Holy Ghost gave spiritual power for men to lead consecrated lives. This was to live in the spirit.

Because this world of the spirit was a new thing, John could write (vii. 39) "the spirit was not yet"; while later Christians, who had forgotten the precision of language of our canonical writers, could say the Holy Ghost was not yet "given." It is unnecessary to examine here every instance of the use of the expression "the spirit." We may, however, observe that in the language of the day it was common to hear such words as "a spirit of infirmity," "a dumb spirit," "an unclean spirit," "an evil spirit," and these may interpret for us "a Holy Spirit." We get further light from our Lord's words, John vi. 63 : "It is the spirit that quickeneth . . . the words that I have spoken unto you are spirit and are life."

On a review of the whole subject two or three observations must be made. Not only is the uniformity of language remarkable, but its testimony to the authenticity of our records is to be noticed. All four evangelists agree in reserving to our Lord's latest weeks His reference to the Holy Ghost as a person. This cannot be accident, nor is it easy to suppose that if He had spoken in Aramaic, all should have expressed in their Greek a distinction which was not explicit in His language. Incidentally it may be remarked that Syriac and Latin cannot express simply and straightforwardly the distinction we have noted in the Greek, and it is not without significance that the versions in those two languages are responsible for the erroneous text in John vii. 39.

At this point the reader may remember the words in the Nicene Creed, "was incarnate by the Holy Ghost," and may ask what sense these words will bear in the light of what we have been saying. A reference to the Greek shows that, since the article is not used, the words according to the view we have indicated above exclude the direct assertion made in the English translation. They do not state that the Holy Ghost, the Third Person of the Blessed Trinity, effected our Lord's Incarnation. They say no more than that the Blessed Virgin's conception was brought about by a spirit of holiness, not by a spirit of lechery and lewdness. We are led to look further and to ask on what Scriptural authority the statement is made. It is based upon the words in the First Gospel, where again the article is not present. St. Joseph is told that his wife is not guilty of sin. More than two centuries ago Bishop Pearson declared that every clause in the creeds must be understood in the sense of the scriptural passages on which it was based. We must therefore add nothing in our interpretation of the Creed to what the words used in the first Gospel express. It will be observed that, interpreted thus strictly, the Creed says something less than is often asserted by those who have the English translation only in mind.[1] Some other words recorded by Luke as spoken by the angel at the Annunciation require consideration, but some will certainly argue that they are not so definite and conclusive as to require our subscription to the accepted understanding of the matter. One point, however, must be made clear. Whenever and wherever men are actuated by a spirit of holiness, that spirit proceeds from the operation of the Holy Ghost. It follows that however strictly we interpret the words of the Creed, we shall still believe that it was the Holy Ghost Himself who directed, controlled and suggested whatever the Blessed Virgin did or suffered in virtue of the spirit of holiness through which she conceived our Lord.[2]

Excursus IV

The Second Advent

IT will not be inopportune here to survey the three accounts given us of our Lord's prophecies respecting the signs which would warn His disciples that the demolition of the Temple buildings was impending. Mark tells us that the apostles asked two questions, the date of the catastrophe and the signs that would presage it. In reply Christ described the disturbances of nature and of society that would for some time precede the collapse of the Jewish state. Then the Son of Man would be seen triumphantly dominant, and all this would come about within that present generation. The signs would be as easy to read as the indications of spring are in the burgeoning of the trees. On the other hand, the Father alone knew the date of "*that day.*" Does this mean that the fall of Jerusalem could be anticipated, but the end of the world could not? Before answering this question, it will be well to notice two points in the Marcan account. The second Advent is manifestly identified with the destruction of Jerusalem, and is scheduled to take place before that generation passed away. We cannot avoid associating this utterance with the declaration that some should not taste of death till they had seen the kingdom of God come with power. The inerrancy of His prophecy our Lord asserted in words too often misunderstood. It would be easier for heaven and earth to pass away than for His words. His disciples therefore should be vigilant, for though the event was certain and arriving in their age and lifetime, they knew not the precise day or hour. When we

[1] It is not without significance that this form of expression is invariably used in the apocryphal Gospel of Nicodemus, which never by any chance strays into the equivalent of what the English translation of the Latin creed has made bold to say. For the use of the preposition ἐκ reference may be made to Rutherford's preface to his translation of the Epistle to the Romans.

[2] See further *C.Q.R.*, vol. cxlix, pp. 127 ff.

turn to Matthew we find that in his usual fashion he has expanded and explained the disciples' question. He makes them ask "when shall these things be and what shall be the sign of Thy coming and completion of this age?" The common translation of this amplification of Mark's words has led the ordinary English reader to strange misinterpretations of Christ's words. It must be noticed in the first place that the single definite article in the Greek makes the "coming" and the "completion" inseparable and not two events at different dates. Moreover, the completion or consummation or winding up of the age is not what is suggested by the words "the end of the world." It is such a mutation in human society as, e.g., Froude has portrayed in his penetrating description of the passing of the Middle Ages. Thus we must understand Matthew to intend us to see in the Advent the ending of the age in which the Temple was the religious centre of the world and the ushering in of a new age in which Christ was acknowledged as the plenipotentiary vicegerent in God's kingdom. When we thus read Matthew's account, all falls into place and we find the same instruction as in Mark. The good news of the kingdom was, as Christ foretold, published in all the civilized world, or Roman Empire, before the downfall of Jerusalem. While His coming to end the age was certain within their lifetime, the exact moment of this coming was hidden even from His human consciousness. This warning, with its necessary corollary that they must be vigilant, Matthew says that our Lord reinforced by the Parables of the Ten Virgins and the Talents. We need not concern ourselves with the fact that here, as usual, Matthew brings in some other sayings of our Lord which Luke shows to have been spoken on earlier occasions. "That day" then in Matthew, no less than in Mark, means not the Great Assize at the end of the world, as ordinarily conceived, but the catastrophic end of that age and the then existing structure of society.

Luke makes the matter yet plainer. He represents the disciples' question as specifically referring to one thing and one thing only—the destruction of the Temple. They asked, as he tells the story, "When shall these things be and what shall be the sign when these things will come to pass." And this question springs, as all three Synoptists tell us, from our Lord's declaration that not one stone of the Temple shall be left upon another. In our Lord's reply Luke depicts, in even more sombre and alarming language than the other evangelists use, the commotions which are to precede the fall of Jerusalem. The disciples would be able to find confirmation of their Lord's prophecies in the persecutions which would befall them. As to "that day," Luke says nothing about the angels and even the Son Himself being ignorant of its precise date, but merely has the warning that the disciples should not be "overcharged with surfeiting and drunkenness" lest it should overtake them as a snare, adding that it will come in that manner upon the whole land, not, as the Authorized Version has it, "earth."

It deserves consideration whether Luke omits the words about the Son's ignorance in consequence of his copy of Mark, whether written or oral, being defective here or whether he regarded it as an unchronological doublet of Acts i. 6–8. In either case we may hesitate to discuss whether our records suggest that knowledge of the precise time of the catastrophe was hidden from our Lord's human consciousness while He was subject to the limitations of this life, but that after He was risen He had resumed His pre-existent deity. On this it would be temerarious to dogmatize, but we shall believe ourselves to be on surer ground if we adopt the view developed in another chapter, that it was after His ascension that the Word, who had confined Himself at His incarnation within the conditions of mortal life, took with Him forty days after His resurrection the consciousness and memory of that life into the temporarily secluded consciousness of His God-head. Here we may doubt whether Luke owes more to intercourse with John or with Paul, for while the latter speaks of Christ as emptying Himself of His deity, the former, who insists that the Word was God and records Peter's declaration that Christ knew all things, nevertheless preserves for us, in the story of the raising of Lazarus, our Lord's question, not to be explained away by any Docetic affectation of ignorance, "Where have ye laid him?" The Quicunque Vult of Western Christendom expresses our orthodox faith by stating that our Lord is one Christ: one not by conversion of the Godhead into flesh but by taking of the manhood into God. Yet when we are studying the records of His mortal life with our attention focused on the development of His human consciousness, we come at last to a point at which we are driven to speak of a reattachment of the divine and the human conscious-ness in our Lord. The Scriptures do not supply us with the evidence which can determine for us unequivocally in what sense this reattachment is to be understood, nor when it took place, but however these questions are to be answered, we have to moot two further questions. First does "that day" in Christ's words always mean, as it is clear it does here, the critical period which ended that age? It is possible to give an intelligible sense to the prophecies of judgment and the harvest as pictures of the discriminating fates which would come upon different types of people in that testing time of crisis, and this will explain how it was that the first generation of Christians concentrated their thought on the Second Coming as a final Advent. The facts of history interpreted for them the essential truth which the pictorial language of the parables conveyed, and later ages have accordingly read other meanings into it. In particular, the parable of the sheep and the goats has been universally treated as an image of the Great Assize. Yet in all the writings of the New Testament except those which are manifestly sub-sequent to A.D. 70 the original idea persists. The Church had to be gradually taught truth in the same way that the apostles had to be taught. The second question is this: did Christ Himself share the apostles' incomprehension of the temporary and limited character of that Advent, or rather of the fact that His kingdom would only in long stretches of time extend itself over the wills of men, with great moments of crisis occurring at intervals when He would manifest again and again His indisputable supremacy over whatever was inimical to God's will? Such crises, as Bishop Westcott said, are to be seen in such events as the collapse of Rome, the onrush of Islam, the break-up of the Middle Ages and, we may add, the French Revolution and the two great wars in our own time. A sober answer would seem to be that Jesus as a human prophet foresaw the fall of Jerusalem in the near future, but had no clear vision of the future history of the world. On the other hand He had such affinity and identity of will with the Father that He knew and propounded to His disciples the principles which lie at the heart and core of God's government of the world. Thus Christ's parables show us not merely how judgment would fall on good and bad in A.D. 70, but how at all times and finally men would reap the fruit of their doings.

EXCURSUS V

The Third Day

IN the phraseology of the Hebrews, as in that of other nations, certain expressions acquired idiomatic significance which could not be inferred from a mere lexical study of the individual words. Thus in Jeremiah xxv. 4 we read: "The Lord hath sent unto you all His servants the prophets, *rising early* and sending them," where a literal interpretation of the phrase would manifestly pervert the sense. In the same way the expression "on the third day" or "after three days" had lost its verbal precision in much the same way as with us "half a moment" and "in a second" have become blunted till they mean no more than the "anon" of Stuart times.

In Luke xiii. 32-33 our Lord says: "Go ye, and tell that fox, Behold I cast out devils, and I do cures today and tomorrow, and the third day I shall be perfected. Nevertheless I must walk today, and tomorrow, and the day following." When He told the Jews (John ii. 19), "Destroy this temple and in three days I will raise it up" the expression meant for Jewish ears nothing more precise than "soon" or "presently." Scrupulous scholars have searched the Old Testament to discover what might have suggested the prophecy, and Hosea vi. 2 has been claimed as the authority for stating that the Resurrection on the third day was according to the Scriptures. Without dwelling upon the fact that a single passage would be properly described in Greek as "the Scripture," we may say that what the Creed asserts is that the Resurrection was in accordance with the Scriptures. That the event took place on the third day is a matter of historical fact, but that fact of date we need not look to find in the Old Testament. When we examine the Gospel story we seem to observe first a round declaration that the destruction of the Temple shall be soon followed by its restoration. Accepting John's interpretation that the Temple is the Lord's body, we shall have in mind the Psalmist's words, "Thou wilt not suffer thy Holy One to see corruption," and from what we read about Lazarus in the grave we infer that our Lord could deduce that He must be raised again before the fourth day. Later, meditation on Jonah's story would again introduce the familiar expression, so that our Lord said "as Jonah was three days and three nights in the whale's belly, so shall the Son of Man be three days and three nights in the heart of the earth." Keeping in view the idiomatic use of the expression (something like the Welshman's use of "couple" for a small number) we shall not be troubled over the concurrent and contradictory use of the two expressions "after three days" and "on the third day." We shall recognize the Scriptural predictions of the Resurrection, and that a speedy resurrection, and shall adhere to the historical statement which dates the Crucifixion on Friday and the Easter Rising on Sunday.

PART FIVE

WAYSIDE JOTTINGS

Chapter One

SIMON ISCARIOT, LEPER AND PHARISEE, AND HIS SON JUDAS

THE Fourth Gospel tolls the knell of Judas' expiring discipleship by repeating in sinister cadence the description of him as Simon's son. Why, we may ask, does the evangelist reiterate so insistently what might be thought a trivial detail? Did he feel that in some way it made sadder and more sombre the story he had to tell of his one-time fellow-disciple? Perhaps certain possible interpretations of incidents in the Gospel history may furnish the explanation and reasons of the evangelist's dwelling on the identity of Judas' father.

Iscariot in spite of various other interpretations may in view of the Syriac translation be taken to mean that his home or birthplace was Kerioth and this may with some confidence be regarded as a township in Judaea. It is, then, an attractive theory to identify Simon Iscariot with the Pharisee Simon who, as Luke relates, invited our Lord to dinner. Following the raising to life of the widow's son at Nain, our Lord's teaching in John v. 21–29 acquires fresh significance and this fact seems to lend support to the view that Simon the Pharisee's house was in the neighbourhood of Jerusalem, where our Lord was attending a feast.[1] Mr. Trench has pointed out that the comment in John xi. 2 that Lazarus' sister Mary was the woman who anointed the Lord is hardly to be viewed as preparatory to the account that then follows of the anointing in Bethany. It may more naturally be held to refer to what Luke relates, whose account, like some other parts of his narrative, may fittingly be considered to be derived from John. In that case Mary, Lazarus' sister, is to be identified, as Origen unquestionably identifies her, with the Magdalene.[2] It would follow from this

[1] See also p. 338.
[2] It should be noted that since our Lord in His address to Simon is showing that He was aware that Mary was a great sinner, an adequate

that Simon had been forgiven a little—but in what way? Now in Mark's account of the later anointing, he tells us that it took place in the house of Simon the leper. It is possible that he has confused the two incidents, and that while the second anointing was in Lazarus' house,[1] the first was in Simon the leper's. This may identify the Pharisee with the leper whom our Lord had previously cleansed. His gratitude led him to entertain the Prophet who had healed him. His son had then already become a disciple and had been selected for apostleship. Yet at the end he proved ungrateful, forgetful both of the kindness done to his father and of the distinction bestowed upon himself. Even if we could suppose that he expected our Lord to emerge victorious from His ordeal and merely wished to pick up a little money by precipitating the crisis, he remains in his own words guilty in that he had sold innocent blood.

As for Mary, we are driven to suppose that she was born at Magdala, and, to distinguish her from others, was given the surname of Magdalene,[2] but that her family and she settled later at Bethany. It is noticeable that Luke first mentions Mary Magdalene after telling the story of the anointing in Simon the Pharisee's house.

It is not inconceivable that Luke's knowledge of the leper's identity and domicile lies behind two details in his writing. In iv. 44 he abstains from declaring that the synagogues in which our Lord preached were within the limits of Galilee. In v. 12 he is careful to dissociate the leper's healing from the neighbourhood of Capernaum. It is curious to observe that a similar procedure in the way of selecting and arranging historical material may apparently be detected in another instance. Luke records a visit of our Lord to Nazareth early in His public Ministry, before Simon Peter and his companion were called to leave their fishing. Mark, followed by Matthew, mentions a visit of our

translation would emphasize the subordinate clause (as has often to be done in translating from Greek), the sense being "her sins which are forgiven are many, for she loved much." This logical connexion removes what has been a stumbling-block. Her love proves her forgiveness, but, as St. Ignatius says, faith is the beginning, love is the end.

[1] Mr. Trench may be right, however, in supposing that the Bethany supper was held in Simon's house where Lazarus also was a guest.

[2] The surname Iscariot and the addition "the daughter of Clopas" may serve as parallels.

Lord to His own country after the first parables had been spoken and before the sending out of the Twelve disturbed the conscience of the Baptist's murderer. An unprejudiced study of the details seems to show that these are not variant accounts of a single incident. On the first occasion the animosity of the congregation sprang from a jealousy of Capernaum and a fanatical fury at the suggestion that Gentiles might receive readier help than they themselves. The second time the people were contemptuous and critical. Luke mentions that Capernaum had witnessed signs before the visit, yet is at no pains to explain his words. Mark particularly states that Jesus passed from Capernaum to His old home. In our view the two records are complementary[1] in the same way as the two accounts of Mary's anointings. It will be seen that Luke, having recounted the earlier visit, omits the second at the point where Mark has it, just as he leaves out the feast in Bethany. Mark, deriving his story from Peter, says nothing of the first visit, which in any case preceded the apostle's definitive call.

To recur for a moment to the "little" forgiven to Simon the Pharisee, we have seen on another page that in the Jewish view the forgiveness of sin and the healing of sickness marched step by step alongside of one another. The uncanonical Gospel fragment published by Messrs. Bell and Skeat tells that the leper explained his condition as induced by contact with others in a caravanserai, as if he would urge that his contraction of the contagion was venial and no wilful running into danger. His grudging and ungracious reception of his Guest is explicable as an example of how, as Dean Vaughan said many years ago, we are prone to lose only too soon our sense of gratitude for deliverance from peril or disease.

Miss Dorothy Sayers with a dramatist's penetrative intuition has represented Judas as led to put his Master in the Jews' hands because he mistakenly supposed that Jesus had at last succumbed to the temptation to seize worldly power. This is an interesting reading of the apostle's character, but it does not square very deftly with our Lord's description of him as a backbiter nor with John's flat statement that he was a thief. If we are to superimpose anything on what these aspects of his character

[1] But see p. 116, note.

seem to suggest, it would appear proper to invite consideration of another possibility. Was Judas' attachment to our Lord like that of William the Silent's brother? Of him Miss Wedgwood writes: "Louis' affection had nothing of obedience in it. Impetuous and reckless, with a touch of the possessive in his passionate attachment to his brother, he was convinced that he could force William's hand and was compromising him deliberately, as he thought, for his own good." Was Judas' purpose to force his Master to go forward to His victory, from which He might seem to be holding back because of the "baptism" which had first to intervene, and incidentally while doing this service to his hesitating Lord, why not spoil the enemy by taking what money they were ready to give. This would be some cover against the chance of Jesus' failure.

Chapter Two

WAS THE "YOUNG RULER" SAUL OF TARSUS?

SOME while since the thesis was tentatively put forward that the rich youth[1] who went away sorrowful from our Lord was afterwards the apostle St. Paul. Such an identification is so interesting as to deserve further ventilation and thorough discussion.

Before examining the records of the interview between our Lord and the young man one or two observations must be made. According to both the First and the Third Gospels our Lord had previously taught His hearers that they should "do good," i.e. going beyond the codified duties deduced by the Rabbis from the Mosaic legislation and observed by the Pharisees, His disciples were to be generous and gracious as is our heavenly Father. Subsequently to this, as Luke relates, a scribe puts the question, "What must I do to inherit eternal life?" Referred by our Lord to the Law, he himself summed up man's duty in the two commandments: "Thou shalt love Jehovah" and "Thou shalt love thy neighbour." When he sought to circumscribe the range of the second duty, our Lord uttered the parable of the Good Samaritan. Luke further relates that, a week or two before the incident of the Young Ruler, our Lord spoke the parable of the Rich Man and Lazarus. That some reports of these addresses reached the young ruler's ears is a reasonable probability. It is noticeable that his question is in substance that of the lawyer.[2] The successive appeals to prefer unselfish philanthropy to sequestered ease may be thought to have pricked the youth's conscience. If they did not win Judas from his cupidity or the Pharisees from their respectability and acquisitiveness, they woke in him a stirring sense that here was something

[1] Our knowledge that he was young rests on the testimony of Matthew xix. 20, 22.

[2] It is tempting but fantastic to suppose the lawyer to be Paul's master, Gamaliel. We might more reasonably perhaps identify Gamaliel with the scribe who in Holy Week was not far from God's Kingdom.

worthier of effort than he had hitherto known, a better ideal towards which a man should aspire. The dialogue between him and our Lord may perhaps have followed this course:

Gracious Rabbi, what must I do to inherit eternal life?

Why callest thou me gracious: none is good and gracious but One, that is God.

Rabbi, what gracious thing must I do to inherit eternal life?

Why askest thou me of what is good and gracious? Thou knowest the Commandments: Thou shalt not commit adultery, kill, steal, bear false witness, thou shalt honour thy father and mother.

All these have I observed from my youth up.

Thou shalt love thy neighbour as thyself.[1]

This I have observed from my youth up. What lack I yet?

One thing thou lackest. It is blessed to give rather than to receive. If thou wouldst be a finished pupil, go, sell all that thou hast and give to the poor, and come, accompany me.

Several points deserve to be noticed here.

(1) Jesus, we are told, loved him. Paul writes that Jesus loved him and gave Himself for him.

(2) The Lord declared that with God all things are possible and that the last should be first. We cannot doubt that our Lord, who read men's hearts, foresaw the issue of the spiritual conflict in the young man's heart. Paul declared that the Risen Lord appeared last to him, the least or most junior of the apostles, and he adds that he had laboured more abundantly than they all, and elsewhere mentions that on him fell the care of all the Churches (1 Corinthians xv. 8–10 and 2 Corinthians xi. 28).

(3) The parable of the Labourers in the Vineyard (Matt. xx. 1–16) with its concluding words, "The last shall be first, and the first last," is, according to the First Gospel, spoken by our Lord as a sequel to this encounter with the young ruler.

(4) The address "gracious Rabbi" might possibly be tolerated from one habituated to Greek speech (ἀγαθέ), but our Lord repeatedly discouraged platitudes and conventional phrases (Luke xi. 27, 28 and xiv. 15). Were the youth Saul of

---

[1] This is echoed perhaps in Romans xiii. 8–10.

Tarsus, the rebuke must have eaten into his memory so that it was natural for him to write: "Scarcely for a righteous man" (i.e. one who scrupulously fulfils the Law's literal requirements) "will one die: yet peradventure for a good man" (i.e. one who is generous and gracious) "some would even dare to die" (Romans v. 7, where this parenthetic remark about the good and generous man disturbs and confuses the argument for most readers, but is intelligible on our hypothesis).

(5) Paul's remembrance of the poor, his working with his own hands, his καύχησις that he preached the Gospel gratis are significant if they spring from his responding at last to the Lord's call.

(6) We may find in this connexion the utterance of the Beatitude, "It is blessed rather to give than to get" (Acts xx. 35).

(7) The "kicking against the goad" becomes intelligible if St. Paul had at this period been in contact with our Lord's teaching. This would explain his declaration that the Christian no longer saw Christ after the flesh (as on our hypothesis he had once seen Him). Moreover, we may in this case suppose that he had himself heard the Lord's denunciation of divorce, and if this had been a temptation of the young ruler, it may explain why the first commandment cited by our Lord to him is that "forbidding adultery."[1] It will be noticed that in Paul's summary of the commandments this sin is similarly named first (Romans xiii. 9).

[1] It is attractive, if audacious, to suppose that Paul was among the Pharisees who appear in the last six months of our Lord's Ministry as recorded by Luke, and that the apostle is the evangelist's authority. Cf. Luke xi. 53, 54; xvi. 18; Mark x. 1-12.

Chapter Three

THE HIGH PRIESTHOOD OF ANNAS AND CAIAPHAS

THERE are notorious difficulties and puzzling obscurities in connexion with the Biblical statements as to the High-priesthood of Annas and Caiaphas. Luke[1] to identify the epoch of John's call to his Ministry speaks of "Annas and Caiaphas being High-priest." He uses the singular and not the plural, and this perhaps implies that one only acted at one time, that like the Roman consuls they did not hold co-ordinate authority. In the Fourth Gospel Caiaphas alone is said to have been the High-priest in the year of the Crucifixion. Annas, we are told, was father-in-law to Caiaphas. In the Acts (when Peter and John are arraigned before the Sanhedrin) Annas is named as High-priest, and Caiaphas with others as merely an important or influential priest. We know from Josephus that Annas was High-priest from A.D. 7 to 14, when he was deposed as being insufficiently subservient to the Roman authorities. After two others had been nominated in succession and successively relieved of office, Joseph Caiaphas in A.D. 18 was appointed, and proving more compliant and complaisant than his predecessors retained his position till A.D. 37.

It has sometimes been conjectured that Annas was regarded by legitimists as *de jure* High-priest, while Caiaphas held the position *de facto*. It is conceivable that Annas therefore presided in the Sanhedrin when dealing with a matter of faith not requiring capital punishment, while Caiaphas as a *persona grata* to Pilate presided when it was determined to bring our Lord to His death. It is also conceivable that when it was thought that the Roman power might safely be defied or ignored Annas would assume his office, but when it seemed dangerous to be intransigent Caiaphas appeared as supreme. It cannot but be felt that this does not entirely square with John's explicit statement. Nor does Westcott's explanation seem adequately to account

[1] Luke iii. 2.

for the form of that statement, even though the evangelist viewed the year of the Crucifixion as standing out in his memory from all the years of his life. Is it possible that the Roman practice as between their consuls may supply a clue to the enigma? On this hypothesis after Caiaphas had succeeded, and proved himself acceptable and amenable to the Roman governor, he henceforth alternated with Annas in the High-priesthood. The Moderatorship of the Scottish Church will illustrate the matter. This would explain Luke's equation of Tiberius' 15th year (30 August A.D. 28 to 30 August, 29) with Annas' tenure of office, which would end in March A.D. 29[1] and Caiaphas's, which would follow. Further, Caiaphas would be in office from Nisan A.D. 33[1] to Nisan 34, in which year the Lord was crucified. Finally, Annas would be in office again from April 34 to April 35.[1] This the reader will observe, harmonizes perfectly with the other indications of date in the early chapters of the Acts.

Another fact merits attention, for it would appear to be neither irrelevant nor unimportant. If the biennial tenure of the High-priesthood continued throughout Pilate's procuratorship, Caiaphas would be in office again from March A.D. 37.[1] It is Caiaphas, and not another, whom Josephus tells us that Vitellius the Proconsul of Syria deposed from the High-priesthood when he visited Jerusalem in the paschal week, a fortnight later, at the end of March A.D. 37.

It may be of some interest and advantage to tabulate a few dates which may be inferred from what we have just said.

A.D. 33	24 March*	Caiaphas again took office.
	3 April	The Crucifixion.
	24 May	Whitsunday.
34	March*	Annas resumes the High-priesthood.
	April*	The lame beggar healed.
	May*	Ananias and Sapphira.
	June*	The apostles arrested.
	September*	The seven deacons appointed.
	November	St. Stephen martyred; refugees evangelize Phoenicia, Cyprus, Antioch; Philip in Samaria.

[1] It is conceivable (though most of the evidence discountenances the idea) that the year of office ran from Tishri to Tishri, i.e. roughly from October to October. In that case the dates marked with an asterisk should be set six months earlier.

12*

35	January	Peter and John in Samaria; Paul's conversion.
	February	Paul goes to Arabia.
	April*	Caiaphas resumes office; the Ethiopian eunuch converted; Philip to Caesarea.
	May	Peter to Lydda and Joppa.
	June	Peter visits Cornelius at Caesarea.
37	March*	Caiaphas in office, but presently deposed. Tiberius murdered by Gaius.
	April	Herod Agrippa tetrarch of Galilee.
	Summer	Paul returns to Damascus; escapes to Jerusalem and thence Caesarea; later he proceeds to Tarsus.
38	Spring	Some Christian Cypriots having converted non-Jews at Antioch, Barnabas is sent thither.
Between and	Spring 38⎱ Spring 39⎰	Barnabas brings Paul from Tarsus to Antioch.
Between and	Spring 39⎱ Spring 40⎰	Agabus and others come to Antioch.
40	April	Herod Agrippa made king of Judaea also.
41	24 January	Gaius murdered and succeeded by Claudius.
42		James martyred and Peter arrested about Passover, 26 March.
	28 April	Peter enters Rome.
43	5 August	Herod died five days after a great festival show for Claudius' birthday [1] 1 August.
45		Barnabas and Saul take alms to Jerusalem to the Elders, and taking Mark with them, return to Antioch.
		Famine in Judaea.
47	Spring	Barnabas and Saul with Mark sail from Antioch to Cyprus; Mark returns to Jerusalem.
48	Autumn	Barnabas and Saul return to Antioch.
49		Jews expelled from Rome by Claudius.
		Encounter of Peter and Paul at Antioch (Gal. ii. 11–14).
50	Spring*	The Council at Jerusalem; [2] Paul and Silas start from Antioch on second missionary journey.
52	July	Gallio commences his year of office at Corinth.
54	October	Nero's accession.

---

[1] Or perhaps 28 January A.D. 44, five days after the anniversary of Claudius' accession: cf. Eisler, *The Enigma of the Fourth Gospel*.

[2] On this reckoning Paul first met with Peter in the third year after his conversion, and in the fourteenth year after this met other apostles at the Council. In Acts xv. 33 Judas and the other envoys from Jerusalem are said to return to "the apostles": whether any besides Peter and John (Gal. ii. 1, 9) is not clear.

60–62		Paul's first captivity in Rome.
63		Lazarus died, says Epiphanius.
64	July	Great fire of Rome.
67	29 June	Martyrdom of Peter and Paul.[1]

All the evidence accessible to us—the chief statements will be found printed at the end of this chapter—fixes 29 June as the day of Peter's martyrdom. He had then been bishop of Rome for twenty-five years and according to one reckoning two months and three days, and according to another one month and nine days. His episcopate therefore was dated either from 28 April or from 22 May. St. Jerome avers that the apostle came to Rome in Claudius' second year, and this will accordingly give us April or May A.D. 42. From this it follows that the martyrdom was in the summer of A.D. 67.[2] Conclusive proof that this is correct is furnished by the alternative reckonings given for the exact length of time that he was bishop. The Jewish calendar day for Peter's arrival in Rome on 28 April A.D. 42 was the nineteenth day of the second month, thirty-three days after the Passover. That Jewish date in A.D. 67, when Passover was 19 April, was 22 May, and thus the two statements of our authorities are explained and reconciled. This gives us a sure basis on which to rest the other dates.

The province of Syria, with its headquarters at Antioch, included Palestine as one of its departments. The ecclesiastical organization of the Christians shaped itself on the pattern of the political administration. St. Jerome, in calendaring Peter's episcopate at Antioch, is at pains to note that the apostle was a native of the province, born in the district of Galilee and in the Bethsaida quarter. We may infer that he should be reckoned to have been exercising his office in the province of Antioch when he visited Lydda and Joppa and Caesarea. This encourages us to believe that he went to Antioch soon after the Christian faith was preached there, just as he did when Samaria received the word of God. We thus date Peter's episcopate from A.D. 35, and so seven years before he went to Rome. The ten years which is

---

[1] For another scheme of dates from A.D. 42 onwards see *Expositor*, VIII, Series No. 54, pp. 481–497.

[2] Eusebius, *Chronicon*, dates it in Nero's fourteenth year, evidently reckoning his first year from 1 January A.D. 54.

alternatively given may be taken to be reckoned from A.D. 33,[1] all this period being spent in the province of Syria.

We may believe that it was on Peter's motion that Paul went to Caesarea, which Peter had visited and where Philip was settled, and also that it was on Peter's suggestion that Barnabas called Paul to Antioch from Tarsus.

Jerome writes:

"Petrus, ann. xxv, mens. uno, d. viiii. Fuit temporibus Tiberii Caesaris et Gai et Tiberi Claudi et Neronis, a cons. Minuci et Longini usque Nerone et Vero. Passus autem cum Paulo die iii Kl. Iulias, cons. . . . imperante Nerone."

Felician Recension:

"Beatus Petrus, Antiochenus, filius Iohannis, provinciae Galileae, vico Bethsaida, frater Andreae et princeps apostolorum, primum sedit cathedra episcopatus in Antiochia annis x. Hic Petrus ingressus in urbe Roma Nerone Cesare ibique sedit cathedra episcopatus ann. xxv, mens. ii, dies iii. Fuit temporibus Tiberii Cesaris et Gaii et Tiberii Claudi et Neronis. . . . Hic martyrio cum Paulo coronatur."

Cononian Recension:

"Beatus Petrus, filius Iohannis, provinciae Galileae, vico Bethsaida, primum sedit cathedra episcopatus in Antiochia an. vii., deinde in Roma an. xxv. mens. ii. dies iii. Fuit temporibus Tyberii Caesaris et Gai et Tyberii Claudi et Neronis sub quo et passus."

---

[1] Otherwise we might suppose that Peter was for three years in Syria about A.D. 50. Eusebius, *H.E.V.*, 18, declares that the apostles remained twelve years at Jerusalem, a statement which confirms the view taken in the text and agrees with the language of Acts xi. 30, which may be taken to imply that when Barnabas and Saul went to Jerusalem, A.D. 45, no apostles remained there.

Chapter Four

JUDAEA OR JEWRY?

IN St. Luke's Gospel, iv. 44, there is, it will be remembered, a remarkable divergence of reading as to whether Judaea or Galilee was at that point said by the evangelist to be the scene of our Lord's preaching. The text underlying the Authorized Version said Galilee. The Revisers felt the strength of the evidence to favour Judaea. So far as manuscript evidence goes, this statement pretty well covers the facts. There is, however, a further question which is perhaps of still more importance and on the answer to which may turn the question whether, after all, the two readings may mean the same thing. What is the sense or senses which Luke gave to the word Judaea? Can it mean the whole of Palestine, or at any rate all those parts of it in which the Jews (not Samaritans) lived? To answer this it seems to be worth while to examine our author's use, both in the Acts of the Apostles and in the Gospel. If we begin with the Acts of the Apostles, where because we have no extant sources from which we know the writer drew, we must treat the whole work as homogeneous in usage, we find the following passages exhibiting the use of the word:

Acts
- (*a*) i. 8: "Ye shall be witnesses unto me both in Jerusalem and in all Judaea and Samaria."
- (*b*) ii. 9: "And the dwellers in Mesopotamia and in Judaea and Cappadocia."
- (*c*) viii. 1: "All were scattered abroad throughout the regions of Judaea and Samaria."
- (*d*) ix. 31: "Then had the church rest throughout all Judaea and Galilee and Samaria."
- (*e*) x. 37: "Ye know the word which was published throughout the whole of Judaea beginning from Galilee."
- (*f*) xii. 19: "And he went down from Judaea to Caesarea."
- (*g*) xxviii. 21: "We neither received letters out of Judaea."

It will be seen that of these instances, two only seem to distinguish Judaea from Galilee unmistakably. All the rest, except the last, leave it a possible view at any rate that what is meant is all those parts of Palestine which, unlike the Samaritans, regarded Jerusalem as the centre of true religion (this distinction will harmonize with the general view of Mr. L. E. Browne in his *Early Judaism*).

If we now take the Gospel references, we have:

Luke

(a) vii. 17: "This word went forth concerning him in all Judaea and the region round about" (this after the raising of the dead youth at Nain).

(b) v. 17: "Lawyers who did come out of every village in Galilee and Judaea and Jerusalem."

(c) xxiii. 5: "He stirreth up the people teaching throughout all Judaea and beginning from Galilee unto this place."

Before we finally sift these instances in the hope of coming to a definite conclusion, it will be well to look at the passages which occur in other Gospels.

Mark

(a) i. 5: "There went out to him all the land of Judaea and all the men of Jerusalem," which Matt. iii. 5 reflects in the form: "There went out to him Jerusalem and all Judaea and all the region round about the Jordan"; while Luke iii. 3 says: "He came into all the region round about the Jordan." Matt. iii. 1: "John the Baptist came preaching in the wilderness of Judaea." Matt. iv. 23–25: "He went about in the whole of Galilee . . . and the fame of him went into all Syria . . . and great multitudes followed him from Galilee and Decapolis and Jerusalem and Judaea and beyond the Jordan."

(b) iii. 7: "Jesus withdrew to the sea and a great multitude from Galilee followed and from Judaea and from Jerusalem and from Idumaea and beyond the Jordan and about Tyre and Sidon"; which is reflected in Matt. iv. 25 given above and in Luke vi. 17: "a great multitude of the people from all Judaea and Jerusalem and the sea-coast and Tyre and Sidon."

(c) xiii. 14: "Then let them that are in Judaea flee into the mountains," repeated in Matt. xxiv. 16 and Luke xxi. 21.

St. John's use is to be seen in the following passages:

John

(a) iv. 3: "He left Judaea and went away again into Galilee"; and 54: "Having come from Judaea into Galilee."

(*b*) vii. 1 : "After this Jesus was walking in Galilee for He would not walk in Judaea"; and vii. 3 : "Go into Judaea."

(*c*) xi. 7 : "Let us go into Judaea again."

St. Paul has the word four times in his letters :

(*a*) 1 Thess. ii. 14 : "The Churches of God which in Judaea are in Christ Jesus."

(*b*) Gal. i. 22 : "Was unknown by face unto the Churches of Judaea."

(*c*) 2 Cor. i. 16 : "Of you to be brought on my way toward Judaea."

(*d*) Romans xv. 31 : "That I may be delivered from them in Judaea, which do not believe."

On considering all these passages we seem to be led to the conclusion that Judaea, strictly speaking, will mean the southern part of Palestine round Jerusalem, in contradistinction to Samaria, Galilee and even other small sections of country; but besides that it may be used more widely for all those parts of Palestine where Jews were to be found in substantial numbers. We may say, indeed, that this use is not unlike that of England, which at times may mean England as distinguished from Wales and Scotland and yet it may at other times be used to cover at any rate the southern part of Britain. Since drawing this conclusion I have been interested to find the late Mr. T. E. Page commenting on Acts ii. 9 with the words: "Clearly not Judaea as distinguished from Samaria (cf. i. 8) but the land of the Jews, i.e. Palestine and perhaps some part of Syria."

It will seem to follow from this that in the Lucan passage with which we started, while the better reading, Judaea does testify to the writer's acquaintance with the Ministry of our Lord outside Galilee, it may be precarious to infer that at this particular point he wishes us to understand that our Lord left Galilee for Judaea. It will be safer to take the words to mean that our Lord was preaching in synagogues, whether in Galilee or in Judaea, for some time after the healing of the demoniac in Capernaum and before the summoning of Simon and his partners to become Fishers of Men.

Two subsidiary points may be added.

(1) In the Fourth Gospel "the Jews" designates not only residents in Jerusalem and Judaea proper, but Galileans and perhaps others, such as those in Peraea. In other words the expression is as flexible and fluctuating as "English" or

"British" is with us. In the account of the events at the Feast of
Tabernacles we shall suppose that the Jews from Galilee were
agog with speculation whether what had taken place there in
the last six months would now be followed by a challenge to the
authorities at Jerusalem. These Galileans were unaware of the
design to kill our Lord.[1]

(2) The First Gospel states that after the Baptist's imprisonment Jesus came into Galilee. This accords with Luke's description of the Ministry previous to the call of Peter and his
companions as being exercised in "Jewry," i.e. it was not then
limited to Galilee, whereas after this removal from Judaea following upon John's imprisonment, Galilee was almost exclusively
the sphere of our Lord's activities.

[1] Cf. John vii. 11, 13, 15, 20, 21, 25.

Chapter Five

APOSTLE : SENT : SILOAM : SHILOH

CHARACTERISTIC of much of our Lord's teaching as given in the Fourth Gospel is the insistence that He has been sent into the world by God. In the same way, He tells the Twelve, He sends them out. The title apostle expresses this, and whatever shades of meaning may be suggested to us from extra-biblical examples of its use we may be satisfied to believe that the apostles were intended to continue and extend the work for which the Saviour had been sent. In John i. 6 we are told that "there was a man sent from God whose name was John"; and our Lord manifestly avoids any clarification of His function—a proclamation of His Messiahship would have precluded the possibility of a transvaluation of that title—by simply stating that He had been sent to do and teach certain things. In Matt. x. 40 he is reported as saying, "He that receiveth you receiveth me and He that receiveth me receiveth Him that sent me"; and in Matt. xv. 24 He says to the Syro-Phoenician woman, "I am not sent but unto the lost sheep of the house of Israel." In Luke iv. 18 He takes for His text in the synagogue at Nazareth the words of Isaiah lxi. 1 : "He has sent me to heal the broken-hearted, to preach deliverance to the captives, and recovery of sight to the blind, to set at liberty them that are bruised." At Jerusalem we are told that our Lord declared that "the works that the Father hath given me to finish . . . bear witness of me that the Father hath sent me"; and again, "the Father Himself which hath sent me hath borne witness of me." At Capernaum He said, "This is the work of God that ye believe on Him whom He hath sent." At the Feast of Dedication our Lord said, "Say ye of Him whom the Father hath sanctified and sent into the world 'Thou blasphemest', because I said 'I am (the) Son of God'?" The same assertion is repeated in some other half-dozen passages, and we need not pursue the matter further. There is, however, one word in Mark i. 38 which may well receive our attention. Our Lord told those who followed Him, "Let us go into the next town, that I may preach there also: for therefore came I forth." Luke shows that the word ἐξῆλθον means "came forth from God," for he writes, iv. 43, "for therefore am I sent," and we may compare the words in John viii. 42, "I proceeded forth and came from God . . . He sent me."

The blind man in John ix was sent to wash in the pool of Siloam, and the evangelist tells us that the name means "sent." It may not be too presumptuous to hazard a conjecture that we have here the key to the obscure prophecy in Genesis xlix. 10, "The sceptre shall not depart from Judah, nor a lawgiver from between his feet, until Shiloh come; and unto him shall the gathering of the people be." Can it be that the original text concealed under the present reading signified "He that is sent?"

Chapter Six

THE DATE OF ST. POLYCARP'S MARTYRDOM

EUSEBIUS' *Chronicon* dates St. Polycarp's martyrdom in the Olympiad year July 166 to July 167. Nearly half a century ago C. H. Turner satisfied himself that the true date must be 22 February A.D. 156. He argued from the fact that the proconsul under whom the martyrdom occurred entered on his office in the summer of 154, and although the Roman calendar date should have been 23 February, a Sunday, he supposed this to be an error and the day to have been the Feast of Purim. More recently Prof. E. Schwartz, accepting the same date, has regarded it as the Sabbath in the Passover week which was observed before the equinox. This is not impossible if after A.D. 70 the Judaic cycle was used instead of observation to fix the month Nisan. Nevertheless, an entirely different computation may claim to be correct. Three points must be emphasized: (1) The Smyrna letter throughout makes the martyrdom echo the Crucifixion. Hence μεγάλου σαββάτου need not mean a great Jewish festival. A public holiday may be called a Sabbath or rest day. (2) 23 February is the day of the Terminalia festival. An error in the Roman dating is less probable than one in our own computation of the month Xanthicos. (3) Eusebius' Olympiad 235 is explicable as a misreading of 232 (Π for II). Although graffiti at Pompeii and the number of the Beast in the Apocalypse show the modern notation for numbers, there is evidence for the survival of the older system known to us from Athenian temple treasury accounts and the Parian marble. We may conclude, then, that St. Polycarp was martyred on Saturday 23 February, the public holiday of the Terminalia, in A.D. 155, the second year in the 232nd Olympiad. This dating explains the proconsul's holding of public sports in the amphitheatre and the sitting there of Jews cheek by jowl with Gentiles, as they would not have done on a great Jewish feast-day.

Finally, one point must be stated categorically and unambiguously. Since the Seleucid like the Hebrew calendar was lunar, neither Passover at the Nisan Full Moon nor Purim at the Adar is reconcilable with the second day, i.e. the morrow of the new moon, in Xanthicos. Our date, on the other hand, fulfils this condition. In 155 the astronomical new moon fell on 19 February at 8 hours 38 minutes G.M.T., or 11 hours 4 minutes a.m. local time at Antioch. This new moon would be visible, just possibly perhaps, on the evening of the 20th and certainly on the 21st. The Calendar new moon, therefore, was from the evening of Thursday, 21 February, to the evening of Friday, 22nd. This permits at least, and perhaps confirms, the equating of 2 Xanthicos with 23 February 155, and negatives the equating of it with 22 February 156.

In the account of St. Polycarp's martyrdom which was sent out by the Church of Smyrna and which has been preserved to us, it is said that he put an end to the persecution, adding the seal as it were (to other martyrs' testimony) by the testimony he gave at his martyrdom. σχεδὸν γὰρ πάντα τα προάγοντα ἐγένετο, ἵνα ἡμῖν ὁ Κύριος ἄνωθεν ἐπιδείξῃ τὸ κατὰ τὸ εὐαγγέλιον μαρτύριον. This has been translated: "For one might almost say that all that had gone before[1] happened in order that the Lord might show to us from above a martyrdom[2] in accordance with the Gospel." The original, however, would appear to carry a more pointed significance. The word ἄνωθεν regularly reflects the Greek consciousness that the mouths of rivers lie lower than their sources. The reversal of nature is expressed by the poet in the four words ἄνω ποταμῶν χωροῦσι παγαί. Thus "from above" is often a mistaken literalism for "from the source, from the start, anew, again." So Nicodemus is told "ye must be born again." In our passage the point made is that Polycarp showed how from first to last Christians should, like Christ Himself, give the world proof of the truths to which they bore witness. As Christ did not rush upon death, but at

[1] More exactly "all that led up to the martyrdom."
[2] μαρτυρία, "deposition, testimony, verbal evidence," is to be distinguished from μαρτύριον, "proof by action or material object, concrete evidence, exhibit of the English criminal law." The distinction is still observable in respect of the martyrs: all gave proof of their faith by steadfastness in suffering and by death; some also gave verbal testimony.

first withdrew before those who threatened to seize or to stone Him and did not in bravado challenge those at whose mercy He was, so at first Polycarp withdrew from danger and after his arrest showed meekness and modesty in his replies. Not merely in his last moments but in his whole conduct from the beginning of the persecution he, as an instrument in the Lord's hand, exhibited to the Church the way in which Christians should give proof that their faith was true. There would be no occasion to insist on this alternative interpretation of ἄνωθεν were it not that it pretty certainly supplies the clue to the true meaning of what our Lord said to Pilate: "Thou couldst have no authority against me at all, were it not given thee ἄνωθεν: therefore he that handed me over to thee hath the greater sin." Apart from the disingenuous perversion by Caiaphas of our Lord's answer to him, Pilate would have had no ground whatever for pronouncing Jesus a pretender to the throne. Had Pilate had the case before him *ab initio*, he must have dismissed it. It was because a court of first instance had given sentence and remitted the case to Pilate for confirmation that the Governor had any ground for taking action.

Excursus VI

Jeremiah and Ezekiel

OF all the books eventually accepted as canonical by the non-Christian Jews of Palestine, one in particular would seem to have left its impress on our Lord's thought and language. The writings of the prophet Jeremiah are not so well known to modern readers as the prophecies of Isaiah, yet there are many features in Jeremiah's story and utterances which find their counterpart in the Gospels. It will be unnecessary to quote the parallels in our Lord's utterances: they will be familiar to every reader. In the Book of Jeremiah, without pretending to give an exhaustive record, we may mention a number of noteworthy particulars. The prophet declares that the temple at Jerusalem may expect the same fate as Shiloh, because it has been unfaithful to God's voice. He speaks again and again of the visitation which his countrymen must expect to fall upon them from God. He laments over Jerusalem. He denounces the covetousness of the rulers and people. He calls the Temple a den of thieves. For him prophet and priest are conjoined in the way that scribes and pharisees and lawyers are conjoined for our Lord. Jeremiah contemplates the destruction of Israel as of a tree planted by God but failing to yield fruit. He curses his brethren because they are against him, as our Lord's brethren did not believe in Him. His neighbours plot against his life, as the Pharisees against Jesus. He speaks of a woman in travail when he searches for an apt image for bitter pain. He denounces the pride of his contemporaries who exult in their temporal success. He speaks of God being in the midst of those who are called by His name. He declares that he eats God's word—an expression which cannot but remind us of Christ's avowal that His meat was to do God's will. He abjures the comforts and hopes of married life, which again calls to mind our Lord's reply to Peter when he burst out with the impatient "It does not pay to marry." The prophet speaks of "fishers of men," though in a different sense from that given to the words by our Saviour. He infers that all the people of Judah shall perish unless they repent. He foretells that the Gentiles shall come to worship Israel's God. He anticipates swift ruin for those who are concerned merely to amass wealth, and his words find an echo in our Lord's parable of the rich fool. He denounces transport on the Sabbath for purposes of trade: our Lord's rejection of the verbal definitions of the Sabbath obligation illustrates His replacement of a legalistic literalism by a spiritual interpretation. He speaks of the "way of life and the way of death" and from this latter men should make instant escape. He denounces the oppression of widows and the shedding of blood. He speaks of a new covenant when God's words should be written on the heart. He bids his countrymen not to weep for the dead but for the exile, as our Lord told the women not to weep for Him but for their children. He speaks of God as the God of all flesh, for whom nothing is too hard, as our Lord declared that all live unto God and that with God all things are possible. He says that the sinners shall drink the cup of God's fury and that God will send a sword on the earth. The story of the charges against him bears considerable resemblance to the story of our Lord's trial.

Yet some contrasts must be noticed. The prophet asks God not to forgive his enemies. He desires vengeance. He prays that God will pour out His fury on the nations that have not known Him.

The Gospel parallels to all these expressions are mostly to be found in the record of that period in our Lord's Ministry which followed the Transfiguration. It is not to be thought, however, that nothing like them was actually heard before that. On the contrary, our Saviour's life and teaching were so much of a piece throughout that we shall feel sure that the substance of what is analogous to Jeremiah's utterances was present from the first in our Lord's teaching, even if its tone was more sombre in the last half year. Here, then, would seem to be the reason that some who heard Him believed Him to be Jeremiah returned to life.

That our Lord's mind had been influenced by Jeremiah's teaching is further countenanced by a comparison of the relative frequency with which Jeremiah is quoted. If we take as a basis for our examination the list of passages given by Westcott and Hort as quotations from the Old Testament we find that in the four Gospels Christ is recorded to have repeated sayings of Jeremiah five times, one of these quotations appearing in three Gospels and one in two. Ezekiel is thought to have furnished twice only the language used by our Lord, and both of these instances are somewhat unconvincing. Matthew quotes Jeremiah once in his narrative and the other New Testament writers quote him thirty-one times. Ezekiel is quoted forty-five times, but it is to be remarked that most of these examples are where the prophet's imagery, not his theologumena, is drawn upon, and this is especially the case where in the Apocalypse the New Jerusalem is described in figurative language drawn from Ezekiel's description of Jerusalem as it was to be after the return from the Captivity.

It may be thought that unnecessary stress is being laid upon this point, but a recent writer has sought to emphasize the permanent value of Ezekiel and to find spiritual lessons of the highest quality in the post-exilic rabbis. He denies that Jeremiah taught a spiritual doctrine as distinct from an institutional worship of God, and, depreciating the Epistle to the Hebrews as academic and inferring that all the New Testament writers have given a one-sided and defective view of Christianity, would seem to be forsaking Catholic orthodoxy. The Catholic Church accepted the Canon as enshrining our Lord's message to the world. To supersede the Canon on the plea that the Holy Ghost had revealed truth that justified its supersession has more than once been the mark of thinkers unwittingly straying from the path of orthodoxy. Unless we set out to rewrite the New Testament records, we cannot escape from the conclusion that our Lord rejected the post-exilic developments of the Jewish Temple worship as not according with the Father's will, and therefore Christians must rather suspect the teaching of Ezekiel, placed in the Canon of Scripture by anti-Christian Jewish rabbis, than that of the Epistle to the Hebrews, which the Catholic Church has from the first accepted. Yet this statement is itself an overstatement. The Catholic Faith is a full and balanced corpus of divinely revealed truth. It comprises many partial but mutually complementary presentments of truth. It is for us to learn from all, and to reject none. Thus we shall thankfully study the Epistle which develops the truth that the Sinaitic Covenant has been metamorphosed into the New, but we shall still be ready to learn something of Ezekiel. That prophet, for one thing, tells of the valley of dead bones revivified by the Spirit of Jahveh; for another, he constantly refers to himself as the "son of man." The late Mr. R. O. P. Taylor remarked that this apparently is by way of emphasizing that his God-given message coming to the hearers through human lips was only too apt to be rejected. If this be accepted, we shall feel sure that our Lord drew upon Ezekiel as certainly as upon Jeremiah, and we shall therefore welcome whatever we can learn from Ezekiel without depreciating the Epistle.

Chapter Seven

MARRIAGE: GOD'S WILL AND MAN'S WILFULNESS

STUDY of the chronology of events related in Holy Scripture has sometimes been dismissed as merely the satisfaction of archaeological curiosity. Yet at times it curbs and corrects vagaries of Biblical interpretation. An interesting and important example of this may be seen in respect of our Lord's utterances on the subject of marriage and divorce. Here a critical re-examination of our authorities would appear to warrant the following reconstruction of the history.

After the Feast of Tabernacles in A.D. 32, our Lord, challenged to express His judgment as to the appropriate treatment of a woman guilty of adultery, refused to arrogate to Himself the functions of the judicature. He did not confirm the permanence of the law, which demanded the death sentence, but left open the more lenient alternative of giving the unfaithful wife "a bill of divorcement." Thus the position was clarified and defined. Infidelity was not condoned: it dissolved the marriage, but even indisputable guilt was not to be visited with death. The injured husband was presumably left free to marry again, his unfaithful wife being nominally dead; but she was left to live on and, it would seem, if she married again she was to be faithful to her new husband.

An austere critic might consider this more humane procedure to be a lax declension from an original ordinance of God, but our Lord thus gives the sinner an opportunity for amendment, while at the same time ensuring the purity of the family descent. It would appear that Paul had full knowledge of this pronouncement by our Lord, since he declares that when an unconverted partner deserts a Christian, the Christian is left free to marry again. He admits that this judgment of his does not come in set terms from the Lord, but is so plainly parallel to the Lord's refusal to sentence the guilty wife to death that the apostolic counsel is consonant with the dominical command.

How far this more humane dissolution of the marriage tie had become usual by this time we have hardly the means to determine. The frequent mention of second marriages in the royal house,[1] and the record of the woman of Samaria seem to favour the belief that such humane divorce was the procedure usually followed and was common. What we are told of St. Joseph's cogitations tends to support the idea. He was, we are told, δίκαιος, i.e. a scrupulous observer of the Law, yet he was unwilling to bring the Blessed Virgin before the courts, whose sentence, it was provided, was death by stoning. Hence St. Joseph was inclined to the private annulment of the marriage contract.

Our Lord's pronouncement dismissed the suggestion of stoning, but, as it appears, left it open to the injured husband to do like the prophet Hosea, i.e. to take back the wife if she were ready to "sin no more," or, we may suppose, if his love were unequal to this or if her misconduct were obstinate and incorrigible, to give her a "bill of divorcement," so that both he and the wife might marry again. Hosea's story, however, and Paul's counsel exhibit one feature which distinguishes them from what has often been accepted as a sufficient warrant for supposing that divorce is within the unlimited competence of a husband. That competence would seem appropriate and reserved for the cases where the wife was irreformably and irretrievably resolved to leave her husband. We shall see later how Christian charity prompted the following of Hosea's example and on the other hand Christian freedom set limits to the burden which this would have imposed. Meanwhile we must consider the effect which our Lord's words produced.

It was apparently inferred that the new Rabbi in this matter accepted the rabbinic interpretation of the ancient Law. Here, however, arose another question. Some Rabbis had pronounced for such an interpretation as allowed a husband to get rid of his wife not only for proved infidelity, nor yet for infidelity suspected, but for more or less trifling faults or incapacities of the

---

[1] St. John Baptist's condemnation of Herod's union with Herodias would appear to be founded on the fact that she was his brother's wife, and that brother was still alive. The levirate law sanctioned such a union only where a brother had died without issue.

wife, for incompatibility of temper (as we might say), and even so that he might be free to satisfy his own desire for another woman to be his wife. Would our Lord assent to this easier view? Or would He run counter to the appetites of the careless and easygoing? Might a deed of divorcement be executed not merely as a humane commutation of the death sentence, but for the various reasons which some Rabbis had formulated?

For a proper understanding and appreciation of the legal position[1] at the time and of what we may call Christ's reform of it, an attempt must be made to trace with the aid of anthropological science the probable history of legislation. When Israel was consecrated to be Jahveh's special people, it was ordained that they must not be guilty of certain offences which were discordant with His will and name or nature. Those who so offended were cut off or rather cut themselves off from His covenanted care. So in accordance with primitive ideas association with such offenders must be ended: the nation had to secure itself from the contagion by expelling or executing them. It is manifest that in effect this meant that if a wife was guilty of adultery her husband was free to remarry. It is also manifest that a husband who suspected his wife of infidelity might allow her to leave him without making her face the ordeal of a trial and possible death. This practice of dismissal was obviously open to abuse, and the husband's autocracy was eventually restricted by requiring that he execute a formal deed of divorcement. This legal formality made it reasonable to expect that it would be not a hasty act of ill-temper but a well-considered step. Nevertheless self-indulgence and selfishness was still unbanished from men's hearts, and the exponents of the law

[1] The Law demanded that a betrothed woman taken in the act of infidelity should be stoned (Deut. xxii. 23, 24). When the direct evidence of two witnesses was lacking, the procedure had originally been the "ordeal by bitter water" (Numbers v. 11–31), but this had come to mean the public charging of the woman by her husband, first before the local synagogue court and then before the Sanhedrin, in an endeavour to extract a confession of guilt. If the woman did not confess, she could still be compulsorily divorced should the evidence seem sufficient. Mary's supposed crime merited a public "putting away." But a husband who had found "some unseemly thing" (Deut. xxiv. 1) in his wife—which might be almost anything—could privately divorce her, before two witnesses, giving her a "bill of divorcement" (T. Walker, *The Teaching of Jesus and The Jewish Teaching of His Age*, Section 5A, summary, p. 261).

sought to define and make clear for what reasons a wife might be given this formal and legal dismissal, now permitted as an alternative to public execution. Some authorities, as we have said, imposed stricter and narrower limits than others, who might be thought laxer or more lenient. The old sense of national solidarity, social responsibility and communal pollution was largely lost: individual comfort or even passion became the dominant aim and motive of men meditating divorce. The life story of the prophet Hosea exemplifies this change in moral values. Some would judge his conduct uxorious condonation of unfaithfulness, others unextinguishable fondness of affection. The prophet betrays no consciousness of anything but his private and personal obligation: room is found for the wife's repentance, her offence being regarded as exclusively a matter between her husband and herself. There is no thought of her sin polluting and injuring the whole nation.

With the unerring insight of moral transparency our Lord recalled His questioners from the sphere of particular applications concentrating on private and individual duty to the region of the general law of procreative function ordained by the Creator for man. That function and mutual assistance and companionship was the ultimate and basic purpose of sex and marriage.

It was perhaps in the following January when our Lord was in Peraea that Scribes and Pharisees came to Him and asked whether it was lawful for a man to divorce his wife. They quoted as the basis for the belief that such putting away was lawful the Deuteronomic injunction. His reply is unequivocal: the divine will is for a permanent marriage bond. The Deuteronomic statute is a concession in recognition of human infirmities and contumacies, a concession mitigating the harshness of inflicting the death penalty for such infidelity. The rabbinic refinements, therefore, were to be rejected: men might not dissolve their marriage bond, which God had willed. As Mark relates the encounter, the point at issue appears absolute and our Lord's answer uncompromising. The evangelist's fidelity to the facts may be thought to be confirmed by Luke's brief summary and by Paul's equally definite pronouncement as to the Lord's command. The First Gospel, however, opens up a different perspective. Here the question takes the form whether divorce is permissible for any reason, or perhaps rather for any and every reason.[1] Moreover this Gospel inserts in our Lord's answer a caveat which manifestly excludes something from the scope of the command. Upon this caveat attention has long been focused and its significance debated. Guided by our consideration of the chronological order we cannot but judge that Matthew is pointing out that infidelity is not in question: that issue had been dealt with when the priests brought the guilty woman before our Lord. Peter perhaps was absent from our Lord's company almost throughout the period from the Feast of Tabernacles to the final journey to Jerusalem, and in consequence he had no first-hand knowledge of the encounter in the Temple. Mark, his reporter, similarly makes no reference to it. Luke may have known of it, as we may believe of much else, from John, and therefore naturally omits all allusion to the niceties of rabbinic casuistry and expresses with a direct brevity our Lord's condemnation of any dissolution of the marriage tie with the purpose of marrying another partner. The suggestion may be hazarded that, as Mr. Cottam has argued, the original *pericope adulterae* was a first draft of John's recollections and that its appearance in some copies of Luke instead of John is due to the communication of the story from the apostle to the evangelist. Be that as it may, Matthew's caveat would seem to be a justifiable harmonization of Christ's later words with His previous refusal to pronounce the death sentence on an adulteress.

Minds inclined to legalism have been prone to insist that Mark's account was to be preferred, with its flat condemnation of divorce. The spirit of old Rome made its way into the Christian thought of Western Europe[2] and men looked to find in our Lord's fluid instruction the stiff rigidity of law. As a result while some argued that our Lord abrogated all grounds for divorce except one, others argued that even this single exception was not from the Lord Himself, but was an unworthy softening of the command. Those who were obsessed with a

[1] This ambiguity frequently occurs, especially with a negative.

[2] Mark apparently wrote his Gospel in the first instance for the Church in Rome, and this may have something to do with the fact that, as it would seem, Matthew's caveat and the discharge of the adulteress were ignored or disregarded.

Manichean horror of matter and of the procreative instinct not only interpreted our Lord's subsequent words [1] as an encouragement to celibacy, but also favoured the more sweeping view that divorce was always wrong. Modern critical methods were invoked in support of the contention that the First Gospel reflected the rules current amongst Jewish Christians who could not bring themselves to submit to Christ's absolute command. Yet it is admitted that at other points the First Gospel adheres faithfully to the sense of the Saviour's words, e.g. in the Beatitudes and in the Lord's Prayer, although Luke reproduces the actual words. Others, feeling that this critical argument was an insecure basis on which to rest so absolute a prohibition, laboured to find in the single exception something which might be reconciled with an apparently universal condemnation. They have supposed that the exception was where a man found that his wife had been intimate with another man shortly before the wedding.[2] In such a case they conceived that the marriage might be regarded as null and void from the first and thus they could maintain that our Lord's prohibition was absolute, admitting of no exception. This view of the meaning of Matthew's caveat assumes that some persons might have been so perverse as to think it conceivable that, unless our Lord specified this exception, He might have been teaching that a man was committing adultery if he put away such a bride. It also assumes that it would have been a normal and natural manner of speaking to say that "Whosoever putteth away his wife saving for the cause of *adultery* causeth her to commit adultery." It is hard to believe that any speaker or writer would so express himself. Moreover, the word *fornication* is frequently used in the papyri found in Egypt in virtually the same sense as *adultery*, so that its use for a wife's infidelity cannot be challenged. When the Jews were told by our Lord that they were not Abraham's

---

[1] In the *Holborn Quarterly* (1930) vol. xxi, New Series, pp. 380–382, I have contended that the "saying" which Christ bids those to receive who are able to do so is not Peter's blunt comment but the divine words at the creation of man. My friend Mr. Inglis has since pointed out that this interpretation is fortified by the better MSS., which omit τοῦτον and have only τὸν λόγον.

[2] A careful reading of the Mosaic Laws shows that the prime concern is that no child shall be foisted upon one who is not the father (cf. Deut. xxi. 13; xxii. 15).

children, they replied, "*We* were not born of fornication." Although there may here be an innuendo that our Lord Himself was born of an unchaste maiden, the words naturally should mean that the Jews ancestresses had not committed adultery, but had been faithful to their husbands.

We need not dwell upon the fact that under the Mosaic law such a girl should in general have been executed by stoning, but we must notice that in contradiction and correction of the forcing of this interpretation on the Matthean exception, some scholars have urged that the divine will demands even more than fidelity after marriage. They would have it that when there has been a union, even without the marriage bond between a man and a woman, that union should be permanent, or the partner who abandoned it would be guilty of adultery. Such a view, which has been made the theme of one of Maarten Maartens' novels, cannot be maintained without reservation. The victim of incestuous or adulterous seduction or rape cannot be pronounced guilty of adultery if she should marry another man. It may, however, deserve to be a matter of conscience where no such bar or impediment exists to consider whether an illicit union ought not to be made legally binding by marriage. Something more will be said of this presently.

But we must now proceed to consider Matthew's words from another point of view. At the well of Sychar our Lord told the Samaritan woman that she had had five husbands; "and," He said, "he whom thou now hast is not thy husband": in other words, she and this man were living together not in wedlock but in a terminable and precarious relation. It was in fact an instance of what some modern moralists have advocated with euphemistic elegance as "free love." As we shall see, this relation seems to have been styled *porneia*.[1] So far from the word importing casual or single occasions of loose conduct, as the ordinary translation *fornication* suggests, we shall find it used at times for a settled course of conduct, for a man keeping a mistress, and for a woman living under a man's protection. A careful consideration shows that this is what Paul is criticizing in 1 Corinthians v. It can hardly be supposed that the offender

[1] Cf. Gen. xxxiv. 31 : Shechem had asked to marry Dinah, then living with him.

had sinned on one occasion only. Plainly his repentance was to be shown by his ceasing his connexion with his father's late wife. The apostle's words use the same phrasing as we have noticed in regard to the Samaritan woman, and the Baptist similarly described Herod's union with his sister-in-law. That we are following out the true meaning is further indicated by the wording of Tobias' prayer when he is left with his wife Sarah. "And now, O Lord," he says, "I take not this my sister for *porneia* (i.e. indulgence and satisfaction of passion) but in truth : command that I find mercy and grow old with her" (Tobit viii. 7). Here the distinction is unmistakable between a temporary union and life-long wedlock.

In view of this we are justified in understanding the First Gospel to be warning its readers against extending our Lord's categorical prohibition of divorce, meaning the termination of marriage, so as to mean also a termination of the relation known as *porneia*. It must be understood, the evangelist remarks, that this prohibition is expressly concerned with marriage. *Porneia* may or may not be covered by the same rule : it is not immediately in question. The words then mean, to use an Americanism, aside from any question of *porneia*. This interpretation is confirmed by what we read in the Acts. The Jewish Christians who adhered like James to the Mosaic ordinances, except so far as our Lord was known to have expressly modified them, were scandalized by the way in which Jewish and Gentile Christians at Antioch ignored those ordinances. The Jerusalem decree approved the view that Gentile Christians should not observe the Law, but they laid down four points in which they should avoid giving offence to Jewish prejudices. Three of these are concerned with food, and it is to be noticed that they all touch on matters not specifically mentioned by our Lord, if we take the Gospels to exhibit adequately His teaching. Mark declares that our Lord's words abolished the distinction between clean and unclean beasts. But we have no word about things strangled or about draining the blood away and still less about things sacrificed to idols. It is, however, the fourth point which has exercised commentators' minds. It has always been thought startling to have "fornication" (as it has been translated) put on a level with these matters of food. That great and original scholar Bentley felt this so strongly that he emended the text to *porkeia*, but this has not won acceptance and lexicography lends no support to his suggestion. But we can now see how the matter stands. All Christians accepted the Lord's absolute condemnation of divorce, but in Antioch there were those who argued that where before conversion a man and a woman had formed a looser relation than matrimony its dissolution did not fall within the purview of the prohibition. More than that, we may well believe that after conversion some might be tempted to form such a less binding union if only to secure themselves from falling under condemnation by divorcing their partners. Such Gentile laxity of necessity scandalized the Jew. Yet no express mention of this question had been made by our Lord. Hence not only does the First Gospel point this out, but the Jerusalem decree does not go further than require Christians to abstain from such lax unions for the sake of other Christians to whom they would give offence. It accords with this suggestion that Paul distinguishes between the Lord's absolute prohibition of divorce and the practical advice he gives himself. Where the one partner does not accept the Christian view of life, the apostle declares that the other partner is free to marry again. The matter of *porneia* he discusses on general grounds, a fact which plainly implies that he too recognized that our Lord had not dealt specifically with it. Yet Mark includes "fornication" amongst the things said by our Lord to make a man unclean and (since we have no reason to doubt that Mark's record is faithful and that Peter gave an authentic account of our Lord's teaching) this goes to show that our view of the question at issue is correct. It was agreed that our Lord condemned episodic and promiscuous intercourse with a prostitute, but some argued that a regular and recognized connection between a man and a woman was not forbidden. Among the Greeks, the Romans and perhaps the Jews such a relation was common. It had not the indissoluble character of marriage. It is possible that Peter's comment on our Lord's prohibition of divorce meant that it would be better not to contract a permanent marriage but to form a terminable connexion. Be that as it may, Paul is concerned to insist that such a connexion, if not permanent like marriage, was fornication and inconsistent with the Christian attachment to his Lord. He is thus carrying further than did the Jerusalem decree the Christian disapproval of such a relation. For such *porneia* is no new discovery of advanced modern thinkers. Economic pressure had forced women two thousand years ago to be content with a position inferior to that of the wife and mother. Christianity was not long in urging, though not compelling, its adherents to enter into no other relation but that of matrimony. The Corinthian whose *porneia* was also incestuous Paul excommunicated from the Christian society and, till he abandoned the intimacy, consigned again to the devil's service. This incident, as we shall see, throws valuable light on the Christian view of divorce, but before coming to that we may gather together what seems to result from what has been said.

Scribes and Pharisees asked whether our Lord was in accord with Moses in making death the penalty for adultery. Our Lord refused to pronounce the death sentence, thus tacitly accepting the milder alternative which allowed the guilty person to live. Some months later[1] some Pharisees asked how far this permission extended. Our Lord ruled out all use of the milder alternative which would make it possible for a man or a woman who desired a new partner to have a divorce. He also pressed home the prohibition of adultery by asseverating that to cherish the desire for the possession of a married woman was in essentials to commit adultery in imagination. Still later the Christians realized that *porneia* was a way of escape from marriage that was for them impermissible.

A few points in this summary deserve comment: the Scribes and Pharisees who produced the guilty woman (without, it will be observed, producing the co-respondent for stoning) appear to have wished to find an excuse for bringing our Lord before the Roman procurator on the ground that He had usurped the Roman power of pronouncing a sentence of death. Further we must notice that the woman is not sent back to her husband nor

---

[1] Here one observation must be made. Jesus was now in Peraea, part of Herod's dominions. That He condemned flatly any divorce designed to make possible marriage with some new bride may well be thought to have been reported to the king. This would lend fresh point to the Pharisees' warning that Herod would kill the new prophet, whose words might indeed seem to confirm the idea that He was John risen again and still denouncing Herod's union with Herodias.

forbidden to marry again. The husband divorces her and is himself presumably free to take a new wife. On the next occasion the implications of our Lord's previous action are to be elucidated. It has already been made clear by our Lord that adultery ends the marriage relation, but Moses' ordinance was constantly used as a method of ending marriage and so opening the way to another marriage. Such chicanery our Lord condemned absolutely. To divorce a wife in order to be free to marry another was adultery. It results from this that adultery is the only ground for ending a marriage. With the interpretation just given to the word *porneia* it will be seen that Matthew's report of our Lord's prohibition of divorce is as absolute as that of Mark, Luke and Paul. The supposed exception does not deal with the permanence of the marriage relation. Thus our view of the possibility of a Christian divorce does not rest on Matthew's words, but on the implications of our Lord's refusal to sanction the death penalty for adultery.

One final point must be considered. It has been held at times that where the one partner has committed adultery the other should not marry again, but wait hoping that the guilty person may "repent." An argument has been drawn from our Lord's words to Peter that he should forgive his brother endlessly. It must be noticed, however, that that commandment expressly deals with cases where the offender "repents." When we remember that in the New Testament repentance is a change of outlook and of purpose, we find no reason for urging an indefinitely long waiting in a vague and vain hope that the offender will change. Actual experience shows that most of those who break their marriage ties leave their homes of fixed purpose. It is seldom that we hear of a momentary and casual lapse of infidelity. The Christian might be urged to condone such a lapse when "repentance" was evident. Where "repentance" is stubbornly refused, divorce is permissible and also remarriage so long as this is not the motive and purpose of the divorce. More than this, it is at least arguable that divorce is a Christian duty, so that the guilty party may be afforded the chance of marriage and not be left hopelessly excluded from anything but a life of insecure dependence on a terminable connexion.

Confirmation of our understanding of our Lord's instruction about the marriage relation comes from an unexpected quarter. In the Church of Rome about the middle of the second century there was a great stir of prophetical activity. One particular prophet, Hermas, was the author of works which at one time seemed on the point of gaining admittance to the New Testament canon. The bishop was his brother and at the time the order of prophets overshadowed the more regular officers of Church government, and this to some extent doubtless explains why the prophet's writings attained so high a reputation. Yet although they must today be felt to be of an inferior authority to the books which the Catholic Church has accepted as Scripture, they are of value as witnesses to the way in which Christians of that age understood their duty. In the *Commands* of Hermas we read, to quote Archbishop Wake's translation:

> "'Sir, if a man that is faithful in the Lord, shall have a wife, and shall catch her in adultery: doth a man sin that continues to live still with her?' . . . 'As long as he is ignorant of her sin, he commits no fault in living with her; but if a man shall know his wife to have offended and she shall not repent of her sin, but go on still in her fornication, and a man shall continue nevertheless to live with her, he shall become guilty of her sin and partake with her in her adultery.' . . . 'What therefore is to be done, if the woman continues on in her sin?' . . . 'Let her husband put her away, and let him continue by himself. But if he shall put away his wife, and marry another, he also doth commit adultery.' . . . 'What if the woman that is so put away shall repent, and be willing to return to her husband, shall she not be received by him?' . . . 'Yes, and if her husband shall not receive her, he will sin: and commit a great offence against himself: but he ought to receive the offender, if she repents; only not often.' . . . 'For to the servants of God there is but one repentance. And for this cause a man that putteth away his wife ought not to take another, because she may repent.' . . . 'This act is alike both in the man and in the woman.'"

When these rules are calibrated with our Lord's words in

Matt. xviii. 15–17[1] and with Paul's in 1 Corinthians vii. 10–17, they would appear to support our view of the matter. It is only later ages which have adopted Hermas' rigid rules in this regard, although they have recognized that his uncompromising denial of pardon for recidivists is not in harmony with our Lord's teaching.

We conclude (1) that the death penalty for divorce has been repealed by Christ, and (2) that divorce is forbidden for any and every cause except adultery. For adultery the innocent party should only seek a divorce when it has been made clear that the guilty party is obstinately resolved on having the marriage annulled. The resolution to end the bond should come from the guilty. After the divorce the innocent party is free to remarry according to Paul though not according to Hermas. The guilty party who desires to marry again should be debarred from Christian marriage, inasmuch as the determination to end the marriage and the unwillingness to repent imply a self-excommunication and extrusion from the Christian community. Finally we shall remark that both those who take the laxer view as to divorce and those who sanction making pre-nuptial unchastity a bar to marriage may be charged with a failure in Christian charity. The former sanction the indulgence of the innocent party's jealous rage, the latter do the same. Neither give room for repentance. Both would perhaps be content to leave the culprit without hope of escape from becoming an unprotected paramour : in other words, they concentrate on the individual's position and ignore the moral effects upon society.

[1] Some critics have declared for rejecting Matthew's record here, arguing that he is giving a Jewish alleviation of Christ's stringent requirement of charity, but such critical tampering with what the orthodox Church has accepted as Scripture seems as unwarrantable here as when Matthew states the one exceptional ground for which divorce is permitted.

INDEX

Abba, Father, 292, 293
Abbott, Dr. E. A., *cited*, 93, 219 *n.*, 224 *n.*
Abgar, 206 *n.*, 235–6, 322
Abomination of desolation, 55
Abraham's seed, 37 *n.*, 267
Adonai, 270
Alexandrian canon, the, 296
Ambrose, St., 74 *n.*, 285 *n.*, 332
Amen, 293
Ana of our Lord, 9, 87
Ananus, 194
Annas, 74–5, 360–1
Annunciation, the, 171, 214–5, 346
Anointed, the, 265
Anointing by Mary, 84, 353; the two anointings, 87, 354, 355
Apocalypse, the, 72, 73, 74, 80, 81, 85, 337
Apocrypha, 300
Apocryphal Gospels, 200–2
Apostles, the, 16, 27, 29, 36, 41, 43, 77, 262, 292, 369; names of the, 205–7; the Twelve and the Lord's brethren, 192, 198 *n.*
Aramaic, 292–3
Ascension, the, 44, 194, 247, 320
Astronomical computations, 147 *f.*, 372
Athanasius, St., 285 *n.*, 300, 331 *f.*

Babylon, 246
Badcock, Dr. F. J., *cited*, 176, 177 *n.*
Balaam, 238
Baptism of our Lord, the, 22, 38–9, 76, 217, 278, 305, 314, 328; historical date, 173, 174, 176
Barabbas, 136–7
Barker, Rev. F. E., *cited*, 110
Bartimaeus, 50, 251, 256, 258, 259 *n.*
Beatitudes, the, 36, 64, 66
Beelzebub, 9, 15, 16, 25, 26, 27, 28, 30, 31, 33, 41–2, 46, 48, 62, 69, 70, 78, 107, 109, 256, 338, 344 *n.*
Bell and Skeat: *Fragments of an Unknown Gospel*, 264, 355
Benedictus, the, 295
Bethany, Feast at, 10, 17, 88, 107
Bethlehem, 21, 38, 266

Blasphemy against the Holy Ghost, 70, 80, 120, 344
Blessed Trinity, doctrine of, 325
Blessed Virgin Mary, 191 *f.*, 251 *f.*, 294, 345, 346; and St. Luke's Gospel, 84
Blind, healing of the, 25, 46, 50, 74, 118, 259 *n.*, 261, 316; man born blind, 261, 316, 325; man of Siloam, 74, 250, 370; *and see heading* Bartimaeus
Bread of Life, 79, 336, 337
Brethren of the Lord, the, 191 *f.*, 305
Browne, Rev. L. E., *cited*, 366
Buckle, Rev. D. P., *cited*, 66 *n.*, 89

Caiaphas, 74–5, 108, 125, 233, 234, 246, 247, 256, 315, 339–41, 360–2, 373
Calendars, 141 *f.*, 372
Cana, 74, 76, 223, 234 *n.*, 254, 255, 283–4, 285, 308
Capernaum, 22, 39, 61; teaching in the synagogue, 328, 336
Carrington, Bishop, *cited*, 72
Centurion's, the, ejaculation at the Cross, 235, 236
Centurion's servant, the, 23, 321–2
Cephas, 322; *see* Peter, St.
Cerinthus, 85
Chreiai, 53, 87
Christ, the, 213–4, 322; Dominical title, 266
Christ's human consciousness, development of, 300 *et seq.*
Christological controversies, 301
Church, the Body of Christ, 245, 247
Church, the true Bethel, 243
Cleanliness, ceremonial, 278–9, 288, 338
Clement, St., of Alexandria, 171, 175; evidence of, for Gospel dates, 154–65, 169, 170 *n.*
Cleopas (Clopas), 194, 198 and *n.*, 252, 253, 259
Clopas' companion, 86
Codex Bezae, 240
Codices, 3, 294
Comte, Auguste, *cited*, 243
Corbishley, Fr. T., *cited*, 175, 177 *n.*
Cottam, Rev. T., *cited*, 89 *n.*, 307 *n.*, 380

389